•
ttsburgh

Pennsylvania

Mason-Dixon Line

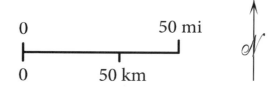

gantown

airmont

M a r y l a n d

Martinsburg
•

airmont
oal field

M O U N T A I N S

Virginia

0	50 mi
0	50 km

N

The Devil Is Here in These Hills

The Devil Is Here in These Hills

West Virginia's Coal Miners and Their Battle for Freedom

JAMES GREEN

Atlantic Monthly Press
New York

Copyright © 2015 by James Green

The author is deeply indebted to the West Virginia and Regional History Center at the West Virginia University Libraries, which granted permission to reprint thirty-seven photographs from their deep and rich collections. It would not have been possible to illustrate this book without the Center and its staff.

Published simultaneously in Canada
Printed in the United States of America

FIRST EDITION

ISBN 978-0-8021-2331-2
eISBN 978-0-8021-9209-7

Atlantic Monthly Press
an imprint of Grove/Atlantic, Inc.
154 West 14th Street
New York, NY 10011

Distributed by Publishers Group West

www.groveatlantic.com

15 16 17 18   10 9 8 7 6 5 4 3 2 1

In Memory of My Father
Gerald R. Green
1922–2012

Contents

CONTENTS

Prologue

O ne autumn morning in 1922, a middle-aged man with wavy hair and horn-rimmed glasses waited in Baltimore's smoky Camden Station for a B&O limited that would take him to Huntington, West Virginia. He looked like an artist or college professor. In fact, James M. Cain had dreamed of being a professional singer like his mother, an operatic soprano, but writing came more easily to him. After editing an army newspaper during the war in France and teaching at a prep school, Cain took a job with the *Baltimore Sun*, covering police court and filing crime stories. But when he boarded the B&O's westbound limited that fall morning, Cain left the city on a different kind of assignment. He was headed over the Allegheny range, bound for the coal country of southern West Virginia. His mission: to search out the truth about what had caused a massive insurrection of armed coal miners the previous summer. In late August 1921, nearly ten thousand workers had marched over fifty miles of rugged terrain to liberate fellow union members who had been jailed under a martial law decree imposed on Mingo County, where a vicious mine war had raged for more than two years.[1]

After the reporter passed through Huntington, he switched railroads and headed due south on the Norfolk & Western, along the Tug Fork River, and into the rugged valley where the Hatfields and

McCoys feuded after the Civil War and "whole families were exterminated," as Cain put it. This bloody history, and the folklore it produced, shaped outsiders' impressions of the wild Tug River country, even after the region had become heavily industrialized and linked to the national economy. The legend of the feud led Cain, like other writers before him, to portray the Appalachian coal country as "an American heart of darkness."[2]

In the prose that would later make him famous as writer of hardboiled murder mysteries and film noir screenplays, Cain described a setting fit for an epic drama.

> As you leave the Ohio River at Kenova, and wind down the Norfolk and Western Railroad beside the Big Sandy and Tug rivers, you come into a section where there is being fought the bitterest and most unrelenting war in modern industrial history.

> Rough mountains rise all about, beautiful in their bleak ugliness. They are hard and barren, save for a scrubby, whiskery growth of trees that only half conceal the hard rock beneath. Yet they have their moods. On gray days, they lie heavy and sullen, but on sunny mornings they are dizzy with color: flat canvases painted in gaudy hues; here and there tiny soft black pines showing against the cool, blue sky. At night, if the moon shines through a haze, they hang far above you . . . They are gashed everywhere by water courses, roaring rivers, and bubbling creeks. Along these you plod, a crawling midge, while ever the towering mountains shut you in.

Above the railbed, blue-black streaks of coal laced the hills for miles, "jumping across rivers and creeks, now broken by some convulsion an eternity ago, now tilted at crazy angles, but for the most part flat, thick, regular, and rich." And along every ascending creek Cain saw curving ribbons of steel rails crawling up the mountainsides to mining operations wedged into the hollows. Here was a region where industry had been organized on a "gigantic" scale. "To see it," he remarked, "is to get the feeling of it: the great iron machinery of coal and oil, the never-ending railroads and strings of black steel cars, groaning and creaking toward destination." There was a "crude outdoor poetry about it," but Cain knew that this marvelous achievement had been marred by a bloody industrial struggle that had lasted more than two years.

On his way up the Tug River Valley, Cain passed coal mines, some of them still closed down by "die-hard union strikers," and he observed "occasional clusters of tents—squalid, wretched places, where swarms of men, women, and children are quartered." And at nearly every train station, men in military uniforms scrutinized each passenger who alighted; they were state policemen, part of a strong force still on duty there, for the bloodshed in this valley had been so severe that Mingo County remained under martial law. The constables always walked in pairs and constantly looked over their shoulders. Everywhere, the reporter felt an "atmosphere of tension, covert alertness, sinister suspicion," and he soon realized why.

In this untamed section of West Virginia two tremendous forces have staked out a battle ground. These are the United Mine Workers of America and the most powerful group of nonunion coal-operators in the country. It is a battle to the bitter end; neither side asks quarter, neither side gives it. It is a battle for enormous stakes, on which money is lavished; it is fought through the courts, through the press, with matching of sharp wits to secure public approval. But more than this, it is actually fought with deadly weapons on both sides; many lives have already been lost; many may yet be forfeited.

Some of the residents who were willing to speak with Cain told him grim tales of what they had witnessed.

[They] will tell you that this struggle has been going on for three years. They will tell you of the bloody day at Matewan, May 19, 1920, when ten men, including the mayor of the town, fell in a pistol battle that lasted less than a minute. They will tell you of guerrilla warfare that went on for months; how Federal troops had to be called in twice. They will tell you of the "three days' battle," which resulted, in May, 1921, in the declaration of martial law. Union partisans will tell you of the exercises on May 30 last [Memorial Day], when the graves of a score of union fallen were decorated with all the ceremony accorded soldiers who have died for the flag. The [mine] operators will tell you . . . how their men have been shot down from behind; how witnesses for trials were mysteriously killed before they could testify.

The "atrocity list" was long and the volume of propaganda was so great that Cain thought it "very hard to sift out the truth."

Frustrated with his inability to explain what had caused this terrible trouble, the reporter from Baltimore chose to entertain his readers with a story he scripted as a three-act play and staged on a frontier set filled with rugged but "lovable" mountaineers who spoke a "quaint language" and fought "strange feuds . . . [for] incomprehensible causes." Onto this wild mountain stage burst the railroads and mining companies, whose agents grabbed the land and forced the frontiersmen into the mines to make a living, according to the rules made by their "new masters." Before long, the coal operators "adopted the law of the rifle themselves, hired armed gentry to watch him and police him and curtail his liberties."

These new boss men were often strangers, flatlanders from strange places up north or back east, men who now told the mountaineer miner "where to go to church and where to send his children to school. They told him what he must take for his labor, how much he must pay for his food, and where he must buy it. Lastly, they told him what organizations he might join, and those that he must not join," particularly the United Mine Workers of America (UMWA).

Act I of Cain's "mine-field melodrama" opened with the appearance of the first UMWA organizers in 1892. These men would return again and again over the next two decades, attempting—always in vain—to win the union pay scale for West Virginia's poorly paid coal diggers. Each foray, wrote Cain, "was repulsed with medieval ferocity by the [coal] operators, who could make more money if they didn't have to pay the union scale."

The union finally broke through in 1902 with a strike that gained union recognition and contractual rights for more than eight thousand miners in the Kanawha County mines near Charleston. Peace prevailed in that district for ten years until coal operators in the Paint Creek Valley refused to give union members a tiny pay raise that other companies had granted their employees. A routine work stoppage followed, but what happened next was anything but routine. When private mine guards started evicting families from their homes, union miners took to the hills and launched repeated attacks against the men they called "gun thugs."

A few weeks later, fighting broke out over the ridge in the Cabin Creek Valley, and by midsummer of 1912, union miners and their employers were engaged in what would become one of the longest and deadliest labor conflicts America had ever experienced. The struggle on Paint Creek and Cabin Creek became a prime example of a development President William Howard Taft had bemoaned in an address to Congress: a situation in which the public and its elected officials allowed an industrial dispute to lead "inevitably to a state of industrial war."[3]

The conflict in West Virginia seemed warlike because of the huge arsenals assembled by both sides, the number of mercenaries the mine operators employed, the guerrilla tactics the strikers adopted, the four deployments of National Guard troops the governor ordered, and the abiding hatreds the clash created. As a result, the first West Virginia mine war embodied all the evils of class warfare that frightened so many Americans during the Progressive Era.

After a thirteen-month struggle, strikers in the Paint Creek–Cabin Creek district won an unexpected victory by practicing a form of solidarity that united white mountaineers, black miners, and Italian immigrants. The spirit of that strike inspired a poet to write a song that became labor's national anthem: "Solidarity Forever." Although the union miners prevailed in the end, their success came at a high cost: twelve strikers and thirteen company men lost their lives in the conflict.

During the first term of Woodrow Wilson's presidency, the UMWA expanded by leaps and bounds in the Kanawha and New River coalfields southeast of Charleston; it was an exciting time when labor activists hoped that progressives in Washington, DC, would enact reforms to protect workers' right to organize. That hope became a reality during World War I when the federal government assumed virtual control of the coal industry and ordered the mine owners not to resist union organization. Those federal controls were still in place when the union launched a new offensive in Logan County in

September 1919, a drive that was met with fierce resistance by the mine operators and an army of deputy sheriffs.

A few months later, miners began forming union locals in Mingo County, where James Cain would later come to write his feature story. Coal company managers immediately fired new union recruits and employed men from the Baldwin-Felts Detective Agency to evict these workers from their homes. The arrival of these detectives provoked a showdown on May 19, 1920, in the little town of Matewan, where the police chief, Sid Hatfield, and his deputies created a national sensation by gunning down seven Baldwin-Felts agents who had just thrown scores of strikers out of their homes. For the next year, a brutal industrial war raged in what came to be known as "Bloody" Mingo County. The fighting subsided only when federal troops, National Guardsmen, state police officers, and hundreds of vigilantes imposed martial law and "began clapping union men in jail" without charges.

Act II in Cain's drama began with thousands of union miners assembling in a valley near Charleston in August 1921, armed and ready to launch their "grand offensive" on company territory. This huge uprising of citizens, unprecedented in modern American history, culminated in a three-day battle on Blair Mountain in Logan County between an insurgent army of at least eight thousand workers and a force of three thousand deputies, volunteers, and conscripts, which had been mobilized to stop the miners' army from invading company-controlled territory. The military conflict on Blair Mountain shocked the nation and embarrassed West Virginia's elected officials.

The Battle of Blair Mountain ended when President Warren G. Harding reluctantly sent twenty-one hundred army infantrymen into West Virginia to halt the warfare and disarm the insurgents. "It was the best second act that had ever been staged," Cain declared, marred only by the deaths of at least a dozen combatants, mostly young coal miners, including two young men who died wearing the army tunics they brought back from France. But this battle was not the end of the show. There was another act to come, wrote Cain: "the great courtroom scene."

A few days after the miners' army dispersed, a grand jury met in special session and "indicted whole pay rolls," according to Cain. Hundreds of insurgents were charged with high crimes and then tried "in the same room at Charles Town where John Brown had been convicted of treason." Cain's "melodrama of coal" ended with those sensational trials, but the same characters—the miners and the union organizers, the mine operators and the company guards— remained onstage throughout the following decade to act out another kind of drama with a much different third act.

The mining industry's domination over its employees during the 1920s troubled a number of prominent liberals, who began to search for some way of saving the coal miners of Appalachia from what they termed "indentured servitude." During this time, no group of American workers attracted more sympathy from reformers than West Virginia's coal miners, and no group stood to gain more when Congress granted industrial workers the right to organize in June 1933. Within days after the law changed, UMWA activists motored through the Mountain State's company towns, sweeping aside all opposition while they organized nearly every coal miner in West Virginia without a shot being fired in anger.

The West Virginia coal miners' story has never been recounted in full from its origins in 1892, when the first UMWA organizers appeared in the coal camps, to those thrilling days in the first spring of the New Deal, when union forces emerged victorious after forty years of struggle.[4] *The Devil Is Here in These Hills* is a history of that enduring struggle and of the diverse community of working people who carried it on for so long.

The events described here took place in Appalachia at the height of the American industrial age, a time when the nation's economy depended entirely upon coal and upon the men who went into the depths of the earth to bring it out; a time when the nation's industrial workers engaged in mass actions on an enormous scale; a time when the nation grappled, as never before, with the moral and political consequences of industrial capitalism and the class hatreds it spawned. But this book is more than a litany of strikes and lockouts, evictions and blacklists, gun battles and armed marches—more than another gruesome chapter in the history of American violence. It is, above all, the story of a people's fight to exercise freedom of speech and freedom of association in workplaces where the rights of property owners had reigned supreme.

During the first years of the twentieth century, writers like James M. Cain and a host of influential Americans recognized that a battle of enormous import was taking place in West Virginia's minefields. The nation's largest labor union and some of America's most powerful corporations had invested millions in winning the loyalty of the state's eighty thousand coal miners. Four governors of West Virginia bent the state's constitution to the breaking point in their efforts to suppress mine worker insurgency, and two presidents of the United States sent federal troops to halt the violence on several occasions. The board of the American Civil Liberties Union, along with some of the most influential journalists of the time, made West Virginia union miners a cause célèbre, and several progressive U.S. senators made the state's coal industry the subject of two exhaustive investigations.

Yet for all the significance the West Virginia mine wars held for Americans during the Progressive Era and the early 1920s—and for all the meaning those conflicts still hold for Appalachians—knowledge of this enduring conflict has been all but lost to American memory. This is surprising because of all the lethal industrial clashes in our history, few were as protracted as those that occurred in West Virginia; few took as many lives (at least seventy-nine men died in those wars); and few attracted as much attention in the halls of Congress. Furthermore, no other strike generated an armed insurrection on the scale of the miners' march in 1921, and no other strike provoked a political crisis that so closely resembled a civil war.[5]

Today, outsiders seem to pay attention to the people of West Virginia when a mine explosion attracts television cameras to some little white church building in the hills, where viewers see the worried faces of the miners' friends and family members awaiting news of their loved ones trapped underground. News reports of impoverished conditions and chronic diseases, flooded creeks and toxic rivers, mine disasters and exploding mountaintops, have conditioned many Americans to see the people of coal country as pitiful casualties of modern history, not as a mindful people who made their own history.

Decades of seeing Appalachia as "a strange land with a peculiar people" have blinded most Americans to the fact that these mountains have been, in the words of author Jeff Biggers, "a stage for some of the most quintessential and daring American experiences of innovation, rebellion, and social change."[6] The Mountain State's mine wars were one of those experiences, a series of rebellions arising from Appalachia that played out on the national stage. This is one of the reasons why the time has come for the West Virginia coal miners' story to be told in full, so that it may finally take its rightful place in the larger history of American freedom.

PART I

Casus Belli, 1890–1911

Chapter 1

The Great West Virginia Coal Rush

1877–1890

After his visit to the "fight front" in Mingo County, James M. Cain returned to Baltimore and attempted to explain to his readers why southern West Virginia had become a war zone "where murder, dynamiting, arson, and insurrection [were the] usual order of the day." It was coal, he concluded; coal had "brought about this state of affairs." For in this part of America, he wrote, coal was the staff of life. "It is coal on which a third of the population depends directly for its living . . . It is coal that has converted the State into one great pock-mark of mines."[1] And it was the cost of mining coal that had turned the rolling hills of southern West Virginia into an industrial battleground.

Virginians had known about the mineral wealth buried beyond the Blue Ridge since the mid-eighteenth century, but it took another century and a half for industrialists to exploit the rich deposits of "black gold" laced through the mountains of the Allegheny Plateau. The wealthy men of the Tidewater first learned of this buried treasure in 1750 from Christopher Gist, a famous explorer and trader, whom they had hired to inventory the most valuable real estate in the territory west of the Alleghenies. Upon his return from the highlands, Gist offered his clients lavish descriptions of the dense forests and fertile valleys he had surveyed, and he presented them with two impressive objects: a tooth from one of the woolly mammoths that roamed the region in the Pleistocene epoch and a lump of coal that had been hardening since the Pennsylvanian subperiod a million years before. Gist's survey put a gleam in the eye of well-endowed investors back east, the kind of men whose capital would one day transform the Appalachian wilderness into a vast industrial domain for the extraction of West Virginia's bounteous natural resources.[2]

The first coal deposits in the region formed during the Late Devonian period, more than 350 million years ago, when forests first covered the mountains of what became the Cumberland Plateau. The woody tissues of dead trees produced accumulations of peat, and the area that later would compose West Virginia became a subsiding basin filled with sediment. As these deposits were buried deeper and deeper, temperature and pressure increased, and over the centuries, the peat deposits became seams of high-quality, relatively low-volatility bituminous coal.*[3]

Few regions in the world were as well endowed with such vast carbon deposits, a commonly known fact by 1765. Thomas Jefferson wrote in *Notes on the State of Virginia* that the whole tract of land beyond Laurel Mountain in western Virginia would yield abundant quantities of the fuel. Three years later, in the Treaty of Hard Labour, the Cherokees relinquished their claim to land south of the Great Kanawha River, where the first coal deposits in western Virginia would eventually be mined by slaves and used as fuel for the salt furnaces south of Charleston.[4]

When the French and Indian War ended in 1763, hundreds of colonial soldiers who fought for the British poured into the lush valleys beyond the Blue Ridge, taking land that the vanquished Cherokee

---

*The bituminous or soft coalfields located in Appalachia, the lower Midwest, and the far West produced most of the nation's fossil fuel. Bituminous coal was classified as thermal fuel used in steam engines and power plants and as metallurgical fuel used to produce coke for iron and steel making. Southern West Virginia mines produced a high grade of low-sulfur "smokeless" soft coal, mainly for export to the national market. Higher-priced anthracite or hard coal contained relatively pure carbon and burned with little flame or smoke; it was mined mainly in eastern Pennsylvania.

people had occupied for centuries. Along with them came hunters and traders, Pennsylvania farmers, Virginia slave owners, German immigrants, and Scots-Irish refugees from the rack-rented counties of Northern Ireland. These Ulstermen would create a new kind of religious movement in the mountains, one led by Presbyterian preachers who emphasized the personal quality of conversion and created a tradition of outdoor festivals, or "holy fairs," that persisted in intensely communal forms of worship characteristic of mountain religion.[5]

Along with these pioneer settlers came the agents from the east who acquired land in great swaths, about three-quarters of Appalachia by 1800. As a result, nearly half of the white settlers worked the land as tenants and day laborers—the ancestors of Appalachia's enduring population of poor whites.[6] But other homesteaders thrived in the lush forests and fertile valleys of Virginia's western counties, notably the Scots-Irish immigrants who brought Ulster's agrarian ways with them to America. They combined livestock herding in "outfields" with raising crops along the creek and river bottoms. Besides growing food for their own consumption, crafty producers also sold various goods out of the region, including livestock, salt, grain, ginseng, hand-crafted wares, and pig iron—commodities that could be shipped via turnpikes and down rivers like the Kanawha that flowed into the Ohio.

Within these western mountain communities, a rough-and-tumble form of frontier democracy flourished, one that would shape the nation's politics during the Age of Andrew Jackson. When the man they called "Old Hickory" threw open the White House to the masses after his inauguration in 1829, the region's highlanders had already earned a reputation as cunning hunters, deadly sharpshooters, and fearless dissenters.

At the start of Jackson's second term as president in 1833, a Virginia farmer named Moses Keeney left the gorgeous hills of Greenbrier County and drove his wagon over the James River and the Kanawha Turnpike until he reached Charleston, a thriving river town with its own little aristocracy of families enriched by selling the salt produced by slaves. When he turned his team up the Kanawha River, Keeney saw salt furnaces belching smoke, mountainsides denuded of trees, long rows of drying sheds, and gangs of black men wheeling barrels and tending furnaces.[7]

A few miles upriver, Keeney entered a largely uninhabited region where thick forests sheltered an endless array of birds and animals—sixty-three species of mammals in all, ranging in size from the rare and tiny flying squirrel to the five-hundred-pound black bear.[8] Wild fruit trees grew aplenty: the crab apple with its sweetly perfumed blossoms, the plum, the mulberry, and the pawpaw with its dark burgundy, bell-shaped blossoms and its sweet, nutritious fruit so highly valued by the Native Americans. Higher on the hillsides grape vines grew so thick they covered parts of the woods in darkness, and farther up the mountainsides were dense stands of eastern white pine, succeeded at higher elevations by black walnut, white oak, chestnut, and red spruce. Some sycamores, red oaks, yellow poplars, and buckeyes reached more than a hundred feet in height with trunks that measured two hundred inches in circumference.

Moses Keeney settled on land in this country, and when he died in 1849, his sons continued to farm, hunt, and cut lumber along Cabin Creek in a place where a little mountain community called Eskdale would emerge. In the mid-nineteenth century, none of the Keeneys could foresee the changes that would come to their valley or to the whole region in the decades ahead, when a wondrously diverse ecosystem would be destroyed by railroads that blackened the air, timber companies that clear-cut the forests, and coal-mining operations that laid waste to the valleys and streams.

Keeney's sons avoided taking sides when the Civil War erupted, even though most residents of Virginia's western counties voted against secession. On June 11, 1861, leading Unionists called a convention in Wheeling, where they formed a provisional government for a new "free state." A month later, federal troops under the command of General W. S. Rosecrans—who had been a pioneer mine operator in the Coal River Valley—triumphed over Confederate forces at the Battle of Rich Mountain. Yankee units then entered the Kanawha Valley, raided the Keeneys' farm, and moved up the New River, where General Rosecrans's soldiers defeated the Confederates at the Battle of Gauley Bridge that fall. A few months later, the state of West Virginia entered the Union with the motto *Montani Semper Liberi*, "Mountaineers Are Always Free," emblazoned on its state flag. Upon the state's great seal, the Founding Fathers placed the image of a coal miner with a pick on his shoulder.[9]

At the end of the Civil War, even the wealthiest landowners and merchants in the new state lacked the access to capital, railroad connections, and land titles they needed to exploit the fabulous wealth of coal reserves that lay beneath their mountains. These men yielded to entrepreneurs from the north and east who would furnish the capital and credit required to build the railroads that would link West Virginia to national markets and open its natural resources to exploitation by industrialists.

During the 1870s, battalions of "steel-drivin' men" like the legendary John Henry tunneled through the mountains and laid down track for the westward extension of the Chesapeake & Ohio Railway from Richmond, Virginia, to its new terminus on the Ohio River at Huntington. The town was named for the great railroad builder Collis P. Huntington, who needed West Virginia's high-quality coal to fire his fleet of locomotives. He also knew that this fuel could be shipped around the world from the enormous coal pier he constructed in Newport News on the Atlantic Ocean, and that it could be taken to Cincinnati, where shippers could float the fuel on boats down the Ohio River or send it on trains to the Great Lakes and Chicago. In 1877, the C&O railroad extension up the Kanawha and New Rivers south of Charleston allowed seven new mine companies to beginning shipping coal to national markets.[10] The great West Virginia coal rush was on.

For the next decade, engineers and surveyors penetrated the Mountain State's remotest valleys searching for coal seams. After the tracts were surveyed, agents followed to buy leases on the land occupied by pioneers, including military veterans who were given wasteland on the western frontier. The state of West Virginia took possession of many old homesteads during the 1880s because the original settlers had not registered their deeds or paid taxes. When outsiders purchased the original deeds and claimed legal ownership, a protracted legal drama unfolded in the federal courts. At first, some judges sided with the pioneers, but when other judges began to rule for the speculators, the original owners started to sell out to agents, representing investors from New York City, Philadelphia, Cleveland, and Cincinnati who coveted the state's bountiful natural resources. Other mountain families signed broad form leases that granted a coal, oil, or timber company the right to use the surface of their land in any way "convenient and necessary" to extract minerals, drill for petroleum, or cut lumber. These leases exempted the holders from taxes and from any liabilities for damages caused directly or indirectly by industrial operations.[11]

In the early twentieth century, absentee owners controlled 81 percent of the collieries in West Virginia's southern counties. In McDowell County, for example, agents acquired forty-five thousand acres of land using capital invested by partners from London; Philadelphia; Hartford, Connecticut; and Staunton, Virginia. These capitalists then leased these lands to five mining companies ready to exploit one of the purest deposits of coal in North America—the low sulfur content of "smokeless" coal from the Pocahontas minefield that would produce the coke essential to steel making and fire the boilers of the nation's locomotives and steamships. Coal production in this region soared to even greater heights after 1895, when another railroad, the Norfolk & Western, reached down from the Ohio River along the Big Sandy River and followed the Tug Fork River deep into the Pocahontas coalfield.[12]

The Pocahontas coal district on West Virginia's southern border with Virginia represented one of that state's four major minefields, defined by surveyors and engineers as distinct and contiguous formations of coal separated from one another by mountains and rivers. North and east of the Pocahontas, the New River minefield stretched over a large section of Fayette County where, by 1900, more than eight thousand workers cut and loaded 5 million tons of coal, much of it going directly into a thousand red-hot beehive coke ovens.[13] To the northwest in Kanawha County, an older coalfield covered both sides of the Kanawha River not far from Charleston, the state capital.

Approximately 140 miles northeast of Charleston lay the Fairmont minefield, which opened during the 1890s when Johnson N. Camden, a railroad builder, oilman, and former U.S. senator from

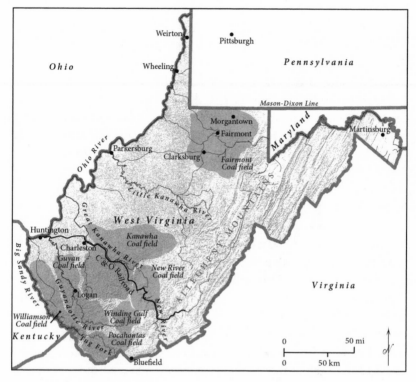

Map of West Virginia during the early 1900s, with cities, railroads, rivers, and coalfields indicated.

West Virginia, formed the Monongah Coal and Coke Company. Camden's engineers cut five mines into the hills and built houses in the town of the same name. By the mid-1890s, Camden's Monongah mines employed the latest machinery and technology, setting the standard for high quality and high productivity.[14] Within a few years, these collieries* would become part of the empire created by the Consolidation Coal Company (often called Consol), whose owners purchased or leased more than fifty thousand acres of coal land. Consol would become the largest producer of coal in the nation by

*A colliery included offices, mine tunnels, tracks, and tipples, where haulage cars were tipped into railroad coal cars. "Collier" was the Old English word for a coal miner, which made its way over to the Pennsylvania anthracite fields in the 1800s.

1907, the same year one of its modern mines, Monongah, exploded and caused the deadliest disaster in America's industrial history.

Meanwhile, new minefields were also being prepared for development north of the Pocahontas field in the unsettled backcountry of Raleigh and Wyoming Counties. To the west, in Logan County, the new Guyan field opened when the C&O extended its line north along the Guyandotte River to the Ohio River. Farther west was the Williamson field, which extended along the Tug Fork River on the Kentucky border. By the time the Norfolk & Western Railway completed its line north to Huntington on the Ohio River in 1895, this new district in Mingo County was predicted to become the coal industry's El Dorado.

Because pioneer industrialists ran their businesses on very narrow margins, they often depended on the profits from their company stores to make up for losses in an unpredictable coal market. And because they had to pay higher transportation costs and absorb the expense of building collieries and whole communities in remote mountain sites, these businessmen depended upon keeping labor costs down so they could sell their coal at low prices and gain an edge in the national market. The operators' insistence on retaining this advantage led them to resist unionization with an extraordinary degree of force and determination.[15]

Small collieries proliferated in West Virginia during the 1890s, but after the turn of the century, syndicates of northern industrialists, bankers, and other investors built modern industrial operations that employed three hundred or more laborers.[16] Like infantry units of an invading army, these well-endowed companies conquered rough terrain, laid down miles of track, opened dozens of mines, erected tipples and company stores, recruited laborers, and constructed entire villages often in less than a year's time.

The rapid development of coal mining created a demographic explosion in sparsely inhabited mountain counties. In McDowell County—which contained most of the Pocahontas field—the population increased by 155.3 percent during the first decade of the twentieth century, compared with a statewide growth of 27.4 percent. The velocity and intensity of industrialization in West Virginia's coal country can be measured with such statistics. What cannot be so readily quantified are the effects this revolution had on mountain people and on the forests and valleys where they were born and raised.

Because industrialists needed to construct new towns in wilderness locations, more West Virginia miners lived in company housing than in any other section of the country—nearly 79 percent, as compared with 24 percent in Ohio. These workers were not ordinary tenants, however, for the state courts had ruled that the mine owner's relationship to his renters was not that of a landlord to a tenant, but rather that of a master to a servant. Therefore, the law allowed the owner to summarily evict families and to inspect miners' houses without a warrant.[17]

The mine operator's power extended over almost every other facet of life as well. He hired and fired his hands at will. He built the schools and selected the teachers, built the churches and selected the ministers, built the store and selected the store manager. He owned or leased every acre of land in and around his town except the creek and the railbed, where a railroad owned the right-of-way. He controlled access to the town and all activity within it, and he hit down with a heavy hand on any activity that might menace his business.

Mine operators like the Virginian W. P. Tams Jr. saw themselves as fair-minded men who were good judges of character and virtue, men who knew right from wrong. If miners had a complaint, "all they had to do was come to me," said Tams many years later. He would hear all complaints, resolve all problems, and levy all penalties, including the ultimate punishment: terminating a miner and, in some cases, putting his name on a blacklist. "To use the expression of the Middle Ages," Tams explained, "I was high justice, the middle and the low." He recalled many occasions upon which he would ask a recalcitrant miner if he wanted to take "company discipline" or face "a court-martial." "A sensible man would always say, 'I'll take company discipline.'"[18]

Mining companies constructed their own stores in most West Virginia coal towns and made sure no independent merchants opened shops to compete with their highly profitable mercantile enterprises. These establishments, often impressively built two-story structures with wide porches, served as community gathering places as well as commercial outlets, where miners purchased equipment and blasting powder and where women shopped for a variety of goods from canned foods to ready-made clothes. Congressional investigators later found that in remote locations, company store prices ranged from 5 to 12 percent more than they were in towns where independent stores existed nearby. Tams recalled that his fellow operators "charged all the market would bear" so that profits on their merchandise would offset losses they often suffered when coal prices fell.[19]

West Virginia mine managers issued their own private currency, called scrip, redeemable only at the company store. Scrip was initially offered as a convenience to miners who could use it to acquire necessary items without having cash in hand and without paying interest on a loan. However, companies would not buy back scrip at face value, and if miners sold it, traders or independent merchants would buy scrip at 25 to 30 percent less than its dollar value. This system generated resentment among many miners, who complained about having to pay high prices at company stores and about lacking the freedom to spend their cash wages freely and buy goods from local farmers and independent merchants.[20]

Company-owned mining communities were unincorporated towns with no elected officials. County sheriffs, commissioners, state representatives, and judges could exercise some legal authority over the area in which the mining camps were located, but these officials generally respected the coal towns as private property and allowed owners to govern the communities they owned. The coal operators assigned law enforcement in these rough company towns to deputy sheriffs, who were actually private guards paid by the coal companies. These men were employed to protect the company's property and to track down thieves. They were also ordered to keep a close watch on the miners, who might slip out of the camps, leaving debts unpaid; on strangers such as peddlers who came to sell their wares; and on "outside agitators" who came to stir up trouble.[21]

These were the facts of life in West Virginia's company-owned mining towns. At first, only a few people questioned the justice of the new order, but as the coal industry matured, the realities of industrial life ground against the experience of native-born Appalachians who had been raised in farming and village communities where various forms of civil society and local democracy had been well established.

Strung along river valleys or creek beds like little black islands in a vast sea of forest, West Virginia mining towns were shadowed by steep mountain slopes with sharp razorback ridges that blocked the rising sun for hours and made the valleys inaccessible to outsiders, except by the rough roads that ran along the streams. Miners' houses were clustered together on bottomland or perched precariously on hillsides in the hollows. Some rows of miners' cabins sat only a few yards from the railroad tracks, so close that dishes crashed to the floor when trains rumbled past. These Jenny Lind houses—named for the coal town where the prototypes appeared—were made cheaply without wall studs, horizontal siding, or insulation (usually provided by straw and plaster), only vertical pine planks. When these boards cured, gaps opened between them and were sealed by nailing narrow battens over the cracks.[22]

Like other mountain villages and commercial towns, mining camps were nested in lovely wooded valleys, but unlike incorporated communities, these settlements had no paved sidewalks, playing fields, grass lawns, shade trees, or flower gardens. But every town featured a colliery tipple that groaned and rattled for hours each day with the sound of coal being funneled into railroad cars. A typical mining town also contained one or two simple whitewashed churches, a boardinghouse for single workingmen, at least one but often several saloons, as well as two one-room schoolhouses, one for white children, the other for "colored" children. Superintendents assigned miners to the segregated sections of their towns, sending new immigrants and blacks to places that came to be known as "hunktown" and "nigger hollow."

For instance, on Paint Creek in the Kanawha field, Quinn Morton and his partners, owners of the Christian Colliery Company in Mahan and the Imperial Colliery Company in Burnwell, set aside some housing for white miners in a section called Frogtown (because it sat so close to the creek that frogs hopped through the doors) and another for blacks called Pecktown, where Imperial's owners built a "colored school." They helped subsidize the construction of a beautiful two-story schoolhouse for whites on the rise above the company houses on the creek bottom, and they supported a YMCA facility, which would help to inculcate Christian values and a sense of fraternity among bosses and miners alike.[23]

The creeks that flowed near the miners' cabins were polluted by mine runoff, manure, and human waste from outhouses. Since hillside privies drained into the streams, bacteria easily invaded bodies and caused diseases like dysentery and smallpox.[24]

The clear, moist mountain air that blew down these valleys now carried a foul combination of smoke from locomotive engines and smoldering refuse dumps, as well as choking gas from superheated coke ovens that produced what one miner's wife called "an awful sickening scent." Cinders from the locomotive boilers fell like rain over the miners' houses, and coal dust from the mine tipples seeped under every door and through every crack, clinging to the miners' clothes and the laundry their wives hung out every day. Coal dust

The Frogtown section of Burnwell with the company-built schoolhouse in the background.

peppered people's food, coated their vegetable plants, and entered their lungs with every breath they took. "The relentless dust," wrote one historian, "never let anyone in a coal camp forget where they were or why the town existed."[25]

Frontier mining towns were often referred to as camps, as though they were military installations on a battlefront, or as coal patches, as though they were no more than sooty smudges on a mountain landscape. They were rough places to live, because they lacked amenities and were isolated from the larger world, but also because they were occupied by large numbers of single men living together in a raw new environment without any of the customs, rituals, and constraints provided by families and churches in settled communities. Most of these men were heavy drinkers—a "hard-bitten lot," one mine superintendent recalled—who fought each other in "frequent brawls that often ended in serious injury, or even death." These altercations were, however, "treated quite casually by local authorities," as were cases of wife beating.[26]

The novelist Mary Lee Settle recorded grim tales of coal town life she heard from her grandmother, the wife of a Kanawha Valley farm boy who had gone into the new mines and, like many of them, had become a drunkard. The miner beat his young wife until she cut out on her own, divorced her abusive husband, and then, like a character in a romance novel, married a wealthy landowner who brought her to his lovely home on Kellys Creek.[27] Other miners' wives were not so daring or so fortunate.

Despite the violence of coal camp life, the women who married coal miners didn't just feed their husbands, bathe and raise their offspring. Many of these wives and their daughters also emerged as strong personalities, especially when there was trouble with the company and collective action was required. These women organized the church activities so important to many mining families, and they played other roles as well, as Bible instructors and tutors, singers and gardeners, seamstresses and laundresses, faith healers and boardinghouse keepers. They were the ones who transformed primitive coal camps into communities of working people, homeplaces where, as one miner recalled, many miners and their families felt like part of a "tribe."[28]

Although coal companies attempted to reproduce prevailing forms of residential segregation in their towns, African Americans, Italians, and Hungarians never lived more than a few hundred yards "up the hollow" from native-born whites, with whom they worked every day in close proximity and mutual dependency. Miners of different races and nationalities all lived in roughly the same type of company house, paid the same rent, and experienced the same hardships of coal town life. "Everybody felt a common kinship," one Appalachian miner remembered, "because they all had to work and fare together the same way." At one time, he added, "there was even a commonship between the mine operators and the men" they employed, but that relationship changed when small operations were consolidated by large corporations, which came to dominate the industry in West Virginia. Later on, during the 1910s, when some mine operators hired welfare workers to investigate their employees' values, one of them would conclude that life in coal camps was "too simple" and "too socialistic," in the sense that people all felt they were on "the same level." Each miner seemed to identify himself as part of a working team, not as a consumer who wanted something his neighbor possessed that he didn't.[29]

Miners who wore overalls and lived in company houses could readily see that they belonged to a class apart from the well-dressed superintendents, who dwelled in well-built two-story homes, and from the mine operator, who lived in a beautiful home—sometimes referred to as "the white house"—on a hillside above the congested camp. And miners who spoke in Appalachian, African American, and Italian dialects could hear their bosses issuing instructions and commands in unfamiliar accents and using big words like "productivity," "efficiency," and "sobriety."[30]

A study of seventy-three colliery operators who did business in southern West Virginia during the early twentieth century indicated that 80 percent hailed from outside of Appalachia. More than half of these men came from the North and nineteen of them arrived from the non-mountain South, including a man named Justus Collins, who left Alabama in 1887 to make his fortune in the mining town of Goodwill, West Virginia. Though he had little formal education, Collins was "endowed with high intelligence and great ambition,"

according to an admirer, and by 1892, he convinced Virginia financiers to back his first solo venture, a colliery he opened at Glen Jean
twenty-five miles to the north in the New River coalfield.[31]

During those early years, Collins adopted a management style he
described in a series of letters to his brother, Jairus, a young mine superintendent. "Habituate yourself to study carefully all the conditions
and details of the business" and "maintain good discipline at all times
at your places, especially around the stores," where men congregated
after work. "We are not running a Christian Endeavor Camp Meeting
nor a Sunday School," Collins remarked, "yet a certain amount of de-
cency and order must be required of our people." Tram cars should be
kept in good repair and well lubricated, haulways drained and cleared,
mules or horses properly cared for at all times. "See that railroad cars
are loaded in the quickest possible time," he added. "Speed saves un-
necessary pay to the army of drivers, trappers, tipple men, etc., and is
a most important factor in the production of cheap coal."

Collins also instructed Jairus to keep a sharp eye on the time
books and on foremen who might hire more men than were required or offer to increase
wages for overtime work.
A mine manager should
"Remember, always, that
to raise wages is a very
simple and agreeable pro-
cess, but to reduce them is
altogether another ques-
tion; in fact, absolutely one
of war." Finally, Collins insisted, "Never lose sight of
the fact that the sole purpose of the organization
is to make money for their
stockholders."[32]

Mine operators like Col-
lins took pride in building
and running well-ordered
communities of workers

Justus Collins, early 1900s.

who would produce coal with all possible speed and efficiency. The men they hired were accustomed to long hours of hard work—as *contadini* in southern Italy, peasants in Hungary, convict laborers in Alabama, and farmers in the hills of West Virginia—followed by periods of rest, for in their rural worlds, the pace of work and the length of the workday varied according to the nature of the task, the weather, and the season of the year. These men had little experience working from dawn to dusk at the same task day after day, month after month. Mine foremen were authorized to fire weaklings, drunkards, and slackers, but they did not exert the kind of supervision exercised by factory foremen. For the most part, miners imposed pressure on themselves to load enough coal to provide an adequate wage to support their families or to send money back home. This compulsion may explain why West Virginia pick and shovel miners were more productive in 1901 than miners using machines.[33]

Nonetheless, mine operators constantly complained about the persistence of "backward traits" among their employees, especially among the single men who had only themselves to feed. Managers were vexed by what they called the "shiftlessness and orneriness" of local folk who did not respond readily to commands or to the lure of earning "big money." Mountaineers accustomed to passing the time hunting, fishing, and visiting did not shed these habits like dead skin when they entered a new industrial world where "time was money" and where time should be "spent" and not "wasted."[34]

During the early 1900s, employers hired far more African Americans and European immigrants than white Americans, hoping these new laborers would be more compliant and productive than the gnarly mountaineers. At the turn of the century, only 554 Italians loaded coal in the Mountain State, but a decade later their numbers had risen to 8,184 and nearly every coal town included a section called "Little Italy" or "Dago Holler."[35] But these new recruits often failed to meet their employers' expectations as well, and in some mines, "greenhorns" gave their supervisors fits. Foremen complained that "colored men" tended to work just long enough to fulfill their basic needs, sometimes only three days a week, and then took time off "to enjoy themselves," wrote one historian. "Foreigners, on the other hand, worked as long and as often as they could but insisted on celebrating numberless religious and national holidays by getting roaring drunk."[36]

Most coal towns had one or two saloons and some had as many as six to eight, places where "a man could get whiskey for a dime a glass" or buy a case of bottled beer for his friends. In addition, the mountaineers produced plenty of corn liquor in moonshine stills and the Italians brewed their own beer and made their own wine. Miners imbibed on many occasions: on paydays, at weddings and christenings, on holidays like Independence Day, May Day, Christmas, and New Year's Day, and on what the immigrants called "saints days" and "Big Sundays," which often led to "Blue Mondays" when absenteeism ran high.[37]

Controlling unruly wage hands was simply a fact of life for mine managers in this frontier industry—an annoying challenge, but not a serious threat. Slackers, weaklings, and drunkards could simply be sent packing at any time. The real troublemakers were the talkers,

Italian miners at a Big Sunday festa at Glen Jean in the New River field.

the agitators, the men who spoke against the boss and who dared to break a taboo by uttering the words, "Boys, we ought to get together and have a union down here."

The first men who talked this way were skilled colliers the coal operators recruited from Pennsylvania, where the earliest miners' union had been formed and where, as one industry historian noted, the mine owners engaged in "a bitter struggle with the Molly McGuires [*sic*], a secret group of Irish terrorists"—his term for an organization of immigrants from Ireland who fought bloody battles with the mine owners and their private police in 1875. In 1880, some troublemakers from the "Molly McQuire fields" organized a march at the mines around Hawks Nest on West Virginia's New River, where they urged other miners to join them in striking for a wage increase. The mine operators beat back this challenge and learned a lesson in the process: They would stop recruiting experienced men from the northern fields, especially British, Scottish, and Irish miners, who were "well schooled in the promotion of strikes."[38]

Union talk began again in 1886, when the Noble and Holy Order of the Knights of Labor organized assemblies of coal miners in the Pocahontas field, where the mine owners employed thousands of black workers without realizing these men had been active in African American labor organizations and civil rights groups like the Union League in the Richmond area. The Knights called two strikes in the Pocahontas field that year in which it became evident to union organizer Michael F. Moran that the "colored men here are not as cowardly as the white men." But black militancy was not enough. Both protests failed and employers imported Hungarians to replace the troublesome African Americans.[39]

To make matters worse, Moran and the Knights also had to contend with a rival labor organization affiliated with the newly founded American Federation of Labor (AFL). Whereas the Knights practiced an inclusive brand of industrial unionism, the AFL affiliates concentrated mostly on recruiting skilled workers. The Knights saw trade unionism as a means to an end—the creation of a "cooperative commonwealth" and a democracy controlled by "honest producers" instead of "plutocrats"—whereas the business-minded craftsmen who founded the AFL's affiliates saw trade unionism as an end in itself. Neither of these approaches proved very effective in the coalfields of the Midwest or Appalachia, and when wage earners conducted a massive general strike for the eight-hour day in May 1886, most of the nation's colliers remained underground hard at work.

In 1890 at the height of the Gilded Age—a year when the AFL declared the nation's coal miners in worse shape than any group of wage earners—the popular social critic Henry Demarest Lloyd drew attention to the plight of these nearly invisible workers in a letter addressed to the public:

> You for whom the coal is dug . . . far away from the toil and trouble of the miner. [The coal diggers] spend ten hours a day in their caverns—pitch dark—except for the flicker and glimmer of the little lamp each carries in the front of his cap . . . They have to work upon their knees, or lying on their side, or stooping low, and sometimes are obliged to lie flat on their backs while digging at the ceiling.
>
> This hard work in a room three feet or three feet six inches high, hundreds of feet below the surface, in the gloom of perpetual night, with air to breathe got only by artificial and imperfect ventilation, is the human price that has to be paid on all our coal. You know this coal only as light, heat, power, profit, comfort, a means of longer life or greater wealth. To the miner it is a black and obdurate enemy, a jailer that imprisons him, shutting out his sunlight . . . ; threatening him daily with death or mutilation in strange and terrible forms, and rewarding his . . . toil with less than the cost of subsistence . . .[40]

American coal miners found their first national champion in Lloyd, but before long these workingmen would choose their own spokesmen from the ranks of tough-minded, self-taught colliers who decided the time had come to form one big union for all the coal miners in North America.

Chapter 2

The Miners' Angel
Winter 1890–Winter 1903

O n the morning of January 23, 1890, scores of short sturdy men wearing black coats and cloth caps filed into the city hall in Columbus, Ohio. Some of these 240 mine workers were English, Scottish, and Welsh immigrants, including many who carried a strong tradition of labor solidarity with them when they left the collieries in Durham, Staffordshire, Yorkshire, Lanarkshire, and the Rhondda Valley. Some were first- and second-generation Irishmen who nursed a grudge over the fate of the Molly Maguires—the twenty immigrant miners hanged in the mid-1870s for crimes they had allegedly committed while waging war against the mine owners and their private police. And many were American-born Protestants who embraced Abraham Lincoln's belief that honest toilers were the backbone of the Republic and that "capital is the fruit of labor."[1]

Half of the delegates were idealistic Knights of Labor like Michael Moran, who came up from southern West Virginia to the convention. The other half were "pure and simple" trade unionists like John McBride from Ohio's Hocking Valley, a founder of the National Federation of Miners and Mine Laborers, who had helped to engineer the first interstate labor agreement for his new union four years earlier.[2] Visionaries like Moran and pragmatists like McBride came to Columbus that winter day in order to merge their rival organizations into one big industrial union that would include all the men and boys who toiled in and around the mines.

After old grievances were aired and lofty speeches delivered, McBride hammered out a fusion agreement, and when the deal was done, pandemonium broke out. "Men banged one another on broad backs," one of the founders reported. They "wept unashamedly, climbed up on collapsing chairs and yelled 'Unity! Unity!'" Two miners who had led rival organizations in Ohio shook hands and swore allegiance to the new union, and then, to demonstrate their sincerity, they kissed each other on the lips. With this gesture of brotherhood, the United Mine Workers of America (UMWA) was born.[3]

Although they were unschooled, the UMWA's founders had honed their intellects by reading newspapers and books, debating politics and religion, and studying economics at the point of production. These colliers had come to a shared understanding of what was happening in their highly competitive industry and what had to be done to protect the men they represented. In the four years preceding the UMWA's founding, railroad mileage had increased by 30 percent and pig iron and steel production had grown by 62 percent—two of the reasons why the demand for bituminous coal soared and output doubled. At the same time, the expansion and reorganization of the large railroad corporations had created an intensely competitive national market for fuel. The nation's largest mine owners and their financiers yearned to corner this market by consolidating the ownership of mines and controlling the means of shipping and marketing the coal.

Union miners had responded to these changes by conducting broader strikes in solidarity with other mine employees, engaging in more job actions aimed at multiple employers, and organizing black and immigrant strikebreakers, who were excluded from most other AFL trade unions. The UMWA's leaders adopted a policy of inclusion, even as a color line was being drawn across the land. "No local union or assembly," the UMWA constitution declared, "is justified in discriminating against any person in securing or retaining work because of their African descent."[4]

Two years later, after the new miners' union gained a foothold in Ohio, Indiana, and Illinois, UMWA executive board member William B. Wilson traveled deep into West Virginia to assist with a recruitment drive headed by Michael Moran, who had hired an African American to work as the district's first paid organizer. Wilson, a Scottish immigrant who would one day become the nation's first secretary of labor, had a keen intellect and sharp eye, and he could see that white miners were laying "back upon their oars . . . of unionism." The most "persistent unionists" in the field were the blacks, he reported.[5]

When he returned from his journey, Wilson asked the national office to send the union's most effective black organizer to West Virginia. Richard Davis was born a free man and raised in Roanoke, Virginia. He later moved to southeastern Ohio, where he loaded coal and joined the union, urging his fellow African Americans to become union men as well. Davis had earned the respect of many white miners, who helped elect him to his district's executive board, where he waged a persistent fight against racism. In one of the many stirring letters he wrote to the new *United Mine Workers Journal*, Davis proclaimed that it was "high time for the color line to be dropped in all branches of industry, for until then, there will be no peace." But he found it nearly impossible to cross that yawning divide in West Virginia's New River field. "The whites say they are afraid of the colored men," Davis lamented, "and the colored men say they are afraid of the whites."[6]

Racial fears and hatreds were not the only obstacles Davis and his fellow activists faced in southern West Virginia. Most of the miners, he reported, were so afraid of their employers he "could do nothing." Although he was a gifted speaker, Davis concluded that it would take more than enthusiasm and "flowery speeches" to move these miners toward unionism.[7]

The possibilities for UMWA expansion vanished in 1894 when a brutal depression caused massive layoffs and deep wage cuts. Forced to defend their members, the union's elected leaders called for a job action in all the bituminous coalfields. But in West Virginia the strike had little effect, and a few weeks after the walkout began, Ohio miners watched, incensed, as long trains of coal cars rolled north filled

34

with "scab coal" from the Mountain State's collieries, where production "increased phenomenally" during the strike.[8]

Three years later, with their organization wasting away, the UMWA's officers took a desperate gamble and called for another general strike; to their amazement, thousands of miners, union and nonunion men alike, responded in what UMWA president Michael Ratchford called a "spontaneous uprising of an enslaved people."[9] A few thousand West Virginia miners answered this call, but most men stayed at work; they were reportedly afraid to attend the meetings since foremen recorded the names of those present and fired them. In any case, union activists were often run out of town by deputy sheriffs or guards paid by the mine operators before they could even rent a hall.[10]

Some embittered UMWA officials blamed West Virginia's miners themselves for the failure of the strike. They complained that these backwoodsmen were "no-good scabs" who were bamboozled by their bosses, intimidated by mine guards, divided by racial hatreds, and ignorant of their true interests as workers. "We have often wondered what kind of animals they have digging coal in West Virginia and have never been able to successfully solve the problem," wrote one disgusted union man. "Their ignorance must be more than dense, their prejudice more bitter and their blindness more intense than that of any other body of miners we have ever heard tell of."[11]

While discouraged union supporters in West Virginia returned to work under the old pay scale, midwestern strikers held firm and compelled the bituminous coal operators to negotiate and sign a trade agreement that would ensure labor peace at a time when coal prices were expected to rise. This historic contract allowed regional market forces to help determine various fair-wage scales in an industry that had been crippled by cutthroat competition. In return for a no-strike agreement by the union, the mine operators sacrificed some of their traditional management prerogatives and granted a host of new job rights to union workers, including the long-desired eight-hour day.[12]

To administer this new agreement, mine operators and union delegates formed an unprecedented "industrial parliament" to govern the nation's most important industry. Infractions by either side would be punished by fines, arbitration hearings would settle disputes, and miners who were judged to have been unfairly dismissed would be awarded back pay. This labor-management accord provided a model for the kind of industrial cooperation favored by political kingmaker Marcus Hanna, national boss of the Republican Party, and by financier J. P. Morgan, the most powerful man in the country at the time.[13]

From the very start, however, there was "a gun pointed at the heart of the industrial government in the bituminous coal industry," as two eminent historians once put it.[14] This was cheap, clean-burning coal that had flowed north from nonunion mines in West Virginia during the 1897 strike. That year, nineteen thousand men produced roughly 12 million tons of fuel in the Mountain State, enough to win some customers away from the midwestern coal companies shut down by the great strike. During the next fifteen years, however, those shipments would appear as little more than ripples in the river of coal that would flow out of West Virginia's collieries; in that period of time, the workforce would expand by fifty thousand and production would rise by more than 1,000 percent.[15]

The threat posed by this swelling volume of "scab coal" pressed hard upon the mind of John Mitchell, the twenty-eight-year-old Illinois miner who had vaulted up the ranks to become the UMWA's acting president. Intelligent, well spoken, and good-looking (some Catholic miners said he looked like a young priest), Mitchell became the union's "boy president" in 1898 with the support of veteran officials who admired his negotiating skills. The new leader promised to work cooperatively with unionized companies and then boldly set out to expand the union's domain into the anthracite coalfields of eastern Pennsylvania, where the mine owners, large eastern railroads, had defeated one organizing drive after another. Moving fast and with devastating effectiveness, union officials pulled out more than one hundred thousand anthracite miners, including thousands of immigrants who idolized "Johnny d'Mitch." It was a surprising show of force that compelled embittered coal companies to accept the UMWA's terms.

John Mitchell, early 1900s.

Later that year, Mitchell decided to remove the gun that had been pointed at the union's heart in the organized fields of the North. He would launch a new offensive in West Virginia headed by two brave men with the know-how and the most experience as UMWA activists in Pennsylvania. The new president believed this venture also required someone with special qualities, someone who could instill courage and hope in the hearts of the frightened men who mined coal in the Mountain State. The person he hired to play that role would have amazed anyone outside the UMWA's ranks, for he chose a woman old enough to be his grandmother to lead this crucial campaign. Her legal name was Mary Harris Jones, but union men all over industrial America knew her as Mother Jones.

Mary Harris was born in 1837 and raised by poor Irish parents who lived off and on in the city of Cork and on a wild, barren country farm where Catholics "incorporated the old pagan gods into the cult of the saints." When she was nine years old, Mary's kinfolk talked in hushed tones of the blight on the potato crop and the stench that rose from the fields. A year later, when the Great Hunger spread, she boarded a ship with her father bound for Canada—two of the two hundred thousand people who left their island homes seeking a new life overseas in the year the Irish called "Black 47."[16]

When Mary's mother arrived in Toronto to join them, she sent her daughter away to a convent school. After two terms, the girl displayed an independent spirit by setting out on her own to make a living as a schoolteacher in Michigan. Prior to the Civil War, this adventurous young woman moved to Memphis, where she met and married George Jones, an ironworker and union man. She gave birth to four children and raised them in the poor white area of Memphis known as "Pinch Gut." Soon after her fourth child was born in 1867, foundry owners took advantage of an economic downturn to close their shops and lock out their union men. George lost his job, and Mary had to find a way to nourish three youngsters and an infant.

As the Jones family struggled to make ends meet, yellow fever raced through the river districts. Wealthy people fled the city, but poor folks in Pinch Gut stayed put and prayed that the angel of death would pass over their houses. Few were so blessed and many succumbed to what people called the "strangers' disease," so named because the fever struck immigrants hardest. One by one, the Jones children fell ill with the disease. First came the chills and aches, and then came the nausea, cramps, and, finally, hemorrhages. One by one, Mary held her babies as they died; one by one, she washed their little bodies and readied them for burial. Then her husband caught the fever and died. "I sat alone through nights of grief," she wrote in her memoir. "No one came to me. No one could. Other homes were as stricken as mine." All day and all night long, she sat in her shanty listening to the grating sound of the death carts' wheels. The experience could have destroyed this thirty-year-old widow, but it didn't.

Leaving Memphis to the dead, Jones made her way to Chicago, where she earned a living sewing dresses for wealthy women until she lost her shop in the Great Chicago Fire of 1871. She picked herself up and started again, but before long a depression gripped the economy and hung on for three years. She suffered through the hard times with her working-class neighbors, all the while hating the aristocrats who employed her because they ignored the plight of the jobless masses wandering the streets.

Chicago was a hotbed of Fenian activity, a place where nationalists set up the "Skirmishing Fund" to finance guerrilla warfare against British authority. The cause had many contributors among the city's immigrants, including those from Jones's native Cork and from other places in western and southern Ireland where the Great Famine and mass evictions had hit hardest and where immigrants were especially apt to see themselves as "exiles" from "British tyranny."[17]

For the next two decades, the widowed dressmaker witnessed wave after wave of protest by Chicago's working people. Jones was there during the depression year of 1874 when the unemployed marched to city hall demanding "Bread or work!," and she was there three years later when the Great Railroad Strike of 1877 rocked the city and the police killed more than thirty men and boys, most of them Irish Catholics.[18]

No city experienced more massive labor unrest during the Gilded Age than Chicago and no city produced more radicals. Mary Jones was destined to be one of them. She joined the Knights of Labor in the 1880s and took to the streets herself in 1894 to support the railroad car builders who lived and worked in George M. Pullman's model city south of Chicago. These well-paid, well-housed workers stunned their patron when they left work to protest a wage cut and a speedup. The strikers asked for support from other trade unions, but only one responded: the American Railway Union (ARU), whose members voted to boycott all trains hauling Pullman's sleeping cars. In a short time, this sympathetic action shut down most of the nation's western railroads and created a national crisis.

Army troops occupied the city to enforce a sweeping federal injunction, and more than thirty Chicago workers died in the streets fighting; it was a tragedy that altered Jones's life. For the next few years, she devoted herself to saving the life of an ARU striker who had been accused of derailing an army troop train. When the union activist was sentenced to death for this alleged act of sabotage, Jones traveled far and wide to seek clemency for him. She even gained access to the White House to plead his case directly to President Grover Cleveland. During the time she spent saving her adopted "son" from the gallows, Jones came to be known as the "Mother of the ARU."[19]

Jones left Chicago for California, where she linked up with a column of unemployed workers as they marched toward Washington, DC, to demand relief. When she joined the tramps that year, Mother Jones kicked off a journey that would put her on the road for the next twenty-five years. She had traveled as far as Kansas with the unemployed when news reports suddenly drew her to the coalfields that surrounded the Birmingham iron and steel district in northern Alabama. There she found a spirited bunch of strikers whose interracial solidarity would amaze her and whose spirit would inspire her. That trip to Birmingham would be the beginning of Mother Jones's lifelong love affair with America's coal miners and their union.

Three years later, when the UMWA declared a general strike in the bituminous coalfields, Jones rushed from one western Pennsylvania coal patch to another, where she demonstrated a captivating speaking ability, organized food donations from local farmers, staged parades with strikers' children, and mobilized wives and daughters to harass strikebreakers.[20] In miners' lore, women brought bad luck or even death to the miners if they were seen around the pits, but President Ratchford was so impressed with Jones's work that he ignored this taboo and hired her to work as a "walking delegate" for the union; then he sent her off to West Virginia to spread the strike below the Mason-Dixon Line.

On July 27, 1897, Jones appeared before seventeen thousand striking miners and their supporters gathered in Charleston under a blazing sun at "a monster" rally. She took the platform that day and stood with the nation's most prominent labor leaders: the crafty little president of the AFL, Samuel Gompers; the aged Grand Master Workman of the Knights, the dignified James Sovereign; and the statuesque socialist Eugene V. Debs, who spoke, bald and hatless, for so long that he suffered from sunstroke. The lanky Debs had become a working-class hero three years before when, as head of the ARU, he had defied the federal government and the nation's most powerful railroads during the Pullman boycott. From then on, Debs and Jones would become two of the most inspirational labor orators and influential socialists in American history.[21]

In 1900, UMWA president John Mitchell promoted Jones to the rank of "international organizer"* at a yearly salary of $500; then he

---

*The UMWA, like many American trade unions of that era, called itself an "international" organization in order to claim jurisdiction over fellow workers in other countries. In fact, the miners' union became a binational body, with strong locals of Canadian coal miners in British Columbia and Nova Scotia.

sent her to West Virginia on another vital organizing mission. In her autobiography, Jones provided a harrowing account of what happened when she entered the Fairmont field that year, a place where union sympathizers were threatened with death if they distributed handbills for her talks. After a few months of work, she left the field with a heavy heart, saddened that "the sacrifices men and women made to get out from under the iron heel of the gunmen were so often in vain!"[22]

When she addressed the UMWA's convention early in 1901, Jones told the delegates gathered in Indianapolis that West Virginia's miners were not the dumb, frightened "animals" and "scabs" other northern organizers made them out be. "You may say what you please about the West Virginia miners being no good," but "I wish you could see how they live." These men worked and survived in wretched conditions and were oppressed by fellows who made the czar of Russia seem like a "gentleman," but she found "these mountain miners" to be "some of the noblest men" she had "met in all the country." In closing, she urged the union delegates not to betray these fellow workers. "My brothers," she concluded, "I shall consider it an honor if, when you write my epitaph upon my tombstone, you say, 'Died fighting their battles in West Virginia.'"[23]

That fall Mother Jones returned to the Mountain State and headed to the Kanawha field, where some of the earliest union efforts had taken place. Her first stop was the little town of Cedar Grove on the Kanawha River about twenty miles from Charleston. She arrived early, before the mist had risen above the water, and walked through a village that had once been a stopping point for pioneers who purchased supplies, boarded one of the town's numerous flatboats, and continued their journey down the Kanawha to the Ohio River.[24] In 1895, when Mary Lee Settle's grandmother, Addie Tompkins, arrived from Charleston in Cedar Grove, it was still a lazy village, but by the time Mother Jones arrived "the roads were already dark with coal dust, ground in by the weather, and the raindrops on the windowsills [of the old Tompkins house] were black." By 1901, this river town with a boatyard and cottages built of slave-made redbrick had become a bustling commercial center, serving hundreds of mine workers who lived and worked in the new collieries located above the village at Ward, where the Kellys Creek Coal Mining Company had built new Jenny Lind houses for the miners and several tall wooden houses on the hillsides for the superintendents. A railroad from Ward's original mine cut the town in half, and on one side of the tracks there were rows of company-built shacks spilling down to the river and the old boatyard.[25]

Only a few early risers noticed the strange woman meandering through the streets with a shawl covering her shoulders and the top of her embroidered dress. She had a pretty face with bright blue eyes and white hair that fell down on her rosy cheeks, and she wore what one observer described as "a nice-lady black pot hat." A woman of average height, sturdily built but not fat, she appeared to be in her fifties, but she marched along like someone much younger.[26]

When the visitor saw a lamplight flickering through a window of a grocery store, she knocked on the door, and the proprietor, a Mr. Marshall, invited her into a back room and offered her some breakfast. She thanked him for his hospitality and then introduced herself as Mrs. Mary Jones, a "walking delegate" for the UMWA. At that moment, the storekeeper realized that he was sitting

New Jenny Lind houses in the Badbottom section of Ward on Kellys Creek.

face-to-face with none other than the notorious Mother Jones, the agitator who had been raising hell up north. "All the time he was frightened and kept looking out the little window," Jones later wrote of the grocer. He told her that if the mine owners knew she was in his store, they would close it down; nonetheless, Marshall offered to help his famous guest by telling her how to get word out to the miners that she would hold a secret meeting on a hillside that night.

At nightfall Jones trudged up the creek bed behind a young miner carrying a kerosene lantern. When she came to the designated spot on a mountain slope, a group of forty men waited for her in the midst of some boulders. While her comrade held a light over her head, Mother Jones spoke about a great union movement that had lifted Pennsylvania coal diggers up out of poverty, and railed about the men and boys who had been "murdered" in a mine explosion at Red Ash by greedy West Virginia mine owners who valued profits more than human lives.[27]

"Mother Jones was always angry," a former coal miner recalled. "She'd swear at anybody," not only at the bosses and their "bloodhounds"—the deputy sheriffs and hired mine guards—but at union officials who cozied up to the employers and sold out their own members. Mine workers who encountered Jones for the first time were thunderstruck when this woman, who looked like a grandmother, spoke to them like a drill sergeant.[28]

That night, on a rocky slope above Kellys Creek, Jones called upon her listeners to stand up and act like men, "not like cringing serfs." She carried on until the time was right to ask who among them would come forward and take the "oath of obligation" to the miners' union. To her delight, all of them lined up, and then one by one each man came before her and raised his right hand and swore to honor the principles of brotherhood; forbear any act of discrimination against a fellow worker on account of creed, color, or nationality and "defend freedom of thought whether expressed by tongue or pen."[29]

Mother Jones retired for the evening feeling pleased with her work, but when she awoke the next morning, a miner burst into her room with terrible news: There had been spies among the miners who took the union oath the night before, and when the men who had taken the pledge reported for work that day, the pit boss told each one to step aside; then he ordered them to clear out of the company's houses. None of them would ever work in the valley again.

"This started the fight," Jones noted years later. It was a fight she would carry to many other coal towns that fall and winter. It was a fight that would brand her "the most dangerous woman in America," a hard and dangerous fight that would link her purpose on earth to the destiny of West Virginia's coal miners, the men she would always call her "boys."

As soon as Jones heard that the Kellys Creek Coal Mining Company had fired all the miners who had taken the union pledge, she planned a protest. "Mr. Marshall, the grocery man, got courageous" and rented his store to her as a place to hold "indignation meetings." When word of this agitation reached company headquarters back in Columbus, Ohio, the general manager hurried down to Cedar Grove on his special railroad car and held a meeting of his own in front of the company store. When he told his miners they should be ashamed of being led around by an old woman, several of them defiantly shouted "Hurrah for Mother Jones!"

The next day was Sunday, and after prayer services ended that morning, Jones sent runners up the valley with word that she would hold a rally to support the men who had been fired. When the miners and their families walked down from the company houses in Ward, Jones gathered them in front of the company's hotel and yelled for the general manager to come out. "He did not appear," she recalled in her memoir, but "two of the company's lap dogs were on the porch. One of them said, 'I'd like to hang that old woman to a tree.' 'Yes,' said the other, 'and I'd like to pull the rope.'"

"On we marched to our meeting place under the trees," she remembered. "Over a thousand people came and the two lap dogs came sniveling along too." Jones began to speak under the crimson cedars, but then stopped suddenly and pointed at the two men who followed the parade. She put her back up against a big tree and called out to them in a stage voice: "You said that you would like to hang this old woman to a tree! Well, here's the old woman and here's the tree. Bring along your rope and hang her!" Jones excelled at this kind of theatrical performance, and her antics thrilled and amused the crowd. By the time the meeting ended, she had gathered even more colliers into her flock.[30]

A few days later, Addie Tompkins glanced out the window of her handsome home on the edge of Cedar Grove to the creek below and saw something that riveted her attention. There in the cold water of Kellys Creek stood Jones. She was wearing miner's boots, holding her skirts up with one hand and gesturing with the other like a bandleader, as she regaled a bunch of miners on their way to town. She had waded into the creek when mine company agents told her she could not speak on the roads or the railroad tracks because they were private property.[31]

By this time, Tompkins had heard many tales of Mother Jones's bravery, accounts of how she once "walked right by a copperhead and never paused," and how she strolled past an unsuspecting foreman and into the mine "with a carbide lamp on a miner's hat she borrowed." Jones found "her boys, sat with them on the gob pile [of slate], and organized while they shared their beans and fatback and cornbread with her." On another occasion, she "had to get out of one mining camp at night because her boys found out that the superintendent and his men were plotting to kill her and an organizer who was with her, [and] burn them in coke ovens . . ." Late in her life, it occurred to Addie Tompkins that Mother Jones behaved like "a woman who had replaced her past with zeal for what she was doing, as if she had already died and had nothing left to fear."[32]

During the winter of 1902, Jones tested her limits by venturing back into the mountain hollows to preach the union gospel to coal town "wage slaves." One rainy night, when she was heading down a steep goat path to a rally, she slipped and slid most of the way down. "My bones are sore today," she wrote to President Mitchell, who replied like a worried son. He pleaded with her to take care and save her strength for this drive, because, he wrote, if the union failed in West

Virginia this time, it would suffer the consequences in its next round of bargaining with the midwestern coal companies.[33]

Mary Jones had reached the age of sixty-five in 1902—at a time when the life expectancy of American women was forty-eight—but she took pride in defying her age, ignoring her sore bones and carrying on. A fellow organizer, who admitted he often whined and thought the battle not worth the effort, reported that Mother Jones never complained: "No mountain seems too high, or path too rugged as long as she can find a receptive audience." As winter turned to spring that year, she found many receptive audiences in the Kanawha coalfield. "Our people are responding like braves," she reported to Mitchell that May. "After three weeks of hard work I feel Kellys Creek is ours . . ."[34]

Mother Jones's self-styled "invasion" of Kellys Creek represented one of the many grassroots campaigns trade unionists were conducting in minefields, rail yards, garment districts, factory towns, and seaports across the land. Prosperity had returned, unemployment had declined, and organized labor was on the march. Strikes and boycotts had never been more effective. By the end of the year, membership in the unions affiliated with the AFL had doubled in the span of just three years and the UMWA had emerged as one of the nation's largest, most diverse labor organizations.[35]

After she evangelized among the miners of Kellys Creek, Jones crossed the Great Kanawha and wended her way through scores of coal camps that lined Paint Creek and Cabin Creek. As her recruiting drive gained

Mother Jones, 1902.

momentum, President Mitchell warned her that the UMWA faced a grave challenge from the anthracite mine owners in Pennsylvania, who refused to discuss an extension of the trade agreement they had grudgingly signed two years before. When the UMWA's executive board reluctantly called for a strike on May 12, President Mitchell wrote to Mother Jones: "I am of the opinion that this will be the fiercest struggle in which we have yet engaged. It will be a fight to the end, and our organization will either achieve a great triumph or it will be completely annihilated."[36]

The great strike in the northern fields excited the newly organized miners of West Virginia, so much so that many of them wanted to act in support of the anthracite miners. Mitchell told them they were not ready to strike, but local union leaders decided to seize the moment anyway. On June 7, 1902, approximately sixteen thousand Mountain State miners shut down 408 collieries in a show of solidarity and in an effort to gain the advantages enjoyed by UMWA members north of the Ohio River. The strikers held firm in the mines

Union miners at a colliery on Cabin Creek.

along Kellys Creek, Cabin Creek, and in the rest of the unionized Kanawha minefield where Mother Jones had done her best work. Employers in this district agreed to terms with union representatives so that their employees could return to work and fill orders from customers who could no longer buy anthracite coal from Pennsylvania. In the nearby New River field, an even more impressive strike by ten thousand newly recruited union miners had stopped production at 80 percent of the collieries in Fayette County.[37]

Mother Jones felt vindicated by her West Virginia boys and she boasted about them in a speech before a special convention of the UMWA.

A great deal has been said for and against them . . . No one has mingled with them more than I have, and no one has heard more of their tales of sorrow and their tales of hope . . . They have their faults, I admit, but no state ever produced nobler, truer, better men under the appalling circumstances and conditions under which they work. Think of the New River field, of the Kanawha River . . . and think of the work the boys have done there. Every wheel there is closed down, and that shows you what good union material there is there. One of the best fellows we have is the black man. He knows what liberty is; he knows that in days gone by . . . his own Mammy wept and prayed for liberty. For these reasons he prizes his liberty and is ready to fight for it.[38]

After several forays into the Mountain State's minefields, Jones had discovered what the first UMWA organizers had learned: black miners held the key to the union's future in that state. It wasn't just a matter of whether whites would ever accept "colored men" as brothers; it was also a question of whether individualistic mountaineers would emulate the black miners by practicing the virtues of solidarity.[39]

The bonds of unity held firm in the New River field where nearly a quarter of the miners were African Americans, but there wouldn't be a quick settlement like the one between the union and the mine owners of Kanawha field. Unlike the operators in the Kanawha field, who ended the strike in a few weeks by agreeing to negotiate, New River's coal magnates pulled up the gates to their garrison towns and prepared for war. "We will let this mine be closed forever," one of them told a reporter, "before we will allow the union to control our business."[40]

The New River employers decided to sit tight and wait for their employees to give up and return to work, but after a few weeks one of these men decided to break the strike. Justus Collins erected iron fences around his colliery at Glen Jean, ordered his lawyers to obtain a federal circuit court injunction against the picketers, and asked a deputy U.S. marshal to command a guard detail on his property. Collins also sued in county court for the power to eject strikers from their rented houses.[41]

Collins's competitors soon followed his example, and within a few days, streams of homeless miners and their families poured out of mine camps like Glen Jean and into the incorporated town of Mount Hope, where the union set up a tent colony for the strikers. Many of the town's residents sympathized with the miners and with their struggle with outsiders like Justus Collins, who had come into Fayette County like soldiers of fortune, established private forms of government in their towns, and ignored elected officials they couldn't bribe.[42] Collins demonstrated his disregard for local authorities when he bypassed the elected sheriff of Fayette County and fortified his property with forty private guards he hired from the Baldwin-Felts Detective Agency in Bluefield, West Virginia.

The agency's founder, W. G. Baldwin, had worked as chief of detective services for the Norfolk & Western Railway and became famous for pursuing outlaws who wrecked trains and robbed their passengers. Baldwin also provided services to judges who wanted fugitives tracked down and brought to justice dead or alive, including the Hatfields accused of slaying the McCoy brothers. On at least two occasions, Baldwin was accused of murdering suspects in cold blood. On another job early in 1900, Baldwin was accompanied by a thirty-three-year-old assistant named Thomas LaFayette Felts, a wavy-haired Virginian. Felts had been sitting behind a desk in the N&W claims department when he signed on to work as a detective.

On his first assignment, Felts joined Baldwin as he tracked an escaped murderer in the wooded mountains of McDowell County. When the agents found their man, he opened fire. In the gunfight that followed, the fugitive put a .45-caliber slug two inches below Felts's heart. The bullet passed through his body and missed his vital organs, but he nearly bled to death. A local newspaper found the story of the shoot-out "most romantic," one that left the correspondent wondering why a man like Felts would "follow a calling so fraught with danger as that of the detective." When it was clear that Felts would live, Baldwin made him partner and put him in charge of meeting the growing demand for detective services from coal operators.[43]

In response to Justus Collins's request, the Baldwin-Felts Agency sent out a band of detectives to Glen Jean. They arrived riding horses, wearing quasi-military uniforms, and bearing Winchester rifles, looking like a troop of U.S. cavalry dispatched to an outpost deep in Indian Territory. The captain of the guards ordered one man to the top of each mine tipple, where Collins had placed searchlights and machine guns; he then ordered one unit to guard the iron gates and sent the others to evict strikers from company housing.

As soon as she heard this news, Mother Jones bought a ticket and boarded a C&O passenger train bound for Mount Hope. The locomotive snaked along the Kanawha River and its gentle falls until it reached a wide lake where the Gauley and New Rivers met to form the Great Kanawha. On both sides of the wild New River, mountains rose three thousand feet above the water, their slopes blazing with a dazzling array of maroon and yellow, crimson and auburn leaf cover. After it passed under the towering rock called Hawks Nest, Jones's train entered the majestic New River Gorge, a grand gateway to the smokeless coalfields of Fayette County.

When she detrained in Mount Hope later that day, the strikers who met her at the station reported that union members were being beaten and shot in the nearby camps. Some men had disappeared without a trace. Thousands of union men had been blacklisted,

A Baldwin-Felts agent at Glen Jean, 1902.

and armed guards had thrown three thousand families out of their houses and onto the roads.[44]

Growing more desperate with each day that passed, the strikers took to the hills and fired on the working miners, wounding two at the Rush Run mine. Near the end of August, a local newspaper called this "the worst reign of lawlessness and terror in the history of the county."[45]

After two Baldwin-Felts agents and two strikers died in a gun battle around the Crane Creek mines, the sheriff declared that it was impossible for him to keep the peace in Fayette County. The governor reacted by sending four hundred militiamen into the New River field. A dozen guardsmen found the situation so frightening that they deserted, but other soldiers reportedly made friends of the strikers; it is said, read a news item, "that some of the militia jeered and taunted the non-union workers on every occasion." On Labor Day, the guard stood aside as thousands of people attended celebrations in Mount Hope and Glen Jean, where the crowds were reported to be "very orderly." A week later, however, the militia effectively cordoned off the mines from the strikers, allowing hundreds of hungry workers to return to the mines without fear of being harassed or assaulted by the union men.[46]

At this point, Mother Jones decided she could do more good in Colorado, where a much larger coalfield struggle was under way. When she arrived in Denver, the miners' magazine hailed this "patron saint" of the workers who toiled in the mines of Pennsylvania and West Virginia; these workers saw her as an "angel of light," and "worshipped [her] with a reverence that is as pure and as holy as ever linked a mother and her sons."[47]

"If she was the miner's angel," wrote the novelist Mary Lee Settle, "she was the owner's devil." They called her an "Old Hag," an evil spirit who bewitched their men. They called her an anarchist even though she was a Christian socialist, but as Settle noted, "no coal operator knew or gave a damn about the difference." Whatever words they used to demonize Mother Jones, the mine owners of West Virginia agreed with a U.S. district attorney who prosecuted her for violating a court injunction that summer. He named her "the most dangerous woman in America" because she could, by her own words and deeds, persuade hundreds of men to walk out the mines.[48]

While she rallied miners in southern Colorado that fall, Jones seethed over the fact that Mitchell and his officers had given up on strikers in the New River field, where the Baldwin-Felts Agency had imposed a "reign of terror," according the *United Mine Workers Journal*. But, as usual, Jones ignored friends who feared for her safety and headed back into the storm. When she reached the New River field, agents tailed her constantly, and one night in early December 1902, when a suspicious fire broke out in the unoccupied hotel room next to hers, Jones narrowly escaped.[49]

Two months later, while she waited for a train to take her to another trouble spot, the clerk told Jones there had been "some shooting" that morning at a strikers' camp near Collins's Glen Jean colliery. She turned in her ticket and found two strikers to take her to the strikers' camp below Stanaford Mountain. When she arrived everything was "deathly still," but then she heard the sound of sobbing and she saw a grieving woman sitting by a cabin that had been riddled with bullet holes. "I pushed open the door," she wrote. "On a mattress wet with blood lay a miner. His brains had been blown out while he slept."[50]

That morning, a large posse of deputies and mine guards had moved upon the camp at dawn, survivors told Jones. They opened fire on the strikers without warning. When the shooting ended, three black miners lay dead in their cabins. A short time later, the witnesses said, the posse killed three white miners.[51]

Justus Collins and his fellow mine operators in the smokeless coalfields assumed that the events at Stanaford Mountain had put an end to their troubles with the UMWA. The New River employers had crushed the strike, blacklisted its leaders, and driven the union from the field, and they had preserved a pay scale that allowed them to undercut their northern competitors in the national market.

For nearly a decade the bloody conflict in Fayette County would be remembered simply as a victory for the mine operators, but a decade later, the struggle would be seen in a different light—as a dress rehearsal for another fight that would take place on a much wider battleground, on a much larger scale, and with far different consequences.

After the slain strikers were buried below Stanaford Mountain, Jones left West Virginia behind and moved on to other causes, but she never forgot what she experienced in the New River field. In speech after speech she would tell her audiences about the horrors of "Medieval West Virginia," with its tent colonies filled with grim-faced men and women and their raggedy little children, and she would often recall that moment when she saw those bullet holes in a black miner's cabin and heard the sobbing of his widow. Of all the cruelties she witnessed in her troubled life, none enraged her more than this one.[52]

Mother Jones had failed in the New River field, and there was blood on the ground to prove it, but her work in West Virginia had not been all in vain. Jones's followers had established scores of union outposts in the mines along Kellys Creek and across the big river on Cabin Creek, where a young mountaineer miner had been inspired to become a leader and take up the fight she had started.

Chapter 3

Frank Keeney's Valley

Winter 1903–Winter 1907

In 1903, Charles Francis Keeney Jr. had been loading coal on Cabin Creek for three years. Short and lean, but sturdy, this twenty-one-year-old mountaineer had straight black hair, piercing blue eyes, strong jaw muscles, and a dimple on his prominent chin. Well-liked for his easygoing ways and his fondness for joking, Keeney seemed like an ordinary young workingman who enjoyed hunting, drinking whiskey, and shooting pool with his buddies. No one imagined then that C. F. Keeney, or Frank as he was known, would one day emerge from obscurity to become a tribune of his people—no one except Mother Jones, who saw something special when she met this "bright-eyed little fellow." Keeney would become one of the many coal camp "boys" she took under her wing. "I gave him a book one Sunday," she recalled in her memoir, "and I said to him . . . 'Go up under the trees and read. Leave the pool room alone. Read and study and find out how to help your fellow miners.' And he did it."[1]

Young Keeney did more than read and study. He became a book lover who worked his way through all of Shakespeare's plays and sonnets and started to write his own poetry. And he did more than help his fellow miners, for he was destined "by birth and by feeling" to become "a genuine leader of his people," as the *New Republic*'s Edmund Wilson remarked many years later.[2]

Like his father and grandfather, Frank was born and raised on land Moses Keeney purchased in 1833 after he drove his wagon from Greenbrier County into the unsettled Cabin Creek Valley. When Moses died in 1849, each of the patriarch's nine sons inherited a parcel of the original homestead, where they cultivated their own subplots, milled lumber, and raised their large families. The Keeney boys carried on with old ways even when life in their valley began to change after the Chesapeake & Ohio Railway ran an extension line up the creek. By 1880, farmers like the Keeneys were outnumbered by 340 coal miners and 160 laborers, including 28 men who worked in the clanking new C&O switching yards at Cane Fork. Moses Keeney's grandson, Charles, was one of those who kept farming on the family homestead with the help of a local girl named Elizabeth, who became the mother of two girls and a boy, Charles Francis Jr., who was born in 1882. But the child would never get to know his father. Charles Sr. died two years later, leaving his twenty-one-year-old wife alone to tend the farm and raise her children.[3]

To get by, the widow took in sewing and relied upon the kindness of the Keeney in-laws and friendly neighbors in the Cabin Creek community called Eskdale. Elizabeth's greatest hope was that her boy would go to school, learn to write and speak proper English, and grow up to be a successful man outside the valley.[4] But when Frank reached the age of ten, his mother did what many others in tight circumstances did. She took her son out of school and sent him to work in the mines. It was a hard choice but a necessary one; the widow and her girls needed the boy's wages. And so, one morning in 1892, little Frank left his cabin in Eskdale with a lunch bucket in his hand and climbed up to a mine portal, where he began working as a trapper boy. His job: opening and shutting tunnel doors for eleven hours a day in a mine on the mountainside above his home.

West Virginia's drift mines were cut into the mountains horizontally and its slope mines descended gradually into the earth. All of these mines included a main entry, or portal, and a second tunnel, or "monkey drift," which provided workers with "ventilation"—a barely adequate suction through a surface grate created by a coal fire that burned all day. "Smoke from explosions of black powder, the reek of oil lamps, and the pervading coal dust made breathable air something of an obsession with the miner," one miner recalled. A trapper like Frank had to pay close attention to his duties, opening and closing the doors regularly to keep the air moving and to allow coal cars to pass back and forth. He also learned not to scare the miners' beloved pigeons or to be afraid of mine rats, because these creatures could sense danger coming before it struck.[5]

One threat the animals and birds could detect was the odor of gas that oozed from the ancient vegetation compacted over the ages. These deposits could produce "firedamp," which contained methane and sometimes carbon dioxide that seeped out of the coal seams. Firedamp, described as "the monster most dreaded by the practical miner," could explode if ignited by sparks or powder blasts, which would send fires raging through mine shafts with hurricane force.[6]

Frank Keeney left no account of how he felt the day he entered the mine portal, but one imagines the dread that might have accompanied a ten-year-old boy's first trip into the hole. For hours on end, a trapper boy's ears would take in the strange sounds made by creaking timbers, rattling coal cars, clopping mules, and thudding blasts of explosions deep in the mine, while his eyes would behold surreal sights, like the white bones of ancient fish skeletons and the remains of tropical plants when they were illuminated by the miners' lamps. Three decades earlier a boy about the same age—a newly emancipated slave—had worked in the same minefield. It was a dreadful experience Booker T. Washington never forgot. He later recalled his terror at being lost in a maze of underground rooms when his lamp went out. Without a match he walked, hands held in front of his body, until, by chance, someone found him and gave him a light. Fearful of the danger, frightened by the "blackest darkness" he could imagine, and repelled by the coal dust that clung to him like a layer of skin, Washington vowed to get an education and rise out of the coal pits, just as he had risen "up from slavery."[7]

Most trapper boys learned how to overcome their fears by watching and listening to the colliers who went underground with them. When young Frank Keeney walked through a mine portal in 1892, perhaps an older miner, maybe a neighbor, offered him some words of consolation or, at least, instruction as they traveled in and out of the mine on what was known as a "man trip." Or he might have heard some words of warning from the older boys who led the mules and coal cars back and forth through the door he tended. At suppertime, youngsters like Frank would sit with the men on a pile of slate and listen as veterans of the mine would sing songs, spin yarns, and tell jokes; they would rib the boys, trick them for laughs, and tell them tall tales of the devilish apparitions that appeared to them down in the hole. The veteran miners, who prided themselves on their toughness, taught the youngest ones how to act like men, how to ignore the pain, and how to laugh away their fears. Boys discovered that serious men turned into jokers when they toiled underground. Acquiring a sense of humor helped mask a worker's dread of the mine, but joking was no substitute for learning how to be careful.[8] In the words of the popular song "Miner's Lifeguard," written by a miner from Oak Hill, West Virginia:

> A miner's life is like a sailor's,
> 'Board a ship to cross the wave;
> Every day his life's in danger,
> Still he ventures to be brave.
> Watch the rocks, they're falling daily,
> Careless miners always fail.[9]

Mule drivers and trapper boys like Frank Keeney set out at six o'clock every morning with the adult miners, who each carried a pick and augur, a can of black blasting powder, fuses, and a tamping rod. The miners dressed in overalls, or "bank clothes," for working the coal banks and wore cloth caps fitted with small oil lamps that lit their way in the tunnels. At dawn, the workers reported to the payroll clerk in the company office, where they were handed numbered brass checks to attach to each coal car they loaded. After checking in, they climbed up a steep trail from the office to the portal of a mine. Then, with their lamps casting a dim yellow light on the dark hillside, the men and boys disappeared one by one into the hole, like ants entering a colony.

Every workday a "panel" of miners, ranging from fourteen to twenty-eight men, passed through a main entry and then turned

A West Virginia trapper boy.

down a side entry. Every three or four hundred feet, passageways were cut, creating narrower, corridor-like rooms that led to a coal face where each miner and his "buddy" worked in their own "room." The colliers left large pillars of coal standing as they cut the face forward and sideways through "breakthroughs" that led to parallel rooms. This was the "room and pillar" method of mining common in the Appalachian bituminous coalfields.[10]

When a miner and his helper approached the entry to their room, danger lurked in almost every move they made. First, the men had to push an empty coal car up wooden rails that they had installed on their own time. "A man sometimes had to get down on his hands and knees, with his left shoulder, well padded, against the car, bracing himself with his toes against the ties and the dirt of the floor," wrote a former miner, while his partner controlled the brakes "to keep the car from rolling back on the pusher if he slipped or grew tired." Back injuries, broken legs, and severed feet and fingers were common.[11]

Next came preparations for extracting the coal. At the far end of the room, the miner lay down on his side and cut under the bottom of the coal face with his pick, inching his way into the cut and hoping the coal was hard enough not to collapse on him. After undercutting the face, the collier turned the crank on a five-and-a-half-foot-long breast auger and pushed with all his weight to bore a hole high on the face. Using a thin iron needle about the thickness of a pencil, he shoved a cartridge of black powder into the hole and pushed a little clay into the hole with a damper; then he carefully withdrew the needle and inserted a wick of waxed paper, a squib, that would burn down to the black powder. When he lit the fuse, the lead miner hollered, "Fire in the hole," and scuttled out of the room with his buddy.

The correct use of explosives depended on the miner's skill and knowledge of how to drill, how much powder to use, and how to damp a charge properly. Besides know-how, the miners depended upon instinct and luck. In some cases, when a shot backfired out of the hole, it ignited coal dust or gas in the miner's room and sent fire bursting into the main tunnel, where it could burn or suffocate the mules and their drivers passing through. This risk increased enormously when inexperienced miners failed to undercut the coal before blasting and took the risk of "shooting on the solid."[12]

A good blast could bring down a ton or more of coal from the fractured face. When the smoke cleared, the collier and his buddy would swing their picks to break up large clumps of coal and shovel the smaller lumps into a mine car; it was back-aching work made more painful by the narrowness of the room. Kanawha County coal seams were relatively thick, so men could often stand or just bend slightly, but some coal cutters had to work bent over all day in "low coal." After sorting out the slate fragments and loading the car, the miner attached his brass check to the side of the car and pushed it out into the main tunnel, where mules or a small locomotive pulled the load out of the mine to the weigh station and then to the tipple, where the coal would be prepared and funneled into railroad cars.

A strong, skilled coal loader might fill five or more cars in a day. In West Virginia's colliers, miners were paid 49 cents per ton of clean coal, compared with 76.1 cents in the unionized mines of Ohio. Under these terms, a hard worker could earn $2.00 for ten to twelve hours of labor, if the work was steady.[13] But on some weeks, a miner might work only two or three days because the railroad failed to supply enough coal cars, or because the mine needed repairs. Even in a good week, there was unpaid work to perform: propping up newly opened rooms with wooden posts, laying track to his room, and lowering the floor of the main tunnel so loaded coal cars could pass through. The miners called this unpaid labor "company work."[14]

The workday ended at 5:30 in the evening when the sunlight had already faded over the mountains. Then the men and boys would gather their tools and trudge down the mountainside to their little cabins to wash off the coal dust that smudged their faces, necks, arms, and hands, and to sit down for an evening meal.[15]

This was the world Frank Keeney entered as a boy. After a temporary escape to attend grammar school, it was the world he reentered in 1900 as an eighteen-year-old man willing and able to load coal for a miner's pay. As a novice, Keeney learned the collier's trade from older craftsmen—the skills of cutting the face, setting the charges, and loading the coal without wrenching his back or crippling himself. He also absorbed the habits and traditions that gave pick and shovel miners a remarkable degree of freedom. Hourly employees were bound to the ten-hour day, but the coal loaders, or "tonnage men," often worked fewer hours and sometimes exercised the right to leave the mine without permission. The carpenters, mechanics, mule skinners, and other mine employees, who enjoyed no such latitude, were known by pit-face miners as "company men." By contrast, the pit-face miners saw themselves as autonomous workmen who labored for themselves as well as for the company.[16]

Mine foremen attempted various forms of industrial discipline to maximize productivity, but in the early 1900s, coal miners experienced little of the supervision foremen and factory managers imposed on workers; in fact, veteran colliers often became surly when a mine foreman came by their place on his little scooter to check on them. Self-respecting craftsmen were even known to stop working when a foreman came by to inspect their room. In some cases, when word came around that a miner had been scolded or punished by a boss, workers would gather on a pile of slate to talk about the incident, and the bolder ones with a "manly bearing toward the boss" would speak up for their fellow worker. Few words meant more to mine workers than "manliness," a quality that connoted "dignity, respectability, defiant egalitarianism, and patriarchal male supremacy," in the words of historian David Montgomery. These were the underground attitudes Frank Keeney absorbed as he entered manhood as a coal miner.[17]

West Virginia miners begin a ten-hour shift with a boy starting his career as a "picker."

The mine operators assumed that if they paid a worker according to the number of tons he loaded, they would foster a competitive climate underground; and in a sense, the tonnage system worked this way. The strongest, most efficient men earned the most money at the end of the day. Frank Keeney wanted to be a first-class tonnage man because he needed to support his widowed mother and two sisters, along with his new wife, a fair teenager named Bessie Meadows, an Eskdale girl who wanted to become a schoolteacher.

A miner's compulsion to load as much coal as possible was tempered by experience, however. Veteran colliers knew competitive individualism bred greed, hostility, thievery, and a disregard for mine safety. Stealing another man's coal was considered a "terrible crime." A thief could commit this offense easily, simply by removing one miner's brass check from his coal car and replacing it with his own; but the miners often detected this kind of trickery and banded together to demand the thief's termination.[18] Taking a mine car out of turn constituted another grave offense. Every workingman was supposed to have his turn when it came to getting an empty coal car, because each collier deserved an equal opportunity to get his load to the weigh station. Coal loaders at the face depended on mule drivers and motor men to honor the old tradition of a "square turn"—"a custom through which colliers sought to control output and equalize earning opportunities by ensuring that each miner would receive the same number of cars during a workday," in the words of a mine industry historian.[19]

Aboveground, many miners suffered at the hands of the company men who short-weighed tonnage a man had loaded or docked his pay because slate was found mixed in with the coal. The need to correct these abuses led the UMWA to demand the employment of a "check-weigh man" whom the miners could trust. A standard tune in miners' lore began with lyric, "You've been docked and docked again, boys / You've been loading two for one," and asked what the miner had to show for working so hard. "Nothing" was the answer, nothing but the miserable life he and his family endured living in

Frank and Bessie Keeney as newlyweds.

rented shanties hard on the railroad tracks. But to those who suffered alone in silence, the chorus offered hope and strength:

> *Union miners, stand together!*
> *Heed no operator's tale!*
> *Keep your hand upon the dollar,*
> *And your eye upon the scale!*[20]

Green miners like Frank Keeney also learned that surviving underground required men to depend upon each other and to honor the wisdom of the most experienced men. The craftiness and deftness of the best colliers was most evident when they performed the riskiest task of all. After workers had advanced the mine face to the end of the seam, veterans began the dangerous work of removing the massive coal pillars that stood between the rooms and helped support the mine top. "Retreat mining" required the rapid destruction of these pillars, each containing tons of valuable coal, before the mine collapsed. As the men removed one pillar after another, the wooden posts used to support the mine top would be strained as the roof started "getting heavy." The wood would then creak and groan and then splinter as the miners heard the roof "working" above their heads and planned their retreat accordingly.[21]

After they loaded coal from the fallen pillars, the colliers and their helpers pushed their cars out into the main entry as fast as possible before sections of the roof collapsed. After the top fell, they returned to break and load the fallen coal before another layer of the top came crashing down with a tremendous roar. "An experienced miner would often work calmly under conditions that would terrify a novice," wrote a veteran of the bituminous mines.[22]

Retreat mining was a risky business, but at least the miners engineered these cave-ins. Under other circumstances, mine tops fell without warning. Even the most skilled miners could not detect the presence of kettle bottoms, the petrified remains of huge ancient tree trunks that could plunge through the roofs and crush workers. During the early 1900s, roof falls in the bituminous coal mines killed an average of 886 workers every year, as compared with the 274 deaths per year caused by explosions and fires. In West Virginia, where mines were cut near the mountaintops, the overburden was looser and more prone to collapse than in the deeper shaft mines of the North.[23]

West Virginia's mine safety laws were the weakest in the nation. One statute required operators to print maps of their mines, but it excluded any provisions for enforcing this requirement. Another statute required employers to hire pit bosses to examine every working place in the mine, but only "as often as practicable." A third rule required the managers to water the coal dust, but only when they detected a dangerous level of gas. The failure of a mine boss to dampen the coal dust was the reason the Red Ash mine blew up in 1905, killing thirteen men and boys on Fire Creek. Red Ash mine was also the location of a disaster in 1900, which killed forty-six miners. This earlier catastrophe outraged Mother Jones, who spoke of it often on her organizing campaign that year, and it had triggered public pressure to improve the state's mine safety laws. The legislature rejected all proposals for reform, however. The lawmakers apparently agreed with West Virginia's Republican governor, G. W. Atkinson, who said in 1901: "It is but the natural course of mining events that men should be injured and killed by accidents."[24]

Young mule drivers in a West Virginia mine tunnel.

Regardless of what their state government might or might not do to protect them, the miners of West Virginia had to rely on themselves and their buddies, rather than on company fire bosses and state mine inspectors, whose numbers were few and whose visits were infrequent. Coal diggers gave up some of their hard-earned pay to aid fellow miners when they were sick or injured, and when a mine exploded, they risked their lives to rescue the survivors trapped inside. If a man died in a mine, they quit work to honor him and to take up a collection for his surviving wife and children. On one hand, the miners' discipline and death-defying courage made them ideal industrial soldiers; on the other hand, the qualities the men forged in underground combat with the elements—bravery, fraternal fealty, and group solidarity—hardened them for aboveground combat with their employers.[25]

The customs and "rituals of mutuality" that young miners like Frank Keeney inherited from older men constituted an ethical basis for taking collective action and for practicing the kind of solidarity the mine workers' union expected from all of its members. Two years after Keeney began working as a coal loader, he joined his fellow workers on the picket line and helped out until the UMWA negotiated a trade agreement with the Kanawha County mine operators. The new contract guaranteed the workers a nine-hour day, tonnage payments verified by a check-weigh man, a promise of freedom from the company store monopoly, and a guarantee that no union activists would be fired or blacklisted.[26]

Two years later, when the officers of UMWA District 17 successfully negotiated a second contract with the Kanawha Valley mine operators, they believed that the employers had agreed to allow a check-weigh man to collect union dues from all mine employees. In other words, the UMWA's leaders assumed they had negotiated a "closed shop" agreement and that, under these conditions, no man would be hired unless he agreed to join the union and pay dues that the employers would deduct from his paycheck. But James M. Kay, the largest mine owner on Cabin Creek, blew up the agreement when he denied that the operators had granted the UMWA a closed shop or that the employers had agreed to deduct, or check off, union dues.[27]

Kay and his fellow operators refused to reopen negotiations on these matters and the officers of District 17 reluctantly ordered Cabin Creek miners to put down their tools and put up picket lines. In response, the employers offered the strikers three choices: they could return to work under the bosses' terms, they could leave the valley with transportation and moving costs paid by the operators, or they could suffer the consequences—termination and eviction from their company-owned houses. Some chose one of the first two options, but other strikers, including Frank Keeney, chose the third. To deal with these defiant ones, Cabin Creek managers hired four Baldwin-Felts detectives to carry out evictions and ensure that union supporters caused no more trouble.[28]

James Kay's decision to stop bargaining with the miners' union was surely influenced by a well-organized, well-funded "open shop" drive the National Association of Manufacturers (NAM) had initiated in 1901. The two-pronged campaign aimed to remold public opinion and turn it against pro-union politicians and their legislative efforts; to reject all closed shop demands; and to resist strikes, boycotts, and organizing efforts with layoffs, blacklists, private armed forces, and court injunctions. Justus Collins and the New River operators had employed all these tactics to crush a strike and maintain low wages in Fayette County collieries in 1902. A reporter calculated that 180 union men were killed on picket lines and marches in a thirty-month period that began in January of that year.[29]

No union miners died during the 1904 strike on Cabin Creek, but when the union's district officers called off the strike in December, diehards like Frank Keeney took the defeat hard, according to a reporter who interviewed him two decades later. "He saw 700 families put out of their houses into the snow. He saw the union broken. He saw the miners denied the right to organize . . . Keeney became vindictive. He became a Socialist."[30]

After his conversion, Keeney found dozens of new comrades who had joined the Socialist Party of America, local men and women who had taken the field that fall to campaign for their party's presidential candidate, Eugene V. Debs, who advocated collective ownership and control of industry and the democratic management of the economy in the interest of all people. Some of these Debs men were union coal miners who had been radicalized by the bitter defeats their union had suffered in the New River field and in the mines along Cabin Creek. Some were immigrant artisans—carpenters, glassblowers, and brewers—who brought their politics with them from Europe. Others were farmers, newspapermen, country schoolteachers, lawyers, ministers, and small-town merchants who had been devoted followers of the Great Commoner, William Jennings Bryan, and his populist campaigns for the presidency in 1896 and 1900, which had ended in failure.[31] These West Virginians had seen their valleys penetrated by the railroad tracks, their farmland gobbled up by outside interests, their virgin forests clear-cut by timber companies. They had seen their free-spirited mountain boys become dependent wage hands who were afraid to speak their minds. And they had seen West Virginia's once contentious two-party political system transformed into what historian Ronald L. Lewis called "a mechanism for the protection of capital."[32]

The most prominent Socialist in West Virginia was cut from a different cloth, however. Harold Houston, a descendant of Sam Houston, the founding father of Texas, was a well-educated gentleman who graduated law school and served as counsel to oil companies operating around his hometown of Parkersburg. But Houston, vexed by the ways capitalist firms extracted profits from his state's natural resources, began to study the writings of the socialists who were Americanizing Marxism and to read radical periodicals like the *Appeal to Reason*, a sensational weekly newspaper published in Girard, Kansas, by J. A. Wayland, one of Mother Jones's closest comrades.[33]

Houston met Frank Keeney after the 1904 strike, introduced him to the *Appeal*, and became his political mentor. From the brilliant lawyer and the socialist classics, the young miner learned the old theory that labor produced all wealth and that wages the capitalist paid the worker represented only a fraction of the value the laborer created. Because experienced colliers understood the technology and labor processes of mining far better than the owners, the Socialists and many others in their ranks believed the miners could operate the coal industry cooperatively and manage it more rationally and safely than the capitalists did. Like Mother Jones—who was hired on as a Socialist Party lecturer in 1904—these workers imagined an industrial order upside down, a new world in which the producers owned and operated the mines, the railroads, the telegraph lines, the newspapers, and "everything else." When that day came, Jones promised the miners, "we will get what belongs to us and not until then."[34]

Until he turned twenty-one in 1903, Keeney's thoughts and actions had been influenced primarily by his experiences on Cabin Creek caring for his mother and his little sisters, toiling with his buddies underground, and living with neighbors and relatives in the little community where he was raised as a free-spirited mountaineer.[35] Over the next eight years, however, the lives of local miners like Keeney would be impacted more and more by the same external forces and events that were affecting thousands of other working people in industrial America.

First came the national open shop drive that encouraged Cabin Creek colliery operators to break the union. Then came stimulus from another outside force: the Socialist Party of America, whose apostles appeared in coal country with news of a "coming nation" in which cooperation and public ownership would replace cutthroat competition and private property. Corporate concentration—the national trend that most worried Socialists and hosts of other Americans—came to Frank Keeney's valley in 1907 when absentee owners located in England acquired eleven mines, including James Kay's collieries, and formed the Cabin Creek Consolidation Coal Company.

With concentration came expansion, as employers recruited thousands of European immigrants and African American migrants to mine their coal in larger mechanized operations. Within six years, the total number of foreign-born and black miners in southern West Virginia collieries would outnumber the total number of white miners. As the demographics of crowded company towns changed, so did the ecology of these mining villages. Eskdale, a pleasant valley settlement when Keeney became a miner in 1900, changed beyond recognition during the decade that followed. "The only thing beautiful about Eskdale was its name," wrote a newcomer in 1912. "It was smoky, sooty and grimy. The constant puff of railway locomotives, the crash and grind of engines, cars, and trains, night and day, produced an atmosphere similar to that surrounding one of the great steel centers . . ."[36]

During those same years, local mine operators struggled to keep the price of labor and the cost of operations low, so their coal could compete with the more expensive product produced in the northern mines. Employers explained to their men that these cost savings also saved jobs, which would be lost if the miners' union returned to Cabin Creek; but this rationale did not prevent local miners from experiencing what one worker would later describe as "a gradual aggravation of conditions."[37]

Mine workers were used to working under dangerous conditions. Men and boys had been injured, and sometimes killed, by slate falls and haulage accidents in Cabin Creek collieries, but none of the mines had blown up until April 20, 1905, when a fire at James Kay's Number 1 mine took the lives of six men. Management blamed a miner for swinging a pick and causing a fatal spark, but many Eskdale people believed the owner was at fault because he had refused to install new, more effective ventilation fans that would have reduced the density of coal dust. Eight months after this disaster, another fire raged through the Horton mine at the mouth of Cabin Creek, leaving the charred remains of John Harvey Crabtree and four other men in the main tunnel. The memory of young Crabtree's death grew sadder when his wife died in childbirth, perhaps, as local lore had it, because of her grief at losing her husband.[38]

The greatest aggravation of all was wage theft. When the miners lost the scale checkers their union contract had provided, they often found a carload of coal short-weighed by a company man, or they found their paychecks docked because a coal load contained slate or other impurities. It was no use complaining about "dockage," the miners said. The boss man's pencil did all the figuring.

After they removed the check-weigh men, Cabin Creek operators decided to measure a ton of coal a new way. They would pay their men the same wage for loading a "long ton" of 2,240 pounds as they had paid them for a standard 2,000-pound ton. Like short-weighing and docking, this pay standard represented another form of what a future attorney general of West Virginia would call "labor larceny." The long ton system confirmed the belief of socialists like Frank Keeney that capitalist employers were inherently greedy and untrustworthy, but a mine worker didn't have to be a socialist to feel cheated when he was not paid for all the coal he loaded.[39]

And yet no one risked speaking out against this new payment system, just as no one risked complaining about the activities of the four Baldwin-Felts mine guards who had been stationed in the valley after the 1904 strike. Charles A. Cabell, who owned the mining town of Carbon, employed two of these guards and had them sworn in as deputy sheriffs to enhance their authority. He later said he hired Baldwin-Felts agents to maintain peace and quiet in the rowdy camps and to keep "undesirables" out of the valley. In Cabell's eyes, these deputies were respectable, conservative men, "very gentlemanly and had good manners," although they were, he said, "men of temper" who resented "any insult or anything of that kind." What the mine owner could not see was that in the eyes of many Cabin Creek people these guards would always be viewed as alien invaders.[40]

Descended from a distinguished West Virginia family, Charles Cabell was raised in Charleston to be a gentleman, a devout Episcopalian, and a paternalist in the tradition of his forefathers. He later claimed that he knew the names of all his men and their families and that all of his employees knew they could come to him if they needed his help. Cabell considered himself a progressive employer. He barred saloons from his town and prevented racial trouble by keeping blacks and whites segregated. He built a church, a school, and a store to provide mining families with essentials. If someone stepped out of line, however, Cabell reacted forcefully. When a candy store owner defied his orders to stop holding dance parties in his shop, the man was pistol-whipped by two mine guards and forced to sell his establishment.[41] And when a spy told Cabell that a boardinghouse keeper named Sarah Blizzard was talking "union talk" and that her husband, Tim, was a UMWA loyalist who had lost his job in the New River field after the 1902 strike, the troublesome couple were warned out of Carbon.[42]

The Blizzards moved down the creek to Frank Keeney's hometown of Eskdale, where Sarah was free to start a new business and find a house that wasn't owned by a coal company. Life was different for the Blizzards in this village. Citizens of Eskdale had incorporated as a township so that they could speak freely in public places, hold open meetings, and elect their own local officials, including Frank Keeney's uncle James, who served as the town's first mayor and post-master, a federally approved position that was usually held by company store managers in privately owned mining towns.[43]

Located on part of Moses Keeney's estate, Eskdale supported ten general stores, a drugstore, a butcher shop, and Ciccareno and Sons, where fresh fruits and confections were sold. There were a few company-owned stores, but they had no monopoly on the retail trade. The town contained company-owned housing as well, but some mining families like the Keeneys lived in their own homes. Local residents built the schools and churches instead of relying upon the mine owners to donate these buildings, and local residents were free to use these buildings as common places to hold meetings and "speakins."

Miners' unions had long flourished in free towns like Eskdale, where merchants, ministers, and professionals knew the workers as neighbors. In communities like these, local residents supported workers when they closed down the mines, for these small-town folks nursed their own grievances against the railroads and mining companies, whose behavior they judged according to their older rural and communal values.[44]

When Eskdale miners like Frank Keeney lost their union protection, they had to be careful about what they said about their employers, for there were spies in the mines who would report them to the bosses. But after work, the colliers could speak with family and friends about their working conditions; about being cheated at the coal-weighing station, being refused their fair turn of mine cars, being kicked off the company store porch by the mine guards, and being sent to work in low coal seams and in rooms with flooded floors, bad air, and "loose tops."[45]

A week rarely passed in coal country without news that a miner, or a group of miners, had been killed or trapped in a slate fall, suffocated by methane, or scorched in a firestorm. During Keeney's first six years as a miner, rock falls, mine gases, train accidents, and explosions killed 1,011 men and boys in the Mountain State's collieries, an appalling loss of life by any measure. But over the next six years, the death rate would double as more inexperienced miners joined the workforce, as more machinery appeared underground, and as foremen pressured the men to increase output. During a time when the state's coal production soared, more than two thousand workers would perish in the mines, a mortality rate twice the national average for mine workers.[46]

Mine company executives and state officials blamed the grim death toll in West Virginia's collieries on careless, inexperienced miners, especially immigrants, who did in fact suffer unusually high rates of injury and death. These officials did not explain, however, that mining became more dangerous every year because coal operators felt compelled by competitive market forces to introduce dangerous new machinery and, at same time, to avoid the cost of making their mines safer.[47]

By 1906, the changes taking place in the coal industry were evident in company towns all over southern West Virginia. Longer and longer coal trains rumbled north out of the Kanawha and Fayette counties and into the Great Lakes trade, which had supplied the nation's industrial core with fuel, and east out of smokeless coalfields in Logan and McDowell Counties to the Virginia coast where it would supply the U.S. Navy's growing armada, including the sixteen new battleships President Roosevelt had requested—a Great White Fleet that sailed around the world in 1907 accompanied by fifty coal tenders.[48]

To meet this demand, mine owners acquired smaller mines, opened new operations, invested in modern machinery, and recruited larger workforces. On Paint Creek in the Kanawha minefield, Charles M. Pratt, the Brooklyn-born secretary of John D. Rockefeller's Standard Oil Company, and George P. Wetmore, a Republican senator from Rhode Island, purchased twenty-one thousand acres of land and leased it to a large mining company owned by Pennsylvania capitalists. By 1912, this firm and a few others employed seventy-five hundred workers who lived in company-owned towns strung out for more than twenty miles up the creek.[49]

In the adjacent New River field, Samuel L. Dixon—an ambitious immigrant from Yorkshire who had given up his work as a Methodist preacher to make a fortune in mining—consolidated twelve mines with backing from the leading coal distributor in New England and from two blue-chip Yankee investment houses, Hornblower & Weeks and Paine Webber.[50] In 1906, Dixon's New River mines yielded an impressive output of ten thousand tons, but since the market could handle much more, the mine owner ordered his engineers to sink shafts deeper into the mountains. In his newer mines, managers replaced mules with motorized engines and installed mechanical cutting machines, which allowed for tremendous increases in productivity. But these innovations also created new dangers. The deafening noise prevented the miners from hearing the sounds that preceded cave-ins, which killed far more miners than explosions. The new cutting machines also produced blinding swirls of fine coal particles that added to the volatility of the already dusty mines.[51]

As they sunk mines deeper into the mountains, Dixon and his pit bosses paid little attention to West Virginia's mine safety laws, including the ban on working more than twenty miners in a mine with only one opening. Nevertheless, on February 8, 1906, one of Dixon's pit bosses sent thirty-five men to work in the Parral mine, which had only one entryway. When an explosion in that operation killed twenty-three men, West Virginia's mining inspector charged Dixon with violating state law.

Eleven months later, in another Dixon shaft mine, something—perhaps an open flame on a miner's lamp—ignited methane gas that had been filling the air in this collier's room. The blast loosened millions of fine coal dust particles, which fueled the fire as it raced toward the elevator, where seventy men and boys were gathered at the end of a shift. When the firestorm arrived, it hurled their bodies against the entry wall and sent the bodies of mules flying down the entryways. Some men who carried blasting powder were dismembered when their loads exploded. When the holocaust reached the elevator cage, it rebounded and roared back up into the mine, killing the men who had survived the first blast. A total of eighty-five men and boys died in the Stuart mine that day. If Samuel Dixon's engineers had created a second tunnel in the mine, as required by law, the blast would have exited the mine through that ventilation tunnel.[52]

Fayette County coroner's juries investigated both the Parral and Stuart mine disasters, but the jurors found no liability on the mine operator's part for the death of 103 men and boys. Instead, the juries concluded that "human error" was at fault in both explosions. It was no surprise when Dixon and his managers escaped punishment, because in his role as the Republican boss of Fayette County, "King Sam," as he was known, had handpicked the jury members largely from the ranks of coal company officers and political cronies.[53]

Blaming careless miners for accidents was so common that in 1906 the *Coal Trade Bulletin* claimed that 99 percent of all mine accidents were "absolutely due to the carelessness or willful negligence of the men employed in them."[54] For its part, the *United Mine Workers Journal* accused the mine operators of ignoring safety laws, and it slammed West Virginia's mining inspector, James Paul, for failing to enforce them. His administration, the *Journal* remarked, had "been marked by one long bloody trail of human slaughter, caused by negligence . . ."[55] But the worst was yet to come.

At 10:30 on the morning of December 6, 1907, a blast shook the ground above the Numbers 6 and 8 Monongah mines owned by the giant Consolidation Coal Company in West Virginia's Fairmont coalfield. The bodies of 361 men and boys were pulled from the rubble, but some estimated the death toll as more than 400. Only four workers survived. "Rescue" crews carried out so many corpses that local undertakers in the area ran out of coffins.[56] Nevertheless, thousands of miners went dutifully back to work in Consolidation's other mines without making any overt protest.

No industrial occupation depended as much on "discipline of a military character," wrote historian Paul H. Rakes, a former miner, because even a small infraction by one individual could lead to the deaths of hundreds. Like soldiers and sailors, miners subscribed to a "sacred code" that, in a disaster, the workers on the surface would volunteer for rescue duty, no matter how dangerous, and would work ceaselessly until the last man was saved and the last dead body was recovered. Coal miners' wives understood the risks their spouses faced underground, and so every day they ritually kissed "their departing husbands goodbye for the fear that they might not see them alive again."[57]

Coffins piled on the streets of Monongah after the disaster in 1907.

Even though colliers acted like obedient soldiers, they did not absolve the mine owners of responsibility for the deaths of their comrades. Each roof fall and explosion strengthened the workers' conviction that the operators were callous men driven only by greed. The tragedy at Monongah provided the miners with a story that confirmed this belief. After the explosion, one miner overheard a foreman ask how many mules the company lost in the disaster. The question this pit boss asked that grim December day became the basis of an adage that would be repeated over and over again in the coal camps by miners who said that coal operators "cared more about a mule than they did a man, because it cost more to replace a mule than it did a man."[58]

The Monongah disaster did not provoke any overt protest from West Virginia's miners, but the event did arouse the first expression of public outrage over the slaughter in the nation's mines and stimulate an industry-led reform movement at the national level. The explosion took place in an operation owned by one of the nation's leading coal corporations at a time when muckrakers were exposing a host of industrial abuses. Indeed, the worst industrial disaster in American history occurred during what President Theodore Roosevelt called "a period of great unrest—social, political, and industrial unrest." Citizens were expressing what he called "a fierce discontent with evil" and showing "a determination to punish the authors of evil, whether in industry or politics." Roosevelt warned, however, that radicals were pushing this "movement of agitation" to dangerous extremes and were causing resentment over the "line of cleavage" that divided those who were well-off from those who were not. Americans should learn, said Roosevelt, to accept "the inevitable inequality of conditions."[59]

Chapter 4

A Spirit of Bitter War

Winter 1908–Summer 1912

T he coal miners who returned to work after hundreds of their cohorts died underground did seem to accept the inequality of working conditions that existed in industrial America. Like foreign-born steel workers, the immigrants who toiled in the Monongah mines found that earning dollars every day compensated for dirty, dangerous labor and long hours. Extreme hardship was a price immigrant laborers were willing to pay if they could accumulate savings and send money home or to the bank for the down payment on a house. But the labor stability in the steel and coal industries depended upon steady work. America, one Polish worker wrote home, "is a golden land as long as there is work."[1]

Appalachian mountaineers and African American farmhands, especially the bachelors among them, were not as dedicated as foreigners were to saving their wages. But married miners like Frank Keeney were just as dependent as the immigrants were on steady work and regular pay. Mine accidents, even horrific disasters, did not disturb this pattern of labor stability. As a result, like collieries throughout the coalfields, the mines on Cabin Creek ran without interruption until late in 1907, when an economic crisis gripped the nation and threatened the stability that had prevailed in the Appalachian coal industry.

That fall a "bankers' panic" swept Wall Street caused by what President Roosevelt called "the speculative folly . . . of a few men of great wealth" who held the public good in "flagrant disregard"; this event triggered a depression that eventually affected everyone who worked for wages, from the miners in Keeney's isolated hometown to the steel workers in the giant mills of Pennsylvania. By Christmas, 600,000 Americans were out of work, and in the course of the next year nearly 3 million people would lose their jobs, 13.5 percent of the nonagricultural workforce.[2] Those who remained at work toiled for reduced hours and sliced wages. "I'd get up every morning at five o'clock to see if the whistle would blow, but that would happen only once or twice a month," recalled one West Virginia miner. "At that rate a man might make five or six dollars a month; and, out of that, they'd take fifty cents for the doctor and fifteen cents for hospital insurance. A man just didn't have anything left at the end of the month."[3]

As 1907 drew to a close, the editor of *Labor Argus*, a socialist weekly published in Charleston, reported that the economic tremors shaking industries like mining were causing more workers than ever to doubt the viability of capitalism. Therefore, the editor predicted, it would become much easier for agitators and organizers to win converts to the Socialist Party and to the UMWA. "I got a lot of new members for both, by pointing out that capitalism was on the way out," recalled A. D. Lavinder, an activist miner from Mount Carbon.[4] Most of the miners who joined the party were native-born mountaineers, including a large number who belonged to the Red Men, a blue-collar version of the Masonic Order. Newcomers from Italy created their own groups and expressed their socialist faith in their own words and customs, like celebrating Primo Maggio with wine and song.[5]

In 1908, Lavinder and his comrades canvassed the coalfields for a Socialist ticket full of candidates who ran on a program calling for public ownership and worker control of all major industries, along with reforestation and land reclamation to create a public domain that would make West Virginia "a more beautiful place to live."[6]

The Republican Party candidate for governor, William Ellsworth Glasscock, who noticed the growth of this new radical party,

Italian miners celebrating Primo Maggio near Sun, West Virginia, 1908.

acknowledged the growing tension between employers and union-ized employees. Glasscock, a slim, balding lawyer and former school superintendent from Morgantown, defended the franchise for black men, which was under attack by the Democrats, and evenhandedly condemned union boycotts and employer blacklists. He proposed a mildly progressive program, which included proposals for higher corporate taxes and stronger mine safety laws to appease miners who were still furious over the slaughter at Monongah.[7]

Glasscock won the election and ensured continued GOP domi-nance over the state government and the Socialist candidate for governor polled a few thousand votes; this tally represented a 100 percent increase in just four years, with the biggest gains recorded in the coal-mining precincts of Kanawha and Fayette Counties. Despite this encouraging sign, socialist miners like Frank Kee-ney passed through the mine portals on the day after the election knowing that nothing had changed. In their frustration, some mine workers turned against political action and toward the strategy of "direct action" practiced by the revolutionary Industrial Workers of the World (IWW). Founded three years earlier by radicals dedicated to class struggle, the Wobblies (as IWW members were known) opposed the strategy of "class collaboration" practiced by well-paid labor leaders like UMWA president John Mitchell, who discouraged strikes and cooperated with the bosses.

This militant minority found a cause in the spring of 1909, when unionized coal operators in the Kanawha Valley demanded a concession from the UMWA. These employers insisted on paying union miners for loading a "long ton" of 2,240 pounds, the same standard their nonunion competitors had adopted. District 17 officials in Charleston called a protest strike in the Kanawha field, but a few days later they called off the job action and accepted the new weighing standard. The next morning union members sullenly returned to the mines, except in the town of Boomer on the Kanawha River, where nearly fifteen hundred Calabrian immigrants dominated the workforce. As far as these Italians were concerned, "the strike was still on," writes historian Frederick Barkey, and, "as if by magic, they produced an amazing supply of rifles they had apparently been accumulating for some time."[8]

The Calabrese mobilized their forces swiftly enough to block several hundred white and black union miners who tried to resume work. The local press described what followed as a riot, but, in fact, the Italian miners acted deliberately by seizing control of the rail line and a blacksmith shop that produced important machinery for the colliery. A large body of strikers paraded through Boomer carrying a huge red-and-black flag (the colors of socialism and anarchism) with gold lettering that read VICTORIA O MORTE.

When the sheriff of Fayette County arrived with a posse of fifty armed deputies and a Gatling gun loaned to him by the Baldwin-Felts Agency, the Italians surrendered peacefully. The sheriff arrested nine ringleaders and took them off to jail, but coal company managers decided they would rather have the men back in the mines than in jail cells. The troublemakers were released on the condition that they return to work for the "long ton." The mine operators in the area dismissed the Boomer incident as a riot by hotheaded "dagoes," without realizing that this remarkable explosion of direct action was a portent of a far more violent uprising.

In 1909, Frank Keeney had been digging and loading coal for eight years without much to show for it. He and his wife, Bessie, had lived their whole lives on Cabin Creek, and they never imagined leaving their home, but with a two-year-old girl in their care and another baby on the way, they decided that Frank would give up on trying to make a living on a miner's pay. The family would head west to make a new life in Arkansas, where they planned to grow and sell cotton.

Cotton planting differed from farming in a mountain valley, and the climate in the Mississippi Delta was nothing like what the Keeneys had known in the mountains of West Virginia. Frank toiled in the hot, bug-infested cotton fields, but then he, his daughter Sybil, and his newborn baby, Mamie, contracted smallpox. Bessie kept her husband and her girls alive, but the family had to abandon their dream of farming their own land.

In 1910, the Keeneys returned to Cabin Creek, and Frank, still weak from illness, went back to loading coal. Things were different now: Mine work was now a life sentence for Frank Keeney, who lost all hope of escaping the pits and going back to the land. Having sold his house and land before he left Eskdale, Keeney was compelled to rent a cabin from the Wake Forest Mining Company and to load coal for the price his boss dictated. At the age of twenty-eight, this proud mountaineer had "no land and no liberty," in the words a descendant.[9]

The following year, Keeney joined ranks with political comrades who were relentlessly canvassing coal towns as they prepared for local elections, and that spring voters elected Socialist mayors in thirty municipalities across the nation, including one in Keeney's hometown of Eskdale. All the changes that been accelerating during the previous decade—corporate consolidation and mechanization, union busting and blacklisting, financial speculation and political corruption—contributed to what one observer called the "rising tide of socialism in America."[10]

Even though the socialist movement was winning over thousands of voters, the party's leader, Eugene V. Debs, believed that electoral campaigns would not matter unless the working class was organized into powerful, inclusive industrial unions. And in 1911, the prospects for labor organizing in West Virginia were dismal. In fact, the UMWA's national officials had decided that conditions were so perilous they would no longer send their men into this black hole. "West Virginia miners will not be organized," one union staffer concluded, "until they themselves have made up their minds that they are going to be organized in spite of all opposition."[11]

In April 1912, northern coal mine owners reached a new settlement with the UMWA that provided for significant improvements in wages and working conditions. Mine company executives in the Midwest agreed to an eight-hour day and a pay increase of 5 cents a ton, to refrain from blacklisting union members, to install accurate scales in all mines, and to guarantee that miners would enjoy free speech and peaceful assembly. Union members in Ohio, Indiana, and Illinois would now earn wages that ranged from 57 cents to $1.27 per ton, while pick miners in southern West Virginia earned 38.5 cents a ton on average for loading coal by the long ton instead of the standard short ton.[12] This new contract presented the leaders of District 17 with an opportunity. If these union officials could negotiate a significant pay increase, they could satisfy their members and strengthen their appeal to the state's nonunion mine workers; but if they failed they might not be able to hold their own, let alone win new recruits to the UMWA's ranks.

When the officers of District 17 sat down to negotiate a new contract with the Kanawha Coal Operators' Association, they requested the same improvements UMWA miners in the North had received. After all, the coal business was booming and the local companies seemed viable and generally profitable. Why wouldn't the employers share some of their good fortune with the men who cut and loaded their coal day in and day out?

The union's logic made no sense to the Paint Creek Operators' Association, whose members wanted to maintain their competitive edge in the national market. When the association's leader rejected all of the union's proposals on April 12, district union leaders caved in and dropped most of their initial demands, except the request for a 5-cent increase in tonnage pay. When the employers refused this proposal as well, District 17's president reluctantly ordered his members to stay out of the collieries on Paint Creek where most of the state's UMWA members toiled.[13]

As soon as the pickets were set up, strike leaders sent some of the strikers over the ridge to Cabin Creek on a secret mission. They were instructed to contact UMWA loyalists in Eskdale and urge them to initiate a sympathy strike. Here was an opportunity Frank Keeney and his Cabin Creek comrades were prepared to seize. They met in Eskdale and drafted a set of demands asking local operators "to restore the miners' right to free speech and peaceable assembly," to end compulsory trading at company stores, to install scales at all mines, to remove the Baldwin-Felts agents stationed in the valley, and to allow the miners to employ their own check-weigh men, as provided by state law. The protestors did not demand a wage increase, which would make the coal they mined more expensive for customers, but they did demand that the mine operators end the "long ton" system of payment and formally recognize the union they had busted in 1904.[14]

The next morning, Frank Keeney and his father-in-law were summoned to the Wake Forest Mining Company's office, where the manager fired them for being ringleaders of the walkout. Both men were told that they would be evicted from company housing and that they would never mine coal on Cabin Creek again. Keeney, now blacklisted and homeless, would have to face the consequences of taking his stand.[15]

After the Keeneys vacated their company house, they joined other strikers taking shelter in a tent camp near Eskdale. They had been living there for two weeks when the strikers received some heartbreaking news. The UMWA's district officers had called an end to the strike against the unionized mines on Paint Creek and the rest of the Kanawha Valley. Union negotiators had withdrawn all of their demands for improved working conditions and had settled for a meager wage increase of 2.5 cents per long ton.

As union miners trooped back to work on Paint Creek and Kellys Creek, Keeney and his fellow strikers found themselves isolated and without any significant support from the UMWA district. The strikers passed a few days pondering their bleak prospects when surprising news arrived in Eskdale: The Paint Creek mine owners had refused to grant even a token 2.5-cent wage increase to their union miners, and District 17 officials had ordered their members back to the picket lines. The strike that had idled collieries all over the Kanawha field would continue, but no one expected a dispute over a meager pay increase to last very long.

On May Day 1912, the men stayed home in towns like Holly Grove, Mucklow, and Burnwell and enjoyed a rare holiday, one that had special meaning for the socialists among them. For the next week, the miners passed the spring days sitting outside their cabins smoking, whittling wood, and talking as the woods along Paint Creek turned endless shades of green and the azalea and dogwood blossoms garnished the valley. A few of the strikers set off to hunt squirrel and possum, others joined together in string bands to play mountain music, and some enjoyed a rare chance to play with their children on the dirt road that ran along Paint Creek.

The strikers assumed that some kind of compromise would be reached, and that they could return in a few days. The Paint Creek Operators' Association and its president, Quinn Morton, had developed a businesslike relationship with UMWA District 17 based on good faith and a willingness to compromise. But on May 3, this relationship was fractured when a contingent of Baldwin-Felts agents arrived at Morton's Imperial Colliery property in Burnwell. When strikers saw Morton lead ten of these men up from the train station at Mucklow with their rifles slung over their shoulders, they knew they had come to evict the strikers from their company-owned homes, and they knew that meant serious trouble lay ahead.[16]

The next day, local residents watched as the Baldwin-Felts detectives drilled military-style in front of the company store in the town of Mucklow. The guards were commanded by Ernest "Tony" Gaujot, a six-foot-four, two-hundred-pound man who wore a black bowler hat to cover an oddly shaped head topped with a bump about the size of a baseball. Having seen combat as a U.S. Army

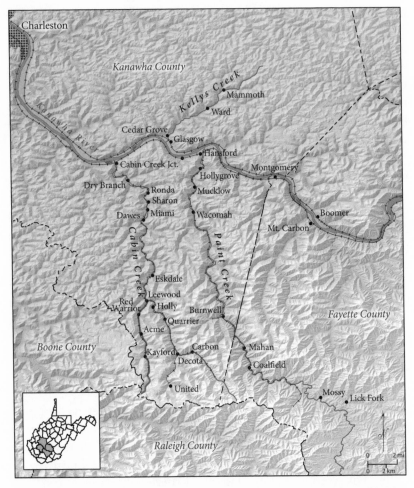

The Paint Creek–Cabin Creek mining district of the Kanawha coalfield.

sergeant in the Spanish-American War, and having served with the occupying forces in the Philippines during the unrelenting suppression of the Filipino nationalists, Gaujot knew how to conduct an occupation.[17]

Alarmed and outraged by this invasion of their community, union leaders convened a meeting of four hundred residents. The citizens who gathered that day decided to appeal to the mine operators and ask them to remove the guards. Brant Scott, a former miner who had lost his leg in a slate fall, led the delegation. A check-weigh man trusted by the miners and the bosses alike, Scott made the community's case to the manager of the largest company in the valley. Surely, he argued, the dispute could still be settled without evictions and without the aggravating presence of private guards. The manager listened quietly to this plea and then told Scott and his delegation that the guards would stay until the miners ended their strike and agreed to work under the old pay scale. When he heard this reply, Scott said that he was sorry, but the union could no longer be held responsible for preserving the peace.[18]

The next day, Gaujot and his men issued eviction notices to the strikers, which gave them ten days to pack up and get out of town. A few days later, on May 14, Baldwin-Felts agents left their quarters in Mucklow just after the sun peeked over the mountains. Carrying rifles, the guards moved from cabin to cabin removing the miners, their wives, and their children and then throwing small pieces of furniture and cookware into the road.[19]

Newt Gump, who had worked in the Paint Creek mines since age eleven, later testified that he saw the guards empty one group of houses while the residents were attending a funeral in Mucklow's church. When the mourners emerged from the service, they saw their belongings piled up outside the church door. Their dismay turned to terror when they looked a short distance away to the porch of the company store and saw guards manning a machine gun pointed directly at the church door. That afternoon Gump and other evicted miners moved down the creek to "free ground" at Holly Grove, where the UMWA had pitched rented tents on the bottomland near the railway tracks. In a few days, long rows of tepees and wall tents nestled along the banks of the stream and even up into the hollows.[20]

A strange silence fell over the coal towns along Paint Creek, places that a few weeks before had been filled with the sounds of hissing and pounding locomotives and the squeal of coal cars on the tracks. But that May, people could hear the stream rushing by full of spring rain and listen to the wind blow through the trees on the mountainsides. This remarkably peaceful scene prevailed, until one day rifle shots boomed in the hills and showers of lead rained down on the

The strikers' camp at Holly Grove near Mucklow on Paint Creek.

Holly Grove camp. Surprisingly, no one was wounded or killed.[21] Gaujot and his men may have assumed that these vulnerable campers would soon take flight. If so, they miscalculated. Not only did the miners stay put, but they also assembled an arsenal and prepared to strike back.

Early in the morning on May 29, as Gaujot and his men ate breakfast in the clubhouse they occupied at Mucklow, rifle fire rattled through the valley. When the detectives ran out to investigate, they were caught in a cross fire coming from the woods on both sides of the creek. Some of them dashed for a makeshift fort where they kept their guns, as bullets kicked up dust around them. A few of the guards fired back, but the spring foliage was so thick on the mountainside that the Baldwin-Felts agents couldn't see any of their assailants—only puffs of smoke rising above the bushes and trees. The firing from the hills would die down for a few minutes and then rev up again; it lasted for forty minutes, until the strikers slipped back into the woods. And so it began, a peaceful strike over a 2.5-cent raise in a remote mountain valley had turned into something else: a life-and-death contest that would last for more than a year.

After the assault on Mucklow, Thomas Felts, co-owner of the Baldwin-Felts Agency, came up from Bluefield to assess the damage. Miraculously, only one guard had been wounded. Felts inspected the guards' well-ventilated fort and realized that his men were at the mercy of strikers shooting at them from higher ground. As a precaution, Felts decided to place a machine gun in the fort as a "means of abating the warfare" and to send out patrols to ambush raiders before they could strike.[22]

On the evening of June 4, several Baldwin-Felts agents returned to Mucklow and reported sighting a column of twenty armed men snaking their way along the ridgeline from the mouth of the creek. A contingent of Italian miners from across the river in Boomer had come to support some of their countrymen on strike in Wacomah, a town located one mile above Mucklow. At 4:40 A.M., Gaujot sent a group of detectives up to intercept the Italian raiding party before it attacked. The guards expected to take the miners by surprise, but the Boomer men had been waiting for them. As the agents approached the ridgeline carrying lanterns, a rifle barked. One of the Italians had fired prematurely, giving away an ambush. The Baldwin-Felts men returned fire, shooting blindly into the dark at the flashes from the miners' rifle barrels. The sound of the gunfight echoed down through the valley for several minutes until the Italians retreated into the darkness and made their way back down the ridge. As the Baldwin-Felts men advanced, they found the body of a young miner lying dead in the hollow. He was later identified as Donato DiPietro, a Calabrian miner from Boomer.[23]

The detectives trailed the miners down the hillside to a cabin in a place locals called "Dago Holler," where they captured five Italians and took them to jail. They were indicted a few days later for attacking the detectives.[24] The death of an immigrant in a remote forest would have been of no account under ordinary circumstances, but on Paint Creek that spring, the killing of Donato DiPietro provided the strikers with a martyr, a man, a "'Taly" (the American miners' word for an Italian), who had died coming to the aid of his fellow workers.

West Virginia's governor, William H. Glasscock, had paid scant attention to the skirmishes on Paint Creek; after all, gun battles had a way of breaking out in the backcountry when the miners lined up against the coal companies and their hired gunmen. But now he had to answer to the royal consul of Italy, who demanded an investigation into the death of DiPietro and the release of the Italian miners who remained in jail after their gun battle with detectives. "For the sake of Justice and Humanity," the consul pleaded, the governor must free the prisoners and prosecute the real "evil doers."[25]

This trouble came at a time when Governor Glasscock's attention was focused on his political hero, former president Theodore Roosevelt, who had launched vociferous attacks on the owners of "predatory wealth" and on federal judges who stoked labor radicalism with sweeping injunctions. GOP leaders were furious with Roosevelt's rabble-rousing, but not Glasscock. He broke ranks and became one of the first to support the former president's quest for the Republican presidential nomination in 1912. Roosevelt thanked Glasscock with a warm note in which he declared that his campaign would be a fight between "the people" and those who sought to "control the people," and in this contest, the candidate predicted: "the people will come out on top."[26]

But the Roosevelt bandwagon jerked to a halt at the Republican Party convention in Chicago, where the Taft machine "steamrolled" the insurgents by disqualifying nearly eighty of the former president's delegates. Governor Glasscock was still fuming over "the Chicago steal" in early July when he was forced to turn his attention back to the strike situation on Paint Creek. Thomas Cairns, the blunt president of UMWA District 17, demanded that the governor remove the mine guards and send in the National Guard. Glasscock refused, but he did agree to deliver a compromise proposal from the union to the Paint Creek Operators' Association. The governor made good on his offer to act as an honest broker, but the association's leaders told him they would not pay their union coal miners even one cent more on the ton. Glasscock had little experience in the coalfields, but he knew that the importation of strikebreakers would cause conflict.

On July 19, a passenger train full of "transportation men" from Kentucky (strikebreakers whose tickets had been paid for by the coal companies) reached Paint Creek Junction and headed up the valley. The locomotive had traveled barely three miles when the passengers heard glass breaking. Men leaped off their seats to the floor as rifle bullets pinged off the metal cars and punctured the windows. After the assault on the replacement workers, the strikers and mine guards returned to their respective armed camps and waited for the next train of transportation men to chug up the valley. Under these circumstances, the last thing Governor Glasscock wanted to hear was that America's most notorious agitator was on her way to Paint Creek, but she was.

When word arrived that she was needed back in the Mountain State, Mother Jones had been speaking on the West Coast rallying support for railroad shop men on strike against the huge Harriman railroad system. "I canceled all my speaking dates in California, tied up all my possessions in a black shawl—I like traveling light—and went immediately to West Virginia." Jones had resigned from her post as a Socialist Party lecturer and rejoined the UMWA staff at the request of her friend John P. White, who had been elected international president of the miners' union in 1911.[27]

After a grueling cross-country trek, Jones reached Charleston, where she told a reporter that when force was used to hinder a worker who was fighting for gains that were rightfully his, he had the right to meet force with force. After she left her calling card in the state capital, Jones took a short train ride up to Paint Creek. On the way, the brakeman told her the story of how the operators put the miners out of their houses at gunpoint, how shots were fired on the Holly Grove camp, and how the miners armed themselves just like the early settlers had against "attacks of the wild Indians." The brakeman warned Jones to turn around and take the next train back to Charleston, but she never paid heed to these kinds of warnings.[28]

By now, Governor Glasscock was hearing from citizens who were disturbed by the news from the strike zone. Roy Smith, a fellow Republican, declared that the suppression of civil rights in the Paint Creek district made a mockery of the state's proud motto *Montani Semper Liberi*. Surely "His Excellency" must know how the guards were treating women and children, Smith added. "I have been up there and I have seen these conditions, and I must say that 'big business,' the capitalists, are writing on the wall the prophecy of their own doom." He closed with a political message: "If the laboring people of Kanawha County get no relief at the hands of a 'Republican' Governor . . . they will bolt the ticket in November and vote with a workingman's party." Smith meant the Socialist Party, whose agitators were already canvassing in preparation for the 1912 election campaign.[29]

Roy Smith represented one of many middle-class Americans who dreaded what one magazine called "a spirit of bitter war" that existed in many of the nation's industrial districts. At the height of the Progressive Era, the United States stood out as the most strike-prone nation in the world. On average, twenty-five hundred work stoppages occurred during the first nine years of the twentieth century when strikes and lockouts often took a bloody turn: thirty silver miners dead in Cripple Creek, Colorado; fourteen coal wagon drivers killed in Chicago; and eleven street car operators slain in St. Louis. Strikers were not the only victims. In 1905, the former governor of Idaho was assassinated for breaking a silver miners' strike, and two years later, leaders of the iron workers' union launched a dynamite campaign that destroyed scores of open shop construction sites; it culminated in the deadly bombing of the building where the anti-union *Los Angeles Times* was published. Twenty people died in the fire that followed the explosion. The fear of being caught in the middle of a class war helped galvanize middle-class citizens like Roy Smith and his friend, the governor of West Virginia.[30]

"This trouble on Paint Creek has been the source of a very great deal of annoyance to me," William Glasscock wrote to another supporter. He deplored the blood that had already been shed, but he believed he had done what he could to maintain order "other than declaring martial law and actually taking possession of Paint Creek."

A few days later, the governor admitted being worn down by his anxiety over the Paint Creek situation. He was under a doctor's care and was told not to take on too much work until he got strong again.[31]

The governor's worries probably grew when he read a Charleston newspaper's alarming description of the situation in the strike zone, where a reporter was impressed by how many strikers and their supporters had access to firearms and by how much the mountain terrain favored them. There were many men on Paint Creek who had "murder in their hearts," he wrote, men who would "pick off" a mine guard or company official as casually as they would sit down to eat an evening meal. After the battle on June 4, the reporter added, the guards "carried their guns in their hands wherever they went." Thus far, only one man, Donato DiPietro, had been killed, but the reporter from Charleston feared that another skirmish might trigger a much bloodier battle.[32]

On the afternoon of July 25, word circulated through the densely packed tent settlement that "gun thugs" were planning to attack the camp that night and that the women and children sleeping there might

Governor William Ellsworth Glasscock.

be killed where they lay. Strike leaders sent runners out across the Big Kanawha to union towns like Ward and Boomer calling for help. That afternoon, scores of armed men crossed the river and moved toward Holly Grove. One bunch of volunteers jumped a C&O coal train and crawled over the cars until they reached the engineer, who was ordered to drop them off at Holly Grove.[33]

That evening, armed sentries went into the hills above the camp, while another detail formed to guard the C&O tracks next to the tent camp in case the Baldwins came down from Burnwell and Mucklow. As twilight faded, miners patrolling the railway noticed something moving in their direction. At 7:45 P.M., a four-wheel cart called a velocipede appeared on the tracks, propelled by two men in business suits. Some of the pickets recognized one of the men as W. W. Phaup, a mine guard. As the two agents rolled past, they saw that the men were holding rifles and they heard one of the strikers shout, "Halt." The detectives kept pedaling and had moved about a hundred yards down the tracks when two rifle shots cracked through the air. Phaup later said that he jerked out his pistol, whirled sideways, fired backward, and then fell off to the side of the tracks with his arm broken by a bullet. As he picked himself up, the guard saw that his partner had been shot through the head and killed.[34]

Phaup managed to drag himself into and across the creek to safety. He later testified that the strikers on Paint Creek were a bad lot who had come to "make a desperate stand there and kill anybody" who threatened their jobs. "I have been through a dozen strikes," he said, but the strikers on Paint Creek "was the meanest class of people . . . the most desperate men I have had to contend with in any strike." After the shooting near Holly Grove, the Baldwin-Felts agents started calling the strikers, their wives, and their children "rednecks."[35]

As soon as Agent Phaup disappeared into the woods, his assailants rushed back from the tracks to the tents and told the men to arm themselves and be ready for anything. Scouts came and went that night reporting on the guards' whereabouts, and then, at about three A.M., the strikers decided to take the offensive. "The next morning a body of approximately 300 men moved quietly out of Holly Grove," one eyewitness recalled, "and after silently wading the waters of Paint Creek, crept into the mountains . . . on both sides of the creek."

When faint morning light glowed above the ridges, the strikers could see the Baldwin-Felts men begin to stir outside of their clubhouse after breakfast, ready to take up their guard posts. The miners were to hold their fire until they heard the sound of a mountaineer imitating the shrill sound of a bobwhite. When they heard the call, the union men poured rifle fire down on Mucklow. The guards ran, zigzagging to find cover and to reach what one reporter described as the "big swivel rifle, known as a 'machine gun,'" a weapon that could kill "at three miles and fire with extraordinary rapidity, being automatically fed by strings of 100 cartridges." Sharpshooters in the hills tried to take out this gun and eventually crippled it by shooting off the cartridge belt. The battle raged for two hours as what one survivor called "a regular hurricane of bullets" swept through the valley.[36]

"Big time on Paint Creek tonight," a Kellys Creek miner noted in his diary on July 26. "Lots of guards got killed by the miners."[37] Newspapers reported that at least six strikers and four guards died in the battle at Mucklow, but reporters could not compile an accurate list of casualties. One of them did, however, provide a chilling description of the scene. "For a distance of 12 miles around the mouth of Paint Creek," he reported, ". . . the inhabitants are said to have lapsed into a state of primitive savagery, spurred on by the depredations of the private guards."[38]

Governor Glasscock learned about the deaths at Mucklow while he was in a hospital recovering from a serious bout of rheumatism. When the Kanawha County sheriff wired a plea for help, Glasscock reluctantly sent a company of the National Guard into the strike zone. When the troops arrived on July 27 aboard a special train, strikers, their wives, and their neighbors swarmed into Mucklow to cheer them. "Grim visaged men, gaunt and hungry from months of privation, danced gleefully as the soldiers marched up the narrow valley," according to one report. "The miners hugged each other, wrung each other's hands and shouted welcome to the militiamen." The strikers rejoiced at the National Guard's arrival because it spelled "an end to the private guard system, which has held sway over the district."[39]

After state militia ended the fighting on Paint Creek, the soldiers began to clean up the filthy camps by digging drainage ditches and making other improvements. Some guardsmen criticized the mine operators for the fetid, slovenly conditions in the camps. A few militiamen even charged that the employers were holding the miners in peonage through indebtedness to company stores and were allowing mine guards to freely commit abuses and even atrocities on the population.[40]

National Guardsmen restored order so swiftly that Glasscock ordered five of the nine militia companies to return to their bases and then asked the commander of the National Guard, Adjutant General Charles D. Elliott, to file a full report from the field.

One of the most prominent men in the Mountain State, Elliott had engaged in the lumber business, gained admittance to the bar, worked as a Secret Service agent, and served as an army officer in the Spanish-American War. In the early 1900s, Elliott, initially a conventional Republican, purchased and published his hometown newspaper in Parkersburg in order to support the GOP. He won an appointment as a U.S. marshal in 1902. Ten years later, he became an ardent progressive and joined Governor Glasscock as a leading supporter of Theodore Roosevelt's campaign to regain the presidency.[41]

When General Elliott returned from his inspection of Paint Creek, he told the governor what he had seen: the cheerless houses, the naked hills, the armed guards, and the tent camps packed with thin, hollow-eyed people. Now, only fifteen miles downriver from this dreary valley, the two officials met at the capitol building in "the civilized city of Charleston." It was a pleasant, prosperous place where people owned automobiles, where well-dressed ladies walked "poodle dogs," and where ministers preached sermons in fine churches filled with good Christians. But Elliott found no signs of "Christian civilization" on Paint Creek, for there, he observed, the mine owners' quest for "dividends" had led to the degradation and impoverishment of their employees. "God does not walk in these hills," the general concluded. "The devil is here in these hills, and the devil is greed."[42]

PART II

The First Mine War, 1912–1918

Chapter 5

The Lord Has Been on Our Side

July 27–September 5, 1912

C harleston, the city General Elliott described with such fine words, appeared to visitors like a sleepy southern state capital. Yet the most prominent buildings—the Burlew Opera House, the huge Masonic Grand Lodge, the formidable Kanawha County Bank, and the luxurious Ruffner Hotel—were more northern than southern in design, and its most prominent businessmen had more contacts in industrial Pennsylvania than they did in the old mother Commonwealth of Virginia. Charleston was the commercial center for a whole region, a city where retail stores did a brisk trade and merchants, large and small, flourished, including scores of Jewish store owners who contributed to the construction of an impressive synagogue downtown. O. J. Morrison's thriving department store on Capitol Street sold everything from overalls and bandannas to gingham dresses and high-powered rifles. Known as "the People's Store," the business catered to building tradesmen, railroad workers, and coal miners from nearby valleys who wanted to avoid the company stores. Charleston's prominent residents included the governor and the state's supreme court justices, as well as bankers, lawyers, engineers, construction contractors, and mining executives like the Cabin Creek mine owner Charles Cabell, who belonged to

Edgewood Country Club and worshipped at the elegant St. John's Episcopal Church.[1]

A government center, a river and rail transportation entrepot, a commercial and financial hub—Charleston was all this and more. The city also provided a corporate headquarters for coal, oil, timber, and railroad company managers who directed vast operations around the rapidly industrializing state of West Virginia. Charleston sat at the edge of the Kanawha minefield and in close proximity to vast stands of timber, natural gas reserves, and oil pools, as well as deposits of iron ore and fire clay—resources that made it cheaper to manufacture goods there than in Pittsburgh. Only 10 percent of the coal mined in West Virginia was sold inside the state; the lion's share of the tonnage was shipped north to the Great Lakes region, where West Virginia mine owners had increased their share of the trade from 1 percent in 1898 to 23 percent by 1912. Similarly, most of the profits reaped from the state's bounteous extractive industries went straight into the bank accounts of investors in Philadelphia, Cincinnati, Cleveland, and New York City.[2]

Nonetheless, Charleston's bourgeoisie thrived on the commerce generated by the railroad and extractive industries. Most miners shopped at company-owned stores, but every Saturday afternoon some of them would put on Sunday clothes and come to shop in the city. Except for these customers, Charlestonians had no contact with mining people or any knowledge of the lives they led up in the industrial valleys. During the summer of 1912, these working people remained largely out of sight, but they were no longer out of mind for the capital city's residents, whose daily newspapers reported alarming news of deadly gunfights on Paint Creek less than twenty miles away.

By the end of July, Frank Keeney and his family had been living under a canvas roof and subsisting on meager meals for more than six weeks. His little girls were still recovering from smallpox; his wife, Bessie, was about to give birth; and his fellow strikers were beginning to despair. They had shut down most of the mines from Eskdale down to the Kanawha River, but the collieries on the upper branches of the creek were still running coal. Keeney and his allies realized that their strike would fail unless they pulled out the miners who lived and worked in all the company-controlled towns.[3]

In desperation, Keeney led a group of strikers to meet with district union officials in Charleston. He assured the UMWA leaders that all the miners in the valley wanted their union back and were prepared to fight for it, but they needed help from the district. But these officials claimed they had no resources to give to the strikers on Cabin Creek, because they had to support the long-standing, dues-paying union members who were on strike along Paint Creek. Keeney, who suspected that the district officials lacked the courage to take up the fight, brushed this excuse aside and barked, "If you men are afraid to make the trip with me, I will find someone with nerve to go with me." As he was leaving, Keeney turned and said: "And I know an old woman who would go up the creek with me."[4]

Late that night, when Mother Jones heard a knock on the door of her Charleston hotel room, she opened it and saw the vaguely familiar face of a young man who introduced himself as Frank Keeney, the same fellow she had once told to get out of the poolroom and educate himself so that he could help his fellow workers. As Jones recalled, Keeney had tears in his eyes when he told her nobody from the district office would come up to Cabin Creek and help the miners. Would she come? Of course, she answered. She had been planning to "break into" Cabin Creek for some time, but where, she wondered, could she hold an open meeting in a valley controlled by the coal companies? When Keeney replied, "Eskdale is free," the young miner and the old agitator hatched a plan.

Jones instructed Keeney to write a handbill announcing her arrival, then have it printed and put in the hands of union railway men on the C&O who could circulate it on their runs up Cabin Creek. "Will freemen submit to being driven and hounded by armed thugs?" the circular began. "Exert your rights as free-born American citizens. Organize yourselves for mutual protection and to protect your wives and babies . . . Only cowards will submit to the wrongs we have suffered. Dare we shrink [sic] these duties and still call ourselves men? . . . [J]oin your striking brothers Tuesday, August 6, and meet in mass meeting at Eskdale on that date."[5]

On August 4, Keeney and his fellow organizers gathered their followers at a baseball park in Montgomery, a railroad town on the Kanawha River near the mouth of Cabin Creek. After a glowing introduction by Keeney, Mother Jones mounted a platform and began to speak by recalling her last visit to the region in 1903, when "gun thugs" murdered three strikers in their beds. She whirled around a wooden stage like a dancer as her audience sat in a circle enjoying the performance. "When I came here ten years ago, we marched into those mountains," she said, pointing to the hills above Montgomery. The mine owners had threatened to get rid of her, but she stayed until the bloody end and she would do so again. "We have some men that will run away," she said, "but you will never get me to run, don't worry about it at all."[6]

Two days later, the residents of lower Cabin Creek looked up from their chores to see Mother Jones pass by in a buggy driven by a coal miner preceded by a detail of National Guardsmen. Governor Glasscock had been persuaded by UMWA vice president Frank Hayes to send the soldiers along to ensure that no harm came to the miners' angel. As this odd procession passed through the coal camps

Mother Jones speaking on a platform in West Virginia.

of Dry Branch, Rhonda, and Sharon, union sympathizers may have sensed that life on Cabin Creek was about to change.

Frank Keeney and his comrades had already gathered a big crowd at Eskdale when Jones and her party arrived at noon. When a UMWA official opened the meeting by asking the miners to be patient and let justice take its course, Jones leaped up and objected, insisting that it was time to rouse all the miners on Cabin Creek. At the end of her speech, she told union members to go home, go to sleep, then wake up and put on their overalls, go to work in the mines and bring the rest of the men out.[7]

The next morning, a Cabin Creek mine manager remembered being stunned as he watched his employees walk out of the drift mouth. He blamed all the trouble on Jones and the "highly inflammatory speech" she delivered at Eskdale. After that, he said, "We never turned another wheel." Another observer marveled at the fact that "the men simply laid down their tools," but "no demands whatever were made upon the operators for higher wages." He did not realize that the strikers wanted much more than the meager raise that had initially caused the strike on Paint Creek. They insisted on winning recognition for their union and they wanted miners in company towns to enjoy the right to exercise free speech and free assembly without interference from private police.[8]

A few days later, Keeney, Jones, and other strike leaders decided it was time to move on to the company towns above Leewood, where the stream split into two branches. And one morning, Jones climbed into a buggy driven by a trapper boy and led a parade of strikers out of Eskdale in the direction of Red Warrior. Aware that nearly a hundred armed guards now occupied the valley, the strikers had prepared for a fight by purchasing surplus arms from the Department of War, including fifty-eight Norwegian-made Krag-Jørgensen rifles, and by buying weapons via mail order at a discount they received after they joined the National Rifle Association.[9]

When Detective Albert Felts—the agency co-owner's brother—heard about the march, he boarded a train at Kayford, along with a justice of the peace, a deputy sheriff, and a dozen men. At Decota, Felts's band was joined by twenty-five more guards. This contingent had moved a short way down the tracks when, as Felts remembered, "we saw a mob consisting of 42 Negroes, Italians, and Americans, carrying Army rifles with bayonets attached," and followed by more than a hundred unarmed strikers.[10]

In her autobiography, Jones recalled that she walked up to the guard manning a machine gun, put her hand on the weapon, and issued a phony threat that the hills were full of sharpshooters with rifles aimed at the posse. Felts's men put up their weapons, and Jones signaled her followers to move on up the creek.[11] In later testimony, Felts remembered the confrontation differently. He said when the armed strikers dropped down in position to fire, Jones stepped forward to negotiate a peaceful retreat. However, it was her heroic version of the story that was passed down the valley and became enshrined in coal country folklore.[12]

After the standoff at Decota, the strike did spread up the main branch of the creek to company towns like Carbon, where the walkout caught mine owner Charles Cabell by surprise. He later testified that his employees had seemed "satisfied."[13] But a coal company physician had a very different impression based on what he heard from miners he treated as patients. Trouble had been brewing in the Cabin Creek Valley for some time, he remarked, because laws were "usurped and contorted" by the employers and the private police they employed. Therefore, the doctor held out little hope that the two parties could settle their differences peacefully.[14] The physician's assessment was sound. Charles Cabell and his cohorts believed that, in spite of the strike, the Baldwin-Felts men could protect loyal employees and keep the mines running, whereas Frank Keeney and the other strikers believed they could drive the scabs, and ultimately the mine guards, out of their valley.

Rocco Spinelli played a large role in the strikers' resistance effort. Standing five feet five inches, weighing 140 pounds, Spinelli had a broad nose, thick lips, and a prominent dimple on his broad chin. Above a pair of long dark eyebrows, a deep scar creased his forehead. Two more scars on the back of his head revealed he was a man who had taken his share of blows. Spinelli had come to West Virginia from Calabria in 1905 and settled so readily into life in Eskdale that he took the unusual step of marrying an American woman, the former Nellie Bowles, who had been born and raised on Cabin Creek.[15]

Nellie and Rocco had leaped into the action that spring as soon as the strike call came from over the ridge in Paint Creek. All summer they traveled from camp to camp "talking to Italian replacements, beseeching them to come out of the creek," in what one historian called "remarkable acts of bravery." On one occasion, the couple persuaded fifty-four Italians to follow them down the stream to the Kanawha River and into Charleston, where UMWA district officers sheltered them in a tent camp set up conspicuously on Capitol Street. One of these men told the press that he had been recruited to work in West Virginia and promised a good house, free coal to heat it, and an easy job as a timekeeper. But when he arrived, he encountered men and women screaming curses at him in English and Italian. On his first day at work, the boss told him there was no office job for him as a timekeeper and that he would go into the hole with the others. After putting in several days of hard labor in a dark mine, the stranger readily followed the Spinellis out of Cabin Creek.[16]

The strangers who arrived on well-guarded trains were not the only threat the strikers faced. Some Cabin Creek miners had refused to join the walkout, including some local African Americans who decided to remain loyal to the bosses who paid them, instead of risking everything by answering a call from an organization led by white men. To help win these men over, the UMWA national officers sent their most experienced black organizer to the scene.

George H. Edmunds had fearlessly entered hostile company territory controlled by white men on many occasions. He had also dared to speak against Booker T. Washington, the acknowledged spokesman for black America, who had urged black mine workers to ally with their employers. A socialist who preached class solidarity, Edmunds touted the UMWA as a rare national organization that banned discrimination in its constitution, elected black men to serve in union offices, and conducted integrated meetings. He spoke with the authority of a man who had risen up out of the pits to become an important union official and self-educated intellectual, a man who read books about socialism and capitalism and contributed articles to the union's journal.

And like Mother Jones, Edmunds spoke of the powerful commitment to unionism made by miners who were slaves or the sons of slaves. These men had been freed from bondage and from the peonage of sharecropping. They were now free to leave their place of employment, and in West Virginia, they were free to vote. But like their white cohorts, black miners found that something of slavery remained in the lives of men who sold their labor and sacrificed their liberty for the right to work for a coal company and live in a company town under the watchful eye of deputy sheriffs and private detectives. A miner, who had been a slave, later testified that the "gunmen" who were "called the Baldwins" did not believe that striking coal miners were citizens, and they took "away from us our rights and privileges" as freemen, "both the black and the white."[17]

While Edmunds relied upon eloquence and logic to make his case for industrial freedom, Dan Chain employed different talents to the same end. Known as "Few Clothes," he weighed more than two hundred pounds, and he knew how to use his fists in a brawl. When the first strikebreakers arrived in Eskdale late in August, Chain joined two other strikers in an assault on a carload of new recruits. After being attacked at the train station, the replacement workers hit the tracks and headed down the creek to a station where they could catch a train that would take them home.[18]

It was rumored that Chain had once belonged to the notorious black army regiment President Roosevelt had discharged in 1906 because some of its members refused to testify against fellow soldiers who were accused of raiding a white neighborhood in Houston. "Anyway," one striker recalled, "[Chain] knew how to handle a gun." And when strike leaders in the Eskdale camp decided they needed to protect themselves from an assault by the guards, they recruited Few Clothes along with ten other experienced marksmen, who became known as the "dirty eleven."[19]

While this band protected the strike community from attack, the miners and their families settled in for what they expected to be a long haul. Ralph Chaplin, a radical organizer and journalist, found the strikers "doing pretty well" in their tent colony. They seemed proud of themselves and even seemed to be enjoying themselves, as they spent long days visiting and sometimes singing together. The scene appalled "local respectables," wrote Chaplin, people who were

Strikers at a store in the Cove section of Eskdale, summer 1912.

not used to this kind of mixing and socializing among men, women, and children of different races and nationalities.[20]

"The Lord has been on our side as far as the weather is concerned," one miner wrote from Eskdale during the last days of summer. "Almost from the first day of the strike, He began to bring forth one of the finest crops of shallot, shonie, dandelion, and other wild greens. Long before the season was over the ground hog was nice and fat. The striking miners have been catching them in large numbers." A popular miners' song captured this man's sense of hope when it promised that "God provides for every miner / When in union they're combined."[21]

Meanwhile, Mother Jones and strike leaders decided to raise a hue and cry in the state capital by marching through Charleston with three thousand strikers and their supporters. At a rally, a stenographer hired by the operators transcribed a speech by Mother Jones, who told the assembly to expect no help from that "goddamned dirty coward" Governor Glasscock, whom, she added wickedly, "we shall call 'Crystal Peter.'" But, "unless he rids Paint Creek and Cabin Creek of these goddamned Baldwin-Felts mine-guard thugs," she warned, "there is going to be one hell of a lot of bloodletting in these hills." Dismayed by these threats, by reports that strikers had ordered a thousand high-powered rifles, and by the fears of his supporters in the business community, Governor Glasscock issued a "Peace Proclamation" on August 20, warning all citizens to disarm, to refrain from gathering together in "riotous or unlawful assemblies" and from "uttering inflammatory speeches calculated to incite riot . . ."[22]

Then Glasscock appointed a commission of three leading citizens to investigate the contradictory claims of labor and management. The commissioners barely had time to digest their charge when they were compelled to investigate a gruesome incident, which revealed to them the full force of the strikers' rage and the depth of support these workers enjoyed from other miners.

On the morning of August 30, the captain of the mine guards on lower Cabin Creek made his daily rounds inspecting company property in Dry Branch, a union stronghold. A balding man with a steady gaze and a professional bearing, Thomas Hines had taken on a responsible position in the valley when he arrived in 1904 after the mine operators abrogated their contract with the union. A company doctor described Captain Hines as "a very pleasant gentleman" who earned the respect of residents by arresting thieves, drunks, and brawlers in the wild coal towns. In time, he married a coal miner's daughter and settled into raising a family in Dry Branch. He was often seen chatting with the miners at the company store and swimming with them in the YMCA swimming pool that coal operator Charles Cabell had opened in Eskdale.[23] In the summer of 1912, Hines's duties abruptly changed when he was charged with evicting his neighbors from their homes and protecting the men the coal operators imported to take their jobs.

That morning, Hines gathered some of his men and set out to track down a check-weigh man from Kayford named Russell Hodge, whom the agent suspected of performing criminal acts on behalf of the strikers. According to a story in the *Charleston Daily Mail*, Hines arrested Hodge and was taking the prisoner back to Dry Branch when a shower of bullets came down from the mountainside and brought the deputy down. When the gunfire from the woods ceased,

Thomas Hines.

other mine guards put their bloodied captain on a train that took him to the Sheltering Arms Hospital, where he died. Later that day, when the district constable went down to investigate the shooting, a hail of sniper fire from the hills drove him away. He vowed not to venture out again until the strike ended.[24]

The killing of Thomas Hines, the first man to die on Cabin Creek, altered the course of events. Thomas Felts ordered up reinforcements from Bluefield, and union forces on the other side of the Kanawha River started moving out of UMWA strongholds at Ward, Cannelton, and Boomer; a few hours later, these men were spied marching "Indian file" along the ridges above Cabin Creek. The governor's commission later issued a vivid description of what happened when the strikers, "seventy-five percent of them with usually cool Anglo-Saxon blood in their veins . . . saw red" and marched out "wild eyed" from union locals and massed on the ridges above Cabin Creek, where they prepared to "sweep down" on Dry Branch and other towns guarded by the Baldwins. In reaction, "the operators hurried in over a hundred guards heavily armed, purchased several deadly machine guns and many thousands of rounds of ammunition."[25]

That afternoon, a company of state militia left National Guard headquarters in Pratt with orders to restore peace around Dry Branch. But when the militiamen arrived they were unable to find, let alone halt, the union forces moving into position for an attack on the mine guards. The next day, strikers tore up the C&O tracks leading up the valley to prevent the influx of more National Guardsmen or hired gunmen, and early that evening union miners took positions on the ridgeline, where they could look down at the lights of Red Warrior and Kayford. The mine owners, well aware of these movements, sent women and children to the cellars and coordinated defense efforts with the Baldwin-Felts operatives. As night fell over Cabin Creek, two armed forces were poised for combat.[26]

After the Kanawha County sheriff visited the valley that night, he reported to the governor that the situation was "beyond his control." Only the National Guard could prevent an all-out war on upper Cabin Creek. Glasscock responded by beseeching Charles Cabell and the other operators to remove their private guards from the territory patrolled by the troops. When the employers refused, Glasscock issued a public proclamation ordering all persons in the Cabin Creek district to lay down their arms. It was no use. The next day, after strikers fired again on trains hauling strikebreakers, and the operators purchased more arms and ammunition, Glasscock took a bold step and declared martial law in the strike zone.

William Ellsworth Glasscock was a scholar and an experienced attorney who knew that only a few governors had dared to suspend the writ of habeas corpus and impose military rule during peacetime. He also knew of the consequences that followed when one governor—Frank Steunenberg of Idaho—did this during a violent silver miners' strike in 1899. His decision provoked withering criticism from labor unions, mainstream newspapers, and congressmen; far worse, it led to the governor's gruesome murder six years later.[27]

Shortly after Glasscock declared martial law, General Elliott, the commander of the National Guard, asked the C&O to outfit a special train he could use to carry away the weapons his soldiers had seized from the Baldwin-Felts men and the strikers. He also planned to use the train to haul military doctors and medical corpsmen up to the valleys to clean up the mine villages, where poor sanitation had created a health menace. Because the general had supported Theodore Roosevelt and his new Progressive Party, the strikers called this train the "Bull Moose Special."

Soon after the militiamen detrained, Elliott ordered the strikers to surrender their arms and told the mine operators to dismiss all Baldwin-Felts agents in their employ. If the coal company executives failed to comply, his soldiers would deport all of these agents from the area. During the first day of martial law, National Guardsmen seized a vast arsenal of 1,872 rifles, 556 pistols, 6 Colt machine guns, and 225,000 rounds of ammunition, as well as 480 blackjacks taken from the mine guards.[28]

Mine operators objected furiously when they were denied their right to employ men to guard their private property and then subjected to rude treatment by militiamen who seemed to regard them as public enemies. "[The guardsmen] thought the miners were really being imposed on," Charles Cabell recalled, "and we were the aggressors in this matter, and that we did not deserve any consideration . . ."[29] By contrast, the soldiers took to the workers' complaints at face value and made them feel that the militia had come to liberate them from what Mother Jones called "thug rule." That evening, five thousand coal miners slept with pleasant dreams for

National Guardsmen with confiscated arms at a mine on Cabin Creek, 1912.

the first time in months, as one reporter put it, knowing that when they awoke the next morning "the day of the mine guards in West Virginia" would be over.[30]

After he declared martial law, Governor Glasscock insisted that the mine operators on Paint Creek and Cabin Creek come to Charleston and meet with UMWA leaders in the statehouse. Several executives grudgingly complied, but they refused to talk with mine union officials face-to-face for fear that this would afford the UMWA some semblance of recognition. Instead, the antagonists sat in separate rooms while the governor engaged in shuttle diplomacy. Glasscock proposed that the miners return to work until a settlement could be reached through arbitration, and as a gesture of good faith, he urged the colliery operators to permanently abandon the private mine guard system. Union negotiators readily agreed to the deal, for they were desperate to end a costly strike, but the employers rejected the governor's proposal on the spot and left the capital in a huff. The next day, the mine operators sent Glasscock a truculently worded letter in which they proclaimed: "We stand for law and order; the UMWA does not. That organization has virtually invaded the State of West Virginia and is carrying on war therein." Then they turned on the governor himself: "You, knowing that it was the purpose of armed bodies of agitators to make assaults upon our people and that we were preparing to resist such assaults . . . placed your troops in the field and declared martial law, disarming all of our people . . ."[31]

The day after Governor Glasscock issued his proclamation, attorneys for the coal companies filed suit in the West Virginia Supreme Court, challenging the governor's authority to declare martial law. Glasscock told a commander of the National Guard he feared that if the court ruled against him, he would have to withdraw the troops, but he hoped that would not come to pass. He had worked all summer to bring together "the warring elements," but the mine operators "refused to do anything," whereas "the miners have always been willing to sit down and adjust their troubles."[32]

To justify their intransigence, the industrialists insisted that the strikes in Kanawha County were the result of a conspiracy between the UMWA and the unionized mining companies in the Midwest. This alleged plot was aimed at destroying the West Virginia coal industry by forcing companies to unionize, which would raise labor costs and drive them out of business. In truth, unionized mining companies in the Midwest did want the UMWA to organize West Virginia's colliery companies in order to negate the effect of cheap coal on the national market, and these coal operators would have been delighted to put their southern competitors out of business. However, the union's official leaders had no intention of destroying Mountain State mine companies. They simply wanted to organize the men who worked for them.[33]

The mine owners publicized a second conspiracy theory as well, one at odds with the idea that northern mine operators and union officials had formed a pact. They charged that Socialists actually controlled the UMWA and were determined to rule or ruin West Virginia's mining industry. To support this claim, the industrialists pointed to a resolution adopted by the UMWA's 1912 convention, which declared that every coal miner was entitled to the "full value" of his labor. The state's mine owners interpreted this to mean that the union's sole objective was to seize their coal mines, abolish wages, and operate the collieries on a socialistic basis. This theory ignored the real politics within the UMWA, however, where the Socialists constituted a vocal minority vigorously opposed by the union's national presidents. In fact, Mother Jones and other Socialist Party leaders had inveighed against former president John Mitchell for joining the business-dominated National Civic Federation, discouraging strikes, and practicing what the radicals called "class collaboration."[34]

On September 6, when Mother Jones addressed a throng of strikers at Court House Square in Charleston, she could see that her followers were excited by the signs that the governor, the National Guard commander, and important private citizens had turned against the mine owners. But she could also feel in her aging bones that it was too soon to declare a victory. What good could possibly come from martial law, she asked, when at that moment the state militia was allowing the mine operators to "bring transportation" up the creeks? Furthermore, the guardsmen wouldn't permit her to go up to Cabin Creek and hold a meeting. Jones said she would not obey this order, and she urged her followers to defy it as well. The strikers must exercise their right to hold "peaceful, law-abiding meetings," even if the governor sent his entire militia to stop them. "We won't surrender that right," she vowed.[35]

Meanwhile, a few blocks away, Governor Glasscock was holding a private session with his attorney general and other advisers about what to do next in the strike zone. The National Guard had disarmed the Baldwin-Felts agents and miners, and yet the strike continued, the strikebreakers kept coming, and the mine owners remained more defiant than ever. The governor retired that night without making a decision.

The next day, Glasscock received a letter from one of his advisers who had attended the meeting. In that session, J. Lewis Baumgartner, a lawyer from Beckley, had urged the governor to arrest all suspected insurgents in the strike district and to put them on trial before a military tribunal. A legal problem had prevented them from taking this drastic course of action. According to the state constitution, a suspension of the civil courts and the imposition of military law required proof of "the actual existence of a state of war." But Baumgartner offered Glasscock a suggestion for how to settle this matter "conclusively for all time." When he had visited the military camp at Pratt on his way home from the capital, the attorney had been impressed when he saw the carloads of guns and ammunition the guardsmen had confiscated from the strikers and the mine guards; then it had occurred to him that no such collection of arms could have taken place under any condition except in an "actually existing" state of war. If the governor could arrange for the publication of photographs documenting this arsenal, he could convince the public that harsh action was necessary and also "disarm any criticism that the most malicious, or carping, [people] might make."[36]

The photographs were duly snapped and sent to newspapers, and the next day National Guardsmen began to arrest civilians, mainly strikers, without warrants. The miners were held on a wide variety of alleged offenses that ranged from trespassing and congregating in groups of three or more to carrying concealed firearms and even

Arms seized by the National Guard on Paint Creek and Cabin Creek.

committing adultery.[37] Soldiers took their prisoners to Pratt and held them in a railway freight house until they could be tried by a military tribunal.

Americans have regarded the right to a jury trial and the right of habeas corpus as birthrights ever since the Founding Fathers adopted the Constitution. Reluctant to violate this tradition, federal government officials suspended these rights only twice, once during the Civil War and once during Reconstruction.[38]

Well aware of this history, UMWA lawyers immediately challenged the military trials as a violation of the West Virginia Constitution, which explicitly prohibited civilians from being tried by military courts. The attorneys failed, however, to secure writs of habeas corpus for their clients, and the strikers remained incarcerated at Pratt without benefit of counsel, without being able to question the vague charges against them, and without being able to summon witnesses who could testify on their behalf.[39] After scores of the strikers imprisoned at the "bull pen" at Pratt were swiftly tried, convicted, and sent off to the state penitentiary at Moundsville, it was painfully evident that Mother Jones's suspicions of martial law were well founded: a brief progressive moment in West Virginia politics had passed.[40]

During the late nineteenth century, governors had called out state militia to stop "labor troubles" on more than a hundred occasions, notably during the lockout at Andrew Carnegie's Homestead, Pennsylvania, steel mill in 1892. This legacy convinced union members that the state's armed forces would inevitably be used to defend private property, but would never be used to protect their liberty. Some trade unions urged their members not to join the National Guard, and in some states, elected officials remained skeptical of appropriating public funds for militia units that would be used to safeguard employers' interests in strike situations.[41]

The military occupation of Paint Creek and Cabin Creek and the military trials at Pratt presented West Virginia's Socialists with a host of political issues to exploit in the coming election season. Seizing the opportunity, party leaders discouraged acts of violence by strikers that would provoke the National Guard and prevent Socialist candidates from campaigning freely throughout the strike zone, where public sentiment seemed to be shifting toward their political party.[42]

Unaware that the Socialists were working behind the scenes as peacekeepers, Glasscock assumed that the strikers were in full retreat and that the mines would soon be in operation. Under these circumstances, he ended martial law in the strike zone, suspended the military tribunal at Pratt, and ordered most of the militia companies to leave the district. To substitute for the National Guard, Glasscock asked General Elliott to create a quasi-military force of reputable, disciplined "watchmen" who would be charged with guarding the mines and preserving order without abusing the strikers. Although the watchmen were to be paid by the coal companies, UMWA district officials accepted these new guards as replacements for the hated "Baldwin thugs."

Governor Glasscock then turned his attention to the state and national election campaigns now in full swing. His idol Theodore Roosevelt was the talk of the nation as he stormed across the country attacking predatory wealth, political corruption, and the competence of his former ally, the incumbent president William Howard Taft, who was campaigning for reelection.[43] Meanwhile, Eugene V.

Debs, the Socialist Party's presidential candidate, attracted enthusiastic crowds with his assaults on the entire capitalist system and the politicians who intended to save it. While Roosevelt and Debs thrilled audiences with their rousing attacks on big business, the Democratic Party nominee, Woodrow Wilson, conducted a cautious and tedious campaign against high tariffs and holding companies. Fearful of Roosevelt's Bull Moose charge, Wilson asked for advice from one of America's most influential progressive intellectuals, Louis D. Brandeis.[44]

Known as "the People's Attorney" for his defense of consumers, women, sweatshop workers, and small businesses being crushed by financial trusts and monopoly corporations, Brandeis believed large capitalists were subverting the freedom of countless American citizens.. These businessmen were accountable to no one, certainly not to their widely dispersed stockholders and not to the government of the United States. Brandeis was particularly concerned about the fate of the nation's wage earners; unless they became "self-respecting members of the democracy," they would remain in a servile condition and America would become a society increasingly divided by class interests and extremist politics. Echoing the words of Mother Jones, Brandeis declared that the conflict between "political liberty" and "industrial slavery" was the most critical social problem facing the nation in 1912.[45]

At Brandeis's urging, Woodrow Wilson embraced the idea of industrial democracy, a vision of a future economic order in which employees would participate in the decisions that affected their working conditions and even in decisions about how businesses should be run. Wilson then took the offensive by attacking Roosevelt's "New Nationalism" program for refusing to legalize trade unions and the right to organize. "What I am interested in," the Democratic candidate announced, "is having the government of the United States be more concerned about human rights than about property rights."[46]

The public had never experienced a presidential campaign in which all the contenders addressed the problems caused by class inequality and corporate irresponsibility. All four candidates advocated various ways of regulating the vast powers acquired by America's huge banks and corporations (through public ownership in Debs's case). And all four men proposed ways of ending outbreaks of violent industrial disputes like the one that had erupted in West Virginia that spring. The fact that this critical presidential election coincided with the escalating struggle in the West Virginia coalfields brought national attention to a strike that would take on an increasing political character as Election Day approached.

Chapter 6

The Iron Hand

September 6, 1912–February 12, 1913

William Glasscock's heart was with Theodore Roosevelt, but his head told him he could not bolt the GOP and campaign for the new Progressive Party. Instead, he ignored the national election and devoted his efforts to electing a fellow Roosevelt enthusiast, Henry Drury Hatfield, to succeed him as governor. Weakened by ill health and discouraged by the strike, the governor looked forward to retiring. Because candidate Hatfield hailed from coal country and because he knew the miners and the operators, Glasscock believed his fellow progressive could bring an end to the bitter industrial dispute, which had spread from Paint Creek and Cabin Creek to 90 percent of the mines in the Kanawha coalfield and more than 30 percent of the collieries in nearby counties.[1]

Trained as a physician, "Drewy" Hatfield had led an effort to build a state-supported hospital for mine workers at Welch in McDowell County, which he later directed. After winning a county office, the doctor earned a reputation as a reformer who worked to clean up the courts, the saloons, and the county's filthy jail cells. Beneath this veneer of reform, however, Hatfield operated like a regular political boss, forging a close alliance with McDowell County coal operators and with local African American leaders who could get black coal miners to the polls, where they provided the GOP with its margin of victory in close elections. During a hotly contested election to the state senate in 1910, Hatfield and his cousins indulged in such flagrant election abuses that the U.S. Congress launched an investigation. No charges were filed, however, and Hatfield served a term as president of a closely divided senate, where he exercised control over federal jobs and funds dispensed by the Taft administration. In 1912, the senator broke with Taft, endorsed Roosevelt, and won the Republican gubernatorial nomination in a field of seasoned GOP politicians.[2]

Henry Hatfield carried with him the burden of his family name, for he was the nephew of legendary clan patriarch William Anderson "Devil Anse" Hatfield, who had led his family in a bloody feud with the McCoys after the Civil War. After the feud ended, Anse Hatfield's political enemies and business rivals took advantage of his vulnerability and went after his land in a series of legal actions. Instead of seeking revenge once again, Anse moved his family from its ancestral homestead near the Tug Fork River on the Kentucky border to a spot twenty miles north in the wilds of Logan County near the town of Sarah Ann. There, on a high ridge above Main Island Creek, Anse constructed a new fortified home and then settled down to a quiet life in his mountain lair, where he kept bees, sold honey, and entertained visitors with tall tales of the old times. Meanwhile, Anse's sons found new occupations in an area being transformed by the coal-mining industry.[3]

Two of Anse's youngest boys, Detroit (Troy) and Elias, had joined the Baldwin-Felts Agency and were killed in Boomer by a shotgun-wielding bootlegger, but Anse's other offspring had stayed out of trouble. Even his notorious son, W. A. "Cap" Hatfield, who led the deadly New Year's Day raid on the McCoys' home in 1888, had settled down and found work as a deputy sheriff in Logan County. By the time Anse Hatfield's nephew Henry ran for governor in 1912, the old "Devil" himself had pulled in his horns and had agreed to be baptized by a Hard-Shell Baptist preacher. If Henry won the election and became governor, the Hatfields—already a political force in three coal-mining counties—would gain more power than any family in the state, and perhaps even a new kind of respectability as well.[4]

Candidate Hatfield supported the direct election of U.S. senators and women's suffrage, advocated a corrupt practices act to take big money out of political campaigns, and proposed a tax on coal, oil, and gas company profits. He appealed to organized labor by proposing a workmen's compensation program modeled after a German law he studied while visiting the Ruhr coal-mining region, promising to restrict the use of private mine guards, and, most important, vowing to bring an end to the deadly struggle in the Kanawha coalfields.[5]

Locked in a tight race, Hatfield kept a wary eye on the Socialist Party's gubernatorial candidate, who suddenly loomed as a vote getter because the mine war in the Kanawha field had radicalized hundreds of miners and their supporters. At the height of the campaign, UMWA vice president Frank J. Hayes reported that coal miners, who represented 40 percent of the voters in Kanawha County, had turned to socialism by the hundreds and that the Socialist Party had an excellent chance of electing its entire ticket. National Guard commander Charles Elliott predicted a similar outcome.[6]

On October 31, hundreds of strikers and other citizens traveled to Charleston, where the great Eugene V. Debs was scheduled to make a campaign stop on his third run for president as the Socialist Party's standard-bearer. A tireless barnstormer and a captivating orator, Debs had already addressed thousands of workers in union halls and railroad yards, tenant farmers in summer encampments, immigrant crowds in city parks, and small-town folks in Main Street opera houses.[7]

Inspired by Debs's campaign, West Virginia Socialists fanned out through the valleys and mining towns to talk to voters about what would happen when capitalist America became a "cooperative commonwealth." Speaking at the Holly Grove tent encampment, Socialist Party state secretary Harold W. Houston asked the miners how many of them intended to vote for Roosevelt, for Wilson, or for President Taft, "a man whose political ideas belong to the 'Dark Ages.'" When no one raised a hand, Houston asked how many would vote for the only union man running for president. Only "Cries of 'Hurrah for Debs'" were heard, according to a stenographer who secretly recorded the speech for the mine operators.[8]

Eugene V. Debs delivering a campaign speech in 1912.

Ralph Chaplin, a writer for the *Labor Star*, a Socialist newspaper published in Huntington, West Virginia, remembered the excitement he felt in the air that fall as he campaigned for Debs and the Socialist ticket. In his autobiography, Chaplin wrote nostalgically about how much he and his family enjoyed the warm hospitality of the local Socialists. But these same kind and gentle "hill people" swore they were ready to take up their rifles to protect their right to vote for Debs. "I don't think," Chaplin remarked, "I have ever encountered such passionate love for freedom as I found in the hills of West Virginia."[9]

On Cabin Creek, a focal point of Socialists' electoral activity, mine owner Charles Cabell felt the campaign's effects in a very different way. He remarked later that in the midst of a violent strike, the Socialist Party candidates injected politics into the conflict in a "bad way." Cabell took the campaign personally because it cost him some friends like the popular local dentist, T. L. "Doc" Tincher. The mine owner had known the dentist all his life and thought of him as a "very respectable man," but in the fall of 1912, when Tincher ran as the Socialist candidate for Kanawha County sheriff, the relationship turned nasty. Cabell had cultivated a reputation as a likable, responsible citizen who was respected by his employees, but that fall the Socialists were suddenly portraying him as a public enemy. The strike had already alienated Cabell's employees from him, and the campaign made it worse: "[I]t was hurting me considerably," he remarked, "because I had been very close to my people . . ." The low point came when he saw a headline in the *Labor Argus* that dubbed him "Czar Cabell of Cabin Creek."[10]

When the election results were tallied, Eugene V. Debs received nearly a million votes, including fifteen thousand in West Virginia, a remarkable increase of 300 percent over his 1908 total; it was the greatest electoral advance the Socialist Party recorded in the 1912 election. Debs ran strongest in the coal-mining counties, especially in free towns like Mount Carbon, where the third party polled 54 percent of the total, and Eskdale, where voters elected Socialists as mayor and as marshal. The Socialist Party's candidates swept the Cabin Creek district, outpolling the Democrats and Republicans combined and winning all the positions as constables and magistrates. In the Paint Creek district, the miners elected the peg-legged check-weigh man Brant Scott, a strike leader, to serve as justice of the peace.[11]

Millions of Americans had participated in an election they thought would change the country. Three-quarters of the electorate voted against the conservative, business-dominated Republican Party and the incumbent president who spoke for the old order. So many Republicans defected from the GOP that Woodrow Wilson won the election and became the first Democrat to occupy the White House in sixteen years.[12]

The newly elected president had big promises to keep, particularly to the UMWA and to other affiliates of the AFL, whose members had helped Wilson and the Democrats win the electoral votes of two critical states, Illinois and Ohio. Wilson also carried West Virginia because Republicans split their vote between Taft and

Roosevelt; however, the GOP's gubernatorial candidate, Henry Hatfield, defeated his Democratic opponent by a narrow margin and became the state's youngest governor at the age of thirty-seven.[13]

After the election, Governor William Glasscock prayed that peace would prevail in the Kanawha minefield until Hatfield took office. With the National Guard withdrawn, the peacekeeping mission would be placed in the hands of the "watchmen" who had replaced the Baldwin-Felts detectives. Many of these watchmen were off-duty National Guard officers who were thought to be fair-minded and public-spirited, men like Major John B. Payne who earned the respect of strikers during the martial law period in September. When that period ended, Payne took a job as a watchman for the Cabin Creek Land Company and moved his wife into one of the firm's houses at Dakota. "It was only after I removed my militia uniform and performed the duties of a watchman that I had trouble with the miners," he later explained.[14]

Captain Guy Levy, a National Guard officer from Charleston, remained in Mucklow on Paint Creek to work as a watchman because his commander, General Elliott, "practically ordered" him to take the job as second in command of a contingent of off-duty National Guardsmen. During the campaign season, Levy and his men had patrolled the mines and railroad depots without encountering much trouble, but after the election, they worked like firefighters, rushing from one spot to another trying to apprehend strikers who had resumed their attacks on replacement workers. On one occasion, armed strikers captured four watchmen and then released them unharmed. Upon their release, the guards reported that some of the strikers had been ready to execute them.[15] On another occasion, gunfire rained down on a C&O train carrying replacement workers from New York, though no one on board was killed or wounded. A reporter for the *Charleston Gazette* observed that the strikers seemed to be aiming at the watchmen guarding the trains, not at the workers on board. By mid-November, Captain Levy said, "the miners thought us just as bad as the Baldwin guards."[16]

In the face of news reports that "guerrilla warfare" had resumed, the coal operators suddenly abandoned their opposition to martial law and demanded that Governor Glasscock reestablish military rule over the strike zone. With the election over, the political risk of declaring martial law for a second time had diminished, and Glasscock ordered the National Guard to return to the Paint Creek–Cabin Creek district. When the troops arrived this time, no miners came out of their tents to cheer them. Perhaps the strikers sensed what lay ahead; perhaps they realized that this time the National Guard was sent to crush them with what a West Virginia attorney called "the iron hand of military rule."[17]

When the National Guard threw a new dragnet over the strike zone, it pulled in scores of men as well as several women who were held without charges at a boardinghouse in Pratt; one of them was Nellie Spinelli, who left five children in the care of her family when she

Watchmen on Cabin Creek with a pet bear.

was arrested. Military authorities also imprisoned Silas Nantz, the Socialist marshal of Eskdale, who was arrested for interfering with a militia captain's attempt to arrest a striker without a warrant. The town's Socialist mayor escaped arrest by fleeing across the Tug River to Kentucky, where he hid out with relatives.[18]

When the military trials resumed in Pratt, Newt Gump, a six-foot-four coal miner who had lived with his wife in the strikers' tent colony at Holly Grove, was sent to the state penitentiary at Moundsville for five years on charges of assaulting a strikebreaker. Dan "Few Clothes" Chain of Eskdale also received a five-year sentence "for obstructing a railroad company in the use of its property." Rocco Spinelli faced the same fate. His wife, Nellie, received a one-year sentence for harassing replacement workers and thereby violating the Red Man Act, a law enacted in 1882 to allow for the prosecution of night-riding vigilantes who had engaged in "a conspiracy to inflict bodily harm on others."[19]

A historian later evaluated these convictions and noted that the officers who presided over the court-martial proceedings in Pratt included several businessmen who "did not know the difference between a felony and a misdemeanor."[20] In any case, no public protest arose against these proceedings except in the pages of Socialist newspapers like the *Labor Argus*, whose editor, Charles H. Boswell, denounced military

Photos of Newt Gump, Dan Chain, and Rocco Spinelli taken after their arrests.

tribunal's actions. "Justice is dead, freedom is a thing of the past, and liberty is but a dream of the future," he declared.[21]

The tough sentences imposed by the military tribunal failed, however, to end the strike or stop the assaults. On November 19, guerrilla warfare resumed on Paint Creek, where snipers fired on a band of strikebreakers. On Cabin Creek, transportation men again faced the fury of the crowds who gathered at the train stations. "They would congregate at every train, ride on the trains and insult men who were working every way they could think of," said one observer, "and if they ever got a chance they would have shot them . . ."[22]

Nor did the sentence imposed on Nellie Spinelli intimidate the wives, mothers, daughters, and sisters of strikers who had joined these congregations. A journalist reported seeing miners' wives screaming insults at the strikebreakers while "drunken mobs" cheered these "unwomanly actions."[23] One of the strikers recalled that the women on Cabin Creek "were about as aggressive as the men were as far as the union was concerned." Sarah Blizzard of Eskdale later admitted that she and some of her women friends snuck out one night and used crowbars to tear up the C&O railroad tracks to prevent trains from bringing in more scabs to work the mines.[24] Women in mining towns were often active on picket lines, for they despised the men who sank low enough to steal another man's job and starve his children. Mother Jones discovered this early in her career as an agitator when she watched immigrant women in coal camps assault a group of scabs with mops, brooms, and iron skillets.[25]

When strikebreakers were black men or immigrants, strikers weighted their epithets with racial and ethnic slurs. Yet these interlopers could also arouse scornful pity in the minds of union activists. In speeches, editorials, songs, and cartoons the scab was characterized as a dupe who was easily fooled by deceptive recruiters. When seen in this human context, the strikebreaker was just another working stiff who could be turned back if he was told the truth; in some cases, a "blackleg" could even be turned around and persuaded to join the union.

Mother Jones wasted little of her venom on the strikebreakers. Indeed, she even recruited two of them to go and tell federal officials how they were lured into West Virginia with deceitful promises.

Jones put all the blame for the violence on the employment agencies whose representatives recruited these men and callously sent them into harm's way. Pressured by Jones and her allies, several Ohio employment agencies recruiting strikebreakers began to abide by state rules that required them to tell recruits they were being sent to work where a strike was in progress.[26]

Americans had been debating the morality of strikebreaking ever since the age of industrial violence began in the 1870s. In 1904, Harvard president Charles W. Eliot proclaimed the strikebreaker a "good type of the American hero"—a worker who demonstrated his "manly instincts" by doing an honest day's work instead of acting like a union man who demanded more pay for shorter hours. Jack London, the most popular writer in America, issued a reply to Eliot in an article for the *Atlantic Monthly*. Furthermore, he is credited for the labor movement's oft-quoted definition of a scab: "After God had finished the rattlesnake, the toad and the vampire, he had some awful substance left with which he made the scab . . . a two-legged animal with a corkscrew soul, a water brain and . . . [a] back-bone made of jelly and glue."[27]

During the second decade of the century, influential thinkers began to express similar views. Walter Lippmann, a founder of the *New Republic*, cited the West Virginia miners' strike in his argument that a worker on a picket line fought a strikebreaker "out of sheer self-protection." It was an ugly thing, he granted, to see a man clubbed by strikers, but it was an uglier thing to see an outsider imported to take away that man's livelihood. When a union forcefully defended its members' jobs, Lippmann maintained, the union acted like a nation protecting its coastline against an invader. "The strikebreaker, then, is not only a peril to the union, he is a peril to the larger interests of the nation."[28]

While she crusaded against strikebreaking agencies, Mother Jones attempted to draw national attention to the ways in which UMWA members had been stripped of their civil liberties by the West Virginia mine operators and by state authorities.[29] Her free speech campaign culminated in Washington, DC, where her friend, the newly elected Democratic congressman from Pennsylvania, William B. Wilson, called a protest meeting in an armory. Before an audience sprinkled with reporters and government officials, Jones detailed the constitutional abuses she had witnessed in the Paint Creek–Cabin Creek mining district. "If such crimes against the citizens of the state of West Virginia go unrebuked by the government," she cried, "I suggest that we take down the flag that stands for constitutional government, and run up a banner, saying, 'This is the flag of the money oligarchy of America!'"[30]

At Christmastime, Jones returned from her incessant travels to visit the people camped at Eskdale and Holly Grove. Arriving on a horse-drawn buggy loaded with shoes, clothing, and presents for the children, she spread as much cheer around the camps as she could; then she took to the road again, leaving her followers alone in the canvas tent colonies to face the winter without her. Among those who remained encamped that Yuletide were Frank Keeney and his twenty-four-year-old wife, Bessie, who was still nursing her baby girl and depending upon family members, friends and UMWA staffers to feed and clothe their three daughters.

Mother Jones with strikers' children at the camp in Eskdale, December 1912.

That winter Ralph Chaplin saw the faces of families like the Keeneys. He and a coal miner buddy hopped freight trains running through the strike zone and dropped bags of leaflets and newspapers over the side to "trusted comrades" waiting at designated drop points. When the train slowed down at coal town crossings, Chaplin looked down at gaunt-looking women and skinny, raggedy children bent over along the tracks with baskets, hoping to find lumps of fuel for their stoves and campfires.[31] These desperate people standing in the snow inspired Chaplin to write a song that would later become famous. His lyrics condemned the capitalists who had "taken untold millions that they never toiled to earn" and praised the workers who had given their labor to make the "greedy parasites" rich. "It is we who . . . dug the mines and built the workshops, endless miles of railroad laid," sings one verse. "Now we stand outcast and starving 'midst the wonders we have made."[32]

When Governor Glasscock returned to Charleston from a family vacation in Florida, he celebrated the New Year with the happy news that the state supreme court had affirmed his decision to declare martial law in September and that a month had passed without any reports of violence in the coalfields. Perhaps he thought the winter weather had cooled off the angry strikers. Relieved by the news that no one had fired upon the trains carrying replacement workers, the governor decided to pull the militia out of Paint Creek and Cabin Creek.[33]

For two weeks, peace and quiet prevailed even though well-guarded trains kept arriving in the strike zone with coach loads of strikebreakers. On January 15, 1913, one of these trains arrived in Eskdale without incident. But as soon as the engine's brakes squealed and the steaming locomotive came to a stop, the station manager heard someone in the crowd curse and then he heard someone holler, "Shoot." An instant later, he said, "Some fellow on the train . . . did shoot, and struck a darky in the head, killing him instantly."[34]

The death of John Miller, an African American striker, threatened to reignite the mine war, but the newly elected town mayor and marshal of Eskdale, both Socialists, defused the situation when they boarded the train and arrested the guard who fired the shot. The two officials then turned over the assailant to the Kanawha County sheriff in Charleston. A few days later, someone put up bail for the guard, and he walked free, reclaimed his guns, and returned to work. Reacting to what it called a "grave injustice," the *Labor Argus* declared that if there was "no law to protect the lives of the workers or to punish those who maim and murder them, then we may say to hell with the law and will advise the working class to take the law in their own hands and redress their own wrongs."[35] The paper's editor, Charles Boswell, closed with a mysterious remark that only a few weeks of winter remained and that soon "the GREEN LEAVES will be out again."

This reference to the seasons may have puzzled some readers, but Ralph Chaplin knew what Boswell meant. In a chilling poem, Chaplin put words into the mouth of a miner who looks out of his tent at the "very bare and cold and lonely" winter hills. The worker tells a buddy that he longs for spring, when the slopes would again "grow fresh and green with every growing thing," because then the thick foliage would provide good cover for strikers who would make the mine guards pay for their crimes.[36]

While advocates of direct action were predicting, if not inciting, violence, Brant Scott, the newly elected justice of the peace on Paint Creek, was trying to prevent actions that would provoke more arrests and military trials. On January 15, Squire Scott fined two strikers for beating up a nonunion man and gave them a "stern lecture." Three days later, he headed up from Holly Grove to the Red Men's lodge in Mucklow with two fraternal brothers to retrieve some records. On the way, Scott issued a warning: "Now boys, of course, we expect to get into trouble because the . . . Baldwins are up there," meaning the watchmen. He told his fellow Red Men to let him do the talking, because he did not think the guards would "beat up an officer of the law." But when they reached the door of the Red Men's "wigwam," guards pulled their guns, saying, "You son of a bitch, don't open that door." When they told Scott they were taking him away, he refused to budge, but his status as justice of the peace meant nothing to the guards. "I am going to give you a good whipping," one of them snarled, and "he did it too," the victim recalled. When he returned to Holly Grove, Scott knew that he could no longer serve as a peacekeeper.[37]

Twenty winter days passed before the fighting resumed on Paint Creek. It started again when union pickets on a mountainside fired on some mine guards patrolling the valley down below. When he heard the shots, Guy Levy, captain of the watchmen, sent a detail to drive the shooters off the ridge. A few hours after Levy and his men returned to their fort at Mucklow, the strikers attacked the guard post from the high ground. No one was harmed and the assault would probably have been forgotten if Quinn Morton, the president of the Paint Creek Operators' Association, had not been in the fort that day; but he was.

Enraged by an assault that could have killed him, Morton ordered Levy and a detail of watchmen to track down the assailants. The guards followed some suspects to the tent camp at Holly Grove. As soon as Levy and his men approached, a group of at least seventy men opened fire on them from a wooded hill. The guards sprang for cover and then retreated to their fort. Asked later if his posse returned fire, the captain replied: "No, sir; they were only too glad to get out of there alive." When Levy returned to Mucklow that afternoon, he looked up into the hills and saw the dark shapes of men moving and shifting along the hillsides as light faded from the valley.[38]

Late that night, Quinn Morton decided it was safe to leave Mucklow for Charleston, where he had arranged to meet Kanawha County sheriff Bonner Hill. When Morton insisted that something had to be done to suppress the insurgents camped at Holly Grove, the law officer was receptive, for he had experienced his own troubles in the camp. A few weeks before, when the sheriff had led a posse of twenty-five deputies up to search the tents, armed miners had confronted the lawmen on the banks of Paint Creek. On that occasion Hill had decided to retreat rather than fight a deadly gun battle. But on February 7, the sheriff decided that Quinn Morton was right. The time had come to move on the tent camp at Holly Grove.

The decision Morton and Hill made that night would haunt them for the rest of their lives, because it unleashed an avalanche of events that had far-reaching consequences not only for the strikers and the mine operators, but also for the state of West Virginia, whose authorities would suddenly find themselves in the spotlight of a federal inquiry into the causes of industrial violence and the uses of government authority during labor strikes.

After he met with Quinn Morton, Sheriff Bonner Hill called the C&O office and asked dispatchers to send the armored train, the Bull Moose Special, over to Paint Creek Junction for a run up to Holly Grove. At this point, few people knew that the Special had been retrofitted at the C&O shops in Huntington with double steel armor below its windows and equipped with the latest model machine gun.[39] That night, when the Special arrived from Huntington, Hill and Morton boarded the train with a posse of well-armed deputies, railroad detectives, and a former Baldwin-Felts agent named Lee Calvin.

Calvin had worked for months riding on trains hauling strikebreakers up Cabin Creek. He later described the men he was hired to protect as "Bowery toughs shipped from New York; gutter snipes," and similar types who "came from Jersey." They were mostly "corner boys," according to Calvin, who wore white collars, of all things. "Miners don't very often wear white collars," he remarked.

Calvin obviously had no respect for the strikebreakers, nor had he any strong sympathy for the mine operators. He simply considered himself a professional willing to do his job—that is, until January 10, when the boss guard on Cabin Creek gave his men "orders to shoot if anyone made a false move or threw a rock or anything." This was too much for Calvin. He confronted the boss after his night run and told him he wouldn't carry out orders like that "for no man . . . not even the Czar of Russia." As a result, Calvin was out of work and lounging around a Charleston hotel lobby when Sheriff Hill recruited him for the late-night run up Paint Creek.[40]

At about ten o'clock that evening, the armored train turned up the valley toward Holly Grove and the engineer killed the running lights. "They were handing the rifles around . . . ," Calvin recalled, "and a fellow came through and says, 'Don't bother raising the windows, boys, you can shoot through the windows in case there is any shooting.'"

As the Special approached Holly Grove, the engineer, perhaps as a warning to the camp, sounded two short blasts from the train whistle. A few minutes later, according to Calvin, some of the men on the train fired at Holly Grove with rifles and a guard opened up with the Gatling gun. After a few seconds, Calvin saw flashes of rifles in the darkness outside and ducked as bullets crashed through the windows and wooden panels of the car. At this point, Quinn Morton shouted at the engineer to "back the train up again until we could give them another round," Calvin later testified; but Sheriff Hill intervened and told the driver to roll on, saying there were women and children in those tents and he would not allow any more firing on the camp.[41]

Francis Francesco Estep and his wife, Maud, lived in Holly Grove in a small cabin on the other side of the creek from the main tent city. Their first two sons had died in infancy and were buried in the Holly Grove cemetery. A third son had been born the previous year and Maud was pregnant again. Cesco, as Estep was known, had been digging coal for 47 cents a long ton, working ten hours a day, six days a week, and renting a company house when he joined the strike. When they were evicted, the Esteps took shelter with friends until Cesco found a cabin on the west side of Paint Creek. He then invited several families of strikers to pitch tents near his place.[42]

On the night of February 7, the Esteps were crowded in their front room with Cesco's two brothers, his cousin, and several friends. They were all "carrying on and talking," Maud later testified, and did not hear the train approach because their doors were closed to the cold. When bullets fired from the train smashed into the frame cabin, Cesco yelled at his wife to take the baby and run to the cellar and then bolted toward the front door of the cabin. Outside, he stopped and turned to holler at Maud to hurry when a bullet struck him in the face. After the firing stopped and Maud heard the train backing up, she crawled out with a lantern and found her husband's dead body.[43]

Eleven strikers had already been killed in the fighting on Paint Creek and Cabin Creek, but the death of Cesco Estep enraged the miners far more than any of the others. The man had been trying to save his wife and baby when a machine-gun bullet, fired from what strikers called the "death train," destroyed his face.[44]

The day after the Special made its deadly run, the C&O manager in Paint Creek Junction informed Governor Glasscock that all telegraph and telephone lines had been cut, and that his "men had simply refused to handle either the local or coal trains" heading up Paint Creek Branch. "Our men had been intimidated, and we had considerable trouble in getting our men to go up the creeks at all," the supervisor later testified; "in fact, we had to dismiss some of them."[45]

The Bull Moose Special's run made sensational headlines that morning and the startling news generated a wave of sympathy for the strikers. One merchant was so horrified by the news that he sent several cases of Springfield rifles and ten thousand rounds of ammunition to the strikers.[46] The assault on Holly Grove provoked outrage far beyond the state's borders as well. In New York, Walter Lippmann cited the raid on Holly Grove in the *New Republic* as a prime example of the tremendous odds workers faced in their struggle for democracy. Unless organized labor gained enough power to win respect, he feared that the working class would be doomed to "a degrading servitude." But with only one-tenth of wage earners organized, the union movement faced gigantic obstacles, because there were no limits to what employers would do to thwart it. A prime example was "that brutal struggle in West Virginia," where, Lippmann wrote, "a gatling gun . . . was run through a mining village at night 'spitting bullets at the rate of two hundred and fifty a minute.'"[47] Under such circumstances, he concluded, guerrilla warfare was the only tactic available to the weak. It would be "idle to talk about industrial peace" until workers won a living wage, protection from their government, and a voice in determining their working conditions.[48]

On February 9, 1913, friends, neighbors, and union brothers attended the funeral and burial of Cesco Estep next to the graves of his two children in the little cemetery at Holly Grove. Maud, his pregnant wife, could not attend because she had been taken to Sheltering Arms Hospital, but Mother Jones appeared to give Cesco Estep's eulogy. According to a Charleston paper, she "sent Cesco on his way to heaven," then told the mourners to get their guns, find the watchmen, and "shoot them to hell."[49]

That evening, a band of strikers gathered in the dark at Beech Grove and made a plan to avenge Estep's death. When Governor Glasscock learned that armed miners arrived in the Paint Creek Valley from across the Great Kanawha and from over the mountain on Cabin Creek, he called a special legislative session to discuss the crisis. Lawmakers answered the alarm and urged the reluctant governor to declare martial law for a third time, and once again, Glasscock ordered National Guard troops to the strike zone.

As the National Guard assembled the next afternoon, a company of several dozen miners made the steep climb to the heights above Mucklow intent on avenging the death of Cesco Estep. Twenty watchmen and company men had prepared for an assault and had staked out a machine gun position in the woods near the fort. "The guards had lever-action Winchesters and . . . a Gatling gun," what one resident called "a fine piece of machinery." When the miners opened fire from the ridges, this witness said he could hear the trees crack and pop just like they did in a winter freeze. The defenders ran "the Gatling gun until it got . . . so hot they [were] afraid the bullets would stick in it." The guards were outnumbered by the strikers, who were equipped with automatic Marvin rifles that allowed each man to fire seven shots without loading. Surprised and outgunned, the company men fled and left the machine gun, which the strikers captured. By nightfall, both war parties had retreated, carrying their wounded away. The Charleston press reported that sixteen men had been killed, but in fact, only one man, Fred Bobbitt, a company clerk, had died in the attack.[50]

The next day, the National Guard arrested forty-seven strikers including the justice of the peace, Brant Scott, and sent them to Pratt. At a rally called to protest the arrests, Mother Jones urged the strikers not to be intimidated by "Governor Crystalcock's militia." She discouraged further acts of violence and announced that she would lead a committee of strikers to visit the governor to protest the new wave of arrests.[51]

The following morning, when Jones and her followers boarded a train bound for the capital, they believed that the outrage over the Bull Moose Special's raid would gain them public support. They left not knowing how much the news of the attack on Mucklow had changed the situation. That morning, the *Charleston Gazette* published a story warning that Jones was leading a mob to Charleston intent on assassinating the governor and dynamiting the state capitol building. Hysteria swept the city after the police chief rang the fire bell as a riot alert and National Guard troops positioned themselves around the capitol building. That same day, lawmen in Charleston arrested John Brown, a Socialist organizer, and two UMWA national organizers on unspecified charges.[52]

Unaware of this activity, Jones and her delegation left the train station and marched peacefully toward the capitol. They had walked a short way when an automobile pulled up in front of them. A marshal stepped out and told Jones she was under arrest for violating General Elliott's martial law decree.[53] Military officers took Jones to Pratt and placed her under round-the-clock guard in a lodging house with several other women who had been accused of harassing strikebreakers. In a few days, nearly two hundred suspects were arrested, including every prominent Socialist in the district. The charges against the alleged ringleaders of the resistance were far more serious than Jones expected. In the coming days she and some of her followers would be placed before a court-martial and tried by a military tribunal for inciting an insurrection and for carrying out a conspiracy to attack Mucklow and commit murder.[54]

During their cold days in confinement at Pratt, Mother Jones and her fellow prisoners held out hope that the new governor, Henry D. Hatfield, would set them free when he took office in March. After all, the governor-elect had campaigned as a friend of the miner and had lobbied the state legislature for a law that would abolish the mine guard system.[55] To put pressure on Hatfield, union lawyers appealed the prisoners' case to a circuit court judge, Samuel D. Littlepage, a Democrat. The judge issued an order prohibiting the military trials scheduled to take place at Pratt, but when his writ was served on the provost marshal in charge of the proceedings, the officer refused to accept it. Littlepage persisted, insisting that it was unconstitutional to try civilians in a military court during peacetime.[56]

Governor Hatfield intervened at this juncture, but not in the way the imprisoned strikers had hoped. "If you don't withdraw your writ," he told the judge, "I will withdraw the troops and the blood-shed will be on your hands." Littlepage backed down, but he refused to concede that justice would be served. "There is no doubt in my mind," the judge lectured the governor, that "peace and good will never be restored to Paint and Cabin Creeks with blood and iron."[57]

Henry Hatfield believed government should find the middle ground in industrial disputes and that elected officials should serve as mediators. When he campaigned for governor, many observers, including some strikers, "were impressed by his personal goodwill toward the miners and his desire to deal fairly with both sides in the dispute." But when push came to shove and radicalism reared its head, Hatfield abandoned the middle ground and, like many progressives, chose to "pressure the weaker contenders." The military trials would take place in Pratt, despite Judge Littlepage's objections, and in the weeks ahead, the strike leaders and their supporters would be subjected to legal prosecution and a campaign of government suppression few American citizens had ever experienced during peacetime.[58]

Chapter 7

Let the Scales
of Justice Fall

March 7–July 29, 1913

T he court-martial proceedings began on March 7 in an unlikely
venue: the meeting room at an Odd Fellows hall in Pratt, which
the National Guard had commandeered for its headquarters. The
makeshift courtroom was littered with strange lodge objects, including a row of metal-tipped spears leaned against the wall. At one end
of the hall, a trio of tightly outfitted military officers sat at a table
waiting to take testimony and pass summary judgment. Above them
hung a metal medallion embossed with the Odd Fellows' symbol,
two hands clasped below an eerie image of a single human eyeball,
which peered out over the proceedings.

Colonel George S. Wallace, the judge advocate in charge of the
trials, made one concession to critics of the proceedings. He allowed the prisoners to be represented by civilian defense attorneys,
but the lawyers would not be allowed to call witnesses in their clients' defense, nor would they be allowed to appeal the sentences
meted out by the tribunal. On the first day of the trials, Mother
Jones and two Socialist comrades turned down legal representation and refused to plead innocent or guilty on the grounds that
they were being treated like "subjects" rather than as citizens with
constitutional rights.

Wallace permitted only one journalist from the *Charleston Citizen* to cover the courts-martial. One day after the trial began, when another reporter shouted a question to Jones as she entered her boardinghouse, the colonel ordered National Guard officers to arrest the snooper and put him in the bullpen with the miners. Later that day, after the guards heard this intrepid reporter interviewing some of the other prisoners, they released him and sent him back to Charleston.

The news of what was happening in Pratt got out, of course, and within days, the court-martial of Mother Jones had become a spectacle. The famous defendant helped her own cause via smuggled messages to her friends on Capitol Hill and by giving an interview to a *New York Times* reporter. Jones told him that, if the officers found her guilty, she could be sentenced to death by a military firing squad; then, exaggerating her age for effect, she said: "I am 80 years old and I haven't long to live anyhow. Since I have to die, I would rather die for the cause to which I have given so much of my life."[1]

A writer for *Survey* magazine reported that he arrived in Pratt with no bias, but he soon sympathized with the strikers after witnessing oppression that he "did not believe could exist in America." And another reporter, Cora Older, the wife of the crusading San Francisco editor Fremont Older, used her influence to get an interview with the celebrated prisoner in the Pratt boardinghouse. Smitten with Mother Jones and troubled by her ordeal, the journalist wrote two magazine articles on the court-martial.[2]

Cora Older also traveled to Washington to voice her concerns to several elected officials, including Senate Majority Leader John Worth Kern, a Democrat from Indiana, who had already received a secret telegram from Jones. Kern promised to demand a congressional investigation into how and why the National Guard "deprived West Virginia citizens of their rights to petition for a writ of habeas corpus and to receive a trial by a jury of their peers."[3] Meanwhile, another friend of Mother Jones's, Secretary of Labor William B. Wilson, a former UMWA officer, was receiving hundreds of letters and telegrams from indignant trade unionists demanding the release of Mother Jones, including one from a veteran miner in Indiana. "I have carried a gun three times in industrial wars in this country," he wrote, "and by the eternal, if any harm comes to the old mother, I'm not too old, nor by the same token, too cowardly to carry it again." Letters like this also arrived in the congressional mailroom and at the White House office of the newly inaugurated president, Woodrow Wilson.[4]

Seemingly unaware of the furor Jones's court-martial was causing in Washington, the military judges in Pratt carried out their assignment with dispatch. The prosecutors produced little hard evidence that a conspiracy among the defendants led to the attack on Mucklow that killed the company clerk Fred Bobbitt. This did not trouble Judge Wallace, who explained that under the state's broadly drawn Red Man Act, conspirators could be convicted of murder without any evidence of "express agreement" between the alleged perpetrators; in other words, a conspiracy could be proved "inferentially, or by circumstantial evidence." Therefore, reasoned the judge advocate, since editorials in the *Labor Argus* and speeches by Mother Jones had inflamed the minds of the miners, then these actions constituted circumstantial evidence that these "expressions" led to Bobbitt's death.[5]

In his closing statement for the court, Wallace astonished the defense by saying that the prisoners enjoyed the same rights in a military court as they did in a civilian court. The judges, he scolded, were not there to "weep" with the defense attorneys who sympathized with the strikers. "We are not here to hear Baldwin guards railed against," he declared. The judges were obligated simply to "weigh the facts and the evidence as it comes and let the scale of justice fall against the prisoners or for them."[6]

Regardless of public opinion, the military tribunal convicted all the men on trial and sentenced them to prison terms of five to twenty years; but this was not all: the judges sent shock waves through the labor movement when they sentenced Mother Jones to the state penitentiary for three years. The verdict and the sentence let loose a new torrent of outrage in labor and progressive circles. Jones's good friend, UMWA president John P. White, took the high road when he declared that the entire court-martial set "a dangerous precedent for civil liberties" in America.[7]

Amid the political furor aroused by the court-martial, Governor Henry Hatfield hesitated to impose the sentences on Mother Jones and her comrades. To win favor with the UMWA, Hatfield released all the men held in the Pratt bullpen, although he did not disband the military commission; nor did he free Mother Jones or any of the eleven Socialist strike leaders. While he pondered the fate of these prisoners, the governor turned to his main objective, settling a long and bloody strike that had caused the state government so much expense and embarrassment in the eyes of the nation. A few days after he took office, Hatfield summoned the coal operators and union officials to Charleston for negotiations. The employers again refused to meet face-to-face with their adversaries and the governor had to serve as go-between. When these talks failed, Hatfield waited a month and then decided to dictate the terms of a compromise.[8]

On April 14, the governor proposed that the mine operators allow the UMWA to organize on their properties, limit the workday to nine hours, place a check-weigh man at the scales of each mine, allow their employees the freedom to trade at independent stores, and establish a grievance procedure. The operators seemed agreeable because they were not being forced to grant union recognition, as did UMWA officials, but thousands of militant miners opposed the deal; they were holding out for formal recognition of the union and a pledge from the employers not to blacklist strike activists or to employ private guards. These militants included a vocal core of socialist miners like Frank Keeney, who spread the resistance movement beyond Cabin Creek, and the editors of the *Labor Argus* and the *Huntington Socialist and Labor Star*, who announced that "Doc Hatfield's agreement" was a "sell out."[9]

Ignoring this noisy opposition, Governor Hatfield

Governor Henry D. Hatfield.

invested the full power of his office in an effort to win support for his agreement. He enlisted the Chamber of Commerce and a host of progressives and businessmen who wanted to heal their state's wounded reputation. He lined up support from the larger coal companies in other parts of the state, whose executives hired a former UMWA official as their spokesman. And he displayed what one historian called "the explosive temper he shared with some of his feudist kinsmen" by issuing an ultimatum to Thomas Cairns, president of UMWA District 17, and his fellow officers. When Hatfield ordered union officials to support his agreement or "face draconian measures against the union and themselves," they caved in and tried to put a good face on this "Hatfield agreement." President Cairns knew how many strikers opposed it, so instead of submitting the proposal for general ratification by the membership, the district president brought it before a hastily convened conference of delegates who debated the contract and then approved the deal. On May 1, district union officials joined Hatfield on a tour of the minefields, where they declared the strike over and ordered the men back to work. The governor went much further and told the miners to return to work in thirty-six hours, or else he would order the National Guard to deport them from the state.[10]

Hatfield's threat infuriated thousands of miners, especially the socialists, who used May Day gatherings to give speeches urging their followers to hold the line and stay on strike no matter what Doc Hatfield and Tom Cairns said. Convinced that socialist propaganda alone fueled the opposition, the governor took a drastic step and ordered soldiers and sheriffs to arrest the editors of the *Labor Argus* in Charleston and to confiscate their presses. Hatfield also sent lawmen to shut down the *Huntington Socialist and Labor Star*, even though the paper was published fifty miles away from the strike zone. After the *Labor Star* suspended publication, officers ransacked the newspaper's office and smashed its printing presses. Such outright suppression of the free press hadn't occurred in America since the Civil War, and it raised a howl of protest from socialists and progressives across the nation.[11]

Radical periodicals denounced Governor Hatfield's "Czar-like methods of persecution" and claimed his actions were worse

Hatfield's Challenge to the Socialist Party

Governor Hatfield has declared that every active Socialist in West Virginia shall be jailed or depórted. Wholesale arrests of Socialists without warrants have already been made; trials by jury denied; our papers confiscated; presses wrecked and Editors jailed. Shall we stand for our comrades being absolutely within the power of this tool of the Coal Trust and the tin soldiers whom he commands?

LAWRENCE DWYER, Socialist and miner. Lost leg in mines. Arrested scores of times for agitating.

By Leslie H. Marcy

A front-page story from the *International Socialist Review* with a photo of Lawrence Dwyer, a UMWA militant from Cabin Creek.

than those being taken by the dictator Porfirio Díaz in "Barbarous Mexico." The mainstream press expressed alarm as well. An exposé published by *Everybody's*—one of the nation's most popular magazines—appeared under the title "'Sweet Land of Liberty!': Feudalism and Civil War in the United States of America, **NOW**."[12]

Harold Houston, state secretary of the Socialist Party, begged the national party office for assistance and then fled the state to avoid arrest. A few days later, a committee of three leading Socialists headed by Eugene V. Debs was appointed to investigate what the party leaders called a "reign of terror" in West Virginia. Meanwhile, the messages Mother Jones snuck out of what she called the "Military Bastille" in Pratt had reached progressives in Washington, notably Secretary of Labor William B. Wilson and Senator William Borah, an influential Republican from Idaho. Senator John Kern read one of her letters into the *Congressional Record* in which Jones begged for the Senate to investigate the crisis in the coalfields.[13]

Some newspaper editors made the same appeal. "This West Virginia outbreak has been of such character, and on so extended a scale; it has cost so much in life, property and business . . . ; it has indicated such a tensity of feeling between the miners and the operators," read an editorial in the *New York Globe*, "that there is a need for the community to know what is was about." Therefore, a federal inquiry should be conducted to explore the issues the mine war raised for the "whole nation."[14]

Feeling the heat, Governor Hatfield released Mother Jones on May 7. The next day she appeared in the Senate gallery and applauded when Senator Kern's call for an investigation passed by a voice vote. Acting largely on her own, one woman had done more than the nation's top union leaders to alert reformers to the suppression of civil liberties in industrial America. Three weeks later, the *New York Call*, a Socialist daily, announced what was "expected to be

Mother Jones in Washington, D.C.

one of the most memorable meetings in the history of this city." It would be held at Carnegie Hall, where Mother Jones, the "angel of the miners," would "tell the story of the great strike of the coal diggers of West Virginia and the suspension of the Constitution and the inauguration of a reign of terror in that State . . ."[15]

Soon after the rally at Carnegie Hall, Eugene Debs and the two other members of the Socialist Party's special investigating committee arrived in Charleston, where Hatfield greeted them warmly and respectfully. He calmed the Socialists' fears by promising that he would release their comrades who remained in prison and that he would allow the suppressed newspapers to reopen. He touted a new state law he had signed banning the use of private mine guards by mine operators and then turned to his main objective: winning the Socialist Party's support for the new contract he had brokered to end the strike. Eugene Debs needed little persuading on the matter. National UMWA officials had already convinced him that it was the best deal the union could get and that the local resistance to the settlement was the work of extremists loyal to the IWW.

Debs had helped to found the IWW in 1905, but he and his Socialist comrades left the organization because the Wobblies advocated sabotage, excoriated mainstream trade unions, rejected electoral politics, and scorned middle-class respectability. Furthermore, they refused to sign any agreements with employers that compromised the right to strike; instead they called for direct action in the form of mass strikes and marches, slowdowns, sitdowns, free speech fights, and acts of civil obedience.[16]

Debs misjudged the opposition to the contract, however. The Socialists leading the strike on Cabin Creek did favor the IWW direct action strategy, and many of them admired the Wobblies' provocative leader, William "Big Bill" Haywood. But Keeney and his comrades were UMWA loyalists who did not share the Wobblies' contempt for established trade unions or for electoral politics. In any case, the Debs committee's report endorsed the governor's proposed agreement, leaving Keeney and other strikers feeling betrayed by the party and the leader they had campaigned for in the fall. In their view, Debs and his comrades had whitewashed Hatfield's repressive actions and endorsed a flawed settlement.[17]

Meanwhile, the governor's political stock soared. The mine war in the Kanawha field had ended with what one journalist regarded as a "nearly complete victory for the miners and something of a triumph, too, for Governor Hatfield." The governor had forced Quinn Morton and the Paint Creek mine operators to accept concessions they had fought against for nearly a year, and at the same time, he had convinced District 17's officers to order the strikers back to work. This was an enormous accomplishment, remarked the *New York Sun*, because it ended what was "probably the most bitter and protracted industrial struggle of the kind in the history of the country." But, the *Sun* warned, this achievement should not be allowed to derail the federal investigation of the bloody events that preceded it.[18]

Encouraged by this kind of publicity, Senator John Kern rose on May 9 to denounce efforts by West Virginia coal companies and their Capitol Hill allies to cancel that investigation. He argued that the governor of that "unfortunate Commonwealth" had nullified provisions of the state and federal constitutions by issuing "arbitrary edicts" that set aside civil liberties in open defiance of the limitations that his state constitution placed upon his powers. "Men are being imprisoned in West Virginia today," he declared, "because they are Socialists . . . and because they belong to a labor union." When citizens were "denied rights for which their fathers fought and died," it was no wonder that the "forces of Socialism multiply."[19]

A few days after Kern's slashing speech, Senator Nathan Goff, kingpin of the West Virginia Republican Party, leaped to the defense of Governors Glasscock and Hatfield. These officials were forced to impose "military justice" because they could not rely upon local law enforcement to suppress the violence on Paint Creek and Cabin Creek. Goff's rejoinder provoked an unusual, and sometimes profound, Senate debate about military law and civil liberties that continued for several more days.[20]

Progressives like Senator Borah joined Kern in making barbed comments about the suspension of civil liberties in West Virginia, but that state's senior senator had the last word. "The name of Mother Jones has been brought into the controversy," said Goff in his closing remarks. "Well, I have no fight with Mother Jones. I am sorry that she feels grieved." She had been a "grand and good friend of the miners. She is the grandmother of them all, but she has certainly been inciting riot and urging insurrection." Furthermore, "Mother Jones was arrested. She was tried. She was convicted," the senator said as he glanced upward. "She is here now looking down from the galleries as she has a right to do." But, Senator Goff added, his state should not be criticized for putting down an insurrection that Jones had helped to create. In any case, he concluded, the whole ugly affair had come to a happy end because "a great section of West Virginia" where the trouble flared was now at peace. "The miners are back at work; most of the grievances they had have been adjusted." Why, he asked, "does our dear old Mother Jones want to stir it up again? Who is dissatisfied?"[21]

The answer was that Frank Keeney and thousands of dissident Cabin Creek miners were dissatisfied. After surviving in tents with mine guards and then soldiers occupying their communities, after seeing scabs take their jobs and watching fellow workers die in gunfights, these die-hard strikers were unwilling to accept the deal Hatfield and his allies tried to impose upon them. In June, dissidents organized large protest meetings in the camps, now free of mine guards, watchmen, and soldiers. At one assembly, three locals called for the removal of the union officers who had pressed the membership into accepting the Hatfield agreement. In the next few days, protests in the form of wildcat strikes erupted in the Kanawha field and at Boomer in the New River field, where Italian miners marched from one colliery to another carrying a red flag and calling fellow workers out on strike. To make matters worse for the employers, union miners who had returned to work on Paint Creek embarked on their own strikes to protest a new contract that had been imposed without a vote by the rank-and-file members. Despite the attempts by the governor and District 17 leaders to keep the miners at work, the wildcat strikes turned into a general walkout.[22]

As "Doc Hatfield's agreement" unraveled in the coalfields, a special Senate subcommittee convened in Washington to investigate the conflict that "had dealt death and destruction in the Paint Creek and Cabin Creek mining districts." It was clear from the start of these hearings that the progressives on the subcommittee intended to make civil liberties violations in West Virginia their primary focus. Senator Borah, whose own state had suffered bloody mine wars, made this point by having certain provisions of the West Virginia Constitution read into the record. The first declared that the constitutions of the United States and the state should always be in effect; the second, that under no circumstances should the right of habeas corpus be denied; the third, that no citizen should be deprived of life, liberty, and the pursuit of happiness; the fourth, that military authority should not supersede civil authority even under plea of necessity; and the fifth, that trial by jury in open court should prevail for all criminal offenses.[23]

The Senate investigation, chaired by Iowa Republican William Squire Kenyon, did not go well for the coal operators, especially Quinn Morton, the owner of the Christian and Imperial Colliery Companies on Paint Creek. Democratic senator James Martine of New Jersey began by grilling Morton about his role on the Bull Moose Special the night Cesco Estep was killed in Holly Grove. When Martine asked the mine owner if he approved of the use of a machine gun, Morton's lawyer objected to the tone of the question. "I have a right to ask that question," the senator replied. "I want to know whether this gentleman, a cultured gentleman and an educated gentleman, approves of the use of a machine gun in a populous village." Morton replied that the senator had done him "a very great injustice," that his conscience was clear, and that he was "tired of being browbeaten." At one recess, Morton and Senator Martine, who seemed inebriated, almost came to blows; their dust-up made news in the *New York Times*.[24]

Several other witnesses offered sober perspectives on the causes of the mine war. The "Czar of Cabin Creek," Charles Cabell, admitted that neither side had clean hands, but he defended the mine guards he had hired as being "very gentlemanly" fellows "with good manners." Former governor William Glasscock refused to blame either side when he replied to a long series of questions from Senator Borah. In the end, though, Glasscock agreed with Borah that the Baldwin-Felts detectives were "the disturbing element" in the creeks.[25]

Perhaps the most affecting testimony the senators heard came from G. C. Cowherd, who had been selling medicines and cigars to company stores on Paint Creek and Cabin Creek for several years. He insisted the "paramount issue" in the strike was what he called the "shotgun system" that had prevailed on Cabin Creek since 1904. The Baldwin-Felts agents were, in his view, "rough and unreasonable" men who denied local residents the privileges other free citizens enjoyed. "When it got worse and worse and worse and worse," the miners struck in order "to do away" with the mine guards.[26] The salesman said he knew the miners of Cabin Creek very well, and he knew they were proud men who resented being driven in any way. "You cannot drive men nowadays," Cowherd told the senators. "You can lead them, but not drive them."[27]

After Senator Kenyon adjourned his committee for the summer, Frank Keeney and his supporters held out for six more weeks until Charles Cabell and the other Cabin Creek mine operators finally agreed to discuss terms that would end the strike. While negotiations got under way, West Virginians celebrated the semicentennial of their "war-born state," rejoicing that "peace and plenty" had replaced the "fierce hatreds" aroused by the Civil War. Governor Hatfield and other jubilee speakers carefully avoided any mention of the lethal mine war that had just ended. But the truth was "that new hatreds were at large in West Virginia in 1913, hatreds just as fierce and threatening as those of 1863 and just as subversive of the state's pride and its sense of community," wrote historian John Alexander Williams. The celebrants chose to ignore these new divisions, "but ignoring them would not drive them away."[28]

The Cabin Creek strikers had nearly reached a settlement with the operators when the hatreds set loose by the mine war resulted in three more deaths. A striker named Cleve Woodrum held a personal grudge against the guards because one night several of them had barged into his cabin while his wife was in labor and demanded that he turn out the lights, as all miners were required to do under the curfew rules imposed by the National Guard. When he refused, they shot out the lights.

A few months later, two watchmen were patrolling the woods around Red Warrior one evening when they came upon Cleve Woodrum and a group of his friends. One of the guards was Don Slater, a former Baldwin-Felts agent, who had earned a reputation among the Cabin Creek miners as a "bruiser."[29] It was still light enough for Slater to see that the four miners had pistols in their hands. He called out to them, saying, "Hello, boys, what are you doing up in here? This is company property," and heard Woodrum reply, "We're picking huckleberries." Before the two guards could digest this improbable response, they heard a revolver cocking. Slater ran behind a tree, but before he could escape, Woodrum put a bullet in his torso and another in his leg. Another miner shot and killed the other watchman, Frank Ginn. After he saw his partner fall, Slater rolled over a little cliff and disappeared from view.

Against the advice of his buddies, Woodrum looked over the edge of the drop to see if Slater was dead. When he did, the guard shot him. The two men, gravely wounded, now lay side by side under the cliff, where they wrestled on the ground until Woodrum stopped breathing. Slater somehow made it back to the company office and was taken to a local hospital, where he told his story and then expired on the operating table. He was the tenth company man killed in the fighting.[30]

Cleve Woodrum and Don Slater died on the eve of a settlement that would end the long struggle on Cabin Creek. A few days later, mine company executives conceded; they agreed not to fire and blacklist strike activists (one particular sticking point), and they also promised to abide by the ruling of a government-appointed arbitration board that would hear appeals on outstanding disputes.[31] Every striker could now return to work under the provisions of the new labor agreement. No ringleaders or Socialist agitators would be blacklisted. Keeney and his supporters did not win union recognition, but after more than a year of striking and fighting, they had finally driven the armed guards out of their valley and brought their union back to life. Their victory came at a high price, however. At least a dozen of their union brothers had been killed in battles with mine guards.[32]

In the aftermath of the mine war, Ralph Chaplin, the radical poet and Wobbly agitator, romanticized the violent tactics miners adopted. But after he left the Kanawha field to edit the IWW's eastern newspaper, Chaplin realized that what impressed him most about the Kanawha miners was not their belligerency, but their extraordinary embrace of that hallowed union virtue: solidarity. It was the strikers' enduring unity that inspired "Solidarity Forever," which Chaplin put to the music of "John Brown's Body." In time, this song would become the national anthem of the American labor movement.[33]

> *When the union's inspiration through the workers' blood shall run,*
> *There can be no power greater anywhere beneath the sun.*
> . . .
> *They have taken untold millions that they never toiled to earn,*
> *But without our brain and muscle not a single wheel can turn.*
> *We can break their haughty power, gain our freedom when we learn*
> *That the union makes us strong.*
>
> *Solidarity forever,*
> *Solidarity forever,*
> *Solidarity forever,*
> *The union makes us strong.*

When Senator Kenyon reconvened his subcommittee's hearings on the causes of the mine war in September 1913, the senators heard surprising testimony from the Kanawha district mine operators who had invested so much in crushing the union; these men now testified that "harmonious relations" prevailed between the employers and their unionized employees. Charles Cabell explained that he had never been "violently opposed to unionism on general principles" and that he was no longer convinced that the UMWA was bent on destroying the West Virginia coal industry. He was willing to work with the union and he believed the new labor agreement removed "any necessity for the mine guards."[34]

When the subcommittee's final report appeared in print, it was bound in two volumes with a total of twenty-three hundred pages of reports, documents, testimonies by dozens of citizens, and a closing comment by the chairman, who placed most of the blame for the trouble on the mine operators' shoulders. They controlled houses, churches, stores, roads, post offices, and cemeteries on private land, and they answered not to elected officials but to the alien owners of the collieries. Instead of relying on official law enforcement, they had hired the private mine guards whose actions provoked the strikers. Union militancy played a role in exacerbating the conflict, stated Senator William Kenyon, but the cause of all the trouble was "deeper and more fundamental." The private ownership of public necessities like coal, "coupled with human greed," had, the senator concluded, "brought about the deplorable and un-American conditions in the West Virginia coalfields . . ."[35]

The first mine war also raised profound constitutional issues. When the state of West Virginia suspended habeas corpus proceedings and jury trials in 1913, it generated what one scholar called "the most comprehensive discussion concerning the use of martial law . . . that ever occurred in the United States." The imposition of martial law, the courts-martial of Mother Jones and strike leaders, and the suppression of the socialist press had aroused serious concerns among attorneys, including one who asked in an article for *Bar*: "Has West Virginia a Republican Form of Government?"[36] After the strike ended, members of the West Virginia Bar Association met and heard their president record an "emphatic protest" against the use of a military court to try private civilians for any kind of crime. And when the Kenyon subcommittee's report appeared, Senator Kern declared that its findings and recommendations would "put an end to military law in this country."[37]

For this reason, and many others, Samuel Gompers, president of the AFL, claimed the strike an epic victory not only for the UMWA but for all organized labor. Scattered groups of miners had rebelled against intolerable conditions, and then, with grim determination, they had united in an "insistent movement" that grew and grew in spite of "suffering and privation." After a long ordeal, these workers forged an agreement with their employers who, with the utmost reluctance, had recognized their right to organize, to spend their wages wherever they pleased, and to have their coal weighed by a fellow miner. But, in Gompers's view, the union miners had accomplished more than this. They had forced the governor and the legislature to enact a law preventing the use of private mine guards as deputies. As a result of their victory, the AFL's president believed that West Virginia's union miners were now poised to enter "a new era of freedom."[38]

At the time Gompers published his assessment of the strike, "peace and quiet reigned" in coal towns like Eskdale where industrial warfare had raged for more than a year. Old wounds were beginning to heal on Paint Creek and Cabin Creek, one of the strikers recalled. And with freedom of speech and freedom of association restored, union membership grew by "leaps and bounds" and spread south and east from the Kanawha Valley into Fayette, Boone, and Raleigh Counties. From this base, the union could mount new campaigns in West Virginia's southern counties where labor organizers had feared to tread for two decades. Gompers believed that the new law prohibiting the employment of private mine guards would now open these fields to union recruiters, but organizers soon realized the new law was useless because it carried no penalty.[39]

Despite the law, Justus Collins continued to employ Baldwin-Felts agents at the mine where these guards had helped him crush the UMWA in 1902. Collins wrote to an associate: "Most of the operators of the state seem to be waking up to the fact that . . . unless we adopt measures . . . to prevent the union from getting hold of us, they will succeed in doing so."[40] The Williamson Coal Operators' Association in Mingo County also defied the new law and reaffirmed the right of its members "to employ secret service men, or detectives, to protect our interests. We want to know what our men are doing, what they're talking about . . . whether the union is being agitated" by activists like John Brown, a Socialist leader in the Paint Creek strike, who suffered a nearly fatal gunshot wound that fall at the hands of two special agents employed by the Consolidation Coal Company. In another incident, New River mine operator Samuel Dixon reacted forcefully when a delegation of miners, led by German socialists, demanded a check-weigh man, as required by a state law. King Sam had them all fired. When their fellow miners struck in protest, Dixon ordered Baldwin-Felts detectives to break up the strike and "kick out all socialist agitators."[41]

The tipple at Justus Collins's colliery at Glen Jean in the New River field.

The effectiveness of the strike in the Kanawha field had horrified and infuriated the executives of some of the state's largest coal companies. Heretofore fierce competitors, these industrialists formed a new regional protective association in the Tug River fields and created a huge fund of $1 million to help elect anti-union public officials and to protect their property from "destruction by Socialists . . . otherwise known as the United Mine Workers of America." Ultimately, the new association intended to drive the "demagogues and radicals" out of the state for good.[42]

These were the forces the UMWA would have to overcome if it attempted to expand its membership beyond the Kanawha Valley. A successful offensive would require an enormous investment by the international union and a unified effort by the leaders and members of District 17. But in 1914, that house of labor was divided against itself. Frank Keeney, his socialist comrades, and his fellow miners on Cabin Creek still distrusted the district officers who had endorsed a "sell out" contract and then refused to put the deal up for a vote by the membership. For their part, District 17 president Thomas Cairns and the international officers decided to purge their radical rivals, consolidate their power, and assure the mine operators that "responsible" officers would keep the industry's interests at heart and keep rank-and-file union members in line.

Cairns and other district officials assumed that Frank Keeney and his fellow dissidents were socialist demagogues or agents of the hated IWW. They would soon discover, however, that Keeney and his comrades were shrewd strategists with a hard core of supporters who had taken up arms to fight for their union and who now believed they, the members, should control the organization their comrades had fought and died for during the recent mine war.

Chapter 8

A New Era of Freedom
Winter 1914–Fall 1918

D uring the early 1900s most American trade unions were democratic institutions, governed by officers elected by their fellow
workers; but as these unions became formal organizations dedicated
to institutionalized bargaining with employers and to the thankless
task of "policing" no-strike contracts, a cadre of career-minded officials emerged. Once elected or appointed to office, many ambitious workingmen clung to their positions, isolated their critics, and
assembled political machines to ensure that they would not have to
return to the drudgery of wage labor. These "business unionists"
were, at best, effective negotiators who delivered on the union's
bread-and-butter demands and then stepped aside as newly elected
leaders took their places. At worst, some took bribes from bosses to
make "sweetheart deals" and some fell in with gangsters who saw
unions as a racket.[1]

The union members who remained loyal to their organizations
and attempted to reform them struggled against long odds. In most
cases, discontented members could be silenced or co-opted, and internal movements for union democracy could often be Red-baited and
defeated; but not always. Frank Keeney and his comrades defied the
odds in the spring of 1913, when they organized thousands of striking

miners into a resistance movement that prevailed over the combined forces of the governor, the National Guard, the mine operators, and the UMWA officials in Charleston. Having proven their mettle during the long strike, these local activists believed they could turn the tables on their enemies and take control of District 17 on behalf of the membership. Some of them were class-conscious union couples like Frank Keeney's Eskdale neighbors Tim and Sarah Blizzard and Rocco and Nellie Spinelli. Others were Socialists like the justice of the peace, Brant Scott, the tireless agitator Lawrence Dwyer, and a pugnacious twenty-six-year-old miner named Fred Mooney who had arrived in Cabin Creek during the midst of the mine war.[2]

Mooney was born in 1888 and raised in a two-room log cabin on Davis Creek in Kanawha County. The boy saw little of his father, who worked cutting timber and digging coal from dawn until dusk for a dollar a day.[3] When Mooney married his boyhood sweetheart, Lillian, in 1908, he described himself as an average coal miner, "husky, strong, and energetic." Ready to assume his role as a breadwinner, the twenty-year-old mountaineer took his teenage bride to a nonunion mining camp in the Kanawha Valley, where the newlyweds rented a company house, bought some furniture from the company store on an installment plan, and started to raise a family. Mooney loaded more coal than anyone else in the mine; yet, at the end of each month, after deductions for his company house, his packaged food, his tools, and his clothes, he could see that he was not getting ahead.

One day, after three years of hard work and self-denial, Mooney slipped out of the coal camp and walked down the valley to look for a better situation. Company officials learned what Fred was up to, and when Lillian went to shop at the company store, the manager told her the Mooneys had no more credit. Stunned because she knew her husband had back wages coming to him, Mrs. Mooney got mad and stormed at the company clerk. When Fred returned that evening, he found Lillian in tears. She told her husband that they had been evicted from their cabin and that it was all her fault for losing her temper. Fred consoled his wife by telling her she had voiced sentiments that had burned at his guts for years, but because of the blacklist, he had kept silent.

The Mooneys packed up and "moved down the creek 'a ways,'" as Fred put it in his memoir, "chasing that ever fleeting shadow, a job, the most elusive thing known to him who toils for a living." Eventually, the young couple moved to Eskdale on Cabin Creek, a place that frightened the children and wore on Lillian's nerves. After Fred Mooney and his family moved into a company house and settled into a routine, he met lots of union sympathizers in the valley, including the local Socialists, like Harold Houston, who became his mentor. He joined the strike in 1912, and while his wife and two babies took shelter in the refugee tent camp, Mooney took to the hills with Dan Chain and the armed volunteers who defended the canvas village.

By 1914, Mooney was eager to join forces with Keeney in the campaign to win control of UMWA District 17. "Keeney was all fire and dynamite," Mooney recalled. "He asked for and showed no quarter." Hanging on for dear life, the district officers in Charleston used their newspaper, the *Miners' Herald*, to attack the dissidents as irresponsible Reds who fomented wildcat strikes in violation of legal labor agreements the district had signed with agreeable employers. District president Cairns dismissed Harold Houston as the union's counsel and had charges brought against Keeney, Mooney, and two other radicals.

Newsboy posing with District 17's newspaper, 1914.

When union officials tried Mooney for disloyalty before the members of his local in Cannelton, his supporters appeared in force, roared their objections, and put a stop to the purge trial. At the district convention in April, the radicals made a bid to take power after Mooney produced a letter from a mine operator who had been assured by Cairns that the dissidents could be controlled and the current contract renegotiated without a work stoppage. This revelation created a tumult among the delegates, but the incumbent officers weathered the storm.[4]

The feud continued in the months that followed, until the radicals decided to break away from the district. Rather than hook up with the renegade IWW, Keeney, Mooney, and Houston reaffirmed their loyalty to the international union and formed UMWA District 30 on Cabin Creek. This organization would be based on two principles: democratic control by the rank and file and the socialist ideal of workers' control over industry. In June 1915, Keeney, Mooney, and other leaders of the new district traveled to Indianapolis and made their case for recognition before the UMWA executive committee. They failed, however, and after several other appeals, the Cabin Creek rebels formed an independent union, the West Virginia Miners Organization.[5]

During the next year, this new union consolidated its position on Cabin Creek, and in the spring of 1916, Keeney decided to press employers to negotiate a contract with his union. He knew that wartime orders were pouring in from Great Britain and France, and he knew that mine owners were making unheard-of profits supplying metallurgical coke to the roaring steel industry. Unwilling to risk a strike, the coal operators came to the bargaining table and granted most of the independent union's demands. Practicing the form of union democracy he preached, Keeney took the contract back to a convention of miners at Eskdale, where the elected representatives of the rank and file approved the deal. The delegates then returned to their locals to ensure that the contract would win majority support at the grassroots.[6]

When the new agreement was ratified, union colliers on Cabin Creek made significantly better wages than union miners in other parts of the Kanawha field, and the UMWA's national officers took notice. Frank Keeney was a socialist and a hard head, but he knew how to make a bargain with the bosses. National president John P. White, who had been supporting the incumbent officers, could see that Keeney's insurgents had won over a large body of the membership. Furthermore, White's good friend Mother Jones vouched for Keeney and denounced the old guard. It was rare for a national union president to side with a group of insurgent radicals against a group of loyal officers, but that is what President White decided to do. He suspended incumbent officers of District 17, appointed Harold Houston as interim president, and ordered a new election. With the Charleston office now in the hands of their socialist ally, the insurgents believed they could win a fair election fight with the district's former officials.

During the summer of 1916, the Cabin Creek miners had many reasons to be hopeful about the future. Three years had passed since the first mine war ended. Hard feelings certainly endured among the miners, and yet, Fred Mooney observed, happiness and contentment prevailed as men worked full days under a new union contract.[7]

No miner would have said it—for fear of bringing on bad luck—but everyone knew that the valley's ninety-two mines had been operating for years without a serious blowout. While the invisible hand of the market provided more work at better wages than Keeney's men had ever known, the hand of God, so visible to people of faith, had spared those men from the lethal forces earth, water, wind, and fire could unleash upon them while they toiled deep within the mountains.

Early in the morning of Wednesday, August 9, it began to rain just as thousands of miners awakened in cabins all along Cabin Creek, from Dry Branch near the mouth of the stream, up the Main Fork to Charles Cabell's Carbon mines, and farther up Fifteen-Mile Fork to Kayford. Rainfall was God's gift to West Virginia. Forty-five inches of precipitation fell over the state each year, on average, filling thousands of mountain streams that fed the state's big rivers: the Coal, the Guyandotte, the Tug, the Big Sandy, the New, and the Great Kanawha. From these rivers came a great portion of the water the Ohio River carried down into the Mississippi. The rainfall that filled these rivers also soaked the Appalachian highlands when gulf winds, supercharged with moisture, moved north and east until they reached the Cumberland Mountains, which deflected them over West Virginia, where the semitropical air met the dry, cold winds blowing down from the Hudson Bay. This conflict of elements generated an abundance of rain that watered West Virginia's fertile fields, orchards, and bottomlands and sustained its dense mountain forests. Sometimes this clash of elements became so intense that it caused furious summer thunderstorms, with electrical displays, wind squalls, hail, and flooding, which was worsened by the destruction of West Virginia's verdant forests by the timber industry and the stripping of hillsides in coal-mining valleys.[8]

So no one paid much attention to the steady rain beating down on the miners as they headed to the collieries at dawn that August day. But M. L. Knox, a collier who worked for a company in United at the highest point in the valley, did snap to attention when the sky above the ridge exploded with lightning strikes, followed instantly by roaring thunder that echoed down the valley for five frightening minutes. The lightning bolts cast a ghostly blue light that illuminated the dark valley below.[9] Within minutes, Knox could hear Cabin Creek rushing and gurgling. He hustled back down the hillside to awaken his wife and children, and when he reached his cabin, water was pouring through the door. By the light of the lamp on his miner's cap, Knox led his loved ones up the hillside in the pelting rain. Then he turned and looked down upon the valley, where he saw five of his fellow miners walking down the railroad tracks to work. One minute they were there, and the next minute gone, smothered by tons of mud and muck that slid down the naked mountainside.

Before he could absorb what he had seen, Knox said he heard the whistle of the 6:15 A.M. C&O passenger train working its way up the creek toward United. Just after he glimpsed the locomotive's headlight searching through the rain, a wall of water crashed down on it, rolling the enormous engine on its side and pushing cars off the tracks. No one in United owned a telephone they could use to call the folks who lived down below or over the ridge in Kayford, where children still slept in their beds and women tended to kitchen chores after bidding their husbands Godspeed.

Torrents from both branches of the creek crashed together at Leewood and filled the entire valley to a level of ten feet above the bed—from one mountainside to the other—as the flood rolled down a twenty-mile culvert toward Eskdale. The floodwater destroyed

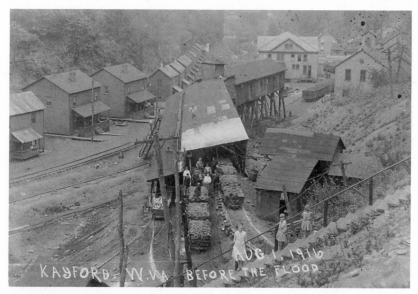

KAYFORD- W.VA. BEFORE THE FLOOD — AUG. 1, 1916

The Tipple at Kayford on Cabin Creek.

the C&O yards at Cane Fork, moving five ponderous yard engines aside, twisting tracks into strange shapes, and swallowing up a hundred heavy coal cars. Mrs. Woody Jarrell, the wife of a C&O engineer, stood in the pounding rain holding her two-year-old child and watched her house and fifty others disappear down the stream, bobbing along like shoe boxes.

At eight A.M. the full force of the cascade descended upon Cabin Creek Junction on the Kanawha River, where the flood caused its worst damage. A wall of gray-green water crashed over the town, knocking out three bridges; it passed through in a remarkably short time, carrying fragments from thousands of houses and several stores and churches, along with a thousand barrels of crude oil—all pushed out into the Kanawha River. The next day search parties pulled fourteen bodies, mostly women, out of the stream above the junction, and horrified West Virginians read of whole families that had perished and of "women and children who had taken refuge in their homes and found their refuges turned into prisons from which escape was impossible and went to their deaths when their little homes were crushed like egg shells by a mighty power."[10]

In the days after the flood, sixty residents of the valleys, mostly the wives and children of coal miners, were laid to rest in graves with modest stone markers made of slate taken from the mines. It had been exactly four years since Mother Jones and her union boys had marched up Cabin Creek to call the miners out on strike, four years since the UMWA created the tent colony on the creek bottom. Now hundreds of people in Eskdale found themselves living in tents once again, but for vastly different reasons. In 1912 mining families became refugees because company guards had evicted strikers from their homes, but in 1916 they became homeless refugees because God called down upon them what valley residents called "a flood of Biblical proportions."[11]

As residents of Cabin Creek began to rebuild their communities that summer and fall, Frank Keeney and Fred Mooney made their bid for union power. "[Once] the campaign was on," Fred recalled, "Keeney and I were slandered by every method known to political tricksters." The incumbents branded their opponents "secessionists" who were no different from the outlaw Wobblies of the IWW. "Yes," Keeney admitted, "I led a secessionist movement against the most degraded group of crooks, drunks, and double dealers that was ever known to infest the body politic of a labor movement . . ." But never, at any point during the insurgency, said Keeney, did he or any of the dissidents foreswear loyalty to the UMWA.[12]

Successful rank-and-file rebellions against union officials were exceedingly rare, but the insurgent miners on Cabin Creek broke the mold. After Keeney won his race for the district presidency and Mooney was elected secretary-treasurer, the victors posed for a photo in which they look justifiably proud of themselves. The twenty-eight-year-old Mooney smiles boyishly at the photographer, looking pleased that he had survived firing, blacklisting, Red-baiting, and a stabbing. Next to him stands thirty-four-year-old Frank Keeney staring confidently at the camera, seemingly proud of the way he clawed his way to power.

Having prevailed in a no-holds-barred power struggle, Keeney and Mooney were ready to take on the enormous challenges that lay ahead of them. The nonunion mine operators had defied state law

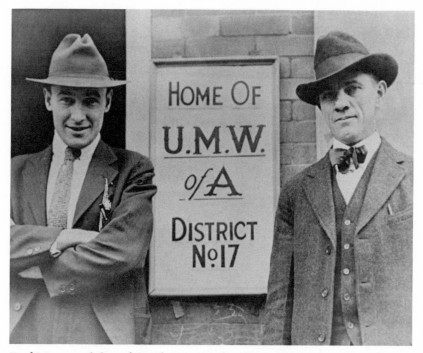

Fred Mooney (*left*) and Frank Keeney after their election to union office.

and beefed up the ranks of their private police, but they also adopted a raft of soft measures to ensure their employees' loyalty. They employed social workers "to bring something of happiness, contentment, and economy" to miners' homes. They built YMCA facilities to provide recreation and to create a "more cultivated character" among hard-living miners. They improved public schools and provided bonuses for the teachers who signed on for hardship duties in the mining districts and instilled the proper moral and social values in the next generation of mine workers. They cleaned up the filthy camps, installed some modern conveniences in miners' houses, and opened movie houses, taking care to select the films to be screened and avoiding what one operator called the "lurid, unreal wild-west type" that made heroes out of "bad men" who used pistols to do their talking. Finally, coal industry leaders launched a concerted offensive against the saloons that had sprouted like mushrooms throughout the coalfields. They were convinced that alcohol was responsible for the miners' lethal attacks on the mine guards and that drunken workers were more susceptible to the appeals of agitators. West Virginia mine company executives led a successful campaign for state-wide prohibition in 1914, a reform that *Coal Age* expected to produce "a notable improvement in the morale" of the mine workers.[13]

When asked, nonunion employees told their bosses they were happy with their living conditions and terms of employment. But one miner expressed a different point of view in a letter to the *United Mine Workers Journal*. "In our town we have many good things," Joe Bruttaniti explained, "there are different kinds of churches and good schools, but there is another thing of much more importance . . . the coal operators have intentionally overlooked—and this is our freedom."[14]

Bruttaniti may have been influenced by national events when he wrote his letter, which appeared in print two days after the 1916 presidential election. President Woodrow Wilson won a second term in the White House that fall after overcoming fierce opposition from the nation's industrialists, who were fighting mad over his support for labor reforms, particularly a bill that mandated an eight-hour day for railroad workers. Boosted by the campaign slogan "He kept us out of war," Wilson's narrow victory over Republican Charles Evans Hughes came in large part from the votes of unionized workingmen mobilized by the AFL, the railroad brotherhoods, and the UMWA. The way now seemed clear for the full implementation of Wilson's "freedom program," including some of the radical labor reforms the U.S. Commission on Industrial Relations had called for in 1915.[15]

The West Virginia coal miners who voted for Wilson also helped elect a Democratic governor, John J. Cornwell. Although he had served for years as legal counsel to the powerful Baltimore & Ohio Railroad, Cornwell ran as a reformer and a Wilsonian in 1916. After winning his party's nomination, the candidate sought an endorsement from Frank Keeney and Fred Mooney, who now held sway over the votes of nearly twenty thousand union miners in Kanawha County. If District 17 supported him, Cornwell promised that he would use the governor's office to strengthen mine safety laws and enact a new statute to ensure that private mine guards were not employed in place of public officials. Furthermore, he offered to aid the UMWA in its effort to organize the nonunion coalfields. The two young union leaders agreed to the bargain, and the votes they mobilized among their members helped Cornwell win by a slight statewide margin of three thousand votes.[16]

Assured of support from the new governor, Keeney and Mooney began making ambitious plans to penetrate company territory and to organize West Virginia's fifty thousand nonunion miners. As a first step, Lawrence Dwyer, president of the new UMWA District 29, launched an expansion drive in the New River field where the union's strongest opponents, Justus Collins and Sam Dixon, had garrisoned their company towns; they asked Mother Jones to help out by revisiting the places where she had seen her followers crushed in 1903. Thirteen years later, she was back in Mount Hope, aiding a campaign that recruited five thousand new members into the UMWA. Dwyer's bravest organizers even penetrated the Pocahontas field in McDowell County, where Tom Felts's agents had rooted out the last pockets of union sentiment a decade earlier. Emboldened by these gains, Keeney and Mooney looked south and west to large, highly mechanized coal companies operating in Logan and Mingo Counties.[17]

Although Keeney and Mooney had supported the Democratic ticket in 1916, they remained socialists at heart; and, like their comrades, they were appalled by the Great War in Europe that pitted the Continent's working classes against each other in a conflict caused by the imperial ruling classes. Other union members shared this belief and opposed the war preparedness program advanced by former president Theodore Roosevelt and leading industrialists. UMWA president John White spoke for many of these trade unionists when he warned his members against the evils of militarism, which he had witnessed in the minefields of West Virginia and Colorado, where soldiers arrested and even attacked American workers. White believed that if the federal government mobilized a standing army and built more great battleships, it would propel the United States into the European war instead of keeping it safe. He "earnestly hoped for the defeat of plans to make our country an armed camp," plans which might easily be used "to extend commercialism abroad and exploit labor at home." When people go to war and are taught to fight, White remarked, "they never rest content until the opportunity is presented to them to demonstrate their prowess . . ." In the winter of 1917, Keeney and Mooney attended a convention of the Kanawha Valley Central Labor Union, where delegates made a novel proposal to the federal government: Since the workers, not the "warmongers," would do the fighting and the dying on foreign battlefields, the convention resolved that no declaration of war should take place until workers could express their opinion in a national referendum.[18]

President Wilson harbored his own fears about the consequences of going to war. As a scholar of history, the president understood Europe's ghastly experiences with war, and as a professor of government at Princeton, he had lectured on the fragility of our nation's constitutional freedoms, especially during the Civil War. "Once lead this people into war and they will forget there ever was such a thing as tolerance . . . ," Wilson remarked privately. "The spirit of ruthless brutality will enter every fiber of our national life, infecting Congress, the courts, the policeman on the beat, the man in the street." The Constitution, the president predicted, "would not survive it . . . free speech and the right of assembly would go."[19]

Nonetheless, the nation's commander in chief put aside his own fears, and on April 2, he walked slowly and solemnly to the podium in the House chamber, where he took the fearful step of "lead[ing] this great peaceful people into . . . the most terrible and disastrous of all wars . . ." This was America's destiny, he declared, because "The world must be made safe for democracy."[20]

The day after Congress declared war on Germany and its allies, a mean-tempered Frank Keeney drank whiskey at the District 17 union office and swore that only the deaths of American boys would tell this country the truth about what he called "this rotten war."[21] Meanwhile, in the statehouse a few blocks away, Governor John Cornwell took an entirely different tone. He denounced the "pacifist prattling" that had led the Germans to believe that Americans were cowards. And he warmly supported President Wilson's call for a military draft as well as his decision to sign the Espionage

Act and the Alien Enemies Act, two laws intended to protect the nation against German Americans and other potential "alien enemies" by allowing citizens to be arrested without warrant for any behavior that seemed disloyal.

In the spring of 1917, as American industry raced to fill war orders, more than six thousand West Virginia collieries produced nearly 90 million tons of coal, a resource valued highly by the War Department. Company profits soared by 500 percent for the West Virginia firms supplying coke to the steel industry and steam coal to the U.S. Navy.[22]

With immigration from Europe restricted by the war and unemployment reduced by nearly 2 million, workers seized the moment to make new demands on their employers. As part of the largest strike wave the country had ever experienced, hundreds of unorganized miners left the collieries in southern West Virginia insisting on union recognition and higher wages. Unofficial walkouts also plagued unionized companies under contract with District 17 of the UMWA. The president of the New River Operators' Association blamed Mother Jones for the trouble. Governor Cornwell complained to federal authorities that her "agitation was producing strikes and tying up coal production," and asked them to remove her from the field. The attorney general refused, explaining that Jones had violated no federal laws.[23]

In fact, by then Jones had decided to rally union miners in support of the federal war effort. "Perhaps I was as much opposed to war as anyone in the nation," she told the UMWA convention in January 1918, "but when we get into a fight I am one of those who intend to clean hell out of the other fellow, and we have got to clean the kaiser up. Now, mind you, I don't mean the German people, I mean the kaiser, the dictator . . ." The poet Carl Sandburg remembered Jones giving wartime speeches in what he called her "singing voice." "Nobody else," he remarked, "could give me a thrill just by saying in that slow solemn orotund way, 'The kaisers of this country are next, I tell ye.'"[24]

If American workers were ever going to gain their freedom, Jones declared, they would have "to stand behind this nation and fight to the last man." When the war was "over over there," the fight in the minefields would resume in southern West Virginia and eventually that "damnable system of industrial slavery" would be broken and miners would be "free for the first time." Like her progressive friends and many of her Socialist comrades, Jones believed the wartime crisis would give the federal government enormous new powers that could be used to unleash the labor movement. An early indication of this possibility appeared in August 1917 when Congress enacted the Lever Act, a statute that gave the president authority to control the production and distribution of food and fuel until the war ended or until 1920, whichever came first. To this end, Wilson created a Fuel Administration to regulate the price of coal and prevent war profiteering. He appointed the UMWA's president, John P. White, to serve as labor's representative on the board.[25]

White believed that the fuel requirements of the war and the federal government's regulation of the industry would enable mine workers to win freedoms and protections they had been denied in peacetime. The UMWA president's hopes were realized a few months later, when the Bituminous Coal Operators of America signed a historic national agreement with the UMWA in which the employers agreed to a one-time wage increase and promised not to discharge employees for union activity.

Elated with the new contract, Keeney and Mooney believed they could now reach out to intimidated West Virginia miners in tightly controlled company towns. The first breakthrough occurred with deceptive ease in the Fairmont field, where Governor John Cornwell brokered a deal between District 17 leaders and Clarence Watson, head of the enormous Consolidation Coal Company. Watson was a Democrat who wanted to be elected U.S. senator, and he needed the UMWA's support for his campaign. In return for the union's endorsement, Watson said he would allow District 17 to unionize his mines.[26]

When the deal was done, union representatives poured into the Fairmont field and organized most of this polyglot workforce in only a few months. Fred Mooney, who led the drive, was especially moved when he learned that in one local the new members spoke twenty-seven different languages. That local was organized in Monongah, where nearly four hundred miners, mostly immigrants, had been killed in the 1907 mine explosion. Within a few months, twenty-two

Newly organized miners with an assembly of local children, 1918.

thousand miners in the Fairmont district had joined the union, and the overall membership of UMWA District 17 had swelled to fifty thousand men.[27]

Keeney and Mooney decided to put aside their socialist principles during the war and make timely alliances with Democrats like John Cornwell and Clarence Watson. They also chose to look away as old comrades in the Socialist Party and the IWW suffered extremely harsh punishment for their opposition to the war. Ralph Chaplin, the Wobbly who had supported and publicized the Paint Creek–Cabin Creek strike, was rounded up along with a hundred other IWW activists. The prisoners were tried and convicted under the Espionage Act for allegedly conspiring to encourage draft resistance and desertion and then sentenced to long terms in federal prison. The postmaster general suspended IWW newspapers and suppressed most Socialist Party publications. A few months later, the Justice Department arrested the party's top leaders including Eugene V. Debs. The four-time presidential candidate was tried, convicted, and sentenced to a ten-year term for delivering a "treasonous speech" in which he declared that it had become "extremely dangerous to exercise the constitutional right of free speech in a country fighting to make the world safe for democracy." Because federal prisons were filled with political prisoners convicted under new federal laws, Debs was sent to the West Virginia State Penitentiary at Moundsville.[28]

Frank Keeney and his associates assumed that their proclamations of loyalty and patriotism would shield them from the repressive forces unleashed by the war effort, and so it had seemed at first. In the spring of 1918, Keeney served as grand marshal of a mile-long Win the War campaign in Charleston, and rode with Mother Jones and the mayor in an open car through the streets. A few days later, they appeared before the state labor convention urging delegates to back President Wilson and buy Liberty Bonds. Rank-and-file miners responded enthusiastically and outpaced their neighbors in buying war bonds. Union members from Ohley on Cabin Creek bought $237 worth of war stamps to "show the world that the United Mine Workers are always in the front in everything the country calls for."[29]

The federal government employed the latest advertising techniques to promote loyalty, to encourage compliance with the draft, and to heighten enlistments. After an initial period of scattered resistance to conscription, thousands of workingmen responded to their nation's call by registering for the draft and volunteering to join the ranks of the American Expeditionary Force. The state of West Virginia claimed the highest per capita volunteer rate in the country. Coal miners were exempt from the draft for the duration of the war, but more than fifty thousand colliers enlisted anyway, including scores of West Virginians who joined the ranks of the Eightieth Blue Ridge Division of the U.S. Army.[30]

On May 18, 1918, the men of the Eightieth boarded troop ships in Lambert Point, Virginia, sailed past the long lines of coal cars waiting in the enormous rail yards of the Norfolk & Western Railway, and then headed out through Hampton Roads into the vast Atlantic. At this point, the German army on the Western Front had been swollen with troops removed from the Eastern Front after the revolutionary government in Russia withdrew from the war. By the end of May, General Ludendorff's troops were camped just forty miles from Paris. During the same month Allied forces were strengthened by 250,000 American soldiers, including its sharpshooting mountaineers of the Blue Ridge Division. With support from the American Expeditionary Force, Allied troops halted the German advance at the Second Battle of the Marne in July, and then counterattacked along the Hindenburg Line. More than 1,800 American soldiers died during the Battle of Belleau Wood, which General John Pershing described as the largest engagement fought by U.S. combat troops since Gettysburg.[31]

In a few days, the first reports of casualties arrived in the coal towns of West Virginia. Among the dead from the Kanawha Valley were Jesse Perdue, who had taken shelter in the Holly Grove tent camp as a boy; Frank Keeney's relative Charles, a marine private; and Corporal Francis Donoghue, the son of an Eskdale coal miner.[32] With news of these losses, expressions of patriotism soared and old enemies outdid each other to express support for the war effort. At Gary, a U.S. Steel company town, mine managers sponsored a huge parade and rally at the ballpark attended by five thousand miners and local residents. A superintendent spoke to the crowd and declared that it was the nation's duty to save those around the world who suffered under the "iron hand of autocracy."[33]

On Labor Day 1918, Frank Keeney addressed his members as a "humble member of the United Mine Workers of America, the largest industrial organization of all time, which has unfalteringly . . . responded to every call of our government and guaranteed to furnish all the coal necessary to victoriously combat the Hun . . . ." Beyond this, UMWA members owed their government another duty: to ensure that all the coal they loaded was "CLEAN COAL," free of slate and other impurities.[34]

Early that November, with the Allied counteroffensive in full stride, Keeney wrote to President Wilson reminding him of the sacrifices his members had made for the war effort.[35] In fact, during the course of the year, when coal production in West Virginia rose to its all-time peak, the number of fatalities in the Mountain State's mines also reached a new high: 437 colliers died that year, raising the death rate to 4.88 per 1,000 miners, as compared with the 2.77 rate in the fully unionized Illinois fields. Commenting on one of the many mine accidents caused by the wartime rush for fuel production, the *United Mine Workers Journal* remarked that these "loyal boys died in the interests of democracy."[36]

While some miners paid the ultimate price for the war effort, many of their employers enjoyed windfall profits. Keeney and Mooney filed numerous complaints against mine operators who refused to pay the wage rate guaranteed by the Lever Act, for disobeying a federal order to place a check-weigh man on each tipple, and for raising prices at their stores. When some of these practices were later investigated by the Department of Justice, fifty-two coal companies in southern West Virginia would be indicted for "war profiteering" and several others for violating the Sherman Antitrust Act.[37] But no one came out from Washington to address the festering grievances of West Virginia's colliers who were loading record tonnages of coal and sacrificing their lives for the war effort without any wage gains to match the skyrocketing cost of living. Beyond this, mine workers were also compelled to surrender many of their personal and constitutional freedoms.

Two years after he had campaigned for governor of West Virginia as an apostle of President Wilson's New Freedom, John Cornwell signed a compulsory work law that forced twenty-seven hundred unemployed people to labor in war-related industries or face arrest. More than eight hundred "vagrants" would eventually be imprisoned for failure to comply with the law. Coal operators soon discovered that the statute could also be used to force miners back to work when they engaged in illegal wildcat strikes to protest various grievances.[38]

Even men who put in a full day's work in the pits found themselves placed under surveillance by the coal companies, who had launched a "Work or Fight" initiative. In Kanawha and Raleigh Counties, employers set up "slacker boards" on which they posted the daily output of each miner. The men with the most tonnage were awarded bonuses and honors, and the men who produced the least were identified and, in some cases, fired and stripped of their draft exemptions.[39]

But repressive wartime measures aimed at essential workers like coal miners and dissenters like the socialists did nothing to rein in the fury of open shop mine operators, who chafed under the new federal rules that protected labor organizers. The secretary of the New River Operators' Association claimed that the wartime scarcity of labor and the union security provided by the federal government spelled disaster for free enterprise. "The socialistic and anarchistic element," he predicted, "will have full power to ruin and oppress one coal company after another . . ." Justus Collins warned Governor Cornwell that further union expansion would restrict wartime production and contribute to a national disaster, but it was not too late to act, for the "political climate" had shifted and now it would be possible to "drive the union out of the New River field."[40]

Cornwell responded to these pleas by pushing through a law that authorized him to call deputy sheriffs into state service if they were required to preserve law and order. When Baldwin-Felts detectives beat two UMWA organizers in Raleigh County, the governor expressed embarrassment but refused to have the guards removed. "The iron hand of autocracy is visible in the Labor world as well as in Germany," wrote a union miner from Thayer in a letter that typified how workers were applying the language of World War I to conditions on the home front. Fred Mooney pounded this drum loudly in a speech before the state labor convention. "Kaiserism shall not dominate a people whose forefathers gave their blood that we might stand free," he declared.[41]

All of this talk about industrial autocracy and workplace democracy made mine operators like Josiah Keeley nervous. As manager of the Cabin Creek Consolidated Coal Company, Keeley had survived the first mine war in the valley and had witnessed the rise of the radical movement led by Frank Keeney and his comrades. In October 1918, the colliery manager warned of an even greater storm to come: "The fight against Kaiserism abroad" had caused the union miners on the home front to "turn to their old enemy," the capitalist mine owner, and then "hang" on him "all the evils of Kaiserism." As the Great War in Europe neared an end, Keeley feared that the seeds of another mine war were being sown in West Virginia's coal towns, where hundreds of miners were taking "the idea of an actual emancipation so literally."[42]

In October 1918, few West Virginians shared Josiah Keeley's worries about what might happen after the world had been made safe for democracy. Public attention was riveted on the news from France, where West Virginia soldiers fought alongside Allied forces as they engaged in a mammoth offensive against German armies dug in along the Meuse-Argonne front. Early that month infantrymen of the Blue Ridge Division had moved through the Argonne Forest, where they had suffered heavy casualties. One of the men in this division wrote home from a field hospital to tell his parents in West Virginia that he had "seen more and gone through more during the last week than most people go through in a life time." The folks at home who read about the battles on the Western Front had no way of knowing how horrible they really were.[43]

After more than a month of fierce fighting, Allied forces had pushed the Germans out of the Argonne Forest, but the advance came at an enormous cost, especially to the large number of U.S. soldiers who had arrived in France without any battlefield experience and, in many cases, without adequate supplies and competent officers. In this, the bloodiest battle U.S. troops fought during the war, 26,277 American soldiers died and more than 95,000 were wounded.[44]

The tide of battle changed during the first days of November when the Blue Ridge Division served as right flank of the American Army's I Corps as it drove the enemy out of the Bois de Bourgogne. In the most rapid advance in the annals of World War I, the Americans forced the Germans back across the Hindenburg Line. News of this success and the spectacular race toward Sedan blazed across newspapers at home, where it was heralded as the beginning of the war's end. Late in the evening of November 11, with the Battle of Meuse-Argonne won, the men of the Eightieth Division camped on the banks of the Meuse River and gathered around bonfires, where they shouted and sang at the news that an armistice had been signed.[45]

Over the next few months, those soldiers who survived the slaughter would cross the Atlantic, leaving their dead comrades behind in graveyards like the 130-acre cemetery in Meuse, where more than fourteen thousand American soldiers were buried.[46] When the troop ships docked and the veterans of the Blue Ridge boarded trains that would take them back to the cities, farm towns, and coal camps of West Virginia, they thought about resuming normal lives as teachers, farmers, miners, husbands, and fathers, but memories of the war ran through their minds. As reminders, these homeward-bound servicemen carried helmets, olive-drab tunics, infantry boots, bayonets, gas masks, Browning automatic sidearms, captured German Lugers, and disassembled parts of Winchester trench guns and Springfield bolt-action rifles. The veterans valued these articles as prizes, as emblems of service, as souvenirs they never imagined using again, for these men believed they had fought and won "the war to end all wars."[47]

Part III

The Second Mine War, 1919–1921

Chapter 9

A New Recklessness

Winter 1919–Winter 1920

The Great War nurtured in millions of American wage earners a desire for a new way of life and for a new democratic order at work. Out of that desire came an avalanche of strikes: 4.2 million workers engaged in work stoppages in 1919—twice as many strikers as there were two years before during what had been a record year for labor unrest. News of these job actions filled the headlines along with reports of ghastly race riots, anarchist bombings, revolutionary uprisings abroad and communist plots.[1] Editors, politicians, industrialists, and other leading citizens reacted, often hysertically, to these events and to rumors of terrors yet to come. As public anxiety rose, a Red Scare gripped the nation and influential Americans demanded drastic action by the government.

In West Virginia, a state legislator drafted a bill that prohibited the teaching of doctrines advocating "the overthrow of organized society" and the displaying of the Red flag "or any other flag, emblem . . . or sign of any nature whatever" that symbolized opposition to government and existing institutions. A first conviction would bring a fine of up to $500 and a year in jail. A second violation of the Red Flag law would be treated as a felony and lead to a prison sentence of one to five years. In the same session, West Virginia legislators created a new state police force on the grounds that without such a constabulary the Mountain State might become a haven for Bolsheviks and anarchists. The UMWA and the Kanawha Valley Central Labor Union condemned the bill, arguing that the proposed state constabulary would become "a permanent military organization," and that it would be used by pro-business governors to break strikes. These laws were enacted but they did nothing to diminish the political fears stoked by the press, the business community, and elected officials.[2]

In the midst of a reactionary storm, Frank Keeney and his advisers made plans to expand the union while federal controls were still in place. During the war, District 17 had added to its hard core of membership in the Kanawha field by unionizing 17,000 miners in the Fairmont field, 6,500 in the New River field, and 1,500 in the Big Coal River area of Boone County, where Bill Blizzard, an aggressive twenty-eight-year-old miner, was placed in charge of a new subdistrict. Fred Mooney distrusted Blizzard because he was "hot-headed and at times irresponsible." But to Mooney's dismay, "President Keeney was inclined to take sides with Blizzard," a family friend whose athletic physique and pugnacious spirit earned him a devoted following back on Cabin Creek, where his mother, Sarah, owned a popular store in Eskdale known as "Ma Blizzard's place."[3]

South and east of Bill Blizzard's base in Boone County lay the Guyan minefield of Logan County, where colliers had produced 10 million tons of nonunion coal during the war, more than the tonnage loaded by unionized miners in the Kanawha field. The UMWA had already established a few locals across the Logan County frontier, which would serve as outposts for the recruitment campaign Keeney and Blizzard were planning. But if District 17 was going to move into the Guyan field, its organizers would need to find a way around or through the formidable defenses erected by Don Chafin, the high sheriff of Logan County.

County sheriffs in West Virginia and other Appalachian states were often powerful politicians, but they were rarely men of means. Sheriff Don Chafin, however, owned stock in the Guyan Valley Bank and lived in a brick house on the slope above the Guyandotte River,

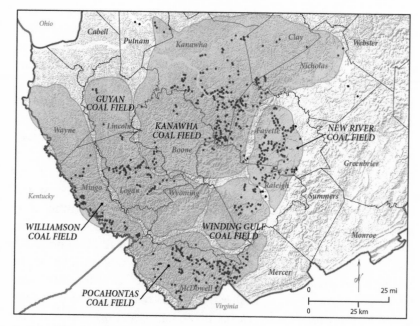

Coal Fields of Southern West Virginia with mines indicated

where the coal company executives resided. A large, round-faced man who dressed in the best linen suits and the finest fedoras money could buy, Chafin cut a dapper figure in Logan, the commercial center of the flourishing Guyan coalfield. He hobnobbed with the best men in town and haunted the luxurious Aracoma Hotel, where a six-course dinner followed by dancing was "all that could be desired" by local patrons.[4]

The Logan County coal operators paid Chafin a huge annual salary of $30,000 to act as their guardian; it was a task he performed with the aid of forty-six active deputies, including John Gore, a former union coal miner, who served as chief deputy because he knew so much about the UMWA. Chafin, who had five hundred more men on the inactive rolls in case they were needed, assigned his men to patrol every rail station in the county to watch for troublemakers and to use whatever means necessary to remove them. When Mother Jones dispatched two national organizers to Logan in 1919, she warned them to be careful and inconspicuous, but to no avail. When Chafin's informers made the visitors out to be agitators, "Don took them up to Blair Mountain Ridge personally," an assistant recalled, and wanted to kill them right on the spot. But a deputy intervened and said, "Don, you can pistol whip them if you want, but I don't think it would be a good idea to kill them." The beaten union men left the county bloodied but alive.[5]

On another occasion, when the chief clerk of the State Department of Mines arrived at a Knights of Pythias meeting in Logan, Chafin's deputies demanded that the visitor state his name and his purpose. When the clerk told them it was none of their business, the officers beat the man with blackjacks and left him on the street unconscious. The assault on a government official and a member of an influential fraternal order made for lurid headlines and scolding editorials in the state's newspapers, but Chafin shrugged off the publicity.[6] Even clergymen feared what critics called "Chafin justice." When the Reverend Alfred Eubanks daringly referred to the UMWA in positive terms to his black congregation at a Saturday night prayer meeting, one of Chafin's spies reported the minister to the sheriff. The next morning a deputy sheriff and two other men pistol-whipped the Reverend Eubanks before he could deliver his Sunday sermon.[7]

The sheriff and his deputies kept particularly close tabs on Logan County coal miners whom they suspected of talking secretly among themselves in their dark rooms deep in the mountains. An African American miner named Luther Mills told a journalist that the sheriff wanted him to spy on his fellow workers to find out who was trying to organize and report back to him. Mills would be a "dead nigger" if he didn't, Chafin warned. But Mills fooled the sheriff and fled from Logan County one night; eventually the miner made his way to UMWA headquarters in Charleston, where Keeney and his associates were plotting against Don Chafin and his patrons.[8]

As a first step toward organizing Logan County miners, Keeney decided to go over Chafin's head and collect on the debt Governor Cornwell owed the UMWA for its crucial support in his election campaign. Since the federal government remained in control of the coal industry, Keeney hoped that Cornwell could use his influence in

Logan County sheriff Don Chafin.

Washington to gain protection for his organizers. The governor discouraged Keeney from attempting any organizing in Chafin's domain, but when pressed, Cornwell asked for a month's leave to see what he could do.[9]

But Keeney, who doubted the governor's intentions, broke his promise and commissioned a squad of fifty seasoned organizers, who were dispatched to Logan County.[10] Perhaps Keeney hoped to catch Sheriff Chafin and the local operators by surprise, but if so, he failed. Large contingents of heavily armed deputies stopped the men from District 17 at the county line and offered them a "choice"—turn back or take their lives in their hands by staying in Logan County. Heads down, the UMWA staffers retreated and returned to Charleston, where they resigned their commissions.[11] Frustrated and humiliated by Don Chafin and his deputies, and rebuffed by his own organizers, Keeney retreated to his office, belted down some extra shots of whiskey, and pondered his next move. There had to be a way into Logan County, and he was bent on finding it.

Keeney knew that mine workers weren't the only Logan County residents who resented Chafin's rule. Local Republicans hated the state's most corrupt Democratic boss, and clergymen objected to Chafin's involvement in the county's illegal saloon business; but these law-abiding citizens had no way of challenging either the sheriff or the coal company owners who paid him tribute. There was, however, one citizen of Logan County who had no fear of Chafin and his minions; indeed, it was often said that this old man had no fear of God.

Anderson "Devil Anse" Hatfield had lived in the backwoods of Logan County for nearly a decade. Two years after his family's feud with the McCoys ended, the patriarch took his wife, Levicy, and their younger children away from the family homestead near the Tug River and headed up-country to find a safer place to live. Hatfield had always been an aggressive businessman and a rugged individualist, and had never shown any interest in what union men like Frank Keeney were trying to accomplish. By 1919, however, word leaked out that the legendary clan leader had taken a dislike to Don Chafin. Hatfield's resentment may have been stoked by his two politically ambitious sons, Joe and Tennis, who envied the sheriff's wealth and power. In any case, Keeney perked up when he learned about Devil Anse's hostility to Chafin.[12]

According to Frank Keeney's daughter Geraldine, her father secretly visited the old man on several occasions. She said Frank would travel through Boone County on horseback through mountain gaps and down creeks, sometimes following lanterns set out by union supporters to let him know the way was clear and safe. Like an intelligence officer operating behind enemy lines, Frank never entered or left Logan County the same way. When he approached the Hatfield home, one of Devil Anse's sons would meet Frank in the woods and escort him up to the house, where the labor leader sat with the old man, drinking whiskey and scheming against Don Chafin.[13]

While Frank Keeney searched for ways into Logan County, he and Fred Mooney also looked for allies in the outside world,

Anderson "Devil Anse" Hatfield, c. 1920.

people who could expose Chafin's regime to the nation. They found one ally by chance in 1919, when Jack Spivak, a reporter for the *New York Call*, appeared in Charleston, where he took a job as a freelancer filing crime stories for the *Daily Gazette*. The redheaded journalist had heard many tales of the West Virginia coalfields, stories about organizers being beaten and killed in the heart of "Hatfield-McCoy feud country" and about a sheriff who ruled Logan County with an iron fist. "I felt that if only a fraction of what these organizers told me were true," he recalled in his memoir, "West Virginia was exciting news about which the country knew next to nothing."

In Charleston, local socialists told Spivak he should talk to the "union boys," Keeney and Mooney, because they could give him the whole "low down." The newsman had met plenty of tough characters in his line of work and in his days as a transient Wobbly, but none of them seemed as rugged as these two mountaineers who wore .45 automatics strapped beneath their suit jackets. Keeney had the hard, deeply lined face of a warrior, Spivak wrote in his memoir. Mooney had the soft voice and smile of a shy mountain boy; but he shocked Spivak by casually mentioning that he had killed a man who had been stalking him ever since the UMWA sent organizers into Logan County.[14]

Spivak volunteered to work for District 17 by investigating abuses of civil liberties in the mining camps. In the weeks that followed, he sent several reports to his friend Roger Baldwin, who was serving a sentence in a federal jail for being a conscientious objector to the war. Before he went to prison, Baldwin and others had founded the National Civil Liberties Bureau to provide legal advice to conscientious objectors and citizens arrested under the Espionage and Sedition Acts during World War I. Spivak's reports convinced Baldwin that Chafin and his men had trampled on the Bill of Rights and that the Civil Liberties Bureau must be alerted to the situation. Pleased with Spivak's work, Keeney hired him to compile a more detailed report on conditions in Logan County and take it to Washington. Somehow Keeney arranged for Spivak to meet with President Wilson's secretary, Joseph Tumulty. When he arrived, the reporter expected to receive "immediate assurances that the awesome power of the Presidency would . . . be used to enforce the Bill of Rights" in

West Virginia. But Tumulty brushed his visitor off and Spivak could only respond with a desk-pounding warning that without support from the federal government, the miners of West Virginia had "no alternative but to defend their rights themselves."[15]

On September 1, Spivak was sitting in the District 17 office going over reports from Logan County when Fred Mooney walked in and calmly reported that armed miners had begun moving out of the union coal towns and were gathering up the river near a little town called Marmet. Spivak drove out to the site with Mooney and Keeney, where he saw thousands of men armed with rifles of every description sitting and standing around numerous campfires. The moon was shining bright and the campfires cast a glow on the faces of angry men. "It looked more like Dante's Inferno than anything I can think of," Keeney recalled, "with the moonlight shining on the rifles." A sprinkling of the miners were "Negroes, Italians, and Hungarians," but most of these volunteers were mountaineers, and a large portion of them were World War I combat veterans who, according to Mooney, had become "disillusioned with the democracy they fought for overseas."[16]

Later that night, the governor arrived at the camp and fearlessly climbed up on a car to address the armed miners. Staring out over the crowd of men in overalls, Cornwell promised to look into their complaints about conditions in the company towns, but he also warned the men that he would call out federal troops if they did not disperse. Keeney followed with his own plea, urging his members to break camp and return to their homes. Some men followed their leader's orders and left Marmet that night, but after Keeney returned to Charleston, he learned that several hundred insurgents had ignored him and marched out of Marmet toward Logan County.

When Cornwell heard that marchers were camped at Danville, ten miles from the Logan County line, he ordered Keeney to rush out and turn them around or suffer the consequences. When Keeney arrived, the insurgent miners gathered around their leader and listened as he urged them, for a second time, to turn around or face certain disaster. Later that day, Keeney told reporters that although he had dispersed his militant members, hundreds of union coal miners were still hell-bent on freeing coal miners in the Guyan field from the regime Chafin and his deputies had imposed upon them.[17]

After the marchers dispersed, Jack Spivak, the ever-curious reporter, asked Keeney and Mooney how so many miners could appear in one spot spontaneously unless there was some kind of "telepathy" at work in the mining valleys. When both men smiled knowingly at this remark, Spivak realized that they had actually called for the miners to move on Logan County, perhaps as some kind of war game or as a demonstration to force state and federal officials to intervene.[18]

The hundreds of miners who defied their governor and ignored their union president by marching toward Logan County acted on their own accord, but employers and government officials like Governor Cornwell saw these men as an armed vanguard of a working class insurgency that seemed more and more threatening with each month that passed. In 1919 wage-earning men and women were angry, restless, and ready to take mass action with or without approval from their elected union leaders. "The most extraordinary phenomenon of the present time . . . ," declared the *Nation*, "is the unprecedented revolt of the rank and file." In January, more than a dozen unions had defied the AFL's president, Samuel Gompers, and shut down Seattle in a general strike. In April, 120,000 textile workers, mostly immigrants, had ignored craft union officials who claimed jurisdiction over the industry, and closed scores of mills in a strike for a shorter workweek. And in July, newly organized steel workers had forced the AFL's cautious officials to call a strike or risk seeing radicals take control. These uprisings made evident to the *Nation* that "The common man, forgetting the old sanctions, and losing faith in the old leadership, has experienced a new access of self-confidence, or at least a new recklessness, a readiness to take chances . . ."[19]

That same reckless mood pulsed through the hearts of many of the two thousand union coal miners sitting in a hot, smoky auditorium in Cleveland on September 9. The day the UMWA's convention opened, the morning newspapers carried reports of growing support among the members for the nationalization of all coal properties; these reports fed a growing fear that established labor organizations were being infected by the disease of

Bolshevism. Even more frightening news came that morning with the news that more than a thousand Boston police patrolmen had voted to strike when the commissioner suspended a dozen union leaders. "Lenin and Trotsky are on their way," warned the *Wall Street Journal*.[20]

When the UMWA's acting president, John L. Lewis, gaveled the convention to order, he not only faced a frustrated mass of delegates; he also had to contend with scores of political and personal enemies on the floor.* Many of Lewis's adversaries were tough union veterans who resented his sudden rise to power; others, especially the socialists in the hall, accused him of being a conservative businessman disguised as a union official. Yet as he stood before this restless assembly in Cleveland, the thirty-nine-year-old chairman showed no signs of being intimidated.

Nearly six feet tall, Lewis filled his dark three-piece business suit with a hefty two-hundred-pound frame. His large head was topped with waves of auburn hair, and his broad brow was dominated by two bushy eyebrows. From the depths of his broad chest came a voice like a bassoon that rumbled through the large auditorium. Lewis spoke in an unusually formal and mellifluous way—a skill he had learned in the theater. Though he was a conservative business unionist at heart, and a Republican by preference, he knew what he needed to know about coal miners; and in the fall of 1919, Lewis knew he had to respond to the belligerent delegates who insisted upon an enormous 60 percent raise in wages, a six-hour day, a five-day week, time and a half for overtime, and double time for Sunday and holiday shifts. Despite his own misgivings, Lewis brought the strike issue to a vote, and the delegates roared their unanimous approval for a resolution to close down the nation's mines on November 1 if the coal companies did not agree to their breathtaking demands.[21]

After the convention adjourned, Governor Cornwell wrote a letter to Lewis claiming that he had evidence proving that Keeney and Mooney had ordered the September 1 march on Logan County.

---

*The executive board had installed Lewis as acting president when the sitting president, Frank Hayes, resigned.

John L. Lewis, c. 1919.

Under these circumstances, the governor believed, Lewis was duty-bound to suspend and discipline the two outlaws along with all the marchers. The UMWA president replied by informing the governor that the recent UMWA national convention had unanimously endorsed a resolution stating that if he, Cornwell, had done his job and upheld the First Amendment in Logan County, it would not have been necessary "for free-born American citizens to arm themselves to protect their constitutional rights." This wire made it clear that Keeney and Mooney had the backing of the nation's largest labor union, an organization with a membership of three hundred thousand men and a chief executive who had at least condoned an attempted insurrection in West Virginia.[22]

After more than a week of fretting over what Keeney might do next, the governor heard the stunning news that a short distance away, at UMWA headquarters, someone had shot and critically wounded Sheriff Don Chafin. Cornwell must have wondered why Chafin had ventured into the lion's den at District 17. The sheriff later explained that he came to Charleston that day to hunt for the "colored miner" Luther Mills, who had fled from Logan after Chafin told him to spy on his fellow miners or end up a "dead nigger." When the lawman and one of his deputies happened to see this fugitive miner on the street, they tailed him to the District 17 office. After the suspect went inside, the two officers from Logan walked in behind him and demanded to see a union officer.[23]

Unfortunately for Chafin, District 17 vice president Bill Petry was in the office that day. Mooney remembered Big Bill as a drunkard who was quick to anger and prone to making "grandstand plays [to antagonize the operators] and then pass the buck." That day, sober or not, Petry acted immediately when he heard that Chafin had entered the building. He grabbed a .32-caliber revolver, stormed into the office where Chafin waited, and, with a curse, shot him four times in the belly. At the same time, two other union officers knocked down the sheriff's deputy, took his gun, and dragged him out of the building. Chafin managed to stand up, walk out the door, and find his way into the lobby of a nearby hotel. After he sat down, his groans attracted attention from guests, who rushed him to a local hospital in time for a doctor to stitch up the sheriff's wounds, remove a bullet lodged in his torso, and save his life.[24]

The governor was appalled and frightened by this outrageous assault on a law officer a few blocks from the state capitol. "For some time I have felt that I am under sentence," he wrote privately in late September. ". . . I firmly believe we are in a crisis [and] that, unless people who believe in law and order . . . assert themselves, not only our Government but our civilization itself is doomed." Cornwell was convinced that certain men in the UMWA would kill him if he did not "stand aside and permit them to unionize the Guyan Coal Fields by force." Even so, the governor vowed to be brave. "If the sacrifice of my life will help stay the tide of Bolshevism and Anarchy, with which the country is threatened," he wrote, "I am not unwilling that the sacrifice, if necessary, be made."[25]

No one attempted to assassinate the governor, but Cornwell and his advisers were more convinced than ever that Keeney and his associates were a menace to society. By contrast, Chafin emerged as a public hero. After he made a miraculous recovery, the sheriff returned to Logan aboard a special railroad car sent by Colonel William Coolidge, president of the Island Creek Coal Company.[26]

It took Frank Keeney a week to find Bill Petry, who had been hiding out with friends in Marmet. Petry surrendered and was indicted for attempted murder by a Kanawha County grand jury; however, the

Governor John J. Cornwell.

district attorney ultimately decided that Petry had fired in self-defense and dismissed the case. The prosecutor, a Republican, may have also been acting out of animus toward Chafin, a powerful Democratic politico. In any event, nearly everyone in coal country had a strong opinion on the shooting of Don Chafin. Some people, especially coal miners and their kin, regarded Petry as a righteous mountaineer bringing a tyrant to justice, while other people, especially property owners and professionals, praised Chafin as a brave peace officer who had survived a cowardly assault by a drunken redneck blinded by class hatred.[27]

By the time Petry returned to his office, Keeney had burned all his bridges with the state's public officials and had lost the public support he had gained during World War I. Making matters worse for the union leader, an unexpectedly massive walkout of 275,000 steel workers on September 22 raised the Red Scare hysteria to a new height. At this inopportune time, Keeney turned to face the toughest challenge of his life: leading West Virginia's union miners in a general strike that promised to be as large and as menacing as any industrial conflict the state or the nation had ever experienced.

"I really think we are facing a desperate situation," said the Ohio Republican senator Warren G. Harding, a leading prospect for his party's presidential nomination. "It looks to me as if we are coming to a crisis in the conflict between the radical labor leaders and the capitalistic system under which we have developed this republic . . ."

Governor Cornwell believed that a national strike would play into the hands of the Bolsheviks and Wobblies, whose strength had been greatly exaggerated by sensational newspaper editorials and misleading reports by state and federal investigators.[28] On Halloween, he asked every sheriff and mayor in the state to form committees of public aid and safety in order to relieve the severe suffering that would be caused by a cessation of coal production and to guard against the "criminal and radical element," who would use the impending crisis to "ply their nefarious trades and to bring about a general social and industrial revolution."[29]

After five weeks of attempting to negotiate a contract with the nation's bituminous mine operators, President Lewis and the UMWA's executive board called for a general strike to begin on November 1. That day, nearly fifty thousand West Virginia miners joined more than three hundred thousand fellow workers in the largest work stoppage the nation had ever witnessed. The enormity of the walkout and the temerity of the miners convinced many observers that the strikers were, as one paper put it, "red-soaked in the doctrines of Bolshevism."[30]

On November 8, a federal judge issued a sweeping injunction that barred all strike actions and named eighty-four national and district UMWA officials, including Frank Keeney, liable for damages. Lewis was furious with President Wilson for abrogating the miners' right to strike; nonetheless, he convened an emergency meeting and asked his executive board to order the members back to work. "We are Americans, we cannot fight the government," he told the press on November 11, the first anniversary of the Armistice. However, the strikers refused to follow Lewis's orders, and as the nation shivered and the economy sputtered, the Wilson administration reacted by offering the coal operators a hundred thousand federal troops to protect miners willing to return to work. That same day, a federal judge ordered the arrest of all the union's district officers. But even these extraordinary actions by federal authorities failed to bring the nation's idle coal miners back to work.[31]

In early December, President Wilson asked Secretary of Labor William B. Wilson and Attorney General A. Mitchell Palmer to work out a compromise with the UMWA and the coal mine owners. The nation had suffered enough; it was time to get the men back in the collieries and put coal back in the furnaces. Lewis and his fellow negotiators jettisoned some of the union's ambitious demands after they gained enough for the members to reach a settlement. The agreement mandated an immediate 14 percent wage increase and promised a further pay raise after a federal coal commission completed an investigation of the industry. Lewis proclaimed the deal a victory and ordered the miners to return to their jobs.

Frank Keeney was dismayed by the settlement, for he had expected the strike to result in much greater gains for the men who had sacrificed so much during the war years. But unlike several other district presidents who attacked Lewis for making compromises and ending the strike, Keeney remained loyal to the UMWA's ambitious acting president.

On January 30, 1920, Lewis appeared with Keeney at a gathering of miners in Bluefield, West Virginia, the headquarters of the Baldwin-Felts Detective Agency. Here in the heart of the Pocahontas field, the UMWA chief threw down the gauntlet. In the months ahead, he announced, the UMWA would target all the nonunion mines in southern West Virginia and in all of Appalachia. "Now is the logical time for this work," Lewis announced, but it would be a daunting task, he warned. "Every agency within the power of the coal companies is expected to be invoked to thwart this movement."[32]

In truth, Lewis's timing defied logic, because that winter seemed like the worst possible time for the UMWA to take on its toughest opponents. A few weeks earlier, Attorney General Palmer had ordered federal agents to conduct raids in twenty-three states, rounding up four thousand suspected subversives, holding them incommunicado, and making plans to deport as many of them as possible. West Virginia's governor joined other elected officials in cheering Palmer's actions, insisting the raids were necessary to nip a Bolshevik revolution at the bud. "There is no time to waste on hairsplitting over infringement of liberty," declared the *Washington Post*.[33]

Furthermore, Keeney and his officers would have to ask nonunion miners to risk their jobs by joining a union in the midst of a severe recession that had gripped the economy beginning that January. But Lewis decided to move on southern West Virginia anyway.

He realized that, now more than ever, cheap coal from the Mountain State's nonunion mines threatened to bring the UMWA to ruin in the North, and he wanted to act while the federal government still regulated the mines under the wartime Lever Act. Lewis also expected the commission set up after the national strike would award union miners with a hefty wage increase that would suddenly make a union contract seem very attractive to nonunion miners. Finally, Lewis knew he had a bold district leader in Frank Keeney, a man who had emerged from the war years as a compelling orator, an influential power broker, and a shrewd strategist.[34]

Keeney returned to Charleston determined to recruit a new force of union organizers who could liberate their "unfortunate brothers in the Guyan field" who were "pleading for freedom."[35] He did not explain, however, why a new venture in the Guyan field would succeed when others had failed, especially in 1920 when Don Chafin had more power than ever and more coal company money to pay labor spies and hire deputies to ride the trains, guard the rail stations, and patrol the main county roads in motorcars. The only other paths into Guyan field lay along rugged mountain roads that led up and over a long, heavily wooded ridge topped by the twin peaks of Blair Mountain.

The Spruce Fork Ridge formed a natural barrier between union country in Boone County and company territory in Logan County, where Chafin's men formed a human barrier. While Keeney and Mooney contemplated these obstacles to expansion, they were taken by surprise when a new opportunity for organizing opened up behind "enemy lines." The hot spot appeared thirty-five miles to the south of Charleston in Mingo County, where coal miners began to grumble about conditions in the mines located along the Tug Fork River, in the same rugged country where the Hatfields and McCoys had once bloodied the soil in their legendary feud.

Chapter 10

To Serve the Masses without Fear

Winter–Spring 1920

When John L. Lewis announced a new offensive in Bluefield that January, Mingo County's mine owners counted on the loyalty of three thousand men who toiled in the churning collieries of the "Billion Dollar" Williamson coalfield, a district that had been opened to mining in 1895 by an extension of the Norfolk & Western Railway south through the Tug River Valley. Mingo County's collieries had operated without disruption during the industrial strife that swept the old coalfields in Kanawha and Fayette Counties during the previous decade.

The high level of mechanization in these modern mines may have affected the workers' behavior. Unlike unionized firms in the Kanawha field, which still employed a large percentage of skilled pick miners—proud craftsmen protective of their underground freedoms and informal solidarities—nearly all the men employed in the Williamson field were machine miners who complied readily with company rules and regulations.[1] Even though machinery gave the employers a new kind of "technical control" over mining operations, coal industry leaders in Mingo County refused to take their employees' cooperation for granted, especially after the mine war erupted on Paint Creek in 1912. These industrialists were horrified in 1913 when a native of their own county, Governor Henry Hatfield, had imposed a union contract on the coal companies operating in the Kanawha field. "Hatfield's personal and political ambitions" had become so large that he turned his back on his old Republican friends in the coal industry and "actually 'arrayed' the masses against the classes."[2]

In a belligerent speech before the Williamson Coal Operators' Association, Colonel Z. T. Vinson explained that the "armed revolution" in the Kanawha field had been partially successful because the mine owners in that district had not cooperated in resisting the UMWA. He urged the employers in the Tug River region to put their competitive ways aside if they expected to resist another union onslaught. "You must have an efficient organization, opposing them at every point and every angle . . . ," Vinson declared. "Your remedy . . . is to fight, and fight boldly, aggressively, defiantly, and unitedly. Working in harmony as a trained army, you can successfully resist the avowed purpose of the United Mine Workers to confiscate your property. If you organize and prepare for war, you will not have labor troubles."[3]

The Williamson operators followed Vinson's advice and enjoyed labor peace for the next six years, but in June 1919, Governor John Cornwell warned these executives not to be too complacent. Miners had been excited by labor's gains during the war, and even loyal employees might cause trouble unless their employers made voluntary improvements in working conditions. Wage increases, better housing, and new schools would do more than anything to block what Cornwell described as a determined effort by radicals to lead union members into a new socialist movement. The Williamson mine company executives responded by improving working and living conditions and by voluntarily granting their employees an eight-hour day.[4] The mine operators found their strategies rewarded when their men stayed on the job during the great coal strike the fall of 1919. The reason, according to Mingo County's Republican congressman Wells Goodykoontz, was that these men were a "favored lot," who mined "thick seams . . . under genial surroundings, at wages, in some cases, higher than the union scale." As a result, the congressman crowed, these miners were "the most happy . . . and contented . . . of all our citizenry."[5]

But if anyone attempted to spread discontent in the ranks of this favored lot, mining companies could turn to a fellow Republican, Mingo County sheriff Greenway Hatfield, a brother of former governor Henry D. Hatfield. Like Don Chafin, Sheriff Hatfield operated a lucrative and utterly corrupt patronage machine that attracted attention from reporters, judges, and federal investigators. In 1916 he and some of his henchmen were ordered to stand trial on charges of coercing campaign contributions, stealing ballot boxes, and stuffing these containers with phony ballots. Two separate juries failed to convict the local bosses, but the prosecutions emboldened local residents who were ashamed to live in "the most corrupt county in the country." In the election that followed the trials, Sheriff Hatfield and his allies were swept out of office and replaced with a slate of Democratic reform candidates led by G. T. Blankenship, a railway union member, who became the new sheriff of Mingo County after campaigning on a promise "to serve the masses regardless of fear or favor."[6]

Although Greenway Hatfield surrendered his position as county sheriff, the family clung to power in its home base in Matewan, a small town on the Tug River where Devil Anse and his family had established their homestead and their timbering business before the Civil War. Another Hatfield, Greenway's brother A.B., had served as police chief and mayor of this wide-open river town, where businessmen served hundreds of miners employed in the coal camps tucked in the hills. But in 1918, the Hatfields lost control of Matewan to a reform candidate for mayor named Cabell Testerman, a popular merchant who ran on a Citizens' Party ticket.[7]

A year later, when the Hatfields made a desperate lunge to regain power, the five-foot-five, 170-pound Testerman stood tall and refused to be intimidated. On Election Day 1919, "Squire" A. B. Hatfield and his relatives assembled a gang of "desperado bootleggers" and "mountaineer ruffians from the wilds of Blackberry Creek" on the Kentucky side, who attempted to "bull-doze" the election for their leader by lining up unregistered voters at the polls. Sheriff Blankenship and his deputies intervened, and when one of his officers put a "hand cannon" to A. B. Hatfield's brain, the former mayor backed down and his gang hustled out of town.[8]

Once Mayor Testerman was reelected, he looked for a man who could keep the peace in a town known for its brawls and Election Day shoot-outs. Ironically, the man Testerman chose for the job was also named Hatfield, but other than his name, the new police chief had nothing in common with the powerful Republican Hatfields.

Albert Sidney Hatfield, or Sid as he was known to his friends, was born in 1893 on Blackberry Creek in Pike County, Kentucky, across the Tug River from Matewan. He was raised there by Jake Hatfield and his wife, who may have had an affair with a drifter. Whatever the circumstances of his birth, Sid was proud to call himself a Hatfield and to tell stories of the legendary sharpshooter Devil Anse Hatfield and his feud with the McCoys. Long after the clan war ended, gun battles continued in the backcountry. When Sid reached the impressionable age of nine, some Hatfields on Blackberry Creek shot it out with a deputy and a detective who had come to arrest the outlaw Ephraim Hatfield, wanted for murder in another state. Both officers of the court were killed in the gun battle, as were Ephraim and his father.[9]

Sid Hatfield attended school irregularly for twelve years and then went to work in a coal mine on Blackberry Creek. On days off, he would climb the twelve-hundred-foot mountain ridge and look across the muddy Tug River at the town of Matewan. By this time, the village had grown from a train stop to a bustling town of eight hundred residents with a Methodist church and a Baptist church hard on the N&W tracks, a new railway depot, a bank, a small department store, and the popular Do-Drop Inn, along with Cabell Testerman's jewelry and candy shop, Reece Chambers's hardware store, and a small hotel.

One day Hatfield crossed the swaying footbridge over the narrow Tug River and found work in a mine where he cut coal in the low seams all day. Here he bonded with his fellow miners as they toiled together in tunnels under the mountains. A wiry man just under five feet six inches in height, Hatfield was an aggressive miner, handy with a pick and an augur. Before long, the young coal loader escaped the depths and started to work aboveground as a blacksmith and then as a handler who sent loaded mine cars down to the tipple at the bottom of the mountain. At night, Hatfield led the rowdy life of a bachelor, shooting pool, playing cards, and drinking liquor.[10]

A gauntly handsome young man with high cheekbones, Sid liked to dress up and court young women in town, buying candies and baubles for them from Cabell Testerman's store. In a few years, he earned enough money to get his rotten teeth pulled and replaced with gold and silver fillings so that when he laughed his mouth shined. Before long, Matewan residents started calling the young Kentucky boy "Smiling Sid." But when he was not laughing and joking, Hatfield could be as mean as a mountain rattlesnake. Quick to anger, he was known as a fast and furious fistfighter and a dead-eyed pistol shooter. Hatfield, who toted two guns, could shoot straight with either hand and would draw down on anyone who crossed him. Soon after he arrived in Mingo County, the young miner had an argument with a mine foreman that resulted in what Hatfield called "a little shooting match" and the pit boss's death. Sid claimed that he shot in self-defense and no charges were pressed. A few years later, at age twenty-six, Hatfield quit drinking when he realized that his fondness for whiskey had slowed down his reflexes. Even sober, Sid was known as a dangerous man, a reputation enhanced by his surname, which linked him with old Devil Anse Hatfield and his son Cap, who had killed a man in Matewan during an Election Day shoot-out in 1896.[11]

But by the time Sid had made a name for himself in Matewan, members of the Hatfield family had settled down, and some had gained political power and a measure of respectability. Although Sid bore the Hatfield name, the "legitimate Hatfields" rejected him as kin. Furthermore, the local power broker Squire A. B. Hatfield hated this young interloper who threw in with his political rivals and replaced him as the town's lawman. Trouble was bound to come of this and it did, after A.B. testified against Sid for making an improper arrest. Indignant over the charge, the police chief confronted the former mayor and gave him "a good pummeling," according to the local newspaper. After the assault, Sid appeared in court to answer a felonious assault charge, but no one came forward to testify against him and he was freed.[12]

The changing of the political guard in Mingo County would eventually have an enormous impact on what the UMWA attempted to do in the Williamson coalfield, but in 1919 union leaders saw no prospects for organizing in the Tug River Valley mines. Though sympathetic to the union cause, Sheriff Blankenship made the same assessment in a letter to Governor Cornwell in which the lawman reported that there would be no labor trouble in the county's collieries unless the operators got "excited" and acted impulsively.[13]

Work in the Williamson coalfield went as usual during the winter months of 1920, but life in the company towns took a bad turn when an influenza epidemic struck the district. At this inopportune time, employers "excited" some hard

Sid Hatfield.

feelings when they decided to hike the compulsory medical fees they charged the miners. Then on March 29 came exciting news from Washington. The U.S. Coal Commission, established as a result of the 1919 strike, recommended a hefty 27 percent wage increase for UMWA members. Commenting on this stunning "award," Mingo County's daily newspaper proposed that it was "only right" for local miners to receive some comparable reward for their sacrifices and hard labors during the war years.[14]

A short time later, workers at the Burnwell Coal and Coke Company requested a 10-cent increase in the tonnage pay rate and the company manager granted them a 9-cent raise, but the next morning the miners discovered that their employer had jacked up the costs of the mining supplies the men needed to buy at the company store. When the first shift arrived at the Burnwell mine, someone had posted a note on the portal saying the nonunion miners who worked there deserved the same substantial pay raise the federal government had granted to union members. After they read the note, the Burnwell miners refused to enter the drift mouth until they could be represented by "an organization of [their] own craft." Later that day, some of these workers contacted Fred Mooney at District 17 and asked for help. Mooney told them to go back to work and wait: union organizers would be arriving soon to begin an all-out campaign in the Williamson field.[15]

A few days later, Mooney appeared in the county seat at Williamson with a seasoned crew from the Kanawha field, along with some tough professionals dispatched by UMWA president Lewis. When they arrived in Matewan, Mooney's men paid their respects to Mayor Testerman and Chief Hatfield, who promised them protection; then they opened an office in town and hired jitneys to bring miners down from the hills and hollows to attend a rally in front of the Baptist church. A few hours later, hundreds of men came down from the coal camps to hear Mooney deliver a stem-winding speech. After a few more UMWA evangelists preached to the men, two or three hundred workers raised their hands and took the oath of obligation to the union.[16]

The morning after the meeting, on April 27, 1920, the Burnwell Coal and Coke Company's managers delivered dismissal notices to the men who had joined the UMWA. The superintendent declared that he would let moss grow over his mine before he would ever "work a union man" underground. That same day, the operator of another colliery tacked a message to the gate that read: "This is a free country . . . but . . . no union men shall be employed by this company."[17]

Two weeks later, on May 8, the Red Jacket Consolidated Coal and Coke Company, Mingo County's largest mining firm, announced that it would not employ any man who joined the miners' union, an organization that taxed "the industrious for the benefit of the indolent" and restrained the employer's "constitutional liberty" to hire anyone he pleased. Many years later, a Mingo miner clearly remembered the spring day in 1920 when he joined the UMWA. "I took the obligation on a Saturday," he recalled, "and we was thrown out on Monday. They told us we'd have to get out or sign the yaller dog, one-or-t'other."[18]

These restrictive labor contracts had first appeared in 1907, when the Hitchman Coal and Coke Company in Fairmont field required its employees to sign them as a way of keeping the union off its property. When the UMWA challenged the legality of these "yellow dog contracts," a federal judge decided that Hitchman had a right to demand these terms of employment because the union could strike, which, in his view, constituted an "illegal conspiracy in restraint of trade" and "a direct violation of the Sherman Anti-Trust Act." To enforce his ruling, the judge issued an injunction prohibiting the union from having any contact with Hitchman's miners. With its very existence as a union in jeopardy, the UMWA took its case to a federal appeals court. There were handshakes and backslapping in union headquarters when the judge overturned the injunction on May 28, 1914. He ruled that organizing and striking did not constitute a criminal conspiracy, and that Hitchman could not, therefore, demand that its employees sign away their right to join the miners' union. But the Hitchman Company stood its ground and asked the U.S. Supreme Court to review the case. On December 10, 1917, Justice Mahlon Pitney read the majority opinion. He wrote that employees enjoyed the right to strike "in principle," but, he added, this "abstract freedom" did not give the union "the right to instigate a strike" against an employer like Hitchman, whose employees had agreed to abstain from union activity. Therefore, a majority of the justices ruled that any attempt by the UMWA to contact or organize these miners constituted a criminal inducement to breach a valid contract.[19]

Justice Louis D. Brandeis, the Supreme Court's newest member, wrote a dissenting opinion in which he argued that the union had pursued peaceful, legal means to a legitimate end; that miners who joined the union had no intention to injure their employer's business; and finally that the UMWA could not be judged an illegal organization under an antitrust law Congress had aimed at monopoly corporations. In Brandeis's view, the court's majority naively assumed that Hitchman's miners freely chose to sign yellow dog contracts. Like his fellow justice Oliver Wendell Holmes Jr., Brandeis believed there could be "no liberty of contract where there was no equality of bargaining position." Under modern industrial conditions, Holmes had

written, it was natural for a worker to believe that he could not se-
cure a fair contract unless he belonged to a union. On this basis,
Justice Holmes and one other member of the high court joined in
Brandeis's dissent.[20]

The editor of the *Yale Law Journal* was stunned by the majority's
reasoning in the Hitchman case because it was based on an old principle of Common Law, which held that a master had a right to take
action against a third party that attempted to seduce a servant from
leaving his service. This "seduction theory" had already been "exploded" by various legal challenges, the editor observed, but apparently this vestige of medieval master-servant law remained alive in
the minds of six Supreme Court justices. *Survey* magazine predicted
that this provocative decision was sure to cause "much bitterness for
the future."[21]

That prediction came true three years later, in 1920, after the
Red Jacket mine superintendent and several Mingo County coal operators insisted that their employees sign new anti-union contracts
and then hired a squad of Baldwin-Felts agents to evict miners who
refused. Sheriff G. T. Blankenship knew what had happened eight
years earlier on Paint Creek when employees of the same agency
had carried out such evictions. Like the editor of the Williamson
newspaper who sensed a "general uneasiness among our laboring
people," the sheriff feared that mass evictions might spark a violent
reaction from union members.[22] As a preventive measure, Blankenship arrested Tom Felts's brother, Albert, when he arrived in Mingo
County on a charge of processing illegal evictions. Buying more
time, the sheriff ordered Felts to appear in magistrate's court with
twenty-seven of his agents. When these agents were released, they
left the county without carrying out their orders, but the sheriff
knew the Baldwins would return. At a public meeting in the county
seat at Williamson, Blankenship told the union supporters to remain
calm and promised them that any eviction notices would be served
by county officials, not private detectives, and the renters would be
given ten days' notice and the right to appeal as the law required.[23]

With the law on their side, union partisans exercised their First
Amendment freedoms to the hilt. Fred Mooney addressed a crowd
of miners in the pouring rain and told them to obey the law and

follow the sheriff's orders, but he also urged them to prevent private gunmen from usurping the law. Later that evening, he telegraphed Attorney General Palmer and demanded federal action. If these unlawful actions continued, Mooney warned, the union could not be held responsible for the consequences.[24]

At another rally, observed by an undercover Baldwin-Felts agent, Hugh Combs, a coal miner and Methodist "exhorter," led the miners in a song and a prayer followed by "a radical talk" insisting that, since mine owners were organized, the mine workers must organize too, or else "they would always be in bondage—to do the bidding of the capitalist." "The Negroes were once in bondage [until] Abraham Lincoln gave them their freedom," Combs declared, "and now the miners, both black and white, were in bondage and that the United Mine Workers were going to give them their liberty." The next speaker, "a Negro preacher named Johnson," said that any man who signed a "yaller dog" contract should "go home and ask his wife to chain him in the yard with the dog," causing "much laughter by his speaking," according to the spy.[25] These two miner-preachers apparently hit the mark, because after the meeting ended, the agent reported to Tom Felts that at least two hundred miners took the oath of obligation to the union.[26]

Five days later, UMWA leaders announced that three thousand Mingo County workers had joined the union, including most of the men who had been evicted from company housing. On May 17, union officials from Charleston arrived with a load of tents and paid to rent land along Lick Creek, the first of several tent camps the union would set up for homeless union families.[27]

On May 19, at 11:47 in the morning, scores of out-of-work miners lined up in Matewan at the front of a store to receive relief funds from UMWA staffers. As they waited, some of them turned to watch the mail train from Bluefield puff into the Norfolk & Western station. Out of one passenger car came a formidable body of men in dark suits carrying valises, each large enough to hold rifles and shotguns. The Baldwins had come back to town.

Albert Felts, wearing a yellow rain slicker, led eleven agents across the tracks to the Urias Hotel. An agency photograph of Felts shows

Strikers lining up to receive union rations in Matewan, May 1920.

a well-dressed, immaculately groomed man in his thirties. His suave looks belied his reputation as a ruthless and highly skilled detective who had performed heavy work for his brother Tom, cleaning out pockets of union support in the New River field and fighting with UMWA guerrillas on Cabin Creek.

Shortly after the first mine war ended, Felts had headed for southern Colorado, where the agency's men were applying the same tactics they had used in West Virginia. After he arrived, Felts had a machine gun shipped out west from Paint Creek and rigged it up on an armored car. C. B. Cunningham, a fellow agent, had manned the machine gun during an assault on striking miners camped at Ludlow. A Greek UMWA organizer died in the attack. The "Death Special," as the miners called it, had been used again when the National Guard launched a far more lethal assault on the camp on April 20, 1914. Seven strikers, two strikers' wives, and eleven of their children died in the Ludlow massacre.[28] Six years later, when Felts and Cunningham climbed down from the train at Matewan Station, none of the local miners realized these two men had left Colorado with blood on their hands.

A few minutes after the train departed, five more detectives arrived in a car driven by Felts's younger brother, Lee, who parked his roadster and joined the other agents in front of the hotel. A few minutes later Albert Felts found Mayor Cabell Testerman and made him a bold proposition. The agent said that if he received permission to put three machine guns on the roofs of stores on Mate Street "to help preserve the peace," his agency would pay Testerman for his cooperation. The mayor turned down the machine guns and the cash.[29]

Felts then moved to the main business at hand, explaining that he had come to evict strikers from Stone Mountain Coal Company houses and that he had an authorization to do so, signed by Magistrate A. B. Hatfield, the ex-mayor of Matewan and enemy of Police Chief Hatfield. Mayor Testerman ignored this remark and claimed that the company houses in question lay within his town's jurisdiction; therefore, the Baldwin-Felts agents had no legal grounds for taking action. At this point, Felts turned away, walked back to the hotel, gathered his agents and led them up to Warm Hollow to evict union families from the Stone Mountain company houses.

After the detectives left, Sid Hatfield telephoned Sheriff Blankenship, who said that Albert Felts had no legal authorization to evict the families and that, as chief of police, Hatfield had grounds to arrest Felts and all of his men. Blankenship promised to send the warrants for these arrests on the next train to Matewan. Two curious teenage telephone operators, excited by the news of the day, were listening in on the conversation between the

Albert C. Felts.

two lawmen and heard Hatfield say: "Those sonsabitches will never leave here alive."[30]

That afternoon, Matewan hummed with the word that the Baldwin-Felts men were carrying out illegal evictions on the Stone Mountain property. When this news reached union men in the area, some of them filtered down from the coal camps into Matewan, armed and ready for trouble. The local school principal dismissed the pupils, and the mayor asked Hugh Combs to recruit a few sober "reliable men to protect the town."

Meanwhile, Mayor Testerman and Chief Hatfield had gone into the hills above town to find the agents. When they located Felts, they asked to see his eviction papers. The detective admitted that he didn't have them, but it didn't matter, he said, ordering his men to continue with the evictions. Hatfield interfered at this point and provoked a heated exchange with Felts. The detective, who was used to having his way with local officials, pulled out his pistol and warned the police chief that he was trespassing on private property. Hatfield stood his ground and Felts kept talking. The agent said that he had been ambushed from the hills when he went into Cabin Creek in 1912, and he warned Hatfield that he would not be "bluffed out" into the open again where he could be gunned down by hidden gunmen. Hatfield replied that if there was to be a fight in Mingo, no one would go into the hills and bushwhack the agents. He told Felts, "The man that kills you'll be lookin' you right in the eye."[31]

Hatfield and Testerman left the coal camp, while Felts and his men continued the evictions. When he returned to Matewan, the police chief and his boyish-looking deputy, Ed Chambers, deputized a dozen men Hugh Combs had rounded up and told them to gather in the hardware store owned by Ed's father, "Daddy" Reece Chambers. They would wait there for the Baldwin-Felts agents to return to town.

Around four o'clock that afternoon, the agents ambled back to their hotel, where they ate supper, rested, and smoked for an hour. They then walked toward the N&W depot to catch the 5:15 afternoon train back to Bluefield.[32] Four of the agents had gun permits and were armed; those who lacked papers had packed up their weapons. As the Baldwin-Felts agents loitered in front of the train station, Sid Hatfield approached Al Felts and claimed he had a warrant for his arrest on a charge of illegally bearing arms within the town limits. The agent replied that he carried a warrant for Hatfield's arrest and that he intended to take him to Bluefield. Hatfield told Felts he would do no such thing, and the men chuckled at each other's pugnacity.

The two men continued to argue as they walked up the street to meet Mayor Testerman, who had asked to see the warrant Felts carried. While the mayor read the document, Hatfield moved back toward the Chambers hardware store. Testerman then stepped toward Felts and said, "This warrant is bogus." The detective had just begun to argue with the mayor when the sound of a pistol shot cracked through the misty air.[33]

Hatfield later testified that Felts pulled out his gun and shot Testerman in the stomach. The police chief said he reacted instantly by firing both of his pistols at Felts. But another witness, a doctor who owned the town's Republican newspaper, told detectives that one of Hatfield's deputies stepped out of the hardware store and shot Albert Felts. There was little disagreement, however, about what happened after Testerman and Felts dropped down on the muddy street. A storm of pistol and rifle fire exploded out of the hardware store, killing Detective C. B. Cunningham when he ran forward shooting at his assailants. At the same time, Lee Felts rushed to his brother's aid, firing his two handguns until Daddy Reece Chambers dropped the detective with one round from his Winchester rifle.

Another Baldwin-Felts agent, A. J. Boorher, wounded in the opening salvo, tried to drag himself away from the field of fire. When one of the deputies in the store—a miner who had just been evicted from his house—saw the detective, he grabbed a loaded pistol, burst outside, ran down the agent, and shot him dead at close range. A fourth detective, J. W. Ferguson, staggered down the street crying, "I'm shot to pieces." A bystander helped Ferguson into a house on Mate Street, where the agent rested briefly until he saw armed men approaching. Ferguson escaped through the back door and was climbing a fence when a deputy knocked him down with a deadly shot to his back. Two other agents died in the storm of bullets let loose by Sid Hatfield and his deputies, and when the shooting stopped, seven Baldwin-Felts men lay dead on Mate Street.

Six other agents escaped. Two of them bolted to Matewan Station and hopped aboard the 5:15 evening train, which crept out of town just after the shooting stopped. Another agent asked for help from a local woman who told him to "split the creek" and swim across the Tug River to Kentucky, and another escaped death by hiding inside an empty barrel and then also swimming to the Kentucky shore.

Chief Hatfield and his men suffered no casualties, but two unarmed miners died in the wild gunfire. After the shooting stopped, citizens walked past the corpses laid out in the N&W station and put Mayor Cabell Testerman on the next train to Welch, where there was a hospital. Testerman did not survive the trip. He died muttering, "Why did they shoot me? I can't see why they shot me."

The next morning, this shooting in an obscure West Virginia river town made national headlines. A front-page story in the *New York Times* quoted Fred Mooney, who said that the bloodbath in Matewan might have been avoided if Attorney General Palmer had responded to his telegram and sent federal marshals to Mingo County. In any case, Mooney remarked, this "terrible affair" might be "a blessing in disguise," an event that would mark the end of "thug rule" in West Virginia's mining communities.[34]

Matewan Station on the Norfolk & Western Railway line.

When Tom Felts heard the heartrending news that his two younger brothers and five of his best agents had been slain, he boarded a train in Bluefield and headed for Matewan with a contingent of heavily armed men. Sid Hatfield expected a counterattack and asked for help from Sheriff Blankenship, who deputized a formidable force of a hundred men to defend Matewan. As the train carrying the Felts and his agents barreled down the Tug River Valley, it seemed certain that an even bloodier battle would soon erupt.

The locomotive engineer had learned, however, that a gun party waited to greet Felts and his men, and he rushed his train past Matewan Station without stopping, despite furious protests from the agents, and rolled on toward Williamson. There, at an undertaker's establishment, Felts viewed the bullet-riddled bodies of his brothers. Afterward, Felts met with the press and told reporters that Hatfield had fired the first shot and that his deputies ambushed Felts's detectives after most of them had packed up their guns. The battle in Matewan had not been "a fair fight," he declared; if it had been, his agents "would have dropped twice as many as the miners did."[35]

The next day a crowd of three thousand attended the Felts brothers' funeral near Tom's farm in Galax, Virginia, where they were mourned as heroes in the war against "criminal syndicalism." The coal operators who had done business with the Felts brothers expressed their horror over the Matewan massacre and demanded the immediate arrest of the police chief and his deputies. On May 24, Sid Hatfield, Deputy Ed Chambers, and seven other men involved in the shooting appeared before Judge James Damron in the courthouse at Williamson. The judge charged Hatfield and his men with murder, but then—to the dismay of Tom Felts and his clients in the coal industry—he released the suspects on $3,000 bail bonds.

Unlike many Mingo County officials, Damron was an independent who had been elected to the judgeship in 1916 after he promised to investigate the corrupt Hatfield machine and to purge the county's registration lists of illegal voters, including "dead men, mules, and tombstones." The judge believed that deputy sheriffs should have conducted risky business like evicting miners from their homes, and he suspected that the Baldwin-Felts agents provoked the strikers by carrying out illegal evictions. Therefore, when Damron impaneled a grand jury to investigate the shootings in Matewan, he asked its members to probe the deeper causes of the violence that exploded on May 19.[36]

The next day, William Ord, the superintendent of the Red Jacket Consolidated Coal and Coke Company, sent Sheriff Blankenship a list of employees he wanted to have deputized to guard his properties. When the sheriff refused because state law prevented him from deputizing private guards, Ord complained to Governor Cornwell that "armed men [were] parading the roads in mobs." Blankenship did some investigating and sent a report back to Charleston. "My dear Governor," he wrote, "The situation remains very quiet in this section." Since most of the mines had been organized, he could not "conceive any reason why there should be further disturbances." Nonetheless, the sheriff planned to swear in extra deputies in order "to handle anything that might arise."[37]

That May, as the magnolias bloomed in the Tug River Valley, Keeney and Mooney felt the wind at their back. Sheriff Blankenship and Judge Damron supported the union cause, as did Samuel Montgomery, the progressive candidate in the Republican gubernatorial primary, who had once served as state secretary of labor and as District 17's legal counsel. Furthermore, Democrats still clung to office in Washington, DC, and even though President Woodrow Wilson was a lame duck, his administration remained accountable to organized labor, which constituted a powerful block within the party. Secretary of Labor William B. Wilson, a former UMWA official and an old friend of Mother Jones's, wanted to encourage bargaining in the Mingo County field before events took another violent turn; to further that end, the secretary sent federal mediators to Williamson to meet with Keeney and Mooney and several mine operators who had agreed to talk with the union officials.

The federal commission's 27 percent wage hike for UMWA members had worked wonders in the minds of unorganized miners, and the coal operators' refusal to negotiate with the union over any wage increase had alienated most of their employees as well as some members of the public. The coal companies had provoked more resentment when they required their men to sign anti-union contracts and then fired those who refused. Hiring "gun thugs" from the hated Baldwin-Felts Agency to carry out the evictions made matters far worse.

Sensing a great chance for a breakthrough in the nonunion fields, John L. Lewis invested even more UMWA money in the campaign and dispatched several experienced organizers to assist in the drive. The results were impressive. "We have Mingo County nearly completed and are breaking into McDowell," Keeney reported in a letter to his president. His forces would not "be blocked, bluffed, or brow-beaten in this campaign" to make every miner in the region a UMWA member. Once the Baldwin-Felts "outlaws were out of the way," the *United Mine Workers Journal* reported, "there was a great rush for membership in the union."[38]

Three weeks later, union organizers moved up the Tug River Valley, signing up the men at the Thacker and Old Ben mines. Over the next few days, UMWA men pushed farther along the river to Glen Alum Creek and as far as War Eagle, the last coal camp on the boundary between Mingo and McDowell County, where the state's largest coal companies mined the fabulous Pocahontas field. On June 17, Lewis received word that his men had entered McDowell County and had passed over what union officials called the "Dead Line," a boundary no organizer could cross and expect to return alive.[39]

After this surge of organizing, UMWA officials contacted the mine operators' association again and asked for negotiations. The employers remained adamantly opposed to talks, and over the next few days, their managers continued to fire union members and evict them from company housing. They retained only those men who signed away their right to join the union.

Faced with such implacable opposition, UMWA leader Frank Keeney and his executive board decided to call for a general strike in Mingo County on July 1. To the surprise of the mine owners, thousands of workers responded. When all the collieries closed down for Independence Day celebrations, union miners and their families and friends gathered for baseball games, traditional pit barbecues, and speeches from union orators like Fred Mooney, who assured them that a new day was dawning in Mingo County.[40]

Chapter 11

Situation Absolutely Beyond Control

July 4, 1920–May 29, 1921

Members of the Williamson Coal Operators' Association were understandably puzzled and utterly infuriated by this turn of events. For the previous six months, they had operated a piece rate incentive system that allowed their best coal loaders to earn wages as high as those of union men. They had answered the governor's challenge by reducing the workday to eight hours, improving housing conditions, and permitting their employees to shop at independent stores outside the company towns. They had done all of this to ensure the loyalty and enhanced productivity of their miners. And now the men they employed and housed had spurned their managers and followed the siren song of socialist agitators from Charleston, who had convinced them they were entitled to an enormous wage increase when, in fact, that federally mandated award was intended only for union miners who had worked under the wartime labor agreement.

The Mingo County operators were being outproduced by the bigger companies in Logan County and the Pocahontas field, and the last thing they could afford was a huge hike in their labor costs. Furthermore, if their men worked under a UMWA contract, the employers were certain that wages would be equalized, piece rate incentives would be banned, and productivity would plunge.[1]

The mine operators of Mingo County stood on the time-honored principle that they had "legal and moral right" to decide how their mines were going to be run. Therefore, they were free to refuse to deal with any labor union, to discharge anybody who caused a disturbance, and to set any terms they wished as a condition of employment. The UMWA raised a hue and cry over the new contracts they called "yellow dogs," but the U.S. Supreme Court had ruled that these contracts were legal.

Frustrated employers also faced an untenable political situation in Mingo County. Although they were influential Republicans with friends in the state capital, the court system, and on Capitol Hill, they had no influence over the pro-union Democrats in control of the sheriff's department and other local offices. As a result, these industrialists could no longer rely upon local authorities to guard their property or enforce their right to employ and house whomever they wanted under whatever contractual terms they chose. In June, Harry Olmstead, labor secretary of the Williamson Coal Operators' Association, complained that "the law was not being enforced and that there was little prospect of its enforcement" by the county sheriff and his deputies.[2]

When the strike began on July 1, the employers attempted to run coal with skeleton crews of "loyal" miners and office personnel while they waited for replacement workers to arrive. But when the first trainloads of strikebreakers reached Williamson, deputy sheriffs told them that a strike was on and that the union would pay their fares home. If the strangers ignored the deputies and left the train depot, they were accosted by crowds of union supporters who subjected them to what one employer called "scathing denunciation, vilification, threats, and in frequent cases assaults."[3]

The superintendent of Red Jacket collieries begged the governor to send units of the new state police force to protect the company's employees from the "verbal vilification" they suffered whenever they encountered the "agitators or malcontents." But Cornwell declined this request on the grounds that state law prohibited the new constabulary from interfering with local law enforcement.[4]

In the meantime, mine superintendents had armed their remaining employees, installed searchlights on their property, and hired professional guards to replace the vanquished Baldwin-Felts agents. By August 1, mining operations were picking up steam, despite the harassing actions of strikers and their local supporters. Three weeks passed without any casualties, and employers thought their troubles might have ended. That hope evaporated on August 21, when strikers attacked the Borderland mine in force. Six company men died at the colliery, located three miles north of Williamson. When Governor Cornwell heard this dreadful news, he realized that a second mine war had begun on the state's western border.

The coal operators again begged Cornwell to send the entire state constabulary into the district. But the state police commander, Jackson Arnold (a descendant of Stonewall Jackson), refused, saying he would not allow his men to act as "stationary guards" for the mine owners' property.[5] With the West Virginia National Guard still federalized, Cornwell turned to the War Department for help. Eight days later, the first federal military forces to enter the territory since the outbreak of the Civil War arrived in Williamson, with orders to guard scores of mines along a fifty-mile stretch of the winding Tug River.[6]

The army's occupation of Mingo County turned the tide against the strikers. Frank Keeney beseeched Secretary of War Newton D. Baker to remove the soldiers because they were being used to break the strike, but he received no reply. By the end of August, the collieries along the Tug were running full again with the help of men who had been thrown out of work by a severe depression. Unemployment, which stood at an unusually low 1.4 percent in 1919, soared to 10 percent the following year and reached an even higher level in the coal-mining industry.[7]

Most union officials would have calculated the odds weighing against them and called off the strike, but Keeney and Mooney realized that if the union was defeated in Mingo County, they would never be able to organize the other open shop fields. Furthermore, the UMWA's president, John Lewis, still honored the UMWA's financial commitment to unionizing all the miners in southern West Virginia. More important, the thousands of miners living in tent colonies still honored the picket lines. Committed to fight over the long haul, Keeney and Mooney urged their followers to hold fast.

Eventually, they promised, the soldiers would leave and the union's fight against the operators could begin again. In the meantime, Keeney and Mooney decided to lay down a few political cards in the deadly poker game they were playing with the Mingo mine operators.

When the electoral campaigns kicked off on Labor Day 1920, pundits predicted Republican victories in most races. The affable but unimpressive GOP presidential candidate, Warren G. Harding, seemed like a sure winner even though he promised to do little more than turn the clock back to the good old days when William McKinley sat in the White House. What America needed, according to Harding, was "not heroics, but healing; not nostrums, but normalcy; not revolution, but restoration; not agitation, but adjustment; not surgery, but serenity . . ." In West Virginia, the Republican gubernatorial nominee, a broad-shouldered, gray-haired Judge Ephraim F. Morgan, joined this call for a "return to normalcy." Morgan had practiced law in Marion County, fought in the Spanish-American War, and later served as public service commissioner under Governor Henry D. Hatfield. A devout Episcopalian, the judge spoke for farmers, merchants, and professionals, but not for the mine owners who backed their own candidate in the primary; but when their man lost, these industrialists donated nearly a million dollars to Morgan's election campaign. It would prove to be money well spent.[8]

Frank Keeney gambled a good deal of District 17's money on the chance that a third-party candidate could somehow win the governor's office and aid the union's cause in the southern coalfields. Electing a pro-labor independent as governor was a long shot, but the UMWA had an impressive candidate in the well-known attorney Samuel B. Montgomery, a progressive Republican who had served as commissioner of labor under Governor Hatfield and as legal counsel to District 17.

That September, Montgomery ran a strong grassroots campaign backed by the state's powerful labor unions. The stocky lawyer appealed to working-class supporters of Eugene Debs and middle-class followers of Theodore Roosevelt, as well as to small farmers and merchants, union members, newly enfranchised women voters, and African American voters, whose leaders were supportive of the UMWA and angry at being taken for granted by the GOP. Montgomery received a surprising total of eighty-one thousand votes in the November election, twice as many votes as the lackluster Democratic candidate. But when all the ballots were counted, Ephraim Morgan was elected by a decisive margin. Keeney and Mooney accused GOP machine bosses of stealing ballot boxes in mining districts and pitching them into the creeks, but in the end, Montgomery had been defeated and District 17's desperate bid for political power had failed.[9]

Two weeks later, Secretary of War Newton Baker withdrew the infantry from Tug River Valley after he concluded that the strikers no longer posed a threat to public order. But as soon as the army decamped, union partisans took to the hills, opened fire, and killed two men at a colliery near the Tug River. One of the victims was a company guard and the other a state trooper whose death would mark a turning point in the struggle. The next day, Governor Cornwell declared Mingo County to be in a "state of insurrection" and announced that army troops would return immediately. This time, he said, the commanding general of the army would govern all civic affairs.[10]

A week later, five hundred army infantrymen detrained in Williamson with orders to occupy the county courthouse, guard the mines, and ban all public assemblies. By Thanksgiving Day, some semblance of normal life had resumed in the Tug River Valley and coal production rose to its normal level. The superintendent at the Red Jacket coal company even found that he could cut wages and still find plenty of men willing to load coal. He could do this because, a few days earlier, lawyers for his company had obtained one of the most sweeping injunctions ever issued in a strike. A U.S. District Court judge barred the union from approaching employees who had signed yellow dog contracts; his order also prohibited Frank Keeney, Sid Hatfield, and all members of the UMWA from "interfering in any way with working miners," from trespassing on company property, or "from advertising, representing, stating by word, by posted notices, or by placards displayed at any point in the State of West Virginia" that a strike was in progress. "If a union cannot make the simple statement that a strike exists in a field covered by an official strike order," Harold Houston asked in despair, "what can it do?" The union could surrender or it could defy the court order and take the legal consequences.[11]

Outraged by the scope of the Red Jacket injunction, Roger Baldwin of the National Civil Liberties Bureau, soon to become American Civil Liberties Union (ACLU), consulted the brilliant Harvard law professor Felix Frankfurter about filing a test case against this "bad law," while another bureau director, Albert DeSilver, proposed a different approach. Realizing that any formal appeal would be negated by the Supreme Court's precedent-setting decision in the Hitchman case, DeSilver called instead for a massive civil disobedience campaign. "Let the miners in West Virginia violate the injunction," he proposed, and "go to jail" in numbers that would undermine any effort to enforce the court order. The legal consequences of defying the Red Jacket injunctions would be enormous, but Keeney decided to give DeSilver's proposal serious consideration.[12]

In late December, Mother Jones arrived at the strikers' camps along the Tug River with words of encouragement and gift-wrapped Christmas presents for the children, who had been living there since July 1. The wives of army officers also took pity on the campers, and several of them volunteered to bring medicine and hand-me-down clothes to the strikers' barefoot children and to assist mothers who were about to give birth in the tents. On Christmas Eve, the army commander relaxed the rules of martial law for a night and allowed a public gathering in Williamson, where a decorated spruce tree stood in the courthouse square. There, together with soldiers and townspeople, the miners and their families sang "Silent Night" and other Christmas carols of joy and hope before they returned to their canvas colonies for the night.[13]

A few days later, a reporter for the *Nation* described the miserable Lick Creek camp as "Labor's Valley Forge." Many tents were pitched on frozen ground with floors covered only by rags or threadbare carpets. "Several children have died of pneumonia and it was pitiful to see any number of new-born babies there—and worst, many women pregnant." And yet, here in this cold, dark industrial valley, the miners of Mingo County were "fighting one of the gamest fights in the history of industrial war."[14]

The stakes in this fight were enormous for the West Virginia mining industry. By 1920, the Mountain State provided nearly one-fourth of the nation's bituminous coal from 1,287 collieries that employed eighty-seven thousand workers. The mine owners had made huge investments in building rail links, buying new machinery, hiring security guards, constructing housing, and erecting new large-scale collieries. As a result, productivity soared from 6.43 tons per man hour in 1910 to 9.98 in 1920, a year when West Virginia coal sales generated a bonanza of $198 million in profits for colliery owners ($2.3 billion in today's dollars).[15] To protect their profits owners and operators of nonunion mines willingly invested huge sums of money to prevent any interruption in production or any form of collective bargaining that raised wages.[16]

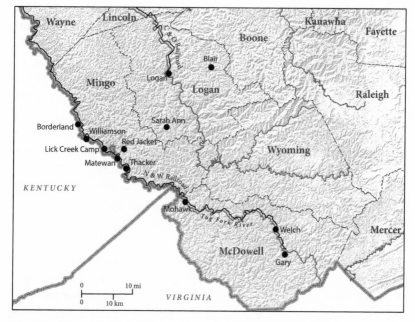

Towns and railways in Mingo, Logan, and McDowell Counties.

The UMWA's national officers were just as willing to invest union money in an all-out organizing drive in southern West Virginia. The union had already contributed the immense sum of $1.3 million to the Mingo campaign, and its leaders were prepared to give more. With an enormous membership of five hundred thousand and a war chest larger than any ever accumulated by an American trade union, President John L. Lewis pledged to give Frank Keeney and Fred Mooney all the support they needed to prevail in Mingo County by assessing each of its active members $1 a month to support the cause.[17] Besides hiring extra organizers, renting tents, supplying rations and medicines, and making strike relief payments, the national office offered to provide full "material and moral support" to Sid Hatfield and his deputies when they faced trial on the charge of murdering Detective Albert Felts in Matewan.[18]

Murder trials often caused excitement in rural county seats, but no one could remember one in which a police chief and his deputies stood accused of committing homicide. Residents of Williamson, the headquarters of the region's major coal companies, viewed the main defendant as an ignorant redneck and dangerous gangster, but in the rest of the county Sid Hatfield had become a hero not only to union miners but also to their neighbors, who resented the behavior of the local "coal barons" and their hired guards. Voters had already shown their admiration for the defendant by electing the twenty-eight-year-old mountaineer constable of the Magnolia district, which encompassed Matewan and the nearby mining towns.[19]

Realizing that many potential jurors sympathized with the police chief and his deputies, Thomas Felts fed the press reports from his detectives, who had interviewed witnesses willing to swear that Hatfield fired the first shot that killed Albert Felts, and others who alleged that the police chief had also fired the bullet that killed Mayor Testerman.[20] According to Felts, the police chief coveted Testerman's pretty wife, Jessie, and wanted to "have her to himself." These allegations had gained credibility when Jessie Testerman snuck away with Sid Hatfield to Huntington just twelve days after her husband died. Felts's agents followed them and reported their whereabouts to the police, who arrested the couple for having illicit relations. Sid

Hatfield explained that he and Jessie had planned on procuring a marriage license but found the city hall closed when they arrived. In any case, by the time the trial opened, Sid and Jessie were married and tending the late Cabell Testerman's store in Matewan.[21]

Defense attorney Harold Houston had to defend his clients against a formidable team of prosecuting attorneys retained by Tom Felts and the coal companies and headed by Captain S. B. Avis, a famous Kanawha County prosecutor known for his skill at convicting men accused of murder. In most counties of the United States, the government's own attorneys prosecuted murder cases, but not in Mingo County, West Virginia, in 1920. Here legal processes could be cut to fit the circumstances at hand.

The prosecution team faced difficulties from the start. First of all, a group of city attorneys paid by big coal companies would have its hands full winning the trust of a jury comprising local men whose neighbors and relatives worked as coal miners. And then there was the problem of evidence: Only a few eyewitnesses had come forward who were willing to testify against Hatfield and his men. One agent reported to Tom Felts that he could not find "any one of the better class" who would appear before the grand jury, because most witnesses were either connected to Hatfield and Sheriff Blankenship or were "in sympathy with them." Others who might have given evidence against the police chief and his deputies had either left town or were afraid to testify, and with good reason. They knew what had happened to a local hotel owner, Anderson Hatfield (one of the many Hatfields named after the family patriarch) when he had agreed to testify for the prosecution. Known as Ancey, the innkeeper had provided hospitality to the Baldwin-Felts agents when they came to town, and he was known to be friendly with the Felts brothers. On a warm August evening five months earlier, Ancey was rocking in a chair outside his establishment, when a rifle bullet blasted through his chest and killed him. A state trooper who happened to be at the scene arrested a miner, who had served as one of the deputies on May 19. Local officers suspected Sid Hatfield's involvement in the innkeeper's killing and arrested him on a charge of being an accessory to murder.[22]

This charge was still hanging over Hatfield's head when he appeared with his codefendants at the county courthouse on a cool January day to stand trial for murder. Looking trim in a tight brown suit and a severe haircut, the defendant willingly gave interviews to reporters and seemed to be enjoying the limelight. Old "Devil Anse" Hatfield had died on Mile Island Creek just two weeks earlier, and some journalists could not resist anointing Sid Hatfield as his successor. But as he stood in the shadow of the courthouse where he would be tried for murder, Hatfield shunned the mantle of "the hoofed and horned devil of popular imagination." Flashing his boyish grin and his metal teeth, the defendant teased the press for labeling him the "Terror of the Tug." When a reporter laughed at one of his jokes, Hatfield remarked disarmingly: "I reckon you thought I had horns."[23]

Selecting an impartial jury proved to be a lengthy and frustrating task. Deputies traveled deep into the hollows to find potential jurors who were not related to any of the defendants. Attorneys eventually examined more than a thousand candidates, but many of them expressed unmitigated hatred for the Baldwin-Felts men and were therefore dismissed. Some lawyers proposed that newly enfranchised females be considered as jurors, but the presiding judge scotched that idea. Someone even suggested that black men be called to serve, another suggestion the judge rejected. Finally, on February 12, twelve men were impaneled as a jury: two schoolteachers, four farmers, five laborers (but no coal miners), and an old backwoodsman who rode down to Williamson on horseback.[24]

The prosecuting attorneys opened the trial by promising to prove that Chief Hatfield and his deputies had committed an act of premeditated murder when they killed Albert Felts. These lawyers built their case on the testimony of one of Hatfield's deputies, who had turned state's witness in return for immunity and a payment, and on that of a man whom Chief Hatfield had considered a friend, a spy named Charles Everett Lively.

Lively had grown up with Fred Mooney on Davis Creek and had joined the UMWA in 1902, but a few years later he left West Virginia and went to work for Tom Felts, jumping from one hot coalfield to another, where he spied on the union and its organizers. A crafty operative, Lively kept his union card and even won office in a Colorado local of the UMWA.

The day after his brothers and his agents were slain in Matewan, Tom Felts sent his ace undercover man to Mingo County and told him to hire on as a miner. Lively worked in a colliery along the Tug River until an unsuspecting owner fired him for allegedly being too friendly with a union supporter. With a perfect cover story in hand, Felts's secret agent turned up one day in Matewan and opened a restaurant below the UMWA office. Lively renewed his acquaintance with Mooney and developed a warm relationship with Hatfield by expressing his loyalty to the union and his hatred for the mine operators and their guards.. No one thought to check up on this new man in town, an out-of-work coal miner who had arrived in Matewan with enough money to open a business.[25]

Lively spent as much time as he could with Hatfield, asking him questions and hoping he would hear incriminating answers. According to the spy's testimony in the Williamson trial, Hatfield told him that he shot Mayor Testerman because he "had the woman he wanted." Referring to Jesse Testerman, the police chief told Lively, "I will have her if I have to go through hell to get her."[26]

Harold Houston.

Roger Baldwin of the ACLU had advised defense attorney Harold Houston to turn the trial into "a prosecution of the coal operators" by "introducing in evidence the entire record of their conspiracy to deprive the citizens of West Virginia of their legal rights." Houston followed this advice and built a case blaming the coal operators and their private guards for the bloodshed on May 19.

At one point during his cross-examination of Charles Lively, Houston forced Lively to admit that he had purchased a machine gun and brought it to Matewan at Tom Felts's request. Leaping on this admission, Houston turned to the local men on the jury and said, "It is time that Mingo County should be governed by the taxpayers, and not by a private detective agency."[27]

After hearing days of wildly conflicting testimony, the jurymen returned with a not guilty verdict and the crowd outside roared its approval. One story has it that the old mountaineer on the jury held out for an acquittal verdict, saying he was ready to sit there all year, "until the mountains turned brown again," before he'd vote to convict a single Matewan boy.[28]

That afternoon, Hatfield and his vindicated deputies arrived in Matewan and the town's entire population turned out to greet their heroes. A "throng that gathered about the hill men when they left the train" swayed back and forth for an hour as people surged forward to grasp the hands of their heroes, while the wives, mothers, sisters, and daughters of the accused men wept "from pure joy at their return."[29]

For nearly a year, the ACLU had been providing services to Frank Keeney in his "fight for free speech and the right to organize" and its director Roger Baldwin had promised Keeney that his organization would "make West Virginia conditions an issue . . . known throughout the United States." To that end, the ACLU recommended that the UMWA petition for a congressional investigation of the First Amendment abuses in Mingo and Logan Counties. District 17's attorney, Harold Houston, collected signatures from union miners and sent their petition on to Washington, but no one in Congress noticed this plea from the coalfields even after Keeney went to Capitol Hill to make a personal appeal to a few senators and to explain to them how "the Constitution had been kicked into disregard in West Virginia."[30]

When Keeney returned, he found the mood in Charleston more threatening than ever. State legislators had voted to double the size of the state police force, and a state representative had reacted to the acquittal of Sid Hatfield by proposing a new statute that would allow a criminal court jury to be selected from residents of a different county. In future trials of union partisans, Harold Houston would not be able to appeal to the sentiments of local people who knew union coal miners as neighbors and relatives.

District 17 leaders and their liberal supporters lobbied against the jury reform bill, but the UMWA had few allies in the state's Republican-dominated legislature, and the bill passed. Everyone knew the new law was aimed at Hatfield, who would soon be put on trial again on the charge of murdering another Baldwin-Felts agent. The next time Hatfield appeared in court, he would not face a jury of his peers from Mingo County. If the law had to be changed, if standard procedures in jury trials had to be altered to ensure his conviction, they would be. This was West Virginia in 1921, and this was how the wheels of justice turned.[31]

While Frank Keeney played politics in Washington and Charleston, Tom Felts's agents reported that Sid Hatfield was moving through the hollows preparing strikers for a spring offensive in Mingo County and that Fred Mooney was bringing money and ammunition into the region from Kanawha County.[32] In April, an army military intelligence officer described the entire West Virginia–Kentucky borderline as "a smoldering volcano with an eruption all the more imminent." The governor of Kentucky, who shared this fear, sent a militia company across the Tug River to assist the West Virginia State Police and to guard his state's border. Nonetheless, citizens on both sides of the river were beside themselves with anxiety and were reportedly "praying for the arrival of federal troops and the promulgation of martial law."[33]

The Kentucky militia could patrol the properties of only a few mine companies, however; the rest were left to their own defenses. Early in May, a large band of men opened fire on one of these unguarded companies located at Merrimac, a few miles downriver from Matewan, while raiders broke into the property and dynamited the firm's power plant. The White Star Mining Company repaired its plant, hired more guards, and resumed operations a few days later. Coal trains rolled out from under the colliery's tipples as usual until May 11, when union partisans returned in force. Some raiders cut down telephone and telegraph lines, and then, at the sound of a cow horn, scores of riflemen launched another all-out attack on Merri-mac from the surrounding hills. Company employees returned fire and the battle raged for the rest of the day and into the night, ter-rifying local residents, including one man who estimated that ten thousand rounds had been fired.[34]

Williamson district coal operators demanded action from the newly inaugurated governor of West Virginia, Ephraim Morgan, who responded by urging the state police commander to move all of his troopers into Mingo County. When Colonel Jackson Arnold refused to usurp the authority of Mingo County's sheriff, Morgan decided to grant authority to another officer of the state police, Cap-tain James R. Brockus. Brockus was a veteran of the U.S. Army's brutal campaign against Filipino nationalists in the early 1900s and of World War I, where he commanded an infantry battalion on the Western Front and where his bravery in combat earned him a pro-motion to captain in 1918. In Brockus, the governor found the tough military man he needed to put down the union insurgency in Mingo County. But soon after he arrived in Williamson, the captain discov-ered what a difficult assignment he had been given. When he led a squad of troopers into the Tug River Valley to conduct his first counterinsurgency operation, the officers' new state police cars got stuck on the muddy road and, as the lawmen tried to move the au-tomobiles, gunfire rained down on them. Dug in for hours, Brockus and his constables finally made their way out of the valley, taking cover behind a coal train moving along the N&W line. That night, Brockus reported to state police headquarters that the situation was far more serious than he had expected. "Arms and ammunition are being purchased daily from the local merchants and shipped in by express," he explained. Unless immediate steps were taken to disarm all persons on both sides of the river, the captain feared that his offi-cers would be ambushed again and that murder would be "commit-ted by the wholesale."[35]

The next morning, Brockus's fears proved justified when gunfire echoed again through the narrow river valley as strikers attacked six Mingo County collieries and one at Mohawk in McDowell County, where saboteurs destroyed a tipple with dynamite charges. Armed combat escalated the next day when two hundred snipers took positions on the Kentucky side of the Tug River's edge and fired at the coal operations less than a hundred yards away. After three days of fierce fighting, authorities arranged a truce and counted the dead. No one could be sure how many men had been killed, but partisans told Frank Keeney "they were bringing dead bodies out of the woods" a week after the battle.[36]

Appalled by the news of what the press called the "Three Days Battle," Governor Morgan sent a wire to President Harding that began with the words "Situation absolutely beyond control of state and county authorities" and ended with another plea for federal troops. The president and his advisers knew, of course, that army units had been sent to Mingo County before without permanently stopping the violence. Harding did not want West Virginia's governors to keep relying on the U.S. Army to do the work of state and local police.[37]

May 19 promised to be "a red letter day" in Mingo County, according to an army intelligence report sent to the governor. That date marked the first anniversary of the Battle of Matewan, a day when more blood might be shed.[38] In response to this report, Morgan invoked the state's emergency public safety law; the statute allowed the governor to suspend the elected county sheriff and his deputies and to place law enforcement in the hands of the state police. That morning, the governor declared that "a state of war, riot, and insurrection" existed in Mingo County, and that it was therefore necessary for him to impose martial law. His executive order prohibited all forms of free speech and assembly that the authorities deemed threatening to public order or private property, and it empowered law officers to arrest and hold citizens in jail at their discretion. Mindful of the legal difficulties Governors Glasscock and Hatfield had encountered in their use of martial law, Governor Morgan allowed the local courts to remain in session. But this concession to civil law would prove to be no more than a fig leaf to cover up the actions of a military regime that would now rule over Mingo County.[39]

As commandant of this new order, the governor appointed Major Thomas B. Davis, a short and stocky man with pudgy cheeks and tiny wire-rimmed spectacles. Although the major looked more like a local grocer than a military commander, he had more experience than most army officers in coping with political protest and domestic unrest. Born in Virginia, Thomas Boyd Davis graduated high school in Huntington and pursued a career as a union machinist in the Chesapeake & Ohio Railway shops until 1898, when he volunteered for the army during the war with Spain. Davis's dreams of seeing action were never fulfilled, but he fell in love with military life and carved out a peacetime career in the state militia, rising from the rank of sergeant to major. During the first mine war in Kanawha County, Major Davis served as provost marshal and the chief enforcement officer to the first military commission that tried strike leaders at Pratt, and on May 9, 1913, he led the raid on the Socialist newspaper the *Labor Star*.[40]

During World War I, when Davis's militia company became part of the U.S. Army and shipped out for France, the major stayed at home, where he commanded four "home guard" units created by the State Council for Defense of West Virginia. These forces paled in comparison, however, with the body of men who served under Davis in Mingo County. In addition to the state's entire police force, the major oversaw a battalion of 800 "special police"—a force comprising white business and professional men and a large number of coal company employees—as well as a 250-member civilian "vigilance committee" consisting of "the better citizens" of the county who had property they wanted to protect.[41]

Under Morgan's martial law proclamation, Davis and his officers had the power to arrest any and all potential troublemakers and hold them in jail without charges and without the benefit of a trial by jury. Soon after he arrived in Williamson, the major stopped the circulation of the *West Virginia Federationist*, the state's official union paper, because it had published an article blaming Governor Morgan for the violence. Police officers even arrested several men for reading that newspaper, along with a few others who were seen reading copies of the *United Mine Workers Journal*. Frank Keeney met with Davis to protest his tactics, but the major stood fast. He would not allow the UMWA to circulate any of its publications, would arrest anyone reading these papers, and anyone holding or attending any public meetings. All the union would be allowed to do under martial law was to distribute relief to the tent colonies under close supervision by Davis's men.[42]

"The big advantage of this martial law is that if there's an agitator around you can just stick him in jail and keep him there," Davis remarked to a reporter from the *Nation*. "He is not only judge and jury," noted the journalist, "he is law-maker besides." Davis could define any activity he wished as a violation of the governor's martial law proclamation, and he could then determine how each offender would be punished. "He claps people into jail and lets them out when he pleases," the reporter observed. "Charges are regarded as superfluous and even the delay and bother of trial by courts martial have been dispensed with." UMWA people called Davis the "Emperor of the Tug" because his rule was "absolute and supreme." However, "ordinary citizens" in Mingo County seemed perfectly content with it because the martial law rules were applied only to union miners.[43]

Chapter 12

There Can Be No Peace in West Virginia

May 30–August 7, 1921

Outraged by the military autocracy Major Davis had imposed in the Williamson minefield, Harold Houston decided to challenge the legality of Governor Morgan's martial law regime in an appeal to the state supreme court. The attorney would base his argument mainly on a case of the arrests of two strike activists, Frank Ingham, an African American community leader, and A. D. Lavinder, the veteran UMWA organizer and socialist agitator.

Frank Ingham had loaded coal in the Mingo mines for fourteen years when the UMWA launched its organizing drive in the spring of 1920. He had become a prominent figure in the community by then, and therefore Ingham had more to risk than others when he decided to join the union. The consequences were immediate. A few days after he took the oath of obligation, Ingham was fired and evicted. After working in Kentucky for a while, Ingham returned to Mingo and pleaded his case to his old mine superintendent. The boss said he respected Ingham as a miner and told him that he could have his old job back, but only if he renounced his oath to the UMWA. The boss declared, "No man would ever poke his head into a drift if he claimed to have a drop of union blood in him."[1]

Before Ingham could make his decision, a law officer arrested him without charges and put him on a train bound for Welch, where he was locked up in the McDowell County jailhouse with other union men who were being held there because the Mingo County lockup was full of strikers and UMWA organizers. When Ingham asked county sheriff William "Bill" Hatfield for permission to call his wife so that she would know he was in jail, the lawman replied, "I am not going to let you out of jail," and then added, "The only message you can get out will be to God . . ."

That night, Ingham tensed as he heard jangling keys and the footfalls of jailers coming his way. Sheriff Hatfield appeared, took Ingham out of his cell and then said to him: "I want to carry you down the road; there is some men down there that want to talk to you." Ingham had spent his life talking to white men and calculating how he could stand up for himself, even under the worst circumstances. He recalled saying calmly and respectfully to the sheriff and his deputies: "Gentlemen, this is a very unusual thing, to take me out of jail and have me make a statement to men down the road. If they want me to make a statement I would prefer to make it here."

While he waited for a reply, a deputy sheriff hit Ingham on the head with an iron club and knocked him down; then two officers dragged him out of the jail and threw him into an idling automobile. A few miles outside of Welch, the deputies pulled Ingham out of the car and beat him on the head with iron clubs until they thought he was dead. Through the whole ordeal, Ingham remained conscious, but he played dead and prayed. "I believe that God heard me," he said later, "and that he answered my prayer . . ." After his assailants drove away, Ingham gathered his strength, lifted himself up, and limped off toward a railroad coaling station, where a locomotive engineer and a fireman were tending their engine. The railroaders, both white union men, picked Ingham up and took him home to Williamson.

Ingham then joined the other strikers in the Lick Creek tent colony, where he worked for the UMWA distributing supplies to the refugees. Before long, Ingham was arrested again by police officers who suspected him of leading men out of the Lick Creek tent camp to cause some kind of trouble. When Ingham's wife, the principal of the local "colored school," visited Major Davis with some relatives and asked for permission to see her husband, he told her the "next nigger" who asked about this prisoner would be jailed as well.[2]

A. D. Lavinder had been sitting in a Williamson ice cream parlor when several state police officers burst in and told him that Major Davis wanted to see him. Having survived years of dangerous living as a socialist and a union organizer in Fayette County, and having lived through a brutal beating at the hands of Baldwin-Felts agents Troy and Tennis Hatfield, Lavinder was not intimidated by the constables. "If the adjutant general wants to see me," he told them, "he can come to union headquarters." The officers ignored this impertinent reply and pulled Lavinder up to his feet, frisked him, took away his handgun, and charged him with carrying a firearm in violation of the governor's martial law proclamation. The constables then sent their prisoner to the McDowell County jailhouse in Welch, where Lavinder remained imprisoned

The Lick Creek tent colony in Mingo County.

until UMWA lawyers tracked him down the next day and filed a habeas corpus petition for his release.

While Houston prepared his appeal to the state supreme court, Major Davis's men continued to arrest miners in Mingo County and hold them without charges. Although these officers manned one of the most repressive regimes ever imposed on a group of American citizens, they were frustrated because, like a foreign army occupying hostile territory, they found it difficult to drive union forces out of the mountain terrain local miners and their supporters knew so well.

When strikers and their allies attacked the Big Splint mine on May 16, Major Davis rushed units to the scene, but by the time they arrived, a militiaman and a state policeman had already been slain. Officers killed one sniper and crossed the river to capture another; they took him back to West Virginia without bothering to seek extradition. "We did not know the State lines down there and we did not care," one constable told the press. "[The prisoner] was lucky to get into the lock-up alive." It was reported that this miner was one of many men who resided in the tent camps created by the UMWA, places of refuge that the authorities "regarded as perhaps the chief obstacle to the maintenance of peace in the Mingo coalfields." Although Davis's men kept close watch on these settlements, it was possible for miners to slip away at night, wade across the Tug, and fire on the collieries from rifle nests in the Kentucky hills.[3]

The day after the killings at Big Splint, Major Davis and the head of the Williamson Coal Operators' Association met with Governor Morgan in Charleston and asked him to approve "a tightening of the reins by military authorities." What Davis had in mind, according to one historian, "was expelling the union families from the tent colonies, commandeering their tents, and resettling the erstwhile occupants in new camps under military control, at what he considered a safe distance from the strike zone and the refuge of the Kentucky border."[4]

For the time being, however, the strikers continued to move in and out of their camps under close watch by the authorities. On the morning of May 30, 1921, lawmen paid little attention when a few unarmed miners and their wives left Mingo County's refugee colonies and crossed to the Kentucky side of the river carrying flowers in their hands. It was Decoration Day, the occasion when Americans traditionally garnished the graves of the Civil War dead with spring bouquets. But on this day, the mourners went to lay garlands at the graves of the union miners who had fallen in the Three Days Battle.[5]

A few miles away in Williamson, Major Davis sat triumphantly on a reviewing stand as a huge parade passed. Captain Brockus headed the line, followed by units of the Kentucky State Militia, state constables in snappy new uniforms, hundreds of civilian special police, and coal company guards attired in hats and business suits. Earlier that day citizens had gathered at the Fairview Cemetery to decorate the graves of Williamson boys who had died in combat in America's wars and to listen to Memorial Day elegies. For decades these orators had used the occasion to grieve over the thousands of lives lost in the War Between the States. After World War I, however, the crushing memory of the Civil War dead had faded, and Memorial Day orators referred less to the young men lost in battle and more to the values the Great War had elevated: an unquestioning loyalty to the government, a new pride in America's military might, and a profound determination to restore law and order to a nation traumatized by the Red Scare. These sentiments weighed heavy on patriotic citizens of Williamson, West Virginia, that Decoration Day.[6]

As Major Davis reviewed his forces that day, he had good reason to believe that the mine war in Mingo County was over. He and his men had suppressed every form of union activity and had bottled up the strikers in closely watched camps. News of events in Bloody Mingo had faded from the headlines, and members of Congress had shown no interest in investigating the major's use of martial law in the Williamson field; but then on June 5 a sequence of events began to unfold that would once again attract attention from journalists and from an important United States Senator.

That day, some of the strikers at the Lick Creek camp saw a car speeding toward their settlement; they feared the auto might be full of vigilantes. A few of the camp guards fired warning shots and the driver, who was apparently lost, made a dusty U-turn and

State police officers and a companion dressed up for a ceremonial occasion in Mingo County, 1920.

sped away. When Captain Brockus heard about this incident, he decided to move on the camp in force; a few hours later he roared into Lick Creek camp with a detail of state troopers who arrested forty miners. Nine days later, Brockus decided to return with Major Davis and arrest one of the strikers who had escaped the first time around. As the officers approached the tent colony, the miner in question appeared outside the camp and brazenly fired a pistol at their car; snipers hidden in the woods opened fire as well. The major told his police officers to strafe the hillside with their Thompson submachine guns, then, humiliated and outraged, ordered them to flee the area.

When he returned to Williamson, Major Davis mustered up a much larger force of state police constables and vigilantes that roared out of town in a caravan of twenty automobiles. When Davis's men reached Lick Creek, some troopers blocked escape routes from the camp, and another body of men climbed to the top of the ridge and began sweeping down the hill. As they moved through the woods, Davis's men came under fire. According to affidavits signed by two strikers, a state trooper named James A. Bowles shot and killed a miner named Arthur Breedlove after he stepped out from behind a tree with hands held up. One of these witnesses reported that Bowles shouted at Breedlove: "Hold up your hands, God damn you, and if you have anything to say, say it fast." When the terrified prisoner murmured, "Lord have mercy," the trooper shot the miner and killed him.[7]

When the gun battle ended, Captain Brockus ordered his officers to search the camp. "They broke into tents where they had doors . . . and where no doors existed they cut their way in," said camp resident William Ball. "They then proceeded to cut the tents all to pieces; break up the furniture . . . dishes, trunks, rifle drawers, and destroy feed and clothing." Ball reported that the raiders poured coal oil in his flour, cut up his army uniform, and stole a Victory medal he had earned for serving in France and his American Legion badge, along with $65 in cash he held as treasurer of his fraternal lodge. Then, according to Ball's affidavit, "They rounded up 56 of us, and after they had destroyed everything we had we drove us at the point of their rifles down through the city of Williamson and put us in the city lockup." The prisoners stood through the night in a twenty-by-forty-foot cell in water polluted with human waste from clogged toilets. Two days later, all but four were released.[8]

News of the raid on the Lick Creek colony and the death of Arthur Breedlove aroused angry protests in the unionized coalfields. A crowd of a thousand people gathered at one town on Cabin Creek, where speakers warned of another impending massacre like the one that had occurred on Stanaford Mountain in 1903. The assembly then approved a resolution that read: "We wish to let the brothers of Mingo County know that . . . we are with them to a man and ready to assist them in any way."[9] At least twenty-six men had died in the Williamson minefield since the gunfight at Matewan Station erupted on May 19, 1920, but Breedlove's death came to mean much more than the others.[10]

★   ★   ★

A few days later, the West Virginia Supreme Court ruled on Harold Houston's challenge to the martial law regime in Mingo County. In a surprise ruling, the justices decided that a governor could not "by a mere order convert the civil officers into an army and clothe them with military powers." Only in cases of actual warfare, said the court, could a governor "set aside the civil laws and rule by his practically unrestrained will." To do so in peacetime smacked of the despotism exercised by "unrestrained monarchial government." Military rule could be imposed upon civilians only if the National Guard or the federal army enforced it. On these grounds, the court declared Governor Morgan's martial law proclamation null and void.[11]

Houston had achieved a stunning legal victory and Frank Keeney suddenly had a reason to hope that his union organizers would be released from jail and that the struggle to organize the mines in Mingo could resume. The Lick Creek raid and the supreme court decision finally provoked a response on Capitol Hill. Senator Hiram Johnson, a maverick Republican from California with close ties to organized labor, had called for a government inquiry four days after Governor Morgan declared martial law, but at that point only a handful of senators showed any interest. But Captain Brockus's raid on Lick Creek outraged Johnson and led him to renew his call for a federal investigation. In an indignant speech delivered on the Senate floor, Johnson denounced the tactics used by Davis, Brockus, and the troopers; they brought to mind, he said, those used by British troops against the Republicans in Ireland. If the stories Johnson had heard from southern West Virginia were accurate, he would have to conclude that there had never been "in our history . . . anything like the conditions that obtain to-day in this territory at our very doors."[12]

The Senate approved Johnson's call for an investigation of the crisis in Mingo County and appointed a subcommittee that would be chaired by Senator William Squire Kenyon, the same man who headed the investigation of the first mine war and wrote the report that identified corporate greed as the underlying cause of the conflict. Suddenly, the field of forces seemed to be shifting in the union's favor.

But before union partisans could celebrate the good news from Washington, the UMWA suffered a crippling setback when Governor

Ephraim Morgan and his attorney general issued a new martial law proclamation designed to overcome the state supreme court's objections. "Military justice" in Mingo County would now be enforced by more than a hundred residents who had been hastily enrolled in a unit of the reactivated National Guard. These instant militiamen would be empowered to arrest miners for any kind of violation of martial law and to hold them without charges, without access to legal counsel, and without the possibility of bail.

Once he regained his old powers, Major Thomas Davis decided to remove the last vestige of the UMWA presence in his district. He ordered his officers to raid the union's office at Williamson, where twelve union officials, some of them from out of state, were meeting to distribute food to strikers.[13] The staffers were charged with unlawful assembly, arrested, denied bail, and sent to Welch in McDowell County, where they were held for several days without benefit of counsel. The UMWA officials who were from out of state were released only after they promised to leave West Virginia and never return.[14]

By this time, events in what the press called "Bloody Mingo" had drawn national attention to the workers locked out of their jobs, hungry children living in tents, mine tipples dynamited by saboteurs, law officers shot from ambush, and citizens being arrested and held without charges or the hope of jury trials. Roger Baldwin's efforts to make conditions in West Virginia "known all over the United States" had met with limited success.[15] But one of Baldwin's allies, a journalist and a civil libertarian, did make the cold war in coal country known far and wide when he published a series of newspaper articles and a widely read booklet in which he explained why "West Virginia is today in a state of civil war."[16]

Known for exposing miserable conditions in federal prisons, Winthrop D. Lane had been sent by the *New York Evening Post* to report on conditions in southern West Virginia. At the same time, Lane fed information to Baldwin and the ACLU. Both sides in the struggle were heavily armed, the journalist noted, and there had been numerous skirmishes, assassinations, and bombings. This conflict had not yet taken the shape of an actual war "being fought by armies in the field, led by military commanders," but it betrayed many characteristics of a civil war in which families and communities were bitterly divided. This cold war was being carried on by other means as well. While the union appealed to the liberal press and to the progressives in Congress, the coal industry waged war on the UMWA "in the courts, through the power to withhold jobs, through ownership of men's homes, through the control of local government." Both sides were determined to win, Lane explained. "There is no prospect of a peaceful solution."

The mine war was a product of clashing economic interests and conflicting ideas of freedom, but it was also the product of men with aggressive personalities. In this cast of belligerent actors, no one's personality mattered more, Lane observed, than that of Frank Keeney, for he embodied everything the operators distrusted about unionism and everything the miners wanted in an aggressive leader. "There is a suggestion of the tiger in Keeney's personality. He seems always ready to spring . . . He is constantly trying to figure out your next move while you talk to him," Lane remarked. "A vehement nature seems gathering itself to reply; you feel in danger of being seized and torn. Keeney is direct rather than subtle. His speech, like his manner, is impetuous. Words roll out of his mouth in torrents . . ."

"I haven't left the class I was born into yet," Keeney declared, "and I hope I never will." He said that people called him a radical and he would not deny that he was, but who, he asked, made him a radical? "I've seen the time when I didn't have the right to eat in this State," he replied in answer to his own question. "I've seen the time when I was refused a job. I've been served with eviction papers and thrown out of my house. I've seen women and children brutally treated in mining camps. I've seen hell turned loose." No one had called Keeney a radical during the Great War, when he asked his union miners to waive their rights and produce all the coal they could. "Now they call me a radical because I insist on holding what the miners in this State have gained."

"I am a native West Virginian," Keeney declared. "There are others like me working in the mines here. We don't propose to get out of the way when a lot of capitalists from New York and London come down here and tell us to get off the earth. They played that game on the American Indian. They gave him the end of a log to sit on and then pushed him off that. We don't propose to be pushed off." If Keeney failed to organize the miners in Mingo County, someone would; West Virginia, he promised, "will be organized and it will be organized completely."

Lane's booklet appeared just a month before the Senate subcommittee opened its hearings, and Keeney had to be pleased with the questions it raised about the struggle in coal country. This was not an ordinary strike over wages, not simply a conflict between men with warlike personalities. A "fundamental question of democracy" lay at the root of the conflict, wrote Lane.[17] In an introduction to the pamphlet, the nation's preeminent labor economist, John R. Commons, noted that Lane's report on the "civil war" in West Virginia made "plain the issue that faces the nation." When a majority of Supreme Court justices validated the Hitchman Coal and Coke Company's restrictive contracts, the jurists had in effect made nonviolent attempts at persuasion by a labor union as illegal as violent methods of coercion. The high court's decision raised "a great issue of public policy" for the Congress to decide, wrote Professor Commons: Should employers be allowed to organize in their associations and, at the same time, be permitted to deny their employees the same right?[18]

Keeney hoped the Senate would take up that question when Senator Kenyon's subcommittee convened its hearings in Washington on July 18, but the coal operators believed they could use the investigation to turn Congress and the public against the miners' union and its leaders. Colonel Vinson of the Williamson Coal Operators' Association opened the proceedings with a long statement in which he described what he called a "reign of terror" brought down on Mingo County by the UMWA. Union forces, he charged, had murdered more than two dozen men, including five law officers. He also claimed that some of the victims had been shot in the back by gunmen imported from neighboring states.[19]

The studious and articulate Mooney was prepared to testify at length about the constitutional abuses his members suffered when they were denied all of their rights under the First, Fourth, and Sixth Amendments. Much to Mooney's dismay, however, the senators seemed less interested in knowing whether workers' civil liberties had been abused than they were in hearing his replies to the questions a coal industry lawyer asked about whether the UMWA was responsible for the bloodshed in Mingo County, and whether the union intended to impose a closed shop in the mines that would mandate union membership for all miners.[20]

After Mooney was dismissed, industry lawyers trained their sights on their main target, Frank Keeney, who replied to their questions coolly and curtly. When one attorney asked Keeney if his organization had a policy of defending any union member against any crime he was accused of committing during a labor conflict, he replied that the union had "the same right to protect our members as the coal operators have to protect the Baldwin guards . . . when they were charged with murder . . ." Keeney not only avoided a trap, but he had affirmed his Americanism, insisting that a miner, like any citizen, was presumed innocent until proven guilty.[21]

Keeney, a man of words, could match wits with his interrogators, but Sid Hatfield, a man of action, answered hostile questions laconically in a barely audible voice. He showed no chagrin when attorneys reminded him of the several criminal charges still hanging over his head, but Hatfield was caught by surprise when he was informed that he would be charged with blowing up a tipple at Mohawk and that he would stand trial for this offense in the McDowell County seat at Welch, where Frank Ingham had been dragged from jail, beaten, and left for dead.

Keeney, Mooney, and their friends left Washington feeling disappointed. The union's witnesses had failed to arouse much indignation among progressive senators. Furthermore, UMWA leaders had now exhausted all avenues citizens normally used to redress their grievances, and yet thirty union organizers still languished in the Mingo County jail. Scores of families still suffered in besieged tent colonies while hundreds of other miners labored under yellow dog contracts. These people had followed Frank Keeney down what promised to be a road to freedom, but now they were trapped in a valley of despair, and Keeney felt responsible. "By the eternal gods," he vowed, "before I sacrifice them, I will go and fight myself."[22]

★   ★   ★

By the time Sid Hatfield left Washington, he had gained even more celebrity in union circles. Young, brave, and happy-go-lucky, "Two-Gun Sid" could be seen as a real-life version of the wildly popular dime-novel character Deadwood Dick, an outlaw who in one yarn helps a community of Black Hills miners outmaneuver a villain-ous corporation.[23] UMWA officials may have had these images in mind when they commissioned a silent film that would star Hatfield himself. In the movie *Smilin' Sid*, Hatfield is seen pointing two long-barreled Colt revolvers at unseen enemies as he walks stiff-legged through a strikers' tent camp, protecting his people from the vicious intruders. This kind of publicity would have gone to the head of any twenty-eight-year-old, especially a poor, uneducated man born on a little creek deep in Appalachia. It might have even made him feel invincible.[24]

If Sid Hatfield arrived on Capitol Hill feeling cocky, he was in a different mood when the Senate hearings ended. Standing in a hotel lobby, waiting for a ride to the train station, Hatfield told his comrades that if he went to trial in Welch he did not expect to leave Mc-Dowell County alive. Sam Montgomery, Hatfield's legal adviser, shared this anxiety, but he told his client to sur-render peacefully and leave his guns at home. The judge who would preside at the trial had promised Mont-gomery that the defen-dants would be protected by the sheriff of McDowell

Sid Hatfield posing with his pistol.

County, Bill Hatfield, and by the Welch police chief, Harry Chafin. On July 29, these two officers appeared in Matewan, arrested Sid, and took him to Welch.[25]

The next morning, when Sid's wife, Jessie, arrived to post bail for her husband, she was relieved to see that he was still alive. When she left the jail, she visited the sheriff's office, where Bill Hatfield gave his personal assurances that he would allow no trouble at the trial. But later that day, he slipped out of town and traveled to Virginia, where he planned to "take the waters" at Craig Healing Springs.[26]

After spending the night at home, Sid and Jessie Hatfield boarded a train at Matewan Station bound for Welch early on the morning of August 1. They were accompanied by Sid's former deputy and codefendant, Ed Chambers, a wavy-haired twenty-two-year-old who looked even younger than his age; Chambers's wife, Sallie; and Jim Kirkpatrick, a Mingo County deputy sheriff who would act as a bodyguard. The train moved slowly along the Tug on the three-hour journey through the coal towns of War Eagle, Panther, and Mohawk, where fierce battles had raged during the previous year.

Ed Chambers.

Soon after the Matewan party checked into a Welch hotel, Hatfield's defense lawyer, C. J. Van Fleet, arrived with the cheerful news that the presiding judge had agreed to order a new venue for the trial. All the defendants had to do was appear briefly before the bench and hear the judge's order; then they could return to

Matewan on the afternoon train. With this news Hatfield decided to heed his lawyer's advice and leave his guns in the hotel room.[27]

At 10:30 A.M., the Hatfield-Chambers party left their hotel in what seemed to observers like a happy mood. Young Ed Chambers led the way as they crossed Wyoming Street, which was clogged with witnesses and spectators headed to the courthouse for the highly publicized trial. As the defendants and their wives approached the stairs leading up to the building, they saw several men standing eight feet above them on the lawn. The sun was at their backs and their faces were dark, but Jessie Hatfield recognized one of them. It was Charles Lively, the secret Baldwin-Felts agent, who had befriended Sid Hatfield and then testified against him when Hatfield and his deputies were tried for murdering Albert Felts.

When Hatfield and his wife reached the first landing, he turned, waved, and shouted a cheery greeting to another group of defendants on the street below, giving them a grin. Before he could drop his hand, the air erupted with pistol fire from the guns of Lively and two other men standing next to him above the stairwell. Lively's first shot winged Hatfield in the arm. The second one found his breast, and Hatfield twisted around, took two more shots in the back, and dropped dead on the courthouse steps.

Ed Chambers had fallen down to the middle landing after being hit in the initial burst of gunfire. "My husband, he rolled back down the steps," Sallie Chambers later testified before a Senate committee, "and I looked down this way and I seen him rolling down and blood gushing from his neck, and I just went back down the steps after him, you see, and they kept on shooting him . . . in the back all the time after he fell."[28]

"SID HATFIELD SLAIN BEFORE COURT HOUSE," read a *New York Times* headline the next morning side by side with news that the great tenor Enrico Caruso had died. According to the reporter in Welch, local authorities blamed the victims saying that Hatfield had vowed to "get Charlie Lively" for being a spy, and that he drew his gun and fired at the detective as soon as he reached the courthouse steps. The McDowell County deputies who investigated the scene told reporters they found a revolver on Hatfield's body with all six bullets fired and that Ed Chambers had also fired two shots from his gun.[29]

On August 3, undertakers put the caskets of Sid Hatfield and Ed Chambers on a train that would take their bodies back to Matewan, where two thousand people crowded around the N&W station to watch. Many of them were striking coal miners who had come down from the tent camps to see their dead heroes return. For hours, miners, townsfolk, and mountaineers filed silently through the parlor of Sid and Jessie Hatfield's house, paying their respects to their police chief. After leaving the Hatfield home, the mourners quickly scattered, because Major Davis had forbidden congregations of more than two people in Mingo County.[30]

By this time, Jessie Hatfield, Sallie Chambers, and Sid's lawyer, C. J. Van Fleet, had told reporters their story of what happened on the courthouse steps. The widows swore that their young husbands had arrived at the courthouse unarmed and were assassinated. The two men were, according to their attorney, "ambushed while peacefully on their way to a court of justice, and murdered in cold blood . . ." Later, when the McDowell County prosecuting attorney examined the affidavits taken from eyewitnesses, he would corroborate Van Fleet's version of the shooting.

On August 4, scores of state police officers stood on alert as twenty-five hundred people flooded into Matewan for Hatfield and Chambers's funeral. The rowdy river town "was never quieter in its history than today," wrote a Wheeling reporter; indeed, he thought the place was too quiet. There was "no talking, no laughter, no congregation of any sort." People were passing their time waiting for the funeral, but they seemed to be waiting for something else, "they knew not what." But this journalist saw signs of trouble ahead in "the cold, hard eyes and the grim set mouths of hundreds of men." Walking down the streets of Matewan that day and seeing these people was the most impressive experience this journalist had ever had. "The deep feeling evident in every individual was so apparent, it could veritably be tasted."

Pallbearers carried the remains of Sid Hatfield and Ed Chambers in massive metal caskets in a funeral procession down Mate Street, over the suspension bridge spanning the Tug River, and to a cemetery in Kentucky, not far from Blackberry Creek, where Hatfield was born. "The strong wire structure swayed and waved beneath the crowds that hurried across in front of the funeral march," wrote one reporter, and "it sagged beneath the weight of the caskets as they were born across it one at a time."

The pallbearers strained as they climbed the steep muddy hillside to the graveyard, where almost three thousand people listened to a eulogy delivered by Sam Montgomery. The attorney mourned these two young men who had been murdered for opposing the Baldwin-Felts Detective Agency and their employers: "Sleek, dignified church-going gentlemen who would rather pay fabulous sums to their hired gunmen to kill and slay men for joining a union than to pay [a bit more] to the men who delve into the subterranean depths of the earth and produce their wealth for them." When another cloudburst soaked the mourners, the speaker paused, looked up, and observed that "even the heavens" were weeping with grief for the bereaved wives and friends of "these two boys." There would be no peace in West Virginia, Montgomery concluded, until the state removed the private detectives and the deputy sheriffs who enforced laws made by the great corporations who owned the mines and the men who toiled in them.[31]

On the day Sid Hatfield and Ed Chambers were buried, the *New York Times* published an editorial on their deaths entitled "THE PRIMITIVE MOUNTAINEER." In the Tug River region of West Virginia, it began, "they carry on clan feuds in ancient way." In a county seat, two defendants had been brazenly assassinated before a courthouse on their way to stand trial. This outrageous crime had not, however, aroused the "neurotic excitement" it would have caused in communities of "ordinary heredity," the *Times* remarked. On the surface, these mountain people seemed a "good-natured folk, simple, religious, or least given to religious observances, and a little careless with firearms." But the "primitive ferocities" let loose by the coal mine war should serve as reminder that these people were "of an inheritance and habit apart" from the rest of America. "Only slow Time can cure them," the editorial concluded, but in the meantime, shootings like the ones in Matewan and Welch were usefully "killing off their most active specimens."[32]

Many other Americans shared this view of the "primitive mountaineer." It was a stereotype that led some observers to believe that the West Virginia mine wars were not "a consequence of exploitation and impoverishment," as historian Altina Waller put it, but a product of a violent "Appalachian culture," that had been evidenced in the brutal Hatfield-McCoy feud. When northerners and easterners portrayed mountaineers as "primitive folk" isolated from the civilizing effects of modern society, it was easier for them to justify the interventions of modern Americans, who arrived to "discover" these "peculiar people," to convert these "Holy Rollers" to mainstream Christian churches, and to modernize their "backward" communities through commercial and industrial development.[33] In fact, the Hatfield-McCoy feud, which had ended nearly three decades earlier, had little bearing on the behavior of twentieth-century mountaineers caught up in West Virginia's industrial revolution and the new grudges it produced.

Of course, West Virginians could not escape all the lingering effects of their troubled history. During the Civil War, when the western counties of Virginia became a free state, an "inner war" erupted as irregular forces from both sides attacked civilians, leaving a legacy of bitterness and hatred festering in the hills. Other aspects of the state's development also fostered gun violence as a means of settling disputes. Weak and corrupt law enforcement and judicial systems failed to defuse or resolve issues before disputants took the law into their own hands. A spoils system in county government raised the stakes in local elections and provoked regular skirmishes between party factions. And, like their neighbors in other parts of the Mountain South, West Virginians resisted federal revenue agents who attempted to collect taxes on mountain distillers.[34]

Moreover, the extremely rapid development of the state's extractive industries, especially mining, created raw frontier settlements far removed from civil authority. In these rough places lethal violence was commonplace, whether men died in roof falls or explosions, coal camp brawls or skirmishes on the picket lines. It is not surprising, therefore, that the mountain states of Appalachia recorded "an extremely high ratio of homicides to population, even when compared with the rest of the South," notes the historian John Alexander Williams. Most observers misinterpreted the problem, however, because they ignored the "social dimensions" of the region's violent history and concluded instead that "there was something inescapably 'savage' about the culture of Appalachian mountaineers."[35]

Union members reacted with grief and fury to the assassinations of Hatfield and Chambers, but no one attempted to avenge their deaths; instead workers vented their rage with angry words and threatening resolutions. "Never in the history of the country," declared the *United Mine Workers Journal*, "did a cold-blooded murder ever create as much indignation as the double murder of Sid Hatfield and Ed Chambers . . ."[36] An expansive claim to be sure, but it may well have been true as far as half a million American coal miners were concerned.

With cries for revenge ringing in his ears, Frank Keeney puzzled over how to respond to the assassinations in Welch. On the one hand, the murders gave the nation a gory illustration of the case the UMWA had been making against the Baldwin-Felts Agency and its coal company clients. The assassinations also gave the union movement two young martyrs. But Keeney didn't want any more of his followers gunned down; so, he decided to postpone a massive civil disobedience campaign he had planned to launch in Mingo County. "My men are willing to go to jail," he said, "but I am not willing to have them killed."[37]

Keeney and Harold Houston believed the union cause would best be served with a cooling-off period to see if justice would somehow prevail. Perhaps the outrageous murders in Welch would finally force Governor Morgan and the Republicans to banish the Baldwin-Felts Agency from the coalfields forever. But Mother Jones would have none of it. The agency's criminal act must be answered, she insisted, especially in light of the fact that the governor had refused to mention, let along condemn, the murders of Hatfield and Chambers.

When she arrived in Charleston, Jones urged Keeney and Mooney to mount a public protest. The two officers agreed to hold an "indignation rally" on Sunday, August 7, at the state fairgrounds near the governor's private residence. They also agreed to go with Jones and make an urgent appeal to the governor. In the meeting that ensued, Jones and the two UMWA officers called for a joint labor-management commission to mediate disputes and negotiate wages, and they urged the governor to finally abolish the mine guard system, fulfilling a pledge the Republican Party had made in 1920 but had failed to keep. There was still time, the visitors argued, for Morgan to make good on that promise and save the state from another spasm of violence.[38]

Chapter 13

Gather Across the River

August 9–August 25, 1921

A s sun baked the coalfields, and union members waited for the
governor's response, Frank Keeney, Fred Mooney, and Harold
Houston prepared for the worst. On August 9, Houston sent a letter
to a UMWA local officer in Blair, the last outpost on the frontier of
union territory. The lawyer asked the secretary of the local's burial
fund to appropriate at least $600 to "purchase the necessary equip-
ment for the Mingo enterprise," meaning, no doubt, another armed
march on company territory. The crusade could not fail this time,
Houston declared. "The boys need guns, etc. Act at once. You can't
trust the bearer of this note. Destroy it as soon as read." A few days
later, reports reached Sheriff Don Chafin indicating that armed miners were patrolling the roads leading from Boone County into Logan
County.[1]

Chafin's chief deputy, John Gore, who had worked as a UMWA
miner in this area, knew that union locals on the county line were
led by angry militants who had been spoiling for a fight. Based on
Gore's report, Chafin requested a detachment of state police to rein-
force his army of deputies and when the troopers arrived in Logan,
he asked their captain to investigate reports of an impending assault
by union forces.[2]

On August 12, five state police officers left town on horseback, rode up the Dingess Run watershed over Blair Mountain, and into Clothier, a union mining community on the Boone County line. As they galloped into the village, one of the riders crashed into an open car, injuring the driver as well as his own horse. The troopers interrogated the motorist "pretty roughly," according to an eyewitness who said the constables "were young and untried boys, loose-mouthed," and they "bragged a good deal of" what they had done to rout the UMWA in Mingo County. The troopers demanded to know if the driver was a union man or a union sympathizer, "which was like shaking a red flag to a bull in that particular locality," stated a local mine manager who overheard the conversation.[3]

After his release, the aggrieved civilian walked home and told his neighbors what had happened, embellishing his story by claiming that fifty or more constables had burst into town searching homes and abusing women and children.

These rumors circulated through Blair and other coal camps along the Spruce Fork River, and within hours a band of armed miners formed along the river and marched into Clothier looking for the constables. When the volunteers approached the town, they saw a car they mistook for a police vehicle and fired at the auto. The driver sped away over the mountain ridge to Logan, where he reported the incident to Don Chafin, who immediately sent a squad of heavily armed troopers back over the mountain to arrest the shooters. But as soon as the sheriff's posse entered Clothier, union supporters surrounded the police car, disarmed the constables, cursed them, and sent them back to Logan unharmed. After giving the state police a "slap in the face," the miners, who expected more raids to come, cut telephone and telegraph lines and beefed up patrols along the roads leading to the union mining towns. Though he was infuriated by these events, Sheriff Chafin ordered no more raids on union country that week; he vowed, however, that one day he would make those redneck miners pay for humiliating the state police he had sent into harm's way.

On August 17, Governor Morgan rejected all the suggestions union leaders had proposed as ways of averting an all-out war. He would not lift martial law or release the union organizers jailed in Mingo

County. He would not take any action against the Baldwin-Felts Agency, nor would he offer any comment on the murders of Hatfield and Chambers or on the fact that the accused assassin, Charles Lively, had been freed on bail. Furthermore, Morgan refused to create the joint commission with labor and management representatives Keeney had suggested because to do so would give the UMWA official recognition, a status the coal operators vehemently opposed. Finally, Morgan absolved the mine owners, the state troopers, and the private guards of any wrongdoing; all the trouble in Mingo County, he insisted, had been caused by agitators who did not reside in the coalfields of southern West Virginia.[4]

A few hours after the governor's announcement, Savoy Holt, a young miner from Cabin Creek, rode up and down the Kanawha Valley calling out union men. Groups of workers in their dirty overalls gathered along the railroad tracks in towns like Ward, Eskdale, Mucklow, and Mount Carbon to listen as Holt read a letter from Frank Keeney. In it the president of District 17 vowed that his union would spend every dollar it had, and spill blood if it had to, in an effort to liberate its imprisoned members in Mingo County. At Boomer, a mine superintendent listened as Holt "told the men about the outrages in Mingo County and how the state had taken over the country; that the miners had gone to Eph Morgan and asked that martial law be revoked, but he had refused to do it." Now, Holt declared, it was "up to them." They would soon be told of the place and time to assemble and prepare for action. "If you are men," he concluded, "you will be there, prepared as instructed."[5]

At Ward on Kellys Creek, where Mother Jones had first preached the union gospel in 1901, Holt called upon seven hundred men to "gather across the river" at Marmet to prepare for another march on Mingo County. The local immediately voted to donate $1,500 to buy supplies for the campaign, and individual members contributed their own money to match that amount. After Holt left, a group of black workers met and listened as their leader told them that if the white men had gotten out their guns, the "black men should not be backward; they ought to get guns too." Within hours, more than two hundred men dressed in overalls marched down Kellys Creek, crossed the Big Kanawha, and headed downriver toward Marmet.[6]

When Governor Morgan learned that the miners were on the move that evening, he may have wondered why a group of men with jobs, homes, and families would risk everything they had to take up arms and come to the aid of strangers who lived halfway across the state. It would have been difficult for a conservative, self-made man like Morgan, an apostle of individualism, to understand why thousands of miners would behave so irrationally. He apparently could not imagine how these union miners felt when two of their defenders were murdered on the steps of a courthouse as they stood next to their wives, or how they felt when people just like them were confined in tent camps like refugees, arrested without charges, and deprived of their rights to free speech, but he was about to find out.

Three days after Governor Morgan turned down the union's demands, six hundred miners had gathered in Lens Creek Hollow, a mile from Marmet and just ten miles from the state capital. These men were the advance guard of an army that would form during the next four days when "coal mining in central West Virginia stopped" as a result of an extraordinary general strike. "Miners with rifles, by the thousand, poured into Marmet, some riding on the tops of passenger trains," wrote one of the first reporters on the scene. At the camp, armed men searched cars for liquor and allowed peddlers and salesmen to make their way through the encampment only if they secured permission from a "committee," a body that "seemed to hold the destinies of the gathering in its hands."[7]

Keeney and Mooney left Charleston on the day the miners began to move toward Marmet. When they returned from a visit to the Fairmont field, Keeney gave a misleading interview to the *New York Times*. "I wash my hands of the whole affair," he remarked, implying that the marchers were beyond his control. Keeney said that he had interfered with such an "enterprise" in 1919 but he would not do so now. "This time," he declared, "they can march to Mingo, so far as I am concerned."[8]

On August 22, Heber Blankenhorn, a reporter for the *Nation*, ventured up Lens Creek where he encountered "a cordon of 100 armed men . . . stretched across the dirt road, the mine railroad, and the creek, barring out officers of the law, reporters, all inquirers." He watched as some miners fired hundreds of shots at a snooping airplane. He could see, at a glance, that the men were white "mountaineers" and "a quarter [were] Negroes." They were wearing blue overalls or parts of khaki uniforms, with red bandannas around their necks, and they were carrying rifles as casually as mine picks. The workers displayed what Blankenhorn called "the usual mining-town mixture of cordiality and suspicion to strangers," but none of the lassitude he had often observed in these cramped settlements. "Lens Creek Valley," he wrote, "is electric and bustling."[9]

Most of the campers appeared to be young men and all of them belonged to the UMWA, except for a few members of the railroad brotherhoods who ran the coal trains through union country. They were "sober looking, sober speaking" workingmen who told Blankenhorn the same story: They were going to Mingo County to stop the killing of miners in the nonunion fields. "This thing's been brewing a long while," said one man, and it came to a boil when Hatfield and Chambers got "killed in front of their wives" after they had been promised safe conduct. "It was a trap," the miner explained. But, the reporter interjected, those killings had occurred several weeks before. It took a while, the man replied, for the word to get around the camps that they let Hatfield's murderer—"that Baldwin-Felts, Lively"—out on bail while scores of union miners were stuck in Mingo County's jail on no charges at all just because of martial law. Although the assassinations at Welch got the miners' blood boiling, the marchers were not simply out for revenge. They had embarked on a mission to free their brothers imprisoned under Major Davis's military regime.

The journalist Blankenhorn left the camp doubting the miners could actually form ranks and march on enemy territory, but Governor Morgan could not be sure the protestors would disband. The newspapers were full of alarming stories of renegade miners "ravishing the country, robbing passers-by, and threatening death to law officers." And Morgan's office was flooded with messages from Charleston residents who feared an invasion by the marchers and from colliery managers whose operations had been shut down when their workers left to join the march. To make matters worse, a "crime wave" was rolling over Kanawha County as bootleggers, bank robbers, gamblers, and pimps ran wild in Ford motorcars, spreading fear and anxiety. Concerned

Undated photo of armed coal miners in camp.

citizens formed a Law and Order League and invited the governor to address its members. Morgan blamed the trouble on three great evils, "moonshine liquor, pistol-toting, and automobiles." To this evil brew, he added the criminal disorder caused by the insurgent miners who had gathered near the city "for the sole purpose of terrorizing the government of the State."[10]

Governor Morgan and his advisers figured that if the miners marched across the mountains into Logan County and clashed with Chafin's men, the death toll in the fighting would be immense, but Morgan felt crippled. With most of the state's new police force tied up in Mingo County and the state's National Guard still under the control of the U.S. Army, Morgan felt compelled to ask Secretary of War John W. Weeks to send federal troops to West Virginia once again. When the secretary refused this request and sent his intelligence chief to investigate instead, Morgan called Don Chafin and asked him to create a home guard. The sheriff mustered hundreds of local businessmen into service, and told his deputies to scour the coal towns and order the miners to join his defense forces or be fired from their jobs. Within a few days, Chafin would have three thousand well-armed men under his command.

As he searched for a way to disperse the "armed mob" gathering at Marmet, Morgan received a telegram from Mother Jones, who surprised him by asking if she could "be of any assistance in restoring order."[11] The governor invited the storied agitator to come to his office, where he apparently convinced Jones that he had the miners' best interest at heart. She offered to help him by contacting President Harding, whom she had met, and asking him to send her a telegram she could bring to the miners' camp in an effort to dissuade the miners from going to war. After the meeting, Jones sent word to the miners at Lens Creek that she would be coming soon to read them a message from the president. When the miners at the Lens Creek camp heard this, they sent a delegation to Fred Mooney's house in Charleston and asked him to see if Jones had actually been in touch with the White House.[12]

An admirer of Mother Jones since the day she came to Cabin Creek in 1912, Mooney became closer with her when they traveled to Mexico earlier in 1921 to attend the Pan-American Federation of Labor conference. When their train approached Mexico City, he had watched with awe as a group of strikers boarded their car and greeted "Madre Yones," covering her with a blanket of red carnations and blue violets. He was even more impressed when he accompanied her to a reception with President Álvaro Obregón, whom Jones had saved from extradition and certain death when he was imprisoned in Arizona during the Mexican Revolution.[13] Mooney also knew that this famous lady had met with former presidents Taft and Wilson and that she was acquainted with President Harding; it therefore seemed plausible to him that she had actually received a telegram from the White House.

On the afternoon of August 24, Keeney and Mooney motored out to the Lens Creek encampment to see what the old lady had to say. When they arrived, Jones was standing on hillside surrounded by a mass of men wearing denim overalls and holding weapons of every description. She was reading a piece of paper she said she had received as a wire from the president, in which he asked the miners to return to their homes and promised that he would use his good offices to "forever eliminate the gunman system from the state of West Virginia." This sounded suspicious to some of the miners, and several asked their union officers to look at the telegram. When Keeney reached up as if to take the paper out of her hand, Jones stepped away and barked at him. "Go to hell. None of your business."

Then, when Keeney turned and said, "Well boys, that telegram is a fake, [and] so is Mother Jones, [so] we will just move on," he and Jones got "into a right smart controversy," according to one observer. Keeney took control at this point and ordered guards to stop anyone from leaving the camp; then he drove back to Charleston with Mooney to see if a telegram had indeed been sent from the White House.[14]

In the meantime, Jones had stormed out of the camp in a rage. She had been rudely confronted and, in her view, badly insulted by two men she had regarded as her adopted sons. She was, no doubt, sincere in her desire to stop the miners from embarking on what seemed to be a suicidal mission, so sincere that she felt justified lying to them. Jones had assumed that she could easily manipulate her followers with trickery, but Keeney and Mooney were now tough-minded, suspicious men, no longer young lads basking in her aura.[15]

The shock of Frank Keeney's "betrayal" was so severe, Jones wrote later, that she suffered a nervous breakdown and an attack of rheumatism so acute that she was laid low for nearly a year. She had indeed been humiliated by Keeney and Mooney, but Jones was responsible for her own downfall; in her hubris, she had assumed that she knew what was best for her "boys." According to biographer Elliott Gorn, "It was the height of self-delusion on Mother Jones's part to think that Morgan was the miners' friend, yet because they were mixed up in this together, to that delusion she clung."[16]

Jones's twenty-four-year odyssey of "going in and out of West Virginia" had come to an end. She would never again return to visit her favorite sons, Keeney and Mooney, for they had chosen to shake off her guiding hand. She later wrote: "Those young fellows, void of any experience in the great industrial conflicts, were carried away thinking they could change the world over night . . . with guns and bullets."[17]

A few hours after he returned to Charleston, Keeney sent word to his lieutenants at Marmet confirming that the "telegram" from Harding was a fake. Later that evening, an advance unit of six hundred miners broke camp, shouldered arms, and moved out of Lens Creek Hollow, marching south and east toward the Logan County line.

On the morning of August 25, cabin dwellers in the wooded hills of Boone County looked on in wonder as long lines of men that stretched out for twenty miles moved along the creek beds. Those who were close by heard the marchers singing a ditty to the tune of "John Brown's Body," rising with gusto to the chorus, "We'll hang Don Chafin to a sour apple tree." The men in this overalls brigade walked at a slow pace, climbing steep grades and following Lens Creek under the canopies of dense foliage that hung over the stream, shading them from the sweltering summer sun. Heber Blankenhorn, who followed the marchers by car, saw another auto pass him by filled with women wearing white headdresses labeled UMW in big blue letters. "They're wives of some of the boys," a miner explained. "They've had experience nursing. They say they'll see this through."[18]

The marchers hiked past some cabins here and there, but they saw no one until farther on, when some Boone County people came out to greet them, offering drinking water, baked dishes, and vegetables from their gardens. At times, the miners stopped and listened to group leaders instruct them on how to avoid machine-gun fire and how to flank the gun nests and take out gunners with high-powered rifles. Unit commanders also warned defectors that they would be treated like deserters from an army engaged in combat. These were not idle threats. One miner had already been executed for failing to carry out an order to steal guns from a company store.[19]

What began as a mass protest march now took on the menacing look of a war maneuver by more than eight thousand armed citizens under the command of miners with combat experience in the Spanish-American War and in World War I. Many of these veterans wore their "doughboy" army outfits and their rounded battle helmets; some even carried gas masks. In one camp, a decorated Marine Corps marksman and a miner wearing the uniform of a captain in

GATHER ACROSS THE RIVER

the Italian army conducted rifle practice.[20] When reporters on the scene noticed that the volunteers all wore red bandannas around their necks, they began referring to the miners as "red necks."[21]

The miners' march made national news that day, when the *New York Times* featured a front-page story about the "terror" in the mine-fields caused by this mysterious movement of "leaderless" miners. Who gave these men their orders? Who was the general of this army, "which is equal to almost an entire army division?" asked a reporter for the *Charleston Gazette*. "Nobody knows."[22]

Even without a commanding officer, the marchers seemed "well organized, like an army of invasion" divided into "squads, platoons, companies, and battalions." For the next few days, reporters made repeated attempts to find out how such a rapid mobilization of armed civilians could have occurred, but even after "careful inquiry," they could not solve the "mystery" of who had marshaled thousands of marchers strung out along the rough mountain roads of Boone County. In fact, each UMWA local president had mobilized his own members and led them to the camp. From Cabin Creek, Bert Castle, a veteran of the 1912 mine war, led a squad of his members out of Eskdale to Marmet. Ed Reynolds, president of Local 404 from Raleigh County, had recruited three hundred of his men for the march to Mingo, and another local officer had formed a column of eighty miners who had marched out of town after raising $600 for food and $130 to purchase high-powered rifles.[23]

Speaking to curious reporters in their Charleston headquarters, Frank Keeney and Fred Mooney maintained the fiction that the marchers had moved spontaneously without direction from District 17. In truth, Keeney and his associates had mobilized the miners and the march did indeed have a general. Twenty-eight-year-old William Blizzard, Keeney's friend from Eskdale on Cabin Creek, had assumed overall command of the army and had led it through Boone County, where Blizzard served as subdistrict director for the UMWA.[24]

Blizzard had lived and breathed unionism his whole life; his father, Timothy, was a blacklisted UMWA loyalist, and his mother, Sarah, had led women out of Eskdale to tear up the C&O tracks after the Bull Moose Special made its deadly run in 1913. When he was ten years old, Bill became active in the union. During the 1902 strike, his mother would send him out to trap and bring back game for the strikers who camped near the Blizzards' home. Bill Blizzard turned twenty-one during the first mine war, when young men like him picked up their rifles to defend the Eskdale tent camp. During Frank Keeney's rise to power in District 17, Blizzard proved himself a serious union man who refused to drink liquor; he also demonstrated his skill as a leader of union miners in Boone County. Keeney regarded Blizzard as a natural leader, a decisive young man even older miners would follow into battle.[25]

American workers had been organizing unions, demanding their liberty, and invoking the virtue of solidarity for nearly a century, but the nation had never witnessed such a large body of workingmen undertaking a militant action on such a massive scale. The miners' march that summer was a huge general strike as well as a massive political protest against the abuse of civil liberties by private employers and government officials. But this movement of nearly ten thousand armed miners amounted to something even more: By August 25, it had become the largest civil insurrection the country had experienced since the Civil War.

A waning moon cast a dim glow over the hills of Boone County that night as the miners trudged on with the lamps on their caps lighting the way. At 2:30 in the morning they reached a campground that had already been prepared along Indian Creek, near Racine, by an advance party of three hundred volunteers under the command of a former officer of the U.S. Army First Cavalry. At daybreak, a hundred miners crowded into the town's general store, buying some items and stealing others, according to the worried storekeeper who saw one miner holding a hand grenade. Ed Reynolds, who commanded a band of three hundred miners, noticed an idle switch engine on a rail siding with three cars attached. Without hesitation, he climbed aboard and ordered the fireman to shovel coal in the boiler. A few minutes later, Reynolds and his men were rolling down the C&O railway toward Madison, a town near the Logan County line.

Meanwhile, the main body of the miners' army streamed out of Racine and crossed the Big Coal River. After going through the community of Peytona, the volunteers passed Tiger Rock and the falls where Drawdy Creek dropped down, sending white spray over two ledges, and from here the marchers swung south toward Work-man Knob and Logan County.[26] Most of the coal miners march-ing through Boone County came from union strongholds in the Kanawha and New River fields, but the union army gained reinforce-ments from farther away as well. Along the railroad tracks entering Logan County from the north, railroad police observed an encamp-ment of three hundred men from out of state "disguised as hoboes." The men gave no explanation of their presence, stating only that they were "on the move."[27]

At this point, Sheriff Don Chafin knew that an army of at least nine thousand men was advancing toward Logan and was still grow-ing as it moved through Boone County. He called the governor to ask for help, and the governor told the sheriff to do whatever he could to defend the county, while he continued to appeal for federal troops. When he hung up the phone, Chafin ordered the town's fire siren to sound the alarm; this was the warning citizens were told to expect if an invasion were under way. The sheriff then mobilized forty-four of his deputies and opened up the arsenal of weapons he had been stockpiling since the first union invasion threat in 1919. The cache in-cluded ten machine guns, a thousand rifles, and sixty-seven thousand rounds of ammunition. That night, deputy sheriffs and more than four hundred volunteers assembled at the courthouse. While these men received orders to move out and take up defensive positions on the ridge outside of Logan, deputies raced through the nonunion coal camps drafting miners to serve in their defense forces. Chafin also sent out orders to the airport for three biplanes he had rented to fly over Boone County so the pilots could report on the movement of the union troops. The sheriff told the press he was prepared to defend his town of Logan with "every engine of modern warfare."[28]

The Boone County sheriff and his deputies made no attempt to impede the marchers, who had imposed their own form of mar-tial law on the area. Many residents of the mountain region, neigh-bors and kin, welcomed the marchers, but others fled in fear. "At any turn you were liable to butt into a colored man with a high-powered rifle," one mine company official recalled. "I had no idea

Sheriff Don Chafin and his deputies in front of the Logan County Courthouse.

what terrorism could be until that anarchy came . . . without anybody to check it . . . The air was filled with the feeling that if you did not do as you were told . . . something would happen."[29]

On the other side of Blair Mountain that night, cars and trucks filled with deputy sheriffs and volunteers roared out of Logan town and climbed up Dingess Run to take control of the high ground along Spruce Fork Ridge above the encamped miners. By nightfall, Sheriff Chafin had seven hundred armed men guarding strategic gaps and high points along a fifteen-mile defensive line facing the northeast. Deputies and vigilantes cut down trees, dug trenches, and built breastworks of dirt and logs. They concentrated a large force of men at the Crooked Creek gap formed by Hewett Creek, at three points above Ethel Hollow at the origins of Beech Creek, and in between the twin nineteen-hundred-foot peaks of Blair Mountain, where a crude road led upward from Blair, through a gap, and down toward Logan town.[30]

After five months in office, President Warren G. Harding was confronted with an almost unimaginable scenario: two armies of civilians—both filled with veterans of the Great War in Europe—were prepared to engage in mortal combat on American soil just two hundred miles from the nation's capital.

Chapter 14

Time to Lay Down the Bible and Pick Up the Rifle

August 26–September 5, 1921

E arly in the morning of August 26, as thousands of armed miners settled down in their camps, Governor Morgan sent a wire to the White House insisting that only the U.S. Army could prevent a colossal disaster from taking place in his state. During World War I, federal regulars had been deployed frequently to suppress labor strikes that local and state authorities believed to be instigated by radicals and aliens, but by 1921 these violations of the Posse Comitatus Act (the law limiting the use of federal forces to uphold state law) were rousing criticisms from conservatives and liberals alike.[1]

The next morning, President Harding met with his staff and with the secretary of war to discuss Morgan's request. The White House had reasons to distrust West Virginia's public officials, who had already called upon the army several times to restore order and who now had a state police force to keep the peace. Instead of sending in the infantry, Harding ordered Brigadier General Harry H. Bandholtz to go out and investigate the trouble. An illustrious warrior, Bandholtz had earned the Distinguished Service Medal leading U.S. forces in battle against the Germans on the Meuse-Argonne front. If anyone could impress the miners, especially the war veterans among them, it would be this formidable four-star general who had recently served as provost marshal of the U.S. armed forces in France.[2]

On the same day General Bandholtz arrived in the state capital, another World War I hero appeared on the scene, reminding Charlestonians of the exciting days in 1918 when their city was awash with soldiers and preparations for war. A crowd gathered at the city's airfield that afternoon to see Brigadier General William "Billy" Mitchell arrive in an airplane from Langley Field. He emerged wearing a pistol on his hip, four rows of ribbons on his chest, and a pair of spurs on his boots—odd accoutrements for the chief of the air corps. Surrounding Mitchell, reporters asked him how he would handle the miners hunkered down in gullies and hollows. "Gas," General Mitchell replied. "You understand we wouldn't try to kill these people at first. We'd drop tear gas all over the place. If they refused to disperse then we'd open up, with artillery . . . and everything."[3]

When Keeney and Mooney met with Bandholtz that day, the general spoke to them bluntly: "You two are the officers of this organization and these are your people. I am going to give you a chance to save them, and if you cannot turn them back, we are going to snuff this out just like that," he said, snapping his fingers under their noses. "This will never do," the general continued. "There are several million unemployed in this country now and this thing might assume proportions that would be difficult to handle."[4]

The general's words reflected an anxiety that lingered in American minds after the Red Scare abated and even after President Harding entered the White House promising a "return to normalcy." General Bandholtz had reason to worry about the nearly 3 million unemployed men roaming the nation that year, the kind of men who were being recruited by the German Nazis and their new führer, Adolf Hitler, and by new political parties formed that year by Italian Fascists and American Communists, whose cadre dedicated themselves to mobilizing "the masses" for a proletarian revolution.[5]

Although their enemies saw them as dangerous Reds, Keeney and Mooney considered themselves to be zealous patriots, and they promised Bandholtz they would try to stop the march. The general decided to accompany them to the front to ensure that the two union leaders carried out his orders. When the three men reached the town of Madison on the Little Coal River, Keeney sent word out announcing a mass meeting at the local baseball field for that afternoon. There, on a hot and dusty diamond, he urged the miners to go home. "You are no longer dealing with state or county governments," Keeney warned. "You are dealing with the United States, the biggest and most powerful government on earth."[6]

A rowdy debate ensued when some miners denounced Keeney for ordering them to turn back like cowards. Perilously close to losing control of the meeting, Keeney acted swiftly. Rather than risk taking a vote by a show of hands, he called for a voice vote. The loudest shout arose for the motion to disband. A short time later, General Bandholtz left Madison believing his mission had been accomplished.[7]

When Don Chafin learned that the miners had voted to end their march, he told his deputies to send the defenders of Logan County home. Meanwhile, authorities in Charleston dallied; they were supposed to contact the C&O and send special railway cars to Madison to take the miners home. With thousands of armed men still roaming the area, Keeney and Mooney were waiting nervously for the trains to arrive, when they saw a man pedaling up the tracks from the south on a four-wheel velocipede. It was Lewis White, a militant union leader who lived in a coal camp on the Logan County line. "[He] was coatless, and carried two Smith and Wesson revolvers of the latest type," Mooney recalled.

"Bad Lewis" White, as he was known, was born on Hell Creek in Mingo County, according to a miner who called him "kin" but without affection. "A regular son of a bitch he was," said Dewey Browning of his relative, "mean as a snake."[8] When he saw the two UMWA officials on the station platform, White shouted, "What the hell you fellows mean by stopping these marchers?" Mooney remembered replying as coolly as he could that they were trying to prevent their members from being slaughtered, and White barked back at them: "Oh, hell! What you two need is a bullet between each of your eyes!"[9]

White issued this verbal salvo and left the station in a rage, telling the miners hanging around in Madison that Chafin's thugs were killing women and children around Blair. He eventually assembled a dozen militants who hijacked a C&O train and used it to pick up more armed miners as it rolled down toward Blair, where White had already assembled three hundred armed miners. Mooney wrote later that he and Keeney were sure Lewis White was an agent pro- vocateur paid by Don Chafin to incite the union miners into mount- ing a premature invasion. In any case, when the sheriff learned that White and his men had arrived in Blair aboard a hijacked train, he sounded the fire siren in Logan, and by the time dawn broke the next day, nearly a thousand armed defenders were back in position at the mountain gaps along Spruce Fork Ridge.[10]

Besides the men Lewis White carried to Blair on the hijacked train, another corps of three hundred miners arrived that night in a column Ed Reynolds and Bill Blizzard led out of Madison. Both of these men believed that Keeney had delivered his ballpark speech merely to satisfy General Bandholtz and to save the union and its officers from prosecution by the federal government. After the vote was taken and Bandholtz left, Reynolds recalled that Keeney told the marchers they could do as they pleased.[11]

Frank Keeney had practiced this kind of deception in 1919 when he lied to Governor Cornwell. Now, he seemed to be trying to have it both ways again by obeying Bandholtz and saving the union from destruction and, at the same time, allowing a vanguard of armed miners to march out of Madison toward the Logan County line.

That afternoon, miners who camped in and around a Baptist church at Blair met with captains, who prepared them for action and provided them with a password to use when they confronted strangers: "I come creeping." That night, some of these men marched along the C&O railroad line on the Spruce Fork of the Little Coal River, stopping residents and asking them for money to aid the fight, and rousing miners out of bed to ask them to join their band.[12]

Well aware of these developments around Blair, Don Chafin called Major Thomas Davis in Mingo County and asked for help. Davis responded by dispatching Captain Brockus to Logan County with a ninety-man force of deputies and state constables. When the troopers arrived in Logan, an officer told all the defenders to memorize a password to use to tell friend from foe. The secret word was "Amen."

Later that day, Chafin made a fateful decision. He decided to arrest the union miners who had brazenly surrounded and disarmed the deputies and constables he had sent to Clothier two weeks earlier. Late in the afternoon on August 27, Captain Brockus and a detail of state police left Logan and moved over Spruce Fork Ridge and down Beech Creek toward Clothier. Before they arrived, the troopers arrested several groups of mine workers and ordered them to march ahead of the posse as a human shield. A few miles later, Brockus halted his men in the little town of Sharples where he saw five miners standing in front of a boardinghouse holding rifles. When the captain asked them who they were, one of the workers growled, "By God, that is our business." After a moment of silence, one of the deputies broke the tension and shouted out, "We've come after you Goddamn miners." An instant later, gunfire rang out as men shot at each other from point-blank range. Caught in the cross fire, ten of the captive miners ran for cover. Three of them fell in their tracks, two wounded fatally.[13]

After the skirmish ended, Captain Brockus ordered his men to retreat, and the constables and deputy sheriffs moved back up the road toward Blair Mountain with five prisoners in their custody. Brockus and his men spent the whole night trekking over the ridge and through the forest to Ethel, a mine camp on the Logan side of the ridge. When daylight came, the captain took the roll call, and, to his dismay, he found that four of his deputies were missing. These men had lost their way in the dark and had been captured by a patrol of union miners, who paraded them through the coal camps, placed them under guard, and then offered to exchange their hostages for the five union men Captain Brockus had taken back to Logan.[14]

Why did Chafin choose to serve arrest warrants on miners located in an armed camp at a time when "only a fool would not have realized that the decision he made was certain to threaten the shaky truce"? asked the historian Robert Shogan. "Whatever else people might think of Chafin, no one considered him a fool," so there had to be some other reason for the raid.[15] The sheriff would later blame

Captain Brockus for being "very anxious to get hold" of the miners who had disarmed the law officers, but it was Chafin who ordered the arrests that would trigger an explosion of events.

On Sunday, August 28, news of the troopers' raid on Beech Creek flew around the Kanawha and New River coalfields embellished by lurid and inaccurate reports of women and children being assaulted in Logan County. Within hours, union mine workers who had ridden trains back home from Madison picked up their rifles again and headed back toward the front. Observers saw men clinging to commandeered trains they called "miners' specials" that hauled flat cars and boxcars "literally covered with armed men." Each man wore "a red handkerchief about his neck—the badge of a fighting miner," and many wore the "stone faces" of combat veterans.[16]

"Large forces are again leaving the Cabin Creek district tonight . . . ," the *Charleston Gazette* reported, "and have destroyed all communications on that creek." At a company store near Holly Grove—the tent colony site in the first mine war—miners stole a Gatling gun and took it with them to the front. As volunteers moved

Miners on train cars moving through Boone County, August 1921.

across Boone County; other contingents set out from the Winding Gulf field in Raleigh County, and more volunteers arrived from the coalfields of Ohio, Indiana, and Illinois. The miners "went through in Ford cars . . . quite fast, with a very set, determined expression on their faces, trying to get to the end of the road as soon as possible," one observer recalled. By the end of the day, military intelligence officers reported that union forces had gained de facto control of a five-hundred-mile area from the Kanawha River to the Logan County frontier.[17]

The next morning newspapers across the nation carried news of the impending showdown in the minefields. "Two heavily armed forces face each other on the opposite sides of a narrow ridge in West Virginia's hills waiting for the other to move," warned the *Huntington Advertiser*. "The first untoward act will set off a bitter industrial war . . ."[18]

The alarming situation in southern West Virginia provoked comments in many leading newspapers like the venerable *Philadelphia Public Ledger*, which stated in an editorial that "an armed mob is dragging itself over the hills of West Virginia toward bloodstained Mingo County," a place that had become a "national stench and disgrace." The rights and wrongs of the long strike in Mingo County had been lost in a fog of gunsmoke, but "industrial disputes are one thing," noted the *Ledger*, "and armed revolt is another." In any case, this benighted section West Virginia "needed some drastic recivilizing."

Average citizens had difficulty understanding "the habits of life in that engagingly barbarous commonwealth," the *Baltimore Sun* observed. Astonishing tales of battles and sudden deaths had poured out of that troubled place for decades, but West Virginia now seemed to have "outdone herself." An armed body of men had been "calmly allowed to gather in one county with the avowed purpose of ending martial law in another county." Why couldn't West Virginia mind her own business? "Why," asked the *Sun*, "does it allow herself to be the happy hunting ground for sanguinary detective agencies, and even more sanguinary miners . . . ?"[19]

On August 29, Governor Morgan renewed his request for federal troops to prevent open warfare from erupting in Logan County. In a wire to the White House he claimed that Chafin's forces would be

"utterly unable to repel" an invasion by an armed force of coal miners. Once again, President Harding declined the request; instead he
issued an unusual presidential proclamation ordering the insurgents
to disperse by September 1. The commander in chief then ordered
General Bandholtz back to Charleston to ensure that the miners
obeyed his order. If they refused, the general had orders to mobilize
the infantry and suppress all "insurrectionary proceedings."[20]

The union miners marching toward Logan County knew nothing of these discussions in Washington, and, even if they had, it
would not have mattered to them. Their course was now set. They
planned to move out of their camps the next day, take the mountain ridge, storm into Logan, kill Don Chafin, and then march on
Mingo County, where they would free their imprisoned comrades.
No one was going to turn them around this time. A man who lived
on Hewett Creek, just over the Logan County line, saw the miners
coming up the dirt road from the train station at Jeffrey that day; they
marched five or six abreast and carried an array of guns. Most of
them said they had come over from Cabin Creek and Paint Creek.[21]

On the evening of Tuesday, August 30, as campfires glowed
around the little town of Blair, Bill Blizzard and his lieutenants sent
two patrols out to climb up to the ridgeline. One of these units was
led by Red Thompson, a local miner dressed in khaki riding pants
and an army shirt and wearing a wide-brimmed hat. The other
scouting party was headed by an elderly man named John Wilburn,
a Baptist minister and part-time coal miner who lived in Blair with
his wife and eight children. Wilburn had not been active in the union
until he heard about the police raid and the miners who were killed
as a result. That was enough for Reverend Wilburn. "The time has
come," he told his friends, "for me to lay down my Bible and pick up
my rifle and fight for my rights."[22]

After darkness fell, Wilburn led a column of seventy volunteers
that included his two sons up the White Trace Branch toward the
south crest of Blair Mountain. After spending the night in a fireless
camp, Wilburn and four other men set out on a dawn patrol on August 31. A blanket of fog still covered the woods as they moved in and
out of the trees, listening intently for men on the move. When the
men in the patrol heard a gunshot, they headed toward the sound,

and before long they could see through the mist three men in civilian clothes standing together holding rifles. These men were Logan County deputy sheriffs led by John Gore, Chafin's right-hand man.

Wilburn did not recognize the men, so he asked them who they were and if they knew the password. When they replied in unison "Amen," Wilburn and his men opened fire, and all three deputies fell where they stood. After Gore hit the ground, he fired his rifle into the back of Eli Kemp, a black union man in Wilburn's group who had turned to run. Wilburn walked over and finished off Gore with a bullet to the head. Then the preacher led his men back down from the ridge carrying Kemp, whose wounds would later prove to be fatal.[23]

News of these deaths did not appear in the morning papers. Instead the press reported welcome news that an all-out war might yet be avoided because "battle planes [had] roared over Boone County early today, showering down upon the masses of armed miners . . . copies of the proclamation issued by President Harding calling upon them to disperse." It was also reported that leaders of the miners' army had sent word to Chafin, proposing that, if the miners still jailed in Mingo County were released, then the four deputies captured at Clothier would be set free. Chafin offered to call a truce until midnight if the four hostages were returned to Logan, but he said nothing about the miners imprisoned in Mingo. In any case, the rumor of a truce meant no more to the miners camped along the Little Coal River than the copies of President Harding's proclamation littering the forests along Spruce Fork Ridge.[24]

For more than a year, union miners had waged their battles in a variety of ways: guerrilla tactics in the field, legal appeals in the courts, petitions to governors, publicity efforts in the press, and lobbying efforts on Capitol Hill. Indeed, much of what Winthrop Lane had called the "civil war" in West Virginia had been carried out in the press and the courts and in fierce gun battles, but not by "armies in the field." That would change on the afternoon of August 31, 1921.

The temperature had reached 90 degrees when columns of miners moved out of their camps and up toward the mountain gaps along the Spruce Fork Ridge. One column moved out of Blair up toward the mountain gap and a rough road that led down to Logan. That afternoon, when fighting erupted on the slopes of Blair Mountain, the headline in an evening newspaper proclaimed "ACTUAL WAR IS RAGING IN LOGAN."[25]

The gunfire seemed relentless to the residents who risked staying put in the valley. "It would echo and roll around so much . . . ," said one miner, "you would think they was right down in Blair." When the machine guns cracked up on the mountain and rifle barrages erupted, it seemed to him like "the whole place was coming down on you." The local doctor, an army veteran, said he heard about as much shooting that day as he had when American forces assaulted Manila in the Philippines during the Spanish-American War. And some of the miners told reporters how much the fighting on Blair Mountain resembled the furious woodland combat they waged against the Germans in the dense Argonne Forest of France.[26]

Meanwhile, a more effective assault was under way farther north, where miners who had marched from Jeffrey moved up Hewett Creek toward Crooked Creek Gap, where twelve hundred defenders had established positions. The invaders encountered heavy fire on Mill Creek that afternoon from hundreds of rifles and two machine guns. Bert Castle remembered this fighting vividly when he was interviewed fifty years later. A socialist and president of the UMWA local at Sharon Hollow on Cabin Creek, Castle recalled leading eighty of his members up Hewett Creek. They had crossed the Logan County line and moved up Craddock Creek when they suddenly dropped down to avoid heavy machine-gun fire ripping through the trees. "Two boys was killed," said Castle. "Both were just out of the service and had on their uniforms. They thought they'd go up around a machine gun and capture the gunner. Evidently they got in his sights . . . because both of them were killed. One boy was hit six or seven times."[27]

A few hours later, Ed Reynolds and his squad moved past the spot where Castle's men died and up the Craddock Fork of Mill Creek toward the gap at the top of the ridge. Reynolds's men dragged with them a Gatling gun stolen from a company store on Paint Creek. Above them in the gap, three hundred Logan County deputies waited with two of their own machine guns; one of them was operated by Tony Gaujot, the veteran Baldwin-Felts agent who had commanded the guards at Mucklow during the first mine war in 1912. Reynolds ordered his riflemen to flank the defenders and then attack. When the miners got into position, they raked the defensive fort with rifle and machine-gun fire. A state police captain, who had seen combat in France and in what a reporter called the "famous Mingo war" of 1920, led sixteen other veterans in a desperate fight against the miners on one hilltop. Afterward, this officer remarked that he had never experienced anything like the battle that took place on that hill. "How our men ever escaped being hit is a mystery to me for bullets were hissing back and forth around our heads . . ."[28] The fighting continued for three hours until Gaujot's overheated machine gun jammed. Fearing they would be overrun, the deputies retreated a half mile in the direction of Logan, where they established another defensive position and held their ground through the afternoon. A few hours later Don Chafin sent cars full of reserves up to Crooked Creek Gap with orders to lay down a second line of defense.[29]

Word that units of the miners' army had broken through Chafin's defenses just two miles away caused a wave of excitement in Logan. "Unless troops sent by midnight tonight the Town of Logan will be attacked by an army of from four to eight thousand Reds and great loss of life and property sustained," warned the president of the Logan County Coal Operators' Association in a wire to Republican congressman Wells Goodykoontz of West Virginia. The representative immediately wired President Harding, telling him that his proclamation was being "contemptuously ignored."[30]

By this time, reporters were demanding answers from the UMWA national officers. In his statement to the press, President Lewis refused to condemn the miners or their tactics, even though their actions jeopardized the union. Instead he addressed remarks by the mine operators and state officials who had branded the insurgent miners an army of Reds. On the contrary, said Lewis, the men who marched on Logan County were descendants of a "race of mountaineers" who had peopled the hill country since colonial times. They held in their hearts an "inborn love of liberty," and it was this spirit, Lewis claimed, that made them rebel against the restrictions upon their freedom imposed by the coal industry and the "notorious Baldwin Felts agency." The UMWA had made repeated protests and attempts to redress the miners' grievances before every sort of government body, but to no avail. "Federal troops may restore order in West Virginia," Lewis concluded, but unless the cause of the recurring trouble—the mine guard system—was removed, "the dove of peace [would] never make permanent abode in this stricken territory."[31]

Later in the night a dusty automobile rumbled up a residential street in Charleston and stopped in front of Fred Mooney's house. Several miners clad in worn overalls clomped up onto the porch and called him out. The men told Mooney they were going to lead more troops to the front no matter what President Frank Keeney or President Warren Harding said to them. "The best thing you can do," they told Mooney, "is to clear out and stay out until we get through here."[32]

After these messengers from the front drove away, Mooney hurried over to Keeney's house, where the two men figured out what to do. They had set the miners' march in motion, but now rank-and-file leaders had taken command. As they talked into the night, Keeney and Mooney discussed some other troubling information provided to them by Harold Houston. A Mingo County grand jury had indicted both of them for crimes, including murder, they had allegedly committed during the Three Days War the previous summer. The two union officers reasoned that if they surrendered to hostile authorities in the midst of an uprising, their odds of surviving would be slim. Under the circumstances, it would be best, as Mooney put it, to "clear out, at least for a little while." And so, in the dead of night on September 1, the two men motored out of Charleston and headed for a hideout in Ohio, leaving behind the insurrectionary movement they had initiated.[33]

It must have been a difficult decision for Keeney to make, for he had, in effect, abandoned his followers just as they marched into harm's way. He had also abandoned his wife, Bessie, his seven children, and his aging mother-in-law, Elizabeth. Before he left town Frank told Bessie to prepare for the worst by making sure to put the revolver he had given her under her pillow at night.[34]

The next day, Labor Day, squads of miners launched new assaults on well-fortified mountain gaps. An Associated Press reporter

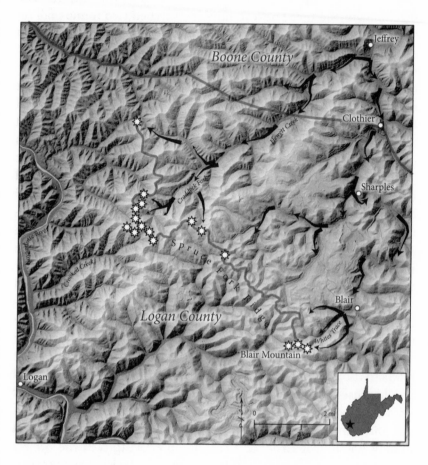

Union Miners

Battle Site

Approximate Location
of Spruce Fork Ridge

The miners' movements and battle sites on Blair Mountain and along the
Spruce Fork Ridge.

embedded among the defenders crouched down behind a log redoubt and looked through field glasses down the valley, where he saw miners attempting to move up and support the assault. As a machine gun clattered next to him, he watched two miners fall on the trail and bullets clip the dust around the bodies as men ran out of the woods to retrieve their comrades. Some deputies on patrol reported that they had shot several riflemen out of the trees where they had been perched. Time and again, the insurgents moved up toward higher ground, and time and again, machine gun and rifle fire drove them back. "So it goes through the day," wrote the AP correspondent. "Men appear and are checked by a veritable wall of fire."[35]

That same day, the miners fighting their way up toward Crooked Creek Gap noticed something different about the airplanes that had been flying over observing their movements. First, one biplane, and then another, swooped low over the mountainside and then banked. As the aircraft engines labored and the planes began to climb again, the miners were startled by the sound of concussions. "My God," one miner shouted. "They're bombing us!"[36] Something extraordinary happened on Spruce Fork Ridge that day: For the first and only time, American citizens were subjected to aerial bombardment on their own soil.

Worried that his defenses would break down, Chafin had ordered pilots to drop two kinds of bombs on the marchers: gas bombs that would cause extreme nausea and bombs made of six-inch pipes filled with black powder, nuts, and bolts that would, if they hit the marchers, "hurt them very badly." The pilots dropped four bombs on a miners' camp near Crooked Creek in an effort to rout the miners located there. One of the bombs that fell on Hewett Creek missed its target: a school the miners were using as a hospital and a barracks. The explosions "virtually shook the steep mountain," creating concussions that "echoed and re-echoed for miles around." Cush Garrett, a boy who lived in the hills, saw the bomb explode near his schoolhouse, and then he heard the miners' high-powered rifles cracking at the planes as they flew over. No one in the miners' army was hurt by the explosions, but the gun battles along the ridge had taken their toll; at the end of the day on September 1, Sheriff Chafin estimated that thirty miners had already died in the battle, along with three defenders.[37]

Outsiders made two separate attempts to stop the union miners' invasion of Logan County that day. The first came at the request of John L. Lewis, who sent UMWA vice president Philip Murray to the front to persuade their members to lay down their arms. But Murray soon realized his own life might be in danger if he interfered, and he returned to safety in Charleston. Meanwhile, General Bandholtz sent two of his officers out to negotiate with the marchers. The soldiers promised the miners they met that if they obeyed President Harding's orders, they would not be "molested" by state police or county sheriffs on their way home. Bandholtz's officers returned with a report that none of marchers had been impressed by the guarantee. When he heard this report, the general decided to take a step President Harding had hoped to avoid. Early on the morning of September 2, Bandholtz wired Washington and requested that army troops "be sent to West Virginia, without delay."[38]

Influential West Virginians were appalled and embarrassed by reports that a "civil war" was raging in Logan County, but they did not agree on who was to blame for the calamity. Many people believed Governor Morgan and state authorities, who accused "outside agitators" for inciting the armed mob that now terrorized thousands of citizens. But others saw the miners as local mountaineers—as reluctant warriors—who had been provoked by Sheriff Chafin. This interpretation would become more popular after General Bandholtz said he believed the invaders would have withdrawn if the special trains the governor called up had arrived in time and if state police had not made an "ill-advised and ill-timed" attempt to serve warrants in Clothier on August 27.[39]

On September 2, the secretary of war ordered a force of twenty-one hundred U.S. Army infantrymen from Camp Dix in New Jersey, Camp Sherman in Ohio, and Fort Knox in Kentucky to prepare for duty in southern West Virginia. It would be the largest peacetime deployment the army had undertaken since 1890, when more than six thousand troops occupied the Lakota Sioux territory to intimidate roughly four thousand followers of the Ghost Dance spiritual movement. The army's massive invasion of the Pine Ridge Indian Reservation resulted in the massacre of 146 Indians at Wounded Knee.[40]

What would happen now? Would a large body of American citizens, many of them combat veterans, actually wage a war against the nation's armed forces? The news from the battlefront, announced in headlines with big bold fonts, was bad enough: "PLANES DROP BOMBS OF TNT ON MINERS," "HARD BATTLE ON TWO FRONTS OF LOGAN COUNTY LINE," "MANY DEATHS AMONG MINERS REPORTED," "IT'LL TAKE THE MINERS A WEEK TO BURY THE DEAD."[41] How much worse could it get if the miners resisted the U.S. Army infantry? How many more men would die?

Heavy fighting continued that day in Crooked Creek Gap and on Blair Mountain, where two units of miners flanked a heavily fortified position near Blair Gap. "The miners pushed the attack desperately; they had no sense of fear," declared one of the men on high ground. Advancing over the crest of the hill in the face of withering rifle and machine-gun fire, they crouched behind trees and huddled down in hastily dug trenches, and sustained their attack for nearly three hours.[42] But at other points along the ridge, word that the army was coming rushed along the firing lines and spread through the hills from mouth to mouth, where it was greeted with cheers from the embattled miners' ranks. "Everywhere it was taken as a signal to prepare to stop fighting," one reporter noted.[43]

The next day Ed Reynolds and his fighters, unaware of the cease-fire, renewed their efforts to break through at Crooked Creek Gap just a short distance from the Guyandotte River and the road to Logan. But the relentless fire from the machine-gun nests kept both units pinned down. "We couldn't fire a shot but what they would rake our line from top to bottom," a Cabin Creek miner recalled. "They must have had car loads of ammo on that hill for they fired hundreds of rounds for every one we sent in their direction." On the evening of September 3, newspapers reported that thirty miners died in the battle of Crooked Creek Gap, but reporters had no way of confirming losses on either side, a confusion that would prevail for a long time after the fighting stopped.[44]

Later that night, Boyden Sparkes, a famous World War I battlefield correspondent, rode the troop train into Madison, "the unionized seat of Boone County," and took note of what he saw. Infantrymen buckled on heavy packs, dropped down on the cindered right-of-way, and formed up in patrol units that a young captain sent into the hills. When he finished giving his orders, the captain turned to a young, wiry, dark-eyed man he saw approaching him. He wore a weather-beaten, narrow-brimmed black felt hat pulled low over his forehead, a rumpled suit that looked like it had been slept in for days, and a soiled necktie knotted on the wrong side of his dirty shirt collar. He identified himself as William Blizzard, subdistrict president of the UMWA. When a soldier asked him, "Are you the general of the miners' army?" Blizzard smiled and replied, "What army?"

But the union official in a rumpled suit admitted that he had influence over the insurgent miners; indeed, Blizzard claimed that he could get all of his men out of the hills by daybreak if the captain in charge sent a detail of soldiers with him. When the officer promised that union members who possessed legal gun permits would be allowed to keep their weapons, Blizzard objected because he knew that most of his men did not have permits. If they turned in their weapons, and if Don Chafin's "thugs" were allowed to keep their guns, the union men would be unarmed and defenseless. Even though he failed to resolve this problem, Blizzard agreed to go back into the hills, talk to his men, and see what he could do to stop the fighting.[45]

The next afternoon Sparkes observed groups of "miner fighters" pouring out of the hills to line up and surrender to the soldiers. Only a few of them turned in their guns; most volunteers hid their weapons after Blizzard explained that Chafin's defenders would not be disarmed. "That's why you don't see the guns," Blizzard told the regimental commander. "When we need 'em again, we'll know where to look for 'em."[46]

Sparkes's report indicated that young Bill Blizzard was in fact the "generalissimo" of the miners' army. The historian C. Belmont Keeney believes Frank Keeney, his great-grandfather, and Fred Mooney "managed events behind the scenes," while Blizzard played a "key role" in the field. But at the height of the battle, these two union officials were far away from the action and could have played at best a limited role after they fled the state. In any case, all the union commanders agreed that the miners' army would not fight Uncle Sam's army.[47] When federal troops moved up Hewett Creek later that day, miners all along the line put down their weapons and greeted the infantrymen by yelling, "We're glad you're with us buddies," and proclaiming they would not fight Uncle Sam. That morning after church services, residents of Huntington read in the Sunday paper that fifty miners had been killed and fifty wounded in the attempt to invade Logan County. "Peace is settling over West Virginia's Valley of Death," declared the editor. "The orgy of blood is at an end. The federal troops are in control."[48]

On Sunday afternoon, the boom of rifles and the clatter of machine guns still reverberated higher up on the ridge in Crooked Creek Gap and near the summit of Blair Mountain, where thousands of shell casings littered the forested slopes. But by dusk that part of the ridge also fell silent and the largest working-class uprising in the nation's history came to a peaceful end. Over the next few days more than fifty-four hundred insurgents surrendered their weapons to federal soldiers, who escaped without suffering a single casualty. Infantrymen searched the woods for bodies, and when they found no corpses, estimates of the death toll dropped drastically.[49]

Meanwhile, the rest of the huge miners' army dissolved into the mountains as the volunteers hitched rides or hiked back home along the creeks, railroad beds, and country roads. "MINERS GAY AS THEY QUIT FRONT" read one report that described insurgents heading home in "cheerful spirits" and vowing to return, if need be, after the federal troops departed.[50] The union workers who fought on Blair Mountain believed they had achieved a political victory in their long struggle to liberate the company towns of southern West Virginia. These men saw themselves as freedom fighters, patriots who had risked their lives to liberate their fellow workers from the twin tyrannies of company domination and military occupation.

Even though they had failed to end martial law in Mingo County or to get rid of Don Chafin, the union miners and their leaders interpreted the arrival of federal forces as a victory, one that would pave the way for a new era in which coal miners would enjoy the rights and liberties the Constitution guaranteed to all American citizens. For the hundreds of World War I veterans who fought on Blair Mountain, that September day might have seemed a bit like Armistice Day, when they celebrated making the world safe for democracy.

In the weeks that followed, the miners' march and the Battle of Blair Mountain elicited numerous assessments by journalists. The "10,000 mountaineer miners" who invaded Logan County had taken the law into their own hands, the *Nation* granted, but they did so because that was precisely what the other side had done when it created a "system of terrorization" in the company towns of southern West Virginia.[51] Even editorials in mainstream newspapers, like the *Washington Star*, sided with the insurgents. "The name of Don Chafin, high sheriff of Logan County . . . struck terror into the hearts of the people in the union fields," the *Star* observed, and it was Chafin "whom the miners and the people of this section place the blame for this latest blot on the State's history."[52]

West Virginia's businessmen and elected officials expected this kind of criticism from liberal outsiders, but they worried about the attitudes of local people toward the insurrection. "The monstrosities alleged against Don Chafin" had led "a large number of men and women, whose own lives are orderly, to openly sympathize with this movement," one prominent editor remarked.[53] This journalist defended Chafin and denied there were any local causes for the rebellion. Another columnist remarked that there had been trouble in the coalfields for a long time, beginning twenty years before with the 1902 strike and the bloodshed at Glen Jean, and that the "warfare" never ceased entirely, but he did not believe those conflicts had led directly to the mine war that erupted in August 1921. The blame for the tragedy rested entirely upon the shoulders of "I.W.W.s and Communists and other agents of disorder" who had "flocked to the region" in 1920.[54]

This commentator followed the lead of Governor Morgan, who had immediately blamed the uprising on a conspiracy of outsiders who intended to overthrow the government. His argument closely resembled the rationale Attorney General Palmer had used to suppress radicalism during World War I and the Red Scare that followed.

Since the alleged conspirators had defied a presidential order, Morgan wanted to make the uprising a "federal case." To that end, the governor asked General Bandholtz to use his troops to arrest miners who had violated President Harding's decree. The general refused, however, on the grounds that his intelligence officers had discovered no evidence of an alien conspiracy; they found only a small amount of IWW and Bolshevik literature in the miners' possession. Furthermore, since federal forces were not supposed to be used in place of state and local police, Bandholtz wanted his troops withdrawn from West Virginia as soon as possible.[55]

The Harding administration also frustrated Governor Morgan by paying attention to UMWA president John Lewis who was attempting to use the insurrection as a reason why President Harding should intervene in West Virginia, compel the coal operators to remove their guards and persuade them to begin contract negotiations with the union. Senator Kenyon, who planned to reopen hearings on conditions in the West Virginia minefields on September 19, told Lewis that the president was sympathetic to the plan and that his subcommittee's inquiry would help build the case for a peaceful resolution to ongoing war in coal country. Before long, however, some of the Mountain State's most influential industrialists convinced Harding that it would be best for him to do nothing.[56]

Unfortunately for Morgan, the president took the same do-nothing course on the legal front. The governor had hoped that the U.S. attorney general would prosecute the insurgent miners for launching an insurrection against the federal government. Lawyers in the Justice Department's criminal division recommended a federal indictment against Frank Keeney, Bill Blizzard, and their confederates. But Harding and his closest advisers decided against prosecution, perhaps because "it was evident to one and all that any Federal investigation into the miners' uprising would inevitably focus public attention on the close ties" between West Virginia coal operators and Republican office holders; and this, the historian Robert Shogan noted, "was a can of worms no one in Warren Harding's government wanted to open."[57]

Governor Morgan and his advisers would have to chart their own course forward without aid from the U.S. Army or the Justice

Department. As weak and incompetent as county sheriffs and state police constables had proven to be, Morgan would need these officers to track down the ringleaders of the miners' insurrection, and he would need to rely upon the state courts and local juries to see that the rebels were punished so severely that the state's tarnished authority would be restored and its restless mine workers taught a lesson they would never forget.

Part IV

The Peace, 1922–1934

Chapter 15

Americanizing
West Virginia
Fall 1921–Fall 1930

A few days after the insurgent miners surrendered to the army, deputy sheriffs from Logan and nearby counties swept through the union coal camps and rounded up hundreds of suspects. "Whole payrolls were indicted," one journalist remarked. Chafin's deputies locked up scores of men in the Logan jailhouse, "where every effort was made to extort confessions from them and induce them to testify against the union leaders," according to a prosecuting attorney from a nearby county.[1]

Frank Keeney and Fred Mooney decided to return to West Virginia from their hideout in Ohio, but only after union officials arranged for them to surrender to Governor Morgan, who had guaranteed their safety. However, John L. Lewis still worried about his officers' well-being, and on September 19, he wired Morgan requesting his formal assurance that Keeney and Mooney would live to stand trial. The next day, Lewis received a chilling reply. "Your silent encouragement of unlawful acts would indicate that Lenin and Trotsky are not without sincere followers in your organization," Morgan declared. "It is a matter of record that you have not lifted your voice in protest against this violence."[2]

Lewis's wire was irritating, but Morgan had a more serious concern: the resumption of Senator Kenyon's investigation of the conditions in West Virginia's coalfields. These hearings would provide another national platform for critics of West Virginia's industrialists and public officials, particularly for UMWA leaders who planned to take full advantage of these sessions by presenting to the senators evidence that the controversial U.S. Steel Corporation had entered into a conspiracy with various operators to deprive coal miners of their constitutional rights. The union even hired the famous radical lawyer Frank Walsh to press their case before Kenyon's committee.

When the sessions opened, Walsh began by reminding the senators that "Mr. Hatfield, a witness who appeared before this committee, was murdered in cold blood by a representative of the Operators' Association in West Virginia." No one could deny, said Walsh, that Charles Lively, the lead assassin, had acted on behalf of the operators, because he "was under their pay." But the shooter was only a pawn in a much larger plot to destroy unionism in the coalfields—"a general conspiracy . . . carried out by the direct command of the United States Steel Corporation," a firm financed by J.P. Morgan and Company and controlled by its president, Judge Elbert Gary. Then, referring to the widows of Sid Hatfield and Ed Chambers who were to appear before the committee, Walsh made a breathtaking announcement: "We expect to show perfectly clearly here that the United States Steel Corporation, in the person of Judge Gary, is as responsible for the death of those two men as if they took action of the board of directors and ordered Lively to murder the husbands of these women."[3]

On the day before, a photographer snapped a picture of Jessie Hatfield and Sallie Chambers when they arrived in Washington to testify; two well-dressed young women from a small river town suddenly found themselves in the national spotlight. Over the objections of coal industry lawyers, Senator Kenyon allowed the young widows to recount the grisly details of what happened when they stood next to their husbands and watched them die on their way to court.[4]

While this drama played itself out on Capitol Hill, Governor Morgan and his attorney general finalized their plans to prosecute the

Jessie Hatfield (*left*) and Sallie Chambers on Capitol Hill, September 1921.

insurgents. Besides charging Keeney, Blizzard, and their followers with murder and various other felonies, state authorities decided to prosecute these miners for committing the high crime of treason against the state of West Virginia. Accusing the ringleaders of the march of such a despicable act would demonstrate that the miners acted not as patriotic freedom fighters but as enemies of the state who were as dangerously subversive as Bolsheviks.[5]

The prosecution of the insurgent miners as traitors would become part of a much grander crusade to "Americanize" southern West Virginia by inculcating the values of political conservatism, corporate capitalism, and "100 percent Americanism."[6] The state's political, industrial, and educational leaders had already funded and implemented a version of this campaign during World War I, when they attempted to instill "the principles and values of industrial capitalism in all citizens, native and foreign-born, and to remove all opposing ideas from public discourse," in the words of historian John C. Hennen. Unlike other Americanization programs that focused entirely on immigrants, the Mountain State campaign targeted native-born black and white workers, whose respect for private property and state authority seemed extremely doubtful to West Virginia's power elite. The political crusade to "Americanize" West Virginia would not only rid the state of redneck rebels like Keeney and Blizzard; it would "re-civilize" the coal-mining districts by silencing all those who had sided with the union cause and reeducating those who had been duped by radical demagogues.[7]

Keeney and his fellow defendants did not realize what powerful forces were mobilizing against them in the winter of 1922, but they knew they would need the best defense attorney they could find to defend them in court. The man they chose was Thomas Townsend, a progressive Republican who grew up working in the mines of Fayette County under what he called the "worst imaginable" working and living conditions; that experience would later shape the course of his career as an attorney. Though he was often invited to serve as a corporate lawyer, Townsend always refused because he had vowed as a youth to devote his efforts to bettering the conditions of his "oppressed friends" in the minefields. As state tax commissioner, he had attempted to reform a system that placed an unfair burden on small property owners while it afforded numerous breaks to large corporations, and as Kanawha County's prosecuting attorney, he honed his skills as a litigator. The lanky mountaineer with a large mustache and a quiet way about him would have to draw upon all of his experience as a defense attorney if he was going to save his notorious clients.

Townsend assembled a formidable team of defense attorneys, including Harold Houston, Sam Montgomery, and C. J. Van Fleet. When the lawyers reviewed the charges against their clients, these lawyers realized that the governor may have overreached when he decided to prosecute the insurgent miners as traitors. In fact, the West Virginia Constitution defined treason very narrowly, "as levying war against the State or in adhering to its enemies."[8]

The defense attorneys were wily politicians who knew their clients would also be tried before the court of public opinion in a state
with a government that had been widely criticized and even ridiculed
in national periodicals. As soon as the legal proceedings began the
New York Times weighed in, accusing the state's attorneys of throwing around indictments for treason as carelessly as indictments for
larceny. To make matters worse for the coal companies, the county
prosecutor assigned to the case resigned after he rejected the legal
propriety of the treason charge. The forthcoming show trials would
be "a waste of scarce resources" in pursuit of "mean-spirited agen-
das," the public attorney remarked.[9]

Roger Baldwin, head of the ACLU, was infuriated by the treason
trials. As far as he was concerned, the real traitors were Don Chafin
and the coal companies that denied coal miners their civil liberties. In
January 1922, Baldwin and the ACLU's executive committee turned
the tables on the coal operators and called upon federal district attorneys to investigate state and county officials who had denied West
Virginia coal miners their constitutional rights.[10]

In response to negative national publicity, West Virginia colliery
owners and some of the state's largest industrialists founded the
American Constitutional Association (ACA) in order to defend the
reputation of West Virginia and its mining industry. "We have been
held up to ridicule and made to appear as a state composed of the
most lawless people to be found in the world," declared one ACA pro-
nouncement. "We have become the Ireland of America in the eyes
of the entire nation." Why? Because investigators from "so-called social and relief committees," "snoops" from scores of big-city periodicals, and even members of the U.S. Senate had concocted reports of
terrible conditions in the coal camps without seeing anything good
in West Virginia, home to "some of the best people in the world." In
fact, said the association's spokesman, "The best blood of the nation,
the purest Anglo-Saxon descendants live in the mountain regions of
the state." The time had come "for every 100 per cent West Virginian to show his colors" and wake up and confront domestic enemies
who were hurling verbal "shrapnel" at the state.[11]

To enhance the moral weight of the ACA campaign, the mine
operators hired Billy Sunday, the nation's most popular evangelist.

Preaching in Logan County that spring, Sunday inveighed against the coal miners accused of treason. "I cannot believe God had anything to do with the creation of these human buzzards," he thundered, adding that he would rather be in hell with John Wilkes Booth than on earth with such "human lice."[12]

While Billy Sunday swept through Logan County, Townsend negotiated with prosecutors and judges to have the treason trials moved from Logan to a new venue outside of coal country in rural Jefferson County near the Maryland border. The proceedings would take place in the same two-columned courthouse in Charles Town where John Brown and four accomplices were convicted of committing an act of treason against the Commonwealth of Virginia. The prosecution had charged that Brown and his men were "moved and seduced by the false and malignant counsels of other evil and traitorous persons, and the instigations of the Devil," to incite a slave rebellion. More than six decades later, Bill Blizzard would face a similar charge in the same venue.[13]

As the rolling hills and rich farmlands of Jefferson County turned green that April, local residents prepared for the great courtroom drama about to unfold in Charles Town. For weeks, these residents had been pestered by reporters, bombarded with propaganda leaflets financed by the coal companies, and visited by traveling "Bible salesmen" who were actually agents Townsend hired with union money to bewail the horrible conditions honest workingmen endured under the rule of "Czar" Don Chafin.[14]

The two experienced lawyers the coal operators hired to prosecute the miners—the "Coal Dust Twins" as the press called them— had wanted to put Keeney and Mooney, the alleged masterminds of the insurrection, on the stand first, but since the two men had fled the state before the fighting started, the prosecutors decided they could make a stronger case against Bill Blizzard, the "generalissimo" of the miners' army. The prosecution had prepared twenty-four test cases, including Blizzard's, and it had more than five hundred to follow if they obtained convictions in the initial trials. "Nothing like it is recalled in history," noted the *Charleston Gazette*.[15]

The day before Blizzard's trial began, Fred Mooney arrived in Charles Town with a somber-looking John L. Lewis as his passenger,

Fred Mooney and his wife arriving in Charles Town with
John L. Lewis.

and later that day, a train—one reporter called it the "Red Special"—
arrived from Logan County carrying Frank Keeney, Bill Blizzard, a
horde of deputy sheriffs, and hundreds of other defendants and witnesses. After the train emptied, all the parties were present for what
promised to be the most unusual legal spectacle the nation had witnessed in many years.[16]

When officers threw open the narrow doors to the Jefferson
County Courthouse on April 25, dozens of men clambered up the
stairs to find seats in the chamber, which was located above the

room where John Brown was tried and convicted in 1859. As William Blizzard sat next to his lawyers that day, he might have wondered if he would follow in Brown's footsteps, all the way to the gallows.[17] But the defendant and his attorney must have taken heart when the presiding judge opened the proceedings by setting a high bar for the prosecution. He instructed the jury that an unlawful assembly, even one that led to violent action, was not necessarily treasonous unless the insurgents conspired to levy war against the government. After the prosecutors outlined the government's case against Blizzard, Thomas Townsend opened by saying that he had read his state's constitution intently and he would prove that its definition of treason did not apply in Blizzard's case. He was prepared to show that his client had not set out to subvert or overthrow the state government and that Blizzard and his associates had, in fact, pleaded with the governor to intervene and solve the crisis in the coalfields peacefully.

Townsend understood the curiously diffident treatment the courts had accorded accused traitors in the past. John Brown's conviction and execution stood out as exceptional when compared with other cases in which the accused traitors were acquitted or else convicted and then pardoned. President George Washington did so for the Whiskey Rebellion's instigators, and later President Abraham Lincoln chose not to prosecute northern Copperheads for disloyalty during the Civil War. Even Jefferson Davis and the rebel leaders of the Confederacy, though charged with treason, never stood trial. Reflecting on this history in an article about the miners' trial, the noted historian James G. Randall explained that American juries and elected officials had taken treason to be "a determined, forcible defiance of the Government, involving a real menace to organized society." Jurors were therefore dubious when it came to convicting and sentencing citizens in cases of "near treason." Furthermore, in a country

Bill Blizzard outside the Jefferson County Courthouse.

born of a revolution sparked by volunteer minutemen—a nation committed to the right of citizens to bear arms and seek redress of their grievances—government officials had tended to grant leniency to those who rebelled against injustice and defied government authorities in doing so.[18]

The prosecutors relied upon the testimony of a few miners who had turned state's witness and testified that Blizzard was in command of the marchers, but there were some cracks in their case. When the state called an infantry captain who had been deployed on Blair Mountain to put down the insurrection, his testimony came "like a bolt out of the sky," according to one reporter. The officer denied hearing any talk from the union men about overthrowing the government; instead he heard the marchers say they wanted to get "the Logan County thugs and protect the women and children."[19]

The coal companies' attorneys did not seem concerned, for they had assumed that jurors from a rural county would not sympathize with a reckless young coal miner from far away in the mountains. The prosecutors might have worried, however, when the judge allowed Blizzard and his codefendants to attend Sunday church services with local worshippers and even permitted the prisoners to play a baseball game with a Charles Town team. Newsmen enjoyed this spectacle enormously, particularly one reporter who listed some of the men on the miners' team along with the charges and bail set for each one:

Dewey Bailey, center field, treason, $10,000
Okey Burgess, second base, murder, $2,500
Cecil Sullivan, first base, murder, $2,500
William Blizzard, right field, treason, murder, etc., $33,000
Frank Snyder, manager, treason, $10,000.[20]

Townsend ignored the carnival outside the courthouse and calmly mounted his defense of Blizzard. The attorney argued that the miners' march had been planned as a peaceful demonstration to eliminate the private mine guard system that prevailed in southern West

Virginia. Captain Brockus's ill-conceived raid into union country on August 27 had provoked the miners to act in self-defense, according to Townsend; had it not been for this incursion, violence could have been avoided. Furthermore, the defense team called a parade of witnesses who swore that they saw Bill Blizzard in Charleston during the march, while others testified that Blizzard had actually helped Keeney turn the marchers around at Madison and had then aided the army in arranging a surrender.

After a trial that had lasted more than three weeks, the prosecuting attorney made his closing argument that Blizzard had led a treasonous insurrection "to subvert the government in whole or in part." The jurymen retired, considered this argument, and rejected it. When the foreman read the not guilty verdict on May 25, the prosecutors and coal operators sat stunned and stone-faced at their table while Blizzard's friends, relatives, and union brothers stood and cheered. Outside the little red courthouse, miners in their Sunday suits hoisted Blizzard on their shoulders and threw their hats in the air. A much grander celebration took place later that day in the state capital, when Blizzard rode through the streets in an open car in the midst of a joyous procession led by a brass band.[21]

Bill Blizzard (*in jacket*) with his fellow defendants before a baseball game in Charles Town.

Instead of vindicating the state in the nation's eyes, Blizzard's treason trial provoked a new wave of approbation in the press. A columnist for the *New York Globe* wondered why the prosecutors were lawyers hired by the coal companies instead of district attorneys. "Government in West Virginia had broken down," wrote another editor, "and its power had passed in part to the mine operators." Even the conservative *New York Times* published an editorial saying that "whatever their offenses, the unionist miners and their leaders were not trying to subvert the Government of West Virginia." Besides, the paper added, Logan County could "scarcely be said to have been under the rule of law or to have had a republican form of government." The liberal *New York Evening World* went even further, when it suggested that Blizzard's attorneys could claim that no crime of treason was possible in West Virginia "because no Government existed" there.[22]

Shocked by Blizzard's acquittal and enraged by reactions in the press, prosecuting attorneys built an airtight case against the next three defendants, John Wilburn and his sons, who were charged with second-degree murder in the deaths of John Gore and his two deputies on Blair Mountain. The defendants were tried, convicted, and sentenced to eleven-year prison terms.[23] In the next trial, Walter Allen, president of the Dry Branch UMWA local on Cabin Creek, faced a jury that included men who admitted having a bias against labor unions. The judge made it easy for the panel to convict Allen of conspiring with various union officials to levy war on the state of West Virginia. The prosecution did not need to show that the defendant actually met with these officials; it only had to show that Allen had been "present" during the armed march. If so, the judge proclaimed, then "the said Walter Allen is guilty of treason."[24]

This ruling outraged James M. Cain, who covered the trials for the *Baltimore Sun* and listened intently for days as the attorneys engaged in a highly unusual and, at times, profound debate over the meaning of treason in America. After he witnessed the prosecution and conviction of Walter Allen, Cain unleashed his rage over what had transpired. "By a jury of his peers," he wrote, "packed against him and bearing instructions virtually proclaiming his guilt; on the flimsiest sort of evidence and with not the ghost of a chance at a fair trial from start to finish, Walter Allen, union miner, has been solemnly adjudged to be a traitor to that section of coal operators' real estate known as the sovereign State of West Virginia."[25]

Cain's reports on the treason trials angered the coal operators so much that they sent a delegation to speak to the *Baltimore Sun*'s editor and demand that the newsman be fired.[26] The editor listened to the executives' complaints, bid the businessmen farewell, and then assigned his man in West Virginia to cover the trials for their duration. The treason trials in Charles Town set Cain off on a coalfield odyssey, one that would bring him back to southern West Virginia in the fall of 1922, when he traveled by train up the Tug River to gather facts for a feature story for the *Atlantic Monthly*. As his journey took him deeper into coal country, he decided to "utilize its bleak, beautiful ugliness" as the setting for an "epic novel." It would be the story of a radical union organizer who marched with Blizzard's army in 1921, the tale of a man with a "compulsion to break things apart, and his final discovery that he couldn't."[27]

The UMWA posted bail for Walter Allen as his lawyers filed an appeal of his conviction with the state supreme court. Then Townsend and his associates concentrated on defending Frank Keeney against the charge of treason. A few members of the miners' army had turned state's witness and were prepared to say that Keeney had set the march in motion and had allowed it to continue, even after he promised General Bandholtz that he had called it off. But before prosecutors could make their case, the judge who was to preside over Keeney's trial made an unexpected announcement. He decided that the political climate in Jefferson County had turned so hostile to the defendant that it would be impossible to find twelve unbiased men to sit on the jury; he therefore transferred Keeney's trial to nearby Morgan County, where, according to one observer, "public sentiment so strongly favored the defendant" that the prosecuting attorneys decided to dismiss the indictment against the miners' ringleader.[28]

Keeney was in no mood to celebrate, however. He still had a murder charge hanging over his head and he was working long hours to maintain a statewide strike that had started on April 1. More than 1.5 million men and women struck that year, more than in the previous banner year when war preparations had created an abundance of jobs and stimulated high hopes among the nation's wage earners. "But 1922 was a year of grimly determined defensive warfare for strikers . . . ," historian David Montgomery explained.[29] Unionized coal companies, plagued by inefficiency and overproduction, faced stiff competition from open shop mines in Appalachia and demanded concessions from the UMWA, but President Lewis vowed that the union would take "no backward step" and his members held firm; the strike even attracted hundreds of nonunion miners who joined in the walkout. When the mine owners grudgingly agreed to maintain the old pay scale in August 1922, Lewis claimed a victory and sent its members back to work.[30]

At this point, all of organized labor in West Virginia turned to Frank Keeney as the man who could lead them through the rough

Defense lawyers and defendants in Charles Town. From left to right, C. J. Van Fleet, (second from left) Thomas Townsend, Sam Montgomery, Harold Houston, Bill Blizzard, John L. Lewis (in front) and Frank Keeney. The other men standing behind appear to be union miners charged with insurrection and treason. Court employees appear on the top step behind the rest.

times that lay ahead. Although he had been indicted for treason and still faced trial for murder, Keeney was nominated president of the West Virginia State Federation of Labor. The other candidates stepped aside and made his election unanimous, a sign that all the state's trade unions supported the miners' march of 1921.[31]

Keeney had little time to devote to his new duties as federation president because his own house was in disarray. The cost of the strike and the legal expense of the treason trials had drained the District 17 treasury. To make matters worse, Walter Allen fled the state and forfeited the $10,000 bond the union had paid. Keeney and Mooney also had to contend with ambitious opponents in the district who accused them of recklessness and incompetence for alienating state and local officials, for saddling the district with crippling financial liabilities, and for failing to save the strikers still marooned in Mingo County refugee camps.

In his article "The Battle Ground of Coal," James M. Cain painted a grim portrait of "some five thousand persons under canvas," whom he left sitting by the Tug River watching mile-long coal trains groan around the river bends, "flotsam cast up by the backwash of a mighty struggle, pathetically loyal to a cause of which they understand nothing."[32]

But some observers saw the encamped strikers and their families as heroic people willing to stand fast for a good cause. The solidarity and tenacity displayed by these people amazed a series of reporters and investigators including Senator Kenyon, who came to Lick Creek to investigate conditions there. He spoke to George Echols, an African American miner who had been born a slave in Virginia and had worked in the mines of Mingo County for four years before the strike began in 1920. He had joined the walkout because the mine boss cheated the men when he weighed their coal cars. In the days that followed, Echols realized that the UMWA believed coal miners, both black and white, should enjoy the same freedoms other citizens exercised. At the first meeting of his racially mixed local, the membership elected Echols vice president. The next day, Echols was terminated and then evicted from his house. When he went to live at Lick Creek, he said that state police came several times, rounded up tent dwellers, and locked them up in Williamson without pressing charges.

"I know the time when I was a slave," Echols told Senator Kenyon, "and I felt just like we feel now." Under the Constitution, the miner remarked, "no man should be condemned . . . until [he is given] a free and impartial trial." Miners were patriotic Americans, he insisted, and it was wrong for them to lose their freedoms when they joined the union. "Now," Echols said to Senator Kenyon, "we are asking you to give them back to us. Let us be free men. Let us stand equal."[33]

The 1922 settlement ignored strikers like Echols and thousands of other nonunion miners who had joined the walkout in other unorganized fields. This betrayal provoked outrage among John L. Lewis's critics in the UMWA, but not from Keeney and Mooney. The West Virginians remained loyal to their union president because he had supported them in Mingo County and in the costly treason trials that followed. However, as soon as the treason trials ended, the national office cut off all funds to District 17. As a result, Keeney and Mooney could no longer support the strike they had called in Mingo County more than two years earlier.

Before the tents came down at the Lick Creek camp, a photographer took a picture of a racially mixed group of men and women sitting together on a rocky slope, with union officials in suits standing with them, waiting to wrap things up. The people who had taken shelter there for more than a year were on their own now. Some found other kinds of work in the Tug River Valley, some went back to their family homes in the hills, and some moved on to work in other coalfields, but none of them would sign yellow dog contracts and return to their old jobs.

By this time, anti-union employment contracts had become nearly universal in southern West Virginia. A year later, the Red Jacket company, in concert with 315 other companies, filed suit to protect these contracts. A judge in the U.S. District Court responded by granting a permanent injunction against all union activities in collieries where miners had signed away their right to join the UMWA. When the U.S. Coal Commission opened its investigations that year, John L. Lewis hoped this official body would find these yellow dog contracts in violation of the Bill of Rights. In their final report, commissioners concluded that these terms of employment were no more "justifiable" than contracts that prohibited membership "in any organization." But the fact remained that Supreme Court had validated these restrictive labor contracts even though they denied union organizers freedom of speech and denied coal miners freedom of association.[34]

Frustrated on this front, the UMWA and the ACLU filed a suit in a state court seeking an injunction that would prevent the coal operators of Logan County from paying Don Chafin and his deputies for their services as mine guards. When the suit failed, the ACLU board decided to launch a free speech fight in Logan, and on March 4, the esteemed Catholic reformer Reverend John A. Ryan and two other prominent liberals addressed city residents on the courthouse steps in the county seat, hoping that the sheriff would arrest them. Refusing to take the bait, Chafin turned the tables on the ACLU speakers and led a chorus of critics who denounced them as outsiders carrying out a plot hatched by Bolsheviks in New York City. It came as a small consolation to the UMWA and the ACLU that Chafin was arrested and

Lick Creek camp dwellers at the end of their long ordeal, fall 1922.

convicted of operating a speakeasy in violation of the Volstead Act later that year, but the sheriff served only a few months in jail and then returned to a "great homecoming celebration" in Logan.[35]

Meanwhile, District 17's leaders had to contend with defections by companies in the unionized sector of the industry. These employers told Keeney they could not remain competitive under the wage scale mandated by the 1922 agreement. Keeney and Mooney decided to plead with President Lewis to permit them to make some concessions to Mountain State companies whose owners had bargained in good faith with the UMWA in the past. "The big boss was consulted and this proposition put up to him," Mooney recalled, but "he tabooed it." The leaders of District 17 returned to Charleston with no choice left but "to fight . . . what everyone knew would be a losing battle" to hold on to a wage scale that had been negotiated in good times.[36]

As Keeney searched for some way to save his beloved district from destruction, he wondered how long he would remain a free man. His future depended upon the verdict of a Fayette County jury whose members would decide if he was guilty of being an accessory to murder. Fortunately for Keeney, his fate also rested in the hands of his gifted attorney, Thomas Townsend, who was a popular man in his home county.[37] Townsend made his case, the prosecutors made theirs, and on March 14, 1924, the jury rendered its verdict. Jimmie Jones, who had followed the murder trial from his home in Ward, marked the event in his diary. "Frank Keeney has been on trial in Fayetteville for 5 weeks," he wrote, "and he come clear today."[38]

Soon after his acquittal in Fayetteville, Keeney found himself facing a different kind of jury and a different kind of judge. Distressed by the loss of union contracts District 17 had suffered, Keeney asked for a formal meeting with President Lewis and the UMWA executive board to see if anything could still be done to save the union in the Mountain State. When the delegation from Charleston arrived at the national office, they were stunned when Lewis turned on them. He berated Keeney and his associates for losing dues-paying members, allowing unofficial wildcat strikes, bankrupting the district treasury, failing to win new contracts, and, above all, "for trying to shoot the union into West Virginia." Pressured by Lewis, Keeney, Mooney, and several other district officers voluntarily submitted their resignations. The UMWA executive board placed District 17 in receivership, and Lewis declared that it would be "a long, long time" before its autonomy would be restored.[39]

Frank Keeney's time in West Virginia had passed. He had risen out of obscurity on Cabin Creek to take control of UMWA District 17 and turn it into a powerful, and sometimes fearsome, organization. John L. Lewis had invested heavily in Keeney's ability to organize the nonunion fields, and he had publicly defended him after the armed march. But in private, the union president had raged at the West Virginian's unauthorized decision to call the union miners to arms. Keeney's insistence on union democracy, his socialist beliefs, and his willingness to wage war on the mine guards and to defy his own government all clashed with Lewis's brand of conservative business unionism and his autocratic approach to union leadership.[40]

After his resignation, Keeney stuck to his principles. Still unwilling to leave the class in which he was born, he turned down a job as a mine superintendent because he believed it would be a "betrayal of his people." Instead, he retired to his home and waited for his chance to leap back into the fight. It came two years later when UMWA dissidents formed a "Save the Union" movement that appealed to Keeney's fighting spirit.[41]

After Keeney resigned from office, thousands of his dedicated followers remained loyal members of the union locals he and Mother Jones had organized during the fight on Cabin Creek in 1912. A few months after their leaders' departure, these stalwart unionists led the fight against Kanawha operators who demanded a devastating cut of 38 percent on tonnage rates.[42] McAlister Coleman, a writer for *Survey* magazine, visited Eskdale on Cabin Creek and Mammoth on Kellys Creek, where he watched deputy sheriffs armed with pistols and eviction notices "setting out" union miners and their families. The reporter saw women and little children wandering about in the mud seeking any sort of shelter and men trying to erect tents in the teeth of a gale, but he did not see a single miner cross the line. At that time, strikes had dropped to a new low, and few union members had the will to resist employers' relentless demands for concessions. It seemed to Coleman that Keeney's old supporters were making a last stand: "Labor's fighting front in America today lies along the Kanawha Valley, in the camps on Cabin and Kelly Creek . . ."[43]

From his home in Badbottom on Kellys Creek, James A. "Jimmie" Jones saw the shape of the future that winter. "The pore miners is throed out of tha houses," he wrote in his diary on December 6, 1924. "No work to do. Very bad all up the river. Miners living in tents and it is very cool weather on the little ones." Two weeks later, more troubling news: "The first car of scab coal come out from Mammoth out of Kellys Creek."

The strikers held on during the winter, but some gave up and left the valley or begged to get their old jobs back. On March 13, 1925, the company superintendent came by the miners' houses on a mission, according to Jones's diary. "Mr. Thomas Minkins had a paper for the miners to sign. The yellow dog!"[44]

Minkins told his employees that any miner who had taken the oath of obligation had to renounce it in order to keep his job; if not, he could pack up and "hit the creek." Some miners held out until the fall, but by then their jobs had been filled by strikebreakers.[45] By September, scores of miners had left the valley, and others had swallowed their pride, signed away their right to belong to a union, and returned to work as company men. It was the beginning of the end for the UMWA in West Virginia.

Mother Jones's autobiography appeared that year with a final chapter she entitled "War in West Virginia." In this section and at earlier points in the book, she highlighted her adventures "fighting for industrial freedom" in the mountains.[46] Oftentimes, she remembered, the union loyalists would be defeated and forced to retreat into the mine camps, where they would lay low, gather their strength, and wait for the right time to strike out again. And so it went in this forsaken land. "There is never peace in West Virginia," wrote Mother Jones, "because there is never justice."[47]

By this time Fred Mooney had decided to leave West Virginia because he could no longer bear to see the miners he once led working for tonnage rates far below the hard-won union scale.[48] Blacklisted by the employers, Red-baited by his enemies, forced to resign his union position by John L. Lewis, Mooney took his second wife and their two babies out west, where he was unknown and where he would be able to find work.

But even with Keeney and Mooney gone and the union movement in full retreat, mine operators in southern West Virginia did not rest assured of their employees' loyalty. Following the trail blazed by the U.S. Steel Corporation in its model mining towns of Gary and Elbert, colliery owners initiated a new wave of reforms in the name of "welfare capitalism." Sanitation, lighting, and housing were improved; swimming pools and gyms were opened; English classes and religious education were offered through the YMCAs; hospitals were established; Boy and Girl Scout troops were formed; and baseball teams were organized. After the miners' armed uprising in 1921, mining companies invested in outfitting different teams and then promoting competition among various communities as a way of enhancing workers' loyalty to the firm and the company town.[49]

The operators' efforts to improve living conditions were also a reaction to an exposé by investigators for the U.S. Coal Commission, who found unhealthy conditions in many Appalachian mining towns, especially some of those in the backcountry of West Virginia. "In the worst of the company-controlled communities," the commission noted, "the state of disrepair at times runs beyond the power of verbal description or even of photographic illustration, since neither words nor pictures can portray the atmosphere of abandoned dejection or reproduce the smells." Besides appealing to public opinion, coal town reforms were intended to place total authority in the hands of management, to remold the personality of the industrial worker and to "prevent him from become class conscious and from organizing trade unions," according to the economist Sumner Slichter.[50]

The effectiveness of UMWA strikes, organizing drives, and resistance campaigns had always relied upon the union's ability to weld together diverse groups of men by convincing them that they had more to gain by working together than they did staying apart. The maintenance of union solidarity had depended upon labor-management agreements that guaranteed blacks and whites virtually the same wages and the same rights on the job, and upon trade union practices that gave both groups the same speaking and voting rights. As the union disappeared from one colliery after another, black and white workers lost the only basis they had ever had for cooperating with one another.[51]

Into the void left by the UMWA came a very different kind of organization riding the winds of paranoia that gripped white Protestant America during the 1920s. "The Ku Klux Klan turned out last night at Mammoth church," observed the miner Jimmie Jones from his home in Ward on Kellys Creek. "They were the first I ever seen." Later on in 1925, he noted, a preacher paid by the KKK delivered a sermon about the assorted evils of bootlegging, wife beating, and race mixing. After the meeting, the Klansmen marched through Ward and burned a cross on Big Mountain above the valley cemetery.[52]

Initially, the Klan had appeared in the commercial towns of West Virginia, communities like Logan and Bluefield—Tom Felts's headquarters—where the mayor welcomed the Klansmen when they gathered at a local theater in full regalia to hear their leader call for total segregation as a way of ensuring white supremacy. After recruiting urban businessmen and professionals, the KKK moved into mining towns like Coalburg, where the hooded order appeared in force after a local mining company hired a new group of black workers. The next morning, "not a Negro was to be found" there.[53]

In the wake of the UMWA's demise, some African American coal miners gravitated toward the Universal Negro Improvement Association (UNIA) and its nationalist leader, Marcus Garvey, whom they regarded as "a Moses." The UMWA's national leaders did not view Garvey's UNIA as a threat to their organization; they did, however, regard the Klan as a serious menace to "union morale and labor consciousness." In response, speakers rose to condemn the KKK at the union's 1924 convention, where the delegates adopted a resolution that would require the expulsion of any members who joined the hooded order.[54]

The KKK's appearance in union locals was one symptom of the grave illness afflicting the UMWA's District 17. During Frank Keeney's last years at the helm, the organization had boasted a membership of fifty thousand strong, but in 1929 it claimed only six hundred

Miners posing outside a colliery at Cannelton (1926), a place where Fred Mooney had once worked and served as UMWA officer.

members.[55] When Percy Tetlow, the man John L. Lewis had appointed president of District 17, appeared before a U.S. Senate committee that year, he estimated that fifty thousand union people had been evicted from their homes in southern West Virginia. Thomas Townsend, who had become District 17's attorney, described the situation more provocatively. If any union organizer or sympathizer attempted to enter "the wilderness of industrial autocracy [that existed] in the smokeless coal fields of southern West Virginia," he would be forced to run a gauntlet of punishment at the hands of injunction-happy judges, labor spies, deputy sheriffs, and mine guards. Even the U.S. senators would not be welcome in these company-dominated towns. There was nothing left for the friends of the union to do, Townsend concluded, "except to invoke divine providence to roll back the waters of the Red Sea and let 'God's people go.'"[56]

The coal operators' victory over the UMWA in West Virginia did not, however, make the Mountain State's mining industry as competitive as the operators had promised it would. Some highly mechanized mining companies supplying coke to the steel industry remained profitable, but hundreds of small firms were played off against each other by the big railroad, steel, and utility companies, who insisted on keeping prices low. Even though West Virginia operators paid their men wages below the union scale, cut pay frequently, and kept company store prices high, they could not recover from a slump that had gripped the coal trade since 1922. On the eve of the Great Depression, the Appalachian coal industry was the sickest of America's sick industries, and the people who made their living in the mines were among the poorest of the nation's poor.[57]

Alfred Reed, a blind musician, had lived his entire life in West Virginia's smokeless coalfields, where he worked as a lay Baptist preacher and as a fiddler who performed at county fairs and church socials. Wherever he went in 1929, Reed heard stories of how people suffered in the coal towns. Even the mine workers who still had jobs complained because they were paying higher prices at company stores with shrunken wages. Out of this experience, "Blind Alfred" recorded his hit tune "How Can a Poor Man Stand Such Times and Live?" a few days after the stock market crashed.[58]

The Wall Street panic in October 1929 made a bad situation much worse in the nation's crippled bituminous coal industry. In the year ahead, people who lived in the Appalachian mining districts would endure a degree of poverty rarely witnessed in the United States. Malnutrition bred diseases, particularly tuberculosis and a sickness known as the "flux," a bleeding form of dysentery that took the lives of many children. Van A. Bittner, a UMWA national staff member whom John L. Lewis had put in charge of District 17, had seen hard times before, but "in all my experiences," he wrote from the Kanawha coalfield, "I have never seen anything to compare with these conditions."[59]

During the spring of 1930, when hunger "began to stalk the hills" of West Virginia, the journalist Malcolm Ross reported that the miners were ready for "any thrust to relieve the agony of underemployment."[60] The most religious among them looked for a

311

new messiah to come and save them, but instead a familiar figure stepped out of the past to revive an old tradition of resistance, a tradition lost but not forgotten among veteran coal miners. Frank Keeney returned to the Kanawha field that spring and sent organizers up the creeks to recruit members for the Reorganized United Mine Workers of America, formed a few months earlier by UMWA dissidents. To aid in the campaign, Keeney called his comrade-in-arms Fred Mooney back from Texas to help him rebuild the old union locals from scratch.[61]

Within a few weeks, Keeney and Mooney convinced many of the men they had once represented that they had to strike to regain the eight-hour day and to stop a pay cut that would reduce tonnage rates to less than half of what they had been in 1923.[62] On August 21, 1930, hundreds of miners risked their jobs by leaving scores of mines in the Kanawha coalfield and joining the Reorganized UMWA, whose leaders held regular meetings on one of the few pieces of land the coal companies didn't own. "Mr. Frank Keeney spoke today at the oil wells & got lots of joiners," the Kellys Creek miner Jimmie Jones noted on October 13. By then the Reorganized UMWA was fighting for its life against Lewis and his forces, and the new union could not send Keeney any more financial aid. Two months later Jones wrote, "The miners is goin' to work on Monday. The strike is over."[63]

On November 30, 1930, word passed through the coalfields that Mother Jones had died in Silver Spring, Maryland. She was mourned by thousands of Americans, especially the nation's hard-pressed coal miners, who were prominent among the forty thousand people who listened on loudspeakers as a Catholic priest eulogized her before she was buried at a miners' cemetery in Mount Olive, Illinois. A young cowboy singer from Texas expressed the sorrow many Americans felt in a song he composed to her memory. Gene Autry performed his ballad "The Death of Mother Jones" that fall on the *National Barn Dance* radio program and then recorded it.[64]

Mother Jones's passing also inspired a young miner and songwriter named Orville Jenks, who had been raised in Big Sandy, West Virginia. A child of Welsh parents, he sang every Sunday in the choir of their Methodist church and on weekdays in the mine, where he tended a trapdoor as a teenager. In 1930, Jenks recorded his best-known composition, "Sprinkle Coal Dust on My Grave." In this song an old coal miner mourns Mother Jones's death, and then, foreseeing his own end, he tells his wife:

> *Don't forget me, little darling,*
> *When they lay me down to rest,*
> *Tell my brothers all the loving words I say.*
> *Let the flowers be forgotten*
> *Sprinkle coal dust on my grave,*
> *In remembrance of the U.M.W. of A.*[65]

Jenks's eulogy for a deceased miner and for his aged guardian angel might have served just as well as a requiem for the union Mother Jones loved so well. For as the first full year of the Depression came to an end, the UMWA had ceased to exist in the coalfields of West Virginia.

Chapter 16

A People Made of Steel

Winter 1931–Spring 1933

As Americans hunkered down during the second winter of the Great Depression, President Herbert Hoover assured his fellow Americans that no one was actually "going hungry." But the president's words brought little comfort to the unemployed masses of Appalachia. By March 1931, 8 million Americans, including 112,000 West Virginia coal miners, were out of work. State, county, and township officials worked desperately to aid the victims of unemployment, but they could not meet the crushing need for aid in mining districts like Cabin Creek, where a reporter found families teetering on "the point of starvation."[1]

The winter of 1931 was the worst possible time to attempt a union revival. And yet that is what Frank Keeney attempted to do. After the Reorganized UMWA disbanded and their leaders rejoined the UMWA, Keeney founded his own organization, the West Virginia Mine Workers Union. In the next few months, battle-tested veterans of the mine wars joined with hundreds of young recruits to help Keeney mount a new organizing drive in the old union precincts like Kellys Creek. Unable to meet anywhere on company property, the miners crowded into the "colored school house" or hiked up the valley to meet on land owned by a petroleum company, where their old leaders held "speakin's" every Sunday afternoon. A journalist noted that the sound truck was always parked next to a cliff "for fear of bullets from behind."[2]

At a time when the official UMWA had failed on all fronts in the Appalachian minefields, Keeney's independents pushed on through the Kanawha district, where they enrolled twenty-three thousand new members during the first six months of 1931. This was a stunning achievement, wrote Louis Stark, a *New York Times* labor reporter. These miners not only suffered from the worst unemployment in the nation, but they had, Stark assumed, been thoroughly intimidated by mine guards, deputy sheriffs, blacklists, and yellow dog contracts.[3] Keeney even ventured across the Little Coal River into Logan County, where he had once traveled on horseback at night to avoid Don Chafin's deputies. Excited by this activity, A. J. Muste, one of the most influential radicals in the labor movement, began to raise funds for Keeney from his liberal allies and provided him with the services of young leftists on staff at Brookwood Labor College in New York.[4]

The Keeneyites also caught the eye of the acclaimed writer Edmund Wilson, who had been sending back edgy sketches of Depression

Union supporters waiting for Frank Keeney on a roadside in Logan County.

America to the *New Republic.* Wilson traveled to Ward on Kellys Creek, where eight hundred people lived in "little flat yellow houses on stilts that look like chicken-houses." These tenants seemed like prisoners to Wilson, "just as much at the mercy of the owners of their dwellings as if they did live in a chicken-yard with a high wire fence around it."[5]

But miners of Ward did not behave like a captive people; they had maintained "a tradition of resistance and a habit of joint action," and they would defend their rights, just like their mountaineer ancestors had in "the old days." The "traditional hostility between the Hat-fields and McCoys" had been replaced by a new kind of antagonism, according to Wilson. "Today there are Hatfields and McCoys on both sides of the economic line-up—both in the mines and among the operators—and members of the same family are found fighting each other as bitterly as the families fought each other in the past."[6]

Like Edmund Wilson, A. J. Muste held out high hopes for the West Virginia Mine Workers Union because it stood "between the Commu-nists, on the one hand, and the corrupt A. F. of L., on the other . . ." Because the new organization sprouted out of native ground in the hills of West Virginia, it was "a spontaneous native labor movement" and a genuine expression of radical Americanism.[7]

Furthermore, these coal diggers had a natural leader with nearly "hypnotic" powers of persuasion. "Frank Keeney is a short man, with a square face and stub-toed shoes," Wilson observed. "He has a straight black bang on his forehead, eyes like fragments of blue bottle-glass, a face as deep-seamed as if the battles of the miners had left their slashes there, and two solid-gold teeth. It has been said of him that he can talk to operators as if they were his own miners, and that he talks to miners like the captain of a ship." In the teeth of the Depression, Frank Keeney left his family in Charleston "to take big chances again"—to see if he could prevail against his enemies or if he would fail and "be crushed with his people."[8]

Keeney knew how to organize miners, but in 1931 he faced a new challenge: saving his followers from starvation. Some of the children at Ward had "gone without food for days and those who did eat sub-sisted on sow belly, potatoes, and pinto beans." Friends, neighbors, and local church groups could provide only so much charity. Some-thing else had to be done, so Keeney took a page out of Mother

Jones's book and led several hundred men, women, and children out of Kellys Creek on a twenty-eight-mile walk down the river to Charleston.[9] As the miners and their allies trod along, they sang an old hymn, "I Shall Not Be Moved," inspired by a biblical verse from Jeremiah. Someone wrote new lyrics for the march—"Frank Keeney is our captain / And we shall not be moved"—and turned this old tune into a modern protest song, one that would become an anthem for the labor and civil rights movements of the future.[10]

After camping outside the city for the night, Keeney and his followers filed peacefully past the handsome brick homes on Kanawha Street and down to the governor's mansion. As they walked along the hot pavement, the miners and their wives attracted hostile looks from well-dressed bystanders, who reportedly feared that this ragtag band of scrawny refugees might bring camp diseases with them to the city. Governor William G. Conley, a Republican who had been the president of a coal company, agreed to meet with Keeney and a delegation of miners. After some of the men from Kellys Creek described their suffering in detail, Conley explained that the state lacked the means to help them; he did, however, take a ten-dollar bill from his wallet and present it to them, along with his assurances that "whatever conditions may be now, we have the best government on earth."[11]

After this discouraging session with the governor, the protestors shuffled slowly back to their camp at Ward, where the West Virginia Mine Workers Union found itself under attack from two directions. UMWA officials reacted to Keeney's independent movement by stepping up their own organizing efforts and Red-baiting their rivals. Meanwhile, the employers reacted by firing and blacklisting employees who had joined the new union.

Always ready to take a big risk, Keeney rallied his followers by the oil derricks and told them they must act before their enemies destroyed their organization. He told them that if they quit work in July, when the operators would normally be filling orders for Great Lakes shippers, they could force their bosses to raise the wage scale, restore check-weigh men to the tipples, and free miners from the obligation to shop at the company store. At his urging, the membership voted to strike on July 6, 1931. The coal companies responded, as expected, by ordering mass evictions, and within a week, eight thousand strikers and their families were camped in tents along Kellys Creek on the few slivers of land the coal companies did not own.[12]

In 1931, few American workers were willing to strike because, as the miners put it, there was a "barefoot man" waiting to take every striker's job. But for Keeney's coal diggers, unionism was not simply a rational calculation; it was matter of principle and an act of faith. According to the constitution of the West Virginia Mine Workers Union, the labor movement was not originated by man; no, those who started it were acting on "a command from God Almighty" like the prophets did thousands of years ago when He told them to lead the Israelites out of bondage to freedom.[13] At one strike rally, a miner-preacher appealed to the strikers' sacred bond with their children, who faced a life sentence in the dark dungeons under the mountains: "I say to you that any man in this gathering today who does not join this strike and stand by it, even until death—for the sake of the children—is not worthy to call himself a Christian because he is not willing to stand up for the Kingdom of Heaven . . . [and] the children are the Kingdom of Heaven."[14]

Convinced they were acting on God's command, Keeney's followers judged the mine operators' actions in moral terms and concluded that these men were false Christians driven by greed and lust for power. Union preachers found plenty of examples to use as parables, including a decision the Winifrede Coal Company made to shut down the church it had built and fire the minister it had hired because he had participated in a prayer meeting with the strikers. When the company posted a No Trespassing sign on the tabernacle door, the strikers replied in a bulletin that read: "You can't even talk about God at Winifrede these days. Who said the coal operators weren't in league with the Devil?"[15]

By midsummer, coal production in the Kanawha minefield fell off on account of the walkout, but the fledgling miners' union had already exhausted its meager resources, and Frank Keeney knew the strike was doomed. Instead of drifting away, as outside organizers often did when their followers were defeated, Keeney rode up the creeks on an empty food truck to tell his people that he had failed them.[16]

While liberal journalists turned their attention away from West Virginia, Malcolm Ross kept an eye on Keeney, and he found him one day sitting in a shabby union office decorated with a campaign poster for the British Labour Party. His desk was cluttered with books and pamphlets, signs that "his knowledge ranged far beyond his native mountains." Keeney assured Ross that although the summer strike had been a failure, he would show the reporter that the spirit of the West Virginia Mine Workers Union had not been crushed.[17]

When the two men arrived at Ward to visit the union men and women who were still camped near the town, miners gave Keeney a lusty cheer and then filed into the "colored school house," where they "squeezed themselves grotesquely into the child-size desk seats." When they settled down, Keeney spoke. "One day," he promised, "there will be no more gun men, no tent colonies, because . . . you people are going through what you are." They had paraded together, sung together, and struck together, and now, he admitted, they had "nothing left but debts and the memory of defeat." Yes, Keeney granted, they had lost the strike that summer, but that did not mean they were a "vanquished" people. As long as they kept their faith in themselves and in one another, he was sure they would have the strength to survive whatever hardships they faced along the road ahead. "People like you," he said, "are made out of steel."[18]

"The time is hard and everybody is looking for work," read a note Jimmie Jones penciled into his diary on a cold day in January 1932. "It is the worse time ever hit the USA." The miners of Kellys Creek sent another delegation to Charleston "to see the governor about grub." When a truck carrying provisions arrived in Ward a few days later, Jones noted the event. "It wair a site to see the people," he wrote. "Some got grub and some none."[19]

By March, one out of every four American wage earners were out of work, and only about one-fourth of them were actually getting relief, mainly canned food, bags of flour, and chunks of coal for fuel. Charities like the Red Cross had run out of resources and public funds were running low. In the midst of all this suffering, President Hoover vetoed a federal relief bill, proclaiming it the most dangerous suggestion Congress had ever entertained. A balanced budget,

Hoover insisted, was the most essential factor in promoting an economic recovery.[20]

Hungry and edgy, American workers took action on multiple fronts that winter and spring. Some mounted hunger marches, blocked evictions, and demanded direct relief from local authorities; and some joined Unemployed Councils or militant new unions organized by the Communist Party. In Indiana, the remaining members of the UMWA struck to protest a 25 percent wage cut and then held seventy strikebreakers as prisoners on mine property until the National Guard freed them. In Pennsylvania, teams of unemployed miners surreptitiously dug small coal pits on company property, removed the fuel, trucked it to nearby cities, and sold it below the commercial price. And in West Virginia, a band of 250 World War I veterans set out from Charleston to join a much larger movement of unemployed servicemen who were marching on Washington, DC. The ex-servicemen aimed to pressure Congress to pass a law that

A West Virginia mining town during winter.

would grant them a special bonus payment for their wartime service they were not scheduled to receive until 1945.[21]

The first group of bonus marchers reached Washington at the end of May, and within a few weeks, twenty-two thousand unemployed men were camped on Anacostia Flats. There, within sight of the Capitol dome, the veterans pitched their tents and created the nation's largest Hooverville. They vowed to stay in Washington until Congress gave them their bonuses.[22]

While Washingtonians adjusted to a ragtag army of veterans camped on their city's outskirts, the usually languid proceedings of the U.S. Congress began to churn with new energy. Inside hearing rooms on Capitol Hill, labor leaders described the growing specter of revolution in America. William Green, a former UMWA official who had become president of the AFL, told a Senate committee that he feared a universal strike and the possibility of class war if Congress failed to address the crisis. "If we do not get at the fundamentals in an orderly, constructive way," Green declared, "we shall be swept aside by a tide of revolt."[23] By this time, the Great Depression had discredited President Hoover and the conservative Republicans who stood in the way of reform. The winds of desperation were howling outside the marble walls of the nation's capital, and some members of Congress were ready to throw open the doors and let those winds blow in.

Senator George W. Norris, a maverick Republican from Nebraska, had his hands full in 1932 trying to help desperate corn and hog farmers in his agricultural state, but this old-fashioned progressive had broader concerns on his mind as well. He believed that judges had created a crisis in American government by issuing injunctions that denied workers freedom of speech and freedom of association.[24]

The senator's interest in the nation's coal miners had developed in 1926, when he broke ranks with his party and traveled to Pennsylvania to campaign for the Democratic senatorial nominee, William B. Wilson, a former UMWA officer who had served as the first secretary of labor. During a campaign tour through a mining district, Norris found himself appalled by what he learned from an old man who had been horribly maimed in a mine disaster and by the epitaph on a miner's grave that read: FOR 40 YEARS BENEATH THE SOD, WITH PICK

AND SPADE I DID MY TASK, THE COAL KING'S SLAVE, BUT NOW, THANK GOD, I'M FREE AT LAST.[25]

After his epiphany in coal country, Norris decided to make the plight of the nation's miners his special cause. As a Lincolnian liberal, the Nebraskan was outraged that the federal courts had sanctioned yellow dog contracts and thereby perpetuated a semifeudal form of master-servant relationship, a form of "involuntary servitude" in clear violation of the U.S. Constitution. From his strategic position as chair of the Senate Judiciary Committee, the "fighting liberal" from Nebraska set out to tackle the two legal powers coal operators had used to keep these workers down: the anti-union contract and the court injunction.

Prepared for a long struggle, Norris called together several legal experts, including the brilliant young Harvard law professor Felix Frankfurter, who had been conducting his own study of the broad use of antilabor injunctions by the courts. The son of Viennese Jews, Frankfurter had worked his way up from the tenements of the Lower East Side of New York. He excelled academically and attended City College and Harvard Law School, where he taught civil rights and investigated the cases of the union radical militant Tom Mooney and the anarchists Nicola Sacco and Bartolomeo Vanzetti. Together, Norris and Frankfurter, two progressive attorneys from extremely different backgrounds, began to draft a bill that would outlaw restrictive employment contracts and prohibit the sweeping injunctions that had made union organizing a crime in hundreds of West Virginia mines.[26]

For six years, Norris attempted to end "government-by-injunction"

Senator George W. Norris.

through an act of Congress, and for six years he failed. By 1932, however, the political landscape had shifted. Democrats had gained control of the House and the Republicans had but a one-vote majority in the Senate; in a close contest, it was Senator Norris who would cast that deciding vote. The Nebraskan sensed that the time had come for a historic change in American labor law. If he succeeded, the consequences would be enormous, especially for the workers who toiled in West Virginia's coal mines.[27]

Norris's anti-injunction bill began with the premise that "the individual unorganized worker is commonly helpless to exercise actual liberty of contract . . . and thereby to obtain acceptable terms and conditions of employment." Wage earners who lived in a democratic country and toiled in an industrial economy should enjoy "full freedom of association" so that they could organize themselves, select their own leaders, and negotiate with their employers without any "interference, restraint, or coercion" by "employers of labor, or their agents." The proposed legislation would also deny the courts jurisdiction in cases when workers peacefully engaged in strikes, joined unions, aided other workers on strike, publicized a labor dispute through advertising, leafleted, or assembled to promote one side in a labor dispute. The yellow dog contracts West Virginia coal companies demanded of their employees violated all of these principles, and Norris drafted his law in a way that made these notorious agreements unenforceable in the federal courts.[28]

On March 1, the U.S. Senate voted in favor of the Norris bill by a stunning margin of 75 to 5. A week later, another maverick Republican, Representative Fiorello La Guardia of New York, introduced the anti-injunction bill on the House floor. The congressman's motion prevailed by an impressive majority of 362 to 14. President Hoover had no choice but to sign the law.

The Norris–La Guardia Act represented the greatest legislative victory for labor in American history, but it had no immediate effect, because trade unions were too weak and their leaders were too timid to test the new law. For the rest of 1932, unions remained comatose, with their leaders suffering from what *Fortune* magazine called "pernicious anaemia, sociological myopia, and hardening of the arteries."[29]

John L. Lewis received more than his share of criticism from liberals; from Communists who had formed a rival miners' union; and from many of his own members in Illinois, who bolted from the UMWA and formed the Progressive Mine Workers of America, a union that attracted some support from Frank Keeney's followers in West Virginia. Lewis's many opponents insisted that he was behaving like a union dictator and acting like the conservative industrialists who were once his adversaries.[30]

During the late 1920s, the UMWA president encouraged northern mine operators to mechanize so they could compete with low-cost coal from the nonunion mines of Appalachia. But the sacrifice of union jobs did not stop the UMWA's slide into oblivion. In 1932, with the coal industry imploding, union membership hitting rock bottom, and with the president's recovery program failing, Lewis decided to jettison his conservative, laissez-faire philosophy and adopt a new political strategy.[31]

In July 1932, the mine union chief arrived on Capitol Hill looking massive in his three-piece business suit. After he sat down at a table, Lewis peered up at members of the Senate Finance Committee and began to outline a carefully prepared plan for the federal government to stabilize the coal industry. The business, he declared, had nearly destroyed itself through cutthroat competition. Production exceeded demand; firms were too small and too numerous; and most owners and operators failed to see beyond their own self-interest. "They have practically no form of organization," Lewis declared. "They have no code of ethics. They are simply engaged in a struggle to continue their existence and remain in business."[32]

Furthermore, said Lewis, these businessmen allowed larger corporations to prey upon the coal industry by selling coal below cost of production and robbing miners of a fair day's pay. The economic reason for the mine owners' behavior was that the demand for bituminous coal was inelastic. Lower prices pushed wages down, but did not increase consumption during the 1920s; the reason was that the market for coal did not expand as rapidly as the nation's economic growth. During the Depression years that market simply collapsed as industrial production fell by nearly 50 percent, plunging from 535 million tons in 1929 to 310 million tons in 1932. But mine owners had invested so much capital in the collieries and other properties that they maintained production, even when they had to sell coal below cost.[33]

During the first three years of the Depression, scores of West Virginia mining firms declared bankruptcy, including the Red Jacket Consolidated Coal and Coke Company in Mingo County; this was the same firm that had demanded the first yellow dog contracts that led to so much labor trouble in 1920. Red Jacket had paved the way for more than a hundred other companies to join together in 1927 and successfully plead in federal court for an injunction that would virtually outlaw the UMWA in West Virginia. The argument industry lawyers made then was that only nonunion, open shop companies could compete profitably in the national market. But even with this advantage, Red Jacket had failed. The lesson, the *United Mine Workers Journal* declared, was that union busting did not pay.[34]

In his testimony before the Senate Finance Committee, Lewis argued that to promote recovery, Congress should suspend antitrust laws, regulate wages and prices, mandate a six-hour day to spread out the work, and, most important, guarantee workers the right to organize. If the union regained its strength, its leaders could negotiate a new industry-wide wage scale that would stabilize labor costs for the largest, most efficient fuel companies and drive the small low-wage firms out of business. This was the same deal Lewis and the UMWA had offered the West Virginia coal operators after World War I as a solution to the chronic instability of coal prices. If the industry put a floor under wages, prices would not fluctuate so wildly, and smaller, less profitable companies would be forced out of the market.[35]

But the nonunion mine owners of West Virginia scorned the UMWA's offer because they hated the union and distrusted Lewis, and because they remained firm believers in a capitalist system unregulated by government agencies or by collectively bargained wage rates and work rules. At first, only a few socialists like Frank Keeney and Harold Houston warned that this system was headed for disaster, but by 1932, many other West Virginians realized that boundless capitalism had run the coal industry into the ground and ruined the lives of thousands who depended upon it.

Appalachian coal miners' average per capita earnings reached $851 in 1923, then fell to $588 in 1929, and hit rock bottom at what one historian called the "unbelievably low point of $235 in 1933." By comparison, the average family income declined to $1,524 that year, and the average yearly earnings for a wage earner in manufacturing dropped to $914. Like the sharecoppers and tenant farmers who became dust bowl refugees, the families who clung to life in the coal towns of Appalachia suffered from the worst of hard times.[36]

By 1932, the prolonged depression had cracked the hegemony of the big-business Republican regime that had seemed so unassailable during the 1920s. In the four years since Herbert Hoover's election to the presidency in 1928, economic catastrophe and governmental paralysis had discredited the old order and its business values, free-market principles, and conservative politics.[37]

When Franklin D. Roosevelt campaigned for the presidency against Hoover in the fall of 1932, he paid little attention to organized labor, which no longer exercised much influence over blue-collar voters. But after his election and his inauguration, Roosevelt found it difficult to ignore insistent labor leaders like William Green of the AFL and John Lewis of the UMWA. During the first one hundred days of Roosevelt's term beginning in March 1933, these union officials and their allies mounted a relentless lobbying effort to win federal assistance for organized labor. They were partially successful when Congress enacted the National Industrial Recovery Act (NIRA) on June 16, 1933.

The centerpiece of President Roosevelt's New Deal, this law exempted coal mining and other industries from antitrust prosecution if businesses agreed to eliminate competition by stabilizing prices, allocating markets, and accepting codes that set minimum wage and maximum hours. These codes included two key sections Lewis had insisted upon: the first guaranteed that employees would "have the right to organize and bargain collectively through representatives of their own choosing," and the second provision stated that "no employee and no one seeking employment shall be required as a condition of employment . . . to refrain from joining, organizing, or assisting a labor organization of his own choosing." The yellow dog contracts thousands of West Virginia miners had signed were henceforth null and void. Federal law had finally granted unions the freedom to engage in organizing and "peaceful persuasion," and given mine workers and millions of other wage earners the "freedom of association" guaranteed by the First Amendment.[38]

President Roosevelt described the NIRA "as the most important and far-reaching legislation ever enacted by the American Congress." The NIRA not only created a recovery administration to regulate industry; it established a relief administration to battle unemployment and authorized an enormous $3.3 billion appropriation for public construction programs ($59.1 billion in today's dollars). The president did not mention the fact that the controversial labor provision of the law—Lewis's "secret weapon"—had survived intact, but joyful union leaders trumpeted the news far and wide. AFL president William Green called Section 7(a) of the NIRA a Magna Carta for the nation's wage earners. The *United Mine Workers Journal* headline proclaimed: "THE OLD ORDER CHANGETH, THE NEW DAY IS AT HAND, LABOR IS BEING EMANCIPATED." Congress had given American workers their own Bill of Rights.[39]

But Section 7(a) was "enabling legislation and nothing more," wrote historian Irving Bernstein, and "its promise would be fulfilled only if the labor movement acted with speed and vigor." Lewis and his UMWA staff had already prepared to exploit the NIRA's promise by putting their toughest activists on the payroll and mobilizing them for an all-out organizing drive in the nation's coalfields.[40]

In West Virginia—always a key to the union's future—outreach work had begun early that spring when District 17's new director, Van A. Bittner, sent his agents out into the coalfields to spread the word that something big would be happening soon. One of his men, Morgan Justice, had worked in Mingo County and had survived numerous scrapes with death in battles along the Tug River. A Logan County miner who had known Justice in 1920 was shocked when he found that, "by some miracle," his friend was "still alive in 1933" and working undercover for the UMWA in the Guyan field. After the two miners exchanged stories about their hard days in the Lick Creek tent camp, Justice promised his long-lost friend that everything had changed since the days of Don Chafin. "All the demons in hell can't keep us from organizing Logan County now," Justice proclaimed.[41]

Bittner was an outsider who was shrewd enough to know that he needed men with local knowledge to lead the union drive in West Virginia. With this in mind, he called upon Bill Blizzard, who had recently been rehired by Lewis as an international organizer, and sent him into Logan County, a place he had tried to overrun by force of arms a decade before.[42] As his assistant, Blizzard chose Milton Hendrix, a miner who had taken guns from the company stores on Kellys Creek to arm the men he led to an insurgent camp at Marmet in 1921. During the spring of 1933, these two veterans of the mine wars eluded sheriff deputies as they worked their way through the hollows, bringing news of the New Deal and of the UMWA's imminent return to the field. As they were leaving one camp, Hendrix recalled hearing a woman shout to her neighbor, "Hey, the union is coming over the mountain next week. You better get ready."[43]

In the weeks that followed, veteran activists like Blizzard, Hendrix, and Justice motored down mountain roads and rumbled into desolate coal camps in beat-up Ford cars boldly announcing on loudspeakers: "The President wants you to join the union." The response they received astounded union officials. A "wave of enthusiasm of mountainous proportions for the United Mine Workers of America is sweeping the areas," the union's journal reported. The flood of new members was "so great" that it was "almost impossible to keep track of it."[44]

In Mingo County, mine workers gathered peacefully and signed union cards in coal towns like Matewan, Red Jacket, Merrimac, War Eagle, and Mohawk, where lethal gun battles had raged in 1920. "It is hard to tell how many men have been killed; how many crimes of one kind or another have come out of the fight for and against unions in the Norfolk and Western region from Bluefield to Kenova," remarked the *Martinsburg Journal*, but in 1933, one act of Congress ended that cruel struggle and brought peace to the Tug River Valley.[45]

The nation's top labor reporter, Louis Stark of the *New York Times*, had visited Kellys Creek in 1931 to report on the rise and rapid disintegration of Frank Keeney's independent union. When he returned two years later, Stark observed something completely different: "This time the operators offered no resistance. Shopkeepers in the coal camps hailed the union organizers with an almost evangelical fervor, supplied them with gasoline for their shabby cars, and gave them a lift in the work of organization."[46]

During that first spring of the New Deal, many mine operators simply surrendered when union forces moved through their company towns. Demoralized by several years of plunging profits, discredited by failed business practices, and deprived of legal support from the federal courts, these employers stood aside and let history take its course. Many of these executives realized that the NIRA codes could stabilize and rationalize their stricken industry, even though these new federal rules also allowed the UMWA to organize their miners. In any case, it was apparent that the movement toward unionization was irresistible.

The miners caught up in the union drive devoted songs, prayers, and poems to their savior, John L. Lewis, and many praised his right-hand man, Van A. Bittner, for finally "organizing West Virginia." In truth, these two national leaders took advantage of circumstances beyond their control—depression conditions that crippled their enemies and new laws that banned yellow dog contracts and proclaimed the right to organize unions—the kind of legal reforms Frank Keeney begged for in 1920 and 1921. Furthermore, Lewis and Bittner commanded a campaign that was actually implemented by savvy local organizers like Bill Blizzard, who drew upon two decades of experience and a vast network of allies. But these veterans of the mine wars received no recognition for doing the hard fieldwork in 1933. They were mere cogs in the machine Lewis and Bittner operated. And, of course, no one in the union acknowledged Frank Keeney for his historic role as leader of the state's union miners. This was no surprise because Lewis and his officer corps had already discredited Keeney "for trying to shoot the union into West Virginia," for bankrupting District 17, and for being a "double crosser" who organized rival unions and "took money from pinks and Reds."[47]

The militant democratic movements Keeney led had failed to accomplish what Lewis's bureaucratic machine had gained for West

Van A. Bittner speaking at a political rally sponsored by a new union local, 1934.

Virginia miners without resorting to the armed violence. When the UMWA won a quick and bloodless victory in 1933, its success owed nothing—or so it seemed—to Keeney or to his comrades who had picked up their guns and fought desperate battles against the coal operators and their armed forces. The gains achieved in these strikes and paramilitary campaigns had all vanished after Keeney left office, but these brutal struggles had not been forgotten by veteran miners who passed on to younger workers an enduring memory of shared hardship and a culture of solidarity. A "tradition of resistance" and a "habit of joint action" had survived even in the hardest of hard times, as Edmund Wilson discovered on his trip to Kellys Creek in 1931; and, as a result, thousands of mining people were well prepared for the task of bringing unionism back to coal country.[48]

While southern West Virginia was being unionized, it was also being Americanized, though not in the way the coal operators and their allies had intended when they launched their own private crusade a decade earlier and cloaked their open shop American plan in the language of loyalty and patriotism. Suddenly, joining the miners' union became a patriotic act, an expression of what one historian called "working-class Americanism." That democratic spirit was reflected in the behavior of West Virginia coal miners who elected their own union officials, asserted new rights in the collieries, spoke freely on the streets of company towns, and voted for candidates who supported organized labor.[49]

Old-timers in the UMWA were not surprised when the union swept through towns like Eskdale, Ward, Mucklow, Boomer, and Mount Hope—the old District 17 strongholds where Frank Keeney was still regarded as a hero. But veterans of the mine wars were amazed at what happened in Logan County, which had always been "the place of terror" for union supporters, as Van Bittner put it. Now, workers throughout the Guyan field "welcomed the union with open arms."[50]

For decades, Logan County's miners had lived in dread of the "overlords that was protecting the companies" whose owners "didn't care nothing for a man's life," Luther Keen, a local worker, recalled. "They was raggedy, hungry, even barefooted," he remembered. "It was beyond imagination. They knew they didn't have anything to lose. They was just ripe for the picking. And I thank the dear Lord that I was able to help him pick!" Some men still held back because they feared losing their jobs, and in those cases, Keen explained, "we'd just get together a few hundred men and go march on that mine that wasn't coming in with us, and we'd give them a little pep talk and just *bring* them in," he added with emphasis. "Once they got the fear of the devil out of them, and they saw this thing for real— and believe me it was—they'd come right behind us."[51]

Within a month, UMWA activists had organized more than ten thousand Logan County miners into scores of union locals. Deciding it was time for a public demonstration of organized labor's new power, UMWA leaders announced a mass meeting at Ellis Ball Park in Logan, where Van Bittner administered the union oath of allegiance to five thousand men over a loudspeaker.[52]

A few days later, on June 23, 1933, hundreds of union coal

miners descended on Charleston from all over Appalachia to attend a historic convention. The 2,500 delegates represented 160,000 new UMWA members. Some of the delegates were Italian and Hungarian immigrants; some were African Americans; and most were white Appalachians of Scots-Irish descent. Hundreds of the conventioneers were young men—the sons and grandsons of colliers who entered mining in the dark decade just passed—and some were veterans of the past mine wars. Looking out over the vast throng gathered in the city's armory, Van Bittner spoke over a loudspeaker and said that with one stroke of the pen President Roosevelt had changed their lives by signing a law that finally gave them the right to organize. "This is our day," Bittner proclaimed; "it is written in the stars that we shall survive . . . You men of McDowell, Logan, Mingo, the Winding Gulf and Kanawha fields . . . you are now free citizens of the United States . . ."[53]

Chapter 17

More Freedom than I Ever Had

Summer 1933–Fall 1934

During the summer of 1933, new union members all over West Virginia met in little schoolhouses, hillside churches, and fraternal lodges to form union locals and elect officers. At one of these meetings in Logan County, two hundred men settled down for a program of speeches and prayer after a string orchestra had played a number of tunes. "We believe there will soon be a time," the local's secretary predicted, "when we miners will be walking the streets of Logan and the merchants will come out and reach out a hand to us and say, 'Come in and buy something.'" When that day came, he remarked, those retailers and professionals who stood by the miners would have their business, but "those who have been against us" should know that "we will be against them . . ." It was time for the people of Logan to decide which side they were on.[1]

After they won over the miners of Logan County, UMWA organizers moved on to the last bastion of the open shop, the Pocahontas minefield in McDowell County. This had been company territory ever since the operators crushed uprisings led by militant black miners in the late 1890s. There had been little labor trouble after that, and in 1933, the field's "captive mines"—collieries owned by large steel companies—remained off-limits to UMWA organizers.[2]

McDowell County mine operators had been able to rely on the loyalty of local mountain whites and blacks from outside the region for nearly four decades. The farmers and hunters who came down from the hills to work in the mines were rugged individualists who took pride in calling their county the "Free State of McDowell," a place where self-reliant mountaineers hated taxes, loved practical jokes, and lived by the adage "What is mine is mine; what is yours is yours."[3] But years of living in tightly controlled company towns and working long days in dangerous mines gradually created a feeling of commonality among these individualists.

One of these mountaineers, Orville J. Jenks, later explained that he had always been a union man at heart, and recalled that in 1930, he wrote a song to memorialize Mother Jones. Three years later, this miner musician was ready to take the oath of obligation as soon as UMWA advance men arrived in the Pocahontas field. Over the next few months, Jenks worked at the union office in Welch, not far from the courthouse where Sid Hatfield and Ed Chambers were gunned down in 1921, while he composed and performed several new songs for the cause, including one tune about his native McDowell County.

> When you hear of a thing that's called union
> You know that they're happy and free
> Some people don't know who to thank
> For this "State of McDowell" that's so free

But Orville Jenks knew: "Give part of the praise to John Lewis," he sang, "And the rest of it to Franklin D."[4]

McDowell County coal companies employed more than 6,000 black miners, the largest total in the state by far. These men had provided labor stability and productivity since the 1890s. "The operators welcomed them," wrote Phil Conley, a journalist and coal industry publicist, because "Negroes made good men for the mines; they were a happy-go-lucky lot who were satisfied with the wages they received and would rather go about their regular work than strike for a few cents more an hour."[5]

For the next three decades, African American ministers and businessmen fervently opposed the white man's union and warned black workers against breaking trust with the coal companies that had made a better life possible for people of color in this region. However, the Depression began to test the African American coal miners' loyalty to their employers and to the local black bourgeoisie. When companies cut wages, kept store prices high, and discarded the vestiges of welfare capitalism, black mine workers in the Pocahontas field began to question their allegiances. They had endured three years of the Depression, a time when they were often the first men to be fired and the last to be rehired by bosses who had once praised them for their loyalty and productivity. Eventually, hundreds of black workers in McDowell County reassessed their options and decided to take sides with their white coworkers in an effort to gain the protection a collective bargaining agreement could provide. When the door to the house of labor was thrown open to them, black miners rushed in and once again became the most "persistent unionists" in the coalfields, just as their forerunners had been when the UMWA first arrived in the Pocahontas field forty years before.[6]

Union organizing in the Pocahontas field blended with community organizing. In Berwind, Henry G. Young, an African American miner, allied with his fellow workers as well as local civic and church leaders in a prolonged effort to organize the miners. Young was a homeowner and pillar in his church, Rosebud Baptist, where he served as choir and Sunday school director, deacon, and trustee. These positions enhanced Young's standing as a community leader and enabled him to play a key role in an interracial civic coalition that would bring the union into the Big Creek district of McDowell County.[7]

Some of the African American coal miners who joined the UMWA sang about their experience gospel-style. In "I Can Tell the World," the United Four Quartet of Barrackville, West Virginia, took on the voice of a miner who tells the nation how blessed he was by what John Lewis's union had done.

> It brought joy, great joy, unto my soul.
> It made me free, it made me glad,
>   Yes it did, my Lord, yes it did.
> An' gave me mo' freedom dan I ever had.[8]

"When the weight of union power settled on Appalachia, a fresh minstrelsy blossomed there," wrote the musicologist George Korson. Brass and string bands, gospel ensembles, and Welsh choirs performed inspirational tunes and old fight songs like "Solidarity Forever" and "We Shall Not Be Moved."[9] There were new tunes performed by guitarists who had learned the blues from traveling crews of black railroad laborers, songs like the mournful "Coal Loadin' Blues" and the rueful "John L. Lewis Blues," sung in the voice of an unfortunate miner who had not joined the union.[10]

For Labor Day 1933, Virginia West, a coal miner's daughter from Mount Hope, composed a song that reflected the new sense of hope surging through the coal camps. West's lyrics celebrated the miners' new freedom from the company store, from the dawn-till-dusk workday, and from the mine bosses and company guards who expected undue deference and blind obedience.

> *Now we don't care what the operators say.*
> *We're goin' to keep fightin' for that six-hour day.*

A church used as a union hall in the Pocahontas coalfield.

Lord, lord, we're independent now.

Now when you meet your boss you don't have to bow,
He ain't no king—never was nohow.

Lord, lord, we're independent now.[11]

Mining town women had traditionally supported union men in their communities by harassing strikebreakers, feeding strikers, marching with Mother Jones, and nursing the wounded during the mine wars. The wives, mothers, sisters, and cousins of coal miners had engaged in these actions spontaneously, but in 1933 females took a more formal role in union affairs by forming ladies' auxiliaries. At Bramwell, loyal union women formed an auxiliary to register working-class females whose votes were just as important as those of men when it came to electing worker-friendly representatives to office. In addition, the seventy-five members of this ladies auxiliary banded together to buy union labor products, discuss their affairs, and sing union songs, "of which," the secretary reported, "we have several written by union miners." They also planned to open a restaurant where those attending a spring celebration could "buy union cooked food and have it served by union women."[12]

Many coal miners' wives shared a belief that the union's coming was a gift from God to those who had kept their faith in Him during the hardest times. One of these women recalled how her spirits soared that spring when the UMWA came into Logan County. From the porch of her house in Mud Fork Hollow, Mandy Porter told a group of curious visitors: "I am an old preacher woman myself and I do believe the good Lord, he watches over the righteous, and he listens to their cries." The misery in the coal camps "was stinking all the way up to heaven," Porter explained, "and the Lord put up with it just as long as he could, and then he just caused things to happen," she concluded. "The Union, I figure, was just a blessing from heaven."[13]

John L. Lewis realized that the miners' wild enthusiasm for the UMWA would wither away or turn to violence if he and his team failed to negotiate a good contract with the bituminous coal companies operating in Appalachia. All through the summer, union and management teams argued into the night at a Washington hotel, but they made no progress, despite encouraging words from President Roosevelt and frequent interventions by Hugh S. Johnson, the truculent, profane administrator of the National Recovery Administration. During breaks in the heated negotiations, Lewis stepped out to phone Van Bittner and other district leaders, "begging and pleading with his agents in the field to keep the lid on a boiling pot and prevent spontaneous strikes."[14]

That summer, Lorena Hickok, an investigator for the Federal Emergency Relief Administration, toured the coalfields of southern West Virginia, where she perceived a frightening level of anger. In an urgent letter to her friend Eleanor Roosevelt, Hickok described the shocking misery she saw in the coal camps. Everyone she met in Logan County seemed anxious and edgy. UMWA organizers had signed up thousands of members and were promising enormous raises and a six-hour workday, but the county's mine operators were

UMWA organizers and local supporters at a rally somewhere in the West Virginia minefields, July 4, 1933.

refusing to make even minor concessions. Hickok thought that both sides seemed reckless and irresponsible, and she warned the First Lady that unless the president intervened and assumed "dictatorial powers," another mine war would explode in southern West Virginia, a conflict that would be far worse than the first two.[15]

Alarmed by Hickok's reports, the First Lady left Washington and crossed the Alleghenies by car to investigate for herself. Eleanor Roosevelt had been following the West Virginia situation since the 1920s, when she sent money one winter to help relieve the misery of evicted strikers living in tents. Guided by old Quaker friends— who had been trying to keep mining families from starving— Roosevelt met and talked with desperate mine workers and their wives in the Fairmont coalfield. Her heart went out to them, and when she returned to Washington, she persuaded her husband and his aides to fund the construction of some model communities for these homeless miners and their families. One of these New Deal towns, Red House, opened a few years later on the Kanawha River; later on, grateful residents would rename the community Eleanor.[16]

Before another mine war could explode in southern West Virginia, John L. Lewis and his team forged a historic agreement with the Appalachian mine operators' association. UMWA negotiators made some compromises on wages and hours, but they also achieved enormous gains for their members. The Appalachian Agreement established an eight-hour day, a forty-hour week, and a base rate of pay for West Virginia miners close to the union scale that prevailed in the older, unionized bituminous mines of Pennsylvania, Ohio, Indiana, and Illinois. Besides granting employees substantial wage increases, shorter hours, and contractual protections for their rights on the job, the coal company executives agreed to "check off" union dues from miners' pay, to accept a four-step grievance procedure, to grant workers the right to select their own check-weigh men, to ban payment in scrip, to free employees from any obligation to shop at company stores, and to not hire boys under the age of seventeen to work in the collieries. Coal town mothers would no longer face mornings like the ones the widow Elizabeth Keeney faced in 1892, when she sent her ten-year-old son, Frank, off with lunch pail in hand, watched him climb to the tunnel, and waited for the rest of the day to see if he came out alive.

When they signed on to the Appalachian Agreement, "the defeated mine-owners agreed to all the things that deputy sheriffs usually shoot people for demanding," wrote Howard Brubaker in the *New Yorker*, a remark that may have left some readers wondering why so many mine workers had been shot and killed for what had been achieved so swiftly and so peacefully during those first spring weeks of the New Deal.[17]

A few months after the Appalachian Agreement took effect, John L. Lewis stood triumphantly before hundreds of UMWA delegates at a convention hall in Indianapolis to report on the union's enormous accomplishments. "The United Mine Workers of America has substantially accomplished the task to which it has been dedicated . . . through forty-four years of its history," Lewis rumbled. "It has at last succeeded in bringing into the fold . . . practically all the mine workers in our great North American continent."[18]

September 4, 1934, was a day to remember in the coalfields of southern West Virginia. Joyful workers and their supporters marched through the streets of company towns and county seats. It was Labor Day, a holiday that many miners had never been allowed to celebrate before. In Mingo County, miners came down from the hills to celebrations in Matewan, Red Jacket, and Chattaroy, where gun battles had raged during the second mine war in 1920. At the county seat in Williamson, a crowd estimated at sixteen thousand gathered in the courthouse square that day, its ranks swollen by delegations of union miners from Kentucky, who had crossed the Tug River to join a parade line that stretched for two miles all the way to a picnic ground outside of town. At Quinwood, a crowd of ten thousand enjoyed a day filled with band concerts and topped off with a nighttime fireworks display. And at Elm Grove, two thousand miners and their families passed the day with baseball games and outdoor dancing to music provided by a UMWA string band.[19] There was much to celebrate on that holiday for the miners had accomplished great things in a miraculously short period of time.

"Well, it was just about heaven when we finally got the union," a retired miner remarked many years later. "A lot of things went to changing in Logan County right away. For one thing, when I first went into the mines, I had to work in water, in cold water, right . . . up to your thighs. Well, you'd get sweaty from all of that heavy work, and hot, and your feet would be in cold water. I got sick from it many a time. But when the union come in, they had to get rid of that water."[20]

The presence of union committeemen in every pit allowed miners to object to working under "loose tops" and in gassy rooms. Furthermore, UMWA lobbyists put pressure on the state to increase its staff of mining inspectors. As a result, West Virginia's mines would no longer be the same hellholes they had been during the 1920s, when 478 workers, on average, died on the job each year. In the six years after the Appalachian Agreement took effect, fatalities in those mines decreased by nearly one-third. If the old death rate had continued during that time period, seven hundred more miners would have died at work during the late 1930s.[21]

Life also changed for the coal operators who had opposed the UMWA so staunchly for so long. Most of these men accepted the new order and grudgingly admitted that wage stabilization would

Union miners marching in a Labor Day parade in Logan, West Virginia.

be good for business. "The experience of 1929–1933 had shown that some method of preventing wage cutting was necessary," wrote mine owner W. P. Tams Jr. many years later, "and the union contract appeared to be the only dependable device to secure this end." But some of the old guard never made the transition. Justus Collins and "King Sam" Dixon, the union's fiercest and most effective adversaries, died in 1934 before they had to cope with the fact that their loyal employees had organized against them. Some old-timers opted out before they gave in. W. R. Thurmond, a coal industry leader who had once allied with Sheriff Don Chafin to keep the UMWA out of Logan County, sold the four mines he owned. Instead of retiring, Thurmond found a place in the New Deal order by accepting an appointment to serve as the state tax collector for the Internal Revenue Service.[22]

When they signed the Appalachian Agreement with the UMWA, the mine owners agreed to end the private mine guard system union members and many others held responsible for the two mine wars that ravaged the region. W. G. Baldwin and Thomas Felts, realizing "the early 1930's were not a good time for private detective agencies," decided to give up their old business of guarding mine properties, protecting scabs, running spies, and intimidating union men. In 1934, Herman Kump, the new Democratic governor of West Virginia, finished the job when he ordered McDowell County sheriff Maginnis Hatfield to disarm and disband nearly two hundred deputy sheriffs who were still being paid by mine operators in the Pocahontas field. The governor's decree applied to the other mining counties as well, where the coal companies had employed hundreds of deputies to keep union organizers out of their mines and to maintain political control over their towns. Reflecting on the evils of the mine guard system, the *Huntington Herald* observed, "It is happily true that conditions which brought it into existence no longer prevail."[23]

By the end of 1934, the UMWA had organized most of West Virginia's coal miners and had expanded its dues-paying membership to more than one hundred thousand men, a ninefold increase in just two years. But there were still a few steep mountains left for union organizers to climb: the "captive" coal operations owned by out-of-state steel manufacturers like the U.S. Steel Corporation, whose subsidiary, the U.S. Coal and Coke Company, employed nearly two thousand men in huge mechanized mines and housed most of them in model towns it constructed at Elbert, Gary, and ten other sites along the upper reaches of the Tug Fork River.[24]

The steel magnates and their mine managers had resisted the 1933 UMWA organizing drive with every means at their disposal. Along with the old methods—labor spies, armed guards, and blacklists—they employed a new weapon: the company-sponsored union or employee representation plan.[25] "[The] worst place we had to organize were the Youngstown captive mines at Dehue, over on Rum Creek," remarked one Logan County union organizer, because "the operators was there with high-powered machine guns and everything." The Youngstown Sheet and Tube Company depended on fuel from its Dehue mine to fire four Bessemer converters, six blast furnaces, and twenty-four open-hearth furnaces in its Ohio mills.[26]

Dehue had remained impervious to union influence when the UMWA swept through hundreds of other company towns in the spring of 1933. During the fall, however, the men who loaded coal at the Dehue mine began to reevaluate their situation when they realized that thousands of union miners would soon be working under a new contract that would provide them with higher pay, shorter hours, and various rights they had never enjoyed. Four years later, thousands of "captive" mine workers exercised the democratic rights afforded them by the National Labor Relations Act of 1935 when they lined up in company towns like Gary and Dehue to vote for the UMWA in "representation elections" conducted by a new federal agency, the National Labor Relations Board.[27]

As industrial relations changed in coal country, so did race relations. Black and white miners and their families remained segregated in their houses, schools, and churches and in most social activities, but union affairs were integrated, perhaps to a greater extent than anywhere else in industrial America at the time. When a writer for *Opportunity: A Journal of Negro Life* conducted a sober assessment of black participation in the union movement, he noted that in the UMWA, the nation's largest union, everyone was admitted "on a basis of complete equality." As a result, this organization's membership of a half million men was highly varied in racial and ethnic composition. "The West Virginia coal fields probably constitute the largest Negro membership in the U.M.W.A. . . ." *Opportunity* reported; and it was here that organized mine workers had "probably made the greatest contribution to the cause of Negro-white unionism."[28]

At one of the largest Labor Day celebrations in 1934, a new UMWA district leader told a crowd gathered in the Pocahontas coalfield that it was the dawn of a new era. In the years ahead, he promised, "the good people of Appalachia" would have the same opportunity as people in the North to earn a living wage. "Instead of having poverty all around us," he promised, "we will have a peaceful and happy people who can pay their debts and look every merchant honestly in the face and say, 'Thank you.'"[29]

A UMWA member and his family, Bertha Hill, Scotts Run, West Virginia.

The union leader's prediction came true over the next seven years when the UMWA's collective bargaining agreement more than doubled the average weekly wage of bituminous coal miners. This represented one of the many achievements a grateful union member from southern West Virginia exalted in a letter he wrote to the *United Mine Workers Journal*:

> What a change has been wrought in this part of the country! Instead of fourteen hours we work seven hours a day. Instead of 20 cents a ton for loading we receive 52.4 cents a ton. I could name many more improvements since the coming of the union, even the dawn of free speech. Thank God for the broad-minded men who have brought these things about.
>
> A.W. McClung
Just a Coal Miner[30]

By 1941, virtually all the nation's coal miners and millions of other wage earners were organized into unions affiliated with the Congress of Industrial Organizations, which had been formed by John L. Lewis and his allies.[31] By that time, West Virginia's coal miners, their wives, their relatives, and their neighbors had enjoyed seven years of peace and freedom; years without bitter strikes and miserable tent camps, without evictions and blacklists, without scabs and gun thugs, without arbitrary injunctions and military occupations, without stool pigeons and yellow dogs. During those years, miners had worked an eight-hour day without laboring under the fear that they could be fired at any time for any reason. A new rule of law now applied underground, a system of labor relations based on contractual rules that set out the miners' rights and responsibilities. And aboveground, a new democracy flourished in company-owned towns, places where miners were now free to assemble in large groups, speak openly in public places, circulate leaflets and newspapers, establish peaceful picket lines on company property, and vote for candidates who supported organized labor.

By 1934, the UMWA's one hundred thousand members in West Virginia represented a formidable voting bloc. As a result, the union's leaders, Van Bittner and Bill Blizzard—a man who had been tried for treason in 1922—emerged as influential power brokers. In the fall elections that year, Bittner and Blizzard engineered the defeat of Frank Keeney's old nemesis, former governor and now senator Henry D. Hatfield, who had condemned the NIRA as a fascist scheme. Hatfield stood for reelection against Bittner's handpicked candidate, a young Democrat named Rush D. Holt, whose father had been a socialist. Senator Hatfield, who was supported by the coal and utility companies, branded his young opponent a Red, but it was no use. Hatfield lost to Holt by a landslide of nearly seventy thousand votes, including thousands of ballots cast by black coal miners who had traditionally supported the GOP and provided Republicans like Hatfield with a margin of victory in close statewide elections.[32]

After more than three decades of struggle and two deadly industrial wars, West Virginia's miners had achieved the kind of freedom they had been striving for since the days of Mother Jones. The Bill of Rights finally had real meaning to the people who lived and worked in the coal country of West Virginia.

During their long march toward freedom, West Virginia's union miners and their families took enormous risks and made great sacrifices. They did so because they understood what a victory would mean for them, for their families, for their neighbors, and for their fellow workers in the mines. What these working people could not have understood at the time was that their struggle would broaden and deepen the meaning of freedom in all of industrial America; nor could they have foreseen that the memory of their struggle would one day become a potent resource for contemporary movements to save Appalachia, its people, and its natural wonders from the forces that have been wreaking havoc in the region for more than a century.

Epilogue

On a warm morning in June 2011, nearly 250 people set out from Marmet, West Virginia, on a fifty-mile protest march to Blair Mountain in Logan County. They planned to take the same route the armed miners had taken on their 1921 march into company territory on a mission to free their fellow workers in Mingo County. When protestors marched along that same route ninety years later, they were armed with different weapons—posters and banners—and bent on achieving a different goal: stopping a mining company from blowing the top off Blair Mountain so that its machines could strip-mine its rich coal deposits. The marchers included local residents, retired coal miners, clergy, artists, academics, historical preservationists, and environmental activists from all over the country, including members of the sponsoring groups, the Friends of Blair Mountain and Appalachia Rising. They wore red bandannas and carried signs that read STOP MOUNTAIN TOP REMOVAL and DON'T STRIP HISTORY. SAVE BLAIR MOUNTAIN. Some men in camouflaged hunting shirts held a white banner labeled UMWA LOCAL 1440, MATEWAN, WEST VIRGINIA.[1]

The marchers were nervous. They knew that during an earlier reenactment of the miners' march, the protestors, including a former Democratic congressman, Ken Hechler, had been attacked and beaten. People on the roadside screamed and cursed at them, called them tree huggers, job destroyers, and worse, but the demonstrators moved on without being physically assaulted. The state police had given the marchers permission to camp out in a park at Racine on the first night, but they were forced out by Boone County sheriff deputies. Soon thereafter the organizers learned that the owners of the campsites they had booked for the five-day march had canceled their reservations. Cell phones buzzed and a complicated plan was hatched to ferry marchers in cars and vans back to Marmet every night and then back to the spot where they had stopped.

By June 9, two hundred more marchers arrived to join the column. Each day they trekked along, sticking to the gravel shoulders of narrow, twisting county roads as ten-ton coal trucks roared by them a few feet away. Despite their fatigue and despite the oppressive heat that settled in the valleys, the protestors vowed to push all the way to Blair Mountain, where some of them would occupy company property and submit to arrest.[2]

For nearly three decades, a small group of West Virginians had attempted to make Blair Mountain a national landmark. After numerous setbacks, the preservationists reached their goal in 2006. Led by Kenneth King, a Logan County resident, they persuaded state archivists and members of the history commission to nominate the mountain for inclusion on the National Register of Historic Places. This appeal was strengthened by the research findings of King and Harvard Ayres, an archaeologist, who discovered weapons, shell casings, and other artifacts on fifteen different battle sites along Spruce Fork Ridge.[3]

Three years later, all the state officials who had supported the National Register nomination were sued by lawyers representing coal industry executives, including Don Blankenship, the CEO of Massey Energy and a fierce enemy of the UMWA whose company had busted many of the union's locals in southern West Virginia.[4] Eventually the coal companies dropped the suits and the site was listed on the National Register. However, Blankenship didn't quit. When his lawyers produced a list of property owners around Blair Mountain who allegedly opposed the listing, the federal government wilted and "delisted" the site. Outraged by this action, West Virginians and citizens from across the nation mounted an even more ambitious crusade to save Blair Mountain.[5]

Blankenship made a host of new enemies when his corporation's Upper Big Branch mine blew up in Montcoal, West Virginia, on April 5, 2010. The explosion in the mine killed twenty-nine workers. A few months later, a federal investigation began, lawsuits were filed, and Blankenship's days were numbered.[6]

A year later, the Friends of Blair Mountain finalized plans for the protest march that would begin at Marmet on June 6, 2011, and culminate on Blair Mountain. When the demonstration got under way, reporters sought out the march's organizers, particularly C. Belmont "Chuck" Keeney, a dark-haired history professor who happened to be Frank Keeney's great-grandson.

In interviews he gave along the march route, Chuck Keeney related the story of how his great-grandfather set off the miners' march of 1921 and explained why this mass protest of yesteryear had become such an inspiration to contemporary groups like Appalachia Rising. Keeney described the 2011 march as a protest against mountaintop removal and as an attempt to recover the lost memory of a struggle for freedom and justice his great-grandfather led long ago.[7]

Interviewers were surprised when Keeney said that his parents never mentioned the exploits of his notorious forefather, and that he never read anything about his great-grandfather or about the mine wars in his eighth grade state history textbook; in fact, the only time he saw the word "union" in the text was when he read about Union Carbide, the chemical company. When Keeney went on to study history in college, he found no mention of the mine wars in his U.S. history textbook or even in the surveys of American labor history he read while attending graduate school at West Virginia University.[8]

This national pattern of neglect has continued in recent years despite the attention paid to the mine wars by scholars of West Virginia history like John Alexander Williams, Frederick A. Barkey, and David Alan Corbin and by creative writers like the acclaimed novelists Mary Lee Settle and Denise Giardina, the legendary poet Don West, the seasoned journalist Lon Savage, and the independent filmmaker and screenwriter John Sayles.[9]

In 2007, Chuck Keeney restored a missing person to his state's history when he published an article on the rise and fall of his great-grandfather, the "redneck radical" from Cabin Creek.[10] As his great-grandson explained, Frank Keeney lived the last years of his life a forgotten man. When the West Virginia Mine Workers Union expired in 1931, Frank joined the Progressive Mine Workers of America, until that union dissolved in 1938. During those years, Keeney had all he could handle seeing his large family through the Depression. He started several small businesses that failed, and the once-powerful labor leader spent the later years of his life living in obscurity working as an attendant in a Charleston parking lot.

It may have been no consolation to Keeney, but he outlived all of his rivals: his toughest industrial adversary, Justus Collins; his political nemesis, Henry D. Hatfield; his mortal enemies, Thomas Felts and Sheriff Don Chafin; and his boss John L. Lewis, who purged him from the UMWA. Although he was a heavy smoker and whiskey drinker, Keeney also outlasted his younger comrades. Fred Mooney became despondent and took his own life in 1952. Bill Blizzard, who had been appointed to fill Keeney's old job as president of District 17, got into a fistfight with Lewis's younger brother and was forced to resign. Three years later, Blizzard succumbed to cancer after refusing to allow the amputation of his infected leg. "He said he'd rather die with his leg," Blizzard's brother recalled, "and he did."[11]

Keeney spent the last decades of his life believing that he and his comrades were no longer remembered as warriors and as pioneers of the labor movement. When he died on May 22, 1970, Keeney's relatives planned what they expected to be a sparsely attended burial service, but to their "great surprise," dozens of elderly miners attended his funeral. Relatives reported that some of these men shed tears as they told youngsters their stories from the mine wars when Keeney called them into battle. "We killed men for him," said one old, peg-legged miner.[12]

Keeney's reputation as an apostle of violence had condemned him in the eyes of government authorities, coal industry executives, and UMWA officials, but not in the eyes of the men who followed him into battle. According to his son-in-law, Cabell Phillips, an acclaimed reporter for the *New York Times*, these men remembered Keeney as a bold fighter and "a fearless and incorruptible Spartacus."[13]

During his later years, Keeney saw some of his worst fears realized in the way John L. Lewis and his successors ran the UMWA. The longtime president and his associates made a fateful decision to collaborate with employers to mechanize the union mines in an attempt to reduce labor costs, enhance productivity, and regain the market share coal companies had lost to oil and gas producers. As a result, the workforce in coal mining dropped from 416,000 workers in 1950 to 180,000 in 1959, the last year of Lewis's long reign as UMWA president.

Economists believe mechanization was necessary to keep the industry competitive, but if it was, Lewis and his officers did little to provide retraining or rehabilitation programs for the thousands of union men thrown out of work as a result. In fact, many dislocated miners found their health and welfare benefits cut and coalfield medical clinics closed. At the same time, the union leadership took funds raised from union dues and invested in large coal companies, making "sweetheart deals" with some of the same firms to drive smaller enterprises out of business. Throughout the decade, Lewis and his team engaged in what critics called "mystery bargaining," a process in which a few union officials met with a few executives and reached agreements they did not bring to the districts or locals for approval. The federal courts would later find these contracts unlawful, but by then the damage had been done.[14]

President Lewis had surrounded himself with men far less capable than he was, including an ambitious aide named W. A. "Tony" Boyle, who "coveted the same authority and control . . . he had seen Lewis wield during his later years in office."[15] After he was elected in 1963, Boyle presided over an administration that reeked with corruption and an organization that seethed with discontent among rank-and-file members who engaged in wildcat strikes to protest concessions they were forced to accept. Leaders of these protests eventually coalesced with members of the Black Lung Association and a host of other dissenters who rallied behind a reform slate headed by Joseph "Jock" Yablonski, a bold reformer who vowed to unseat Boyle and destroy the "corrupt kingdom" he had created within the UMWA.[16]

Boyle's operatives stole the election for their boss, but his tarnished victory infuriated many union members and energized the rank-and-file opposition. Desperate to ensure his future, Boyle gave a surrogate permission to arrange for the assassination of his rival. On New Year's Eve 1969, three hired killers invaded the Yablonski home and murdered Jock, along with his wife and his daughter. After the victims' funeral Jock Yablonski's sons and other mourners decided to organize the Miners for Democracy and build a grassroots movement to get rid of Tony Boyle and his gang once and for all.

Frank Keeney, who turned eighty-eight years old that year, made no public comment on these developments. But he must have been disgusted by the legacy Lewis and Boyle had left to the UMWA, and he must have been gratified that a miner from his own valley had emerged to lead the fight to restore democracy and honesty to the union.

Arnold Miller was born and raised in Leewood just a mile from Keeney's home in Eskdale. As a boy, Miller heard stories of the mine wars from his "grand dad," who had served as president of the same UMWA local Keeney and Mother Jones helped organize in 1912. Later on, when Miller worked as a miner in Eskdale, an old man showed him a photo of Jones conducting a rally from a church porch just before she triggered an uprising. She seemed to know that "once you've got a miner to the breaking point, where he no longer has any fear at all, then you was in big trouble."[17]

By the late 1960s, Miller was retired. He had been disabled by black lung disease and crippled by wounds he suffered in the Normandy invasion. On February 17, 1969, he helped organize thousands of active and retired miners for a march on the state capitol in Charleston with the goal of gaining more compensation for the victims of pneumoconiosis, an extremely common disease among coal miners. When state legislators balked at the demands made by the West Virginia Black Lung Association, ten thousand miners quit work in what came to be known as the Black Lung Strike, the first strike over a health and welfare issue in the annals of American labor history.[18]

If he had lived two years longer, Frank Keeney would have witnessed the triumph of the democratic principles he held dear.[19] In 1972, the federal courts overturned Boyle's election and indicted him for making illegal campaign contributions. (He would later be sent to prison for ordering the murder of Jock Yablonski.) When the Justice Department called for a special election, the Miners for Democracy chose Arnold Miller from Cabin Creek to make another run at Boyle. Miller won the closely supervised election by a narrow margin, but he swamped Boyle in the old union locals of southern West Virginia. When the UMWA reformers triumphed, the *New York Times* declared that "nothing like it had ever happened in the labor movement before."[20]

During the euphoria that followed, a group of young activists who had supported Miners for Democracy decided to recover a forgotten chapter of the union's history by recording the stories of miners who had lived and worked in the mines during Frank Keeney's era. In pursuit of this goal, several journalists associated with a new newspaper, the *Miner's Voice*, drove out of Charleston and into the hollows of Logan County during the summer of 1972.[21] The visitors fulfilled their mission by finding and interviewing scores of retired miners, including a man who recalled the hot days when he fought on Blair Mountain, and then proudly pulled up his shirt to reveal a purple scar left by a bullet from one of Don Chafin's machine guns. They met miners who knew Mother Jones. "She was the cussingest woman you ever heard," one of them recalled, "but the miners loved her," and "they'd do what she said," he added. "She wasn't afraid of the devil and all of his angels," said a coal miner's widow from Eskdale. "She'd come up Cabin Creek here and call out for all the men that wanted to be let out of slavery to follow her. And they did, scores of them."

One of the most eloquent testimonies the Charleston team recorded came from an elderly miner named Ed Perry. The journalists found him living on a Logan County road that hadn't been repaired since 1960, the year the Holden mine blew up and burned eighteen men alive. The Island Creek Coal Company closed its operations after the disaster, and in the next few years, most of Perry's neighbors left town; but he and his wife had remained in one of the last company houses still standing on the mountainside.

"I've always held my head up as high as I could get it," Perry told his young visitors. "I was always 100 percent with organized labor," he added; it was "just as natural as breathing." As long as the miners in Logan County were down and out, the old man explained, they couldn't win anyone's sympathy. "The miner, he had always been kind of like a slave in everyone's opinion, even his own," said Perry. "That all come about to breed a sentiment in their hearts to come up . . . to a place in society where they was acceptable, by their striving." And in Perry's lifetime, the miners did come up to that place, because all the while, he believed, they had nourished "these sentiments of equality" in their hearts.

Acknowledgments

My introduction to the history of West Virginia's miners came in 1978 when I was writing a magazine article about a nationwide coal miners' strike that had erupted that fall. I called my friend, the labor historian David Montgomery, and he told me to look up one of his former University of Pittsburgh doctoral students who lived in Charleston. Fred Barkey greeted me, shared his vast historical knowledge of Mountain State radicalism with me, and introduced me to union officials and strike leaders. Thirty years later, when I began research on this book, Fred was just as helpful. He is one of the many West Virginia residents who have generously provided me with all sorts of valuable assistance.

Kenneth Fones-Wolf and Elizabeth Fones-Wolf welcomed me to West Virginia University and introduced me to two of their brilliant graduate students. Louis Martin and William Hal Gorby not only provided me with meticulous research assistance, but they also guided me around the back roads of coal country and through two wonderful archives: the West Virginia and Regional History Center at the West Virginia University Library and the West Virginia State Archives in Charleston. Professionals in both institutions provided me with excellent guidance and support, especially Dennis Fredette and Catherine Rakowski at the center and Deborah A. Basham at the archives.

Three other graduates of the WVU PhD program also helped me by patiently answering my questions and sharing their deep knowledge of their state's coal industry. Paul H. Rakes, a former UMWA miner, offered advice based on his deep knowledge of the coal industry's dangers. Rebecca J. Bailey took me deep into the culture and politics of Mingo County, the focus of her revealing monograph *Matewan before the Massacre*. And C. Belmont Keeney spoke with me several times about his family's history and his own study of C. Frank Keeney, his great-grandfather.

I am indebted to three other West Virginians as well. Cecil Roberts, president of the UMWA, read my account of events on Cabin Creek where he was born and raised and told me some personal stories of his ancestors, including his great uncle Bill Blizzard. Dale Payne, another native of that valley, generously allowed me to use some images from the great library of family photos he has collected. Dale also spoke with me about how his own family was torn asunder by the first mine war. The activist anthropologist Brandon Nida warned me, with stunning clarity, about the pitfalls of outsiders writing Appalachian history, and he shared with me some of his experiences fighting for economic and environmental justice in the mountains during these mean times. Brandon also took me up to Blair Mountain one day and showed me where to look for the old bunkers on the snow-covered ground and where to look through leafless trees to track the line of march the miners took when they moved up toward Spruce Fork Ridge in 1921.

This book is the product of many drafts and many helpful suggestions by my readers. I am much obliged to historians Fred Barkey, Steve Brier, Ken Fones-Wolf, Lou Martin, Becky Bailey, Chuck Keeney, Beverly Gage, Gregory Downs, Scott Nelson, and Rosemary Feurer, who read the manuscript in various stages and offered valuable suggestions.

Friends, neighbors, and family members supported me in many ways. As always, I am grateful for the help of my friends who read my first very rough drafts: Michael Kenney, Christopher Daly, Andrew Miller, John Hess, Rachel Rubin, Roger House, and, most of all, Jim O'Brien, my first and best reader. Jim also contributed his superb skills as an indexer of books. Ron Joseph carefully proofed several drafts and magically sorted out messed-up endnotes. I owe a special debt to my next-door neighbor, the writer Kelly Horan, for her good cheer and for the fine editing suggestions she provided.

My wife, Janet Grogan, read an early version of the book, offered her assessment, and never wavered in her belief in me and in her understanding of why this book was so important to me. Our son, Nick Green, was my closest reader and toughest critic. He was also my strongest supporter, always willing to talk, especially about Mother Jones and her magic, and always able to pick me up when I was down.

My graduate assistants at the University of Massachusetts Boston— David Fischer, Kelly Saunders, and Jeffrey Robinson—cheerfully and expertly accessed and copied all sorts of material for me. Jeff also sorted out many of my software problems and kept me laughing almost all the time. The Labor Resource Center at UMB supported some copying costs, and the College of Arts and Sciences provided a grant to cover proofreading and map-making expenses and, most important, a sabbatical leave in 2011.

C. Scott Walker, digital cartographer at the Harvard Map Collection, made the maps drawing from a wide range of sources, from topographical and geological surveys to industrial maps. Scott made excellent use of a unique map of troop movements and battle sites on Blair Mountain and Spruce Fork Ridge crafted by anthropologist Harvard Ayres, based on the archaeological research Ayres conducted in Logan County with his students from Appalachia State University. Thanks to Dr. Ayres for granting permission to use his map and for fact-checking my narrative of the battle.

Dr. Elaine Bernard, director of the Labor and Worklife Program at Harvard Law School, has supported my research and has continued to invite me to lecture each year to some of the most talented and dedicated union leaders in this country and around the world. Thanks to her, her staff, and the impressive students who attend the Harvard Trade Union Program.

I am thankful to my publisher Grove Atlantic for a host of reasons. Morgan Entrekin, the publisher and president, and Joan Bingham, the executive editor and vice president, have shown heartwarming enthusiasm for the book. Joan has offered lots of encouragement and guidance from the very start, as has Jamison Stoltz, my careful, insightful, and supportive editor. My agents John Taylor Williams, Hope Denekamp, and Katherine Flynn at Kneerim, Williams & Bloom have been there for me from the start, offering sound advice and much-valued encouragement all along the twisted and sometimes bumpy road to publication.

For some time I thought about dedicating this book to one of the pathbreaking labor historians who inspired me as a young scholar and who supported my work in its early stages. Herbert Gutman and Eric Hobsbawm came to mind, as did David Montgomery, who was a mentor to me as he was to many of my peers; so did my graduate school adviser, the great writer and historian of the South C. Vann Woodward, and my friend Howard Zinn, who encouraged me to take chances and to always write for the public. But when my father passed away in the summer of 2012, I realized that no one could be more deserving of my dedication, because no one cared more about my work, or about this book, than he did. This one's for you, Dad.

James Green
Somerville, Massachusetts
2014

Illustration Credits

LC: Library of Congress
UMWA: United Mine Workers of America
WVRHC: West Virginia and Regional History Center, WVU Libraries
WVSA: West Virginia State Archives

p. 19: Map by C. Scott Walker
p. 24: Dale Payne Collection
p. 27: WVSA
p. 29: Photo by G. W. Trevey, GEM Publications
p. 37: UMWA
p. 42: Colonel William Roosevelt Hudnall
p. 46: LC
p. 47: WVRHC
p. 51: GEM Publications
p. 59: Photo by Lewis Hine, LC
p. 62: Photo by Lewis Hine, LC
p. 63: C. Belmont Keeney
p. 65: Photo by Lewis Hine, LC
p. 76: WVSA

p. 80: GEM Publications

p. 86: Map by C. Scott Walker

p. 88: Dale Payne Collection

p. 93: WVRHC

p. 102: WVRHC

p. 107: Dale Payne Collection

p. 109: WVRHC

p. 111: WVRHC

p. 115: WVRHC

p. 122: Courtesy of Eugene V. Debs Foundation and Indiana State University Special Collections.

p. 125: WVSA

p. 126: WVRHC

p. 129: *International Socialist Review* scan courtesy of Rosemary Feurer

p. 142: LC

p. 144: *International Socialist Review*

p. 145: WVRHC

p. 155: WVRHC

p. 159: WVRHC

p. 163: WVRHC

p. 165: WVRHC

p. 171: WVRHC

p. 183: Map by C. Scott Walker

p. 185: WVRHC

p. 186: WVSA

p. 191: UMWA

p. 193: WVRHC

p. 202: WVRHC

p. 207: WVRHC

p. 208: WVRHC

p. 211: Norfolk & Western Collection, Virginia Tech University Archives

p. 221: Map by C. Scott Walker

p. 225: WVRHC

p. 234: WVRHC

p. 237: WVRHC

p. 244: Public Domain

p. 245: WVRHC

p. 257: Van A. Bittner Collection, WVRHC

p. 264: WVRHC

p. 270: WVRHC

p. 277: Map by C. Scott Walker based on original archaeological fieldwork and map of battle sites and attack routes by Dr. Harvard Ayres.

p. 291: WVRHC

p. 295: WVRHC

p. 296: WVRHC

p. 298: WVRHC

p. 301: WVRHC

p. 304: LC

p. 310: WVRHC

p. 315: WVRHC

p. 320: WVRHC

p. 322: Nebraska State Historical Society

p. 330: Van A. Bittner Collection WVRHC

p. 336: Photo by Marion Post-Wolcott, LC

p. 338: WVRHC

p. 341: UMWA

p. 344: Photo by Marion Post-Wolcott, LC

Notes

Prologue

1. Unless otherwise attributed, quotes that follow are from two articles by James M. Cain, "The Battle Ground of Coal," *Atlantic Monthly*, October 1922, and "West Virginia: A Mine-Field Melodrama," *Nation*, June 27, 1923, reprinted in David Alan Corbin, ed., *The West Virginia Mine Wars: An Anthology* (Charleston, WV: Appalachian Editions, 1990), pp. 144–160.

2. Quote in David C. Duke, *Writers and Miners: Activism and Imagery in America* (Lexington: University Press of Kentucky, 2002), p. 79.

3. Quote in Graham Adams Jr., *Age of Industrial Violence, 1910–15* (New York: Columbia University Press, 1966), p. 32.

4. Previously published accounts—all fully cited in the endnotes to this book—have been episodic or thematic treatments. For example, Jeremy Brecher offered a brief description of the second mine war in his 1972 study of "mass insurgency" in America; John Alexander Williams wrote an insightful chapter on the first mine war in his short history of West Virginia published in 1976; and Richard D. Lunt explored the legal issues raised by the mine wars in a 1979 study. And so it went for the next three decades as university-based scholars like Kenneth Bailey and Edward M. Steel Jr., as well as local historians like Lois C. McLean and Dale Payne, published articles or book chapters on one of the two mine wars or on

related events. David Alan Corbin described both conflicts in his deeply researched 1981 monograph, but the book was not intended to be a seamless narrative of events. Corbin's study, based on his doctoral thesis, was presented as a social history of class conflict in the coalfields of southern West Virginia—the background to the mine wars. More recently, the journalist Robert Shogan has written a lively overview of the miners' 1921 march and the Battle of Blair Mountain; the historian Rebecca J. Bailey has published a thick description of the political and economic tensions in Mingo County that helps explain the oft-mentioned "massacre" of Baldwin-Felts mine guards at Matewan in 1920; and Frederick A. Barkey has given us a revealing study of the state's grassroots socialist movement and what coal miners contributed to it. In addition, publishers have reissued older accounts of the events that led to and through the Battle of Blair Mountain written by H. B. Lee, a coalfield lawyer, and by the journalists Lon Savage, G. T. Swain, and William C. Blizzard.

Curiously, none of these authors provided an account of the struggle over the long haul, beginning in 1892 when the first UMWA organizers arrived, through the ordeal of the 1920s, to the the spring of 1933 when the union movement gained a sudden and sweeping victory.

5. The deadliest labor war in U.S. history began in the fall of 1913 after the UMWA called a strike in the coalfields of southern Colorado. The struggle reached a bloody climax on April 20, 1914, when Colorado National Guardsmen attacked a strikers camp at Ludlow. This raid led to the deaths of five strikers and a UMWA organizer from gunshots and of two women and eleven children from suffocation, when they took shelter in a pit after the tent colony was set afire. In the uprising that followed the massacre, at least fifteen hundred armed miners killed nineteen more men, all mine guards and strikebreakers. Overall, at least seventy-five people died in this conflict, approximately the same total as the lives lost in all of the West Virginia minefield battles from 1902 to 1921. Scott Martelle, *Blood Passion: The Ludlow Massacre and Class War in the American West* (New Brunswick, NJ: Rutgers University Press, 2007), appendix B, pp. 222–24, and Priscilla Long, *Where the Sun Never Shines: A History of America's Bloody Coal Industry* (New York: Paragon House, 1989), pp. 293–94.

6. Quote in Will Wallace Harvey, "A Strange Land and Peculiar People," *Lippincott's Magazine*, October 1973, p. 429. For a study of how visitors, folklorists, and missionaries saw Applachians as a "race" of people

"in but not of America," see Henry D. Shapiro, *Appalachia on Our Mind: The Southern Mountains and Mountaineers in the American Consciousness, 1870–1920* (Chapel Hill: University of North Carolina Press, 1978), pp. xiv–xv. Scholars of modern Appalachian life and culture have worked effectively to correct this stereotype. See Dwight B. Billings, Gurney Norman, and Katherine Ledford, *Confronting Appalachia Stereotypes: Back Talk from an American Region* (Lexington: University Press of Kentucky, 1999). The last quote is from Jeff Biggers, *The United States of Appalachia: How Southern Mountaineers Brought Independence, Culture, and Enlightenment to America* (Emeryville, CA: Shoemaker & Hoard, 2006), p. xv.

Chapter 1: The Great West Virginia Coal Rush, 1877–1890

1. Cain, "West Virginia: A Mine-Field Melodrama," pp. 144–45.

2. Biggers, *The United States of Appalachia*, pp. 28–29.

3. Bascombe M. Blake Jr., "Coal," in Ken Sullivan, ed., *The West Virginia Encyclopedia* (Charleston: West Virginia Humanities Council, 2006), p. 147. Philip M. Conley, *History of the West Virginia Coal Industry* (Charleston, WV: Education Foundation, 1960), pp. 4–5.

4. Conley, *History of the West Virginia Coal Industry*, p. 95.

5. H. Tyler Blethen, "Pioneer Settlement," in Richard A. Straw and H. Tyler Blethen, eds., *High Mountains Rising: Appalachia in Time and Place* (Urbana: University of Illinois Press, 2004), pp. 25–36.

6. Ibid., pp. 20–21.

7. On Moses Keeney and his descendants, see Marlene West Perry and Dale Payne, *The History of Eskdale, Early 1800's–1950's* (Fayetteville, WV: privately printed, 2007), pp. 95–97; on the salt works, see John Alexander Williams, *Appalachia: A History* (Chapel Hill: University of North Carolina Press, 2002), p. 129.

8. Edwin D. Michael, "Fauna," in Sullivan, ed., *The West Virginia Encyclopedia*, pp. 232–34.

9. *West Virginia: A Guide to the Mountain State*, compiled by the Writers' Program of the Works Progress Administration in the State of West Virginia (New York: Oxford University Press, 1941), pp. 48–49, 80–81.

10. Conley, *History of the West Virginia Coal Industry*, pp. 247–66; Ronald D. Eller, *Miners, Millhands, and Mountaineers: Industrialization of the Appalachian South, 1880–1930* (Knoxville: University of Tennessee Press, 1982), pp. 202–203.

11. Ibid., pp. 201–202.

12. W. P. Tams Jr., *The Smokeless Coal Fields of West Virginia: A Brief History* (Morgantown: West Virginia University Library, 1963), p. 19; David Alan Corbin, *Life, Work, and Rebellion in the Coal Fields: Southern West Virginia Miners, 1880–1922* (Urbana: University of Illinois Press, 1981), p. 5; Eller, *Miners, Millhands, and Mountaineers*, pp. 136–37, 202–203.

13. Conley, *History of the West Virginia Coal Industry*, p. 57.

14. Otis K. Rice and Stephen W. Brown, *West Virginia: A History*, 2nd ed. (Lexington: University Press of Kentucky, 1985), pp. 186–87; Festus P. Summers, *Johnson Newlon Camden: A Study in Individualism* (New York and London: G. P. Putnam's Sons, 1937), pp. 367, 371–77.

15. Williams, *Appalachia*, pp. 256–59.

16. Eller, *Miners, Millhands, and Mountaineers*, p. 134.

17. Ibid., pp. 162–63, 193–94; Corbin, *Life, Work, and Rebellion in the Coal Fields*, pp. 66–69, 128–29. For a more positive view of life in the company towns, see Crandall A. Shifflett, *Coal Towns: Life, Work, and Culture in Company Towns of Southern Appalachia, 1880–1960* (Knoxville: University of Tennessee Press, 1991).

18. Quoted in Laurence Leamer, "Twilight for a Baron: Major William Purviance Tams, Jr.," *Playboy*, May 1973, p. 168.

19. Tams, *The Smokeless Coal Fields of West Virginia*, pp. 25, 52.

20. Corbin, *Life, Work, and Rebellion*, p. 32; Lou Athey, "Scrip," in Sullivan, ed., *The West Virginia Encyclopedia*, pp. 156, 644; Deborah Weiner, "'Scrip Was a Way of Life': Company Stores, Jewish Merchants, and the Coalfield Retail Economy," in Jennifer Egolf, Ken Fones-Wolf, and Louis C. Martin, eds., *Culture, Class, and Politics in Modern Appalachia: Essays in Honor of Ronald L. Lewis* (Morgantown: West Virginia University Press, 2009), pp. 31–55.

21. Tams, *The Smokeless Coal Fields of West Virginia*, p. 58.

22. Ken Sullivan, "Jenny Lind House," in Sullivan, ed., *The West Virginia Encyclopedia*, p. 382.

23. Dale Payne, *Pictorial History of Paint Creek: 1750's–1950's* (North Kansas City, MO: Technical Communication Services, 2009), pp. 90–95. West Virginia mine owners embraced Jim Crow as readily as any white men of the era. However, unlike textile mill owners who refused to hire blacks, coal operators mixed races and nationalities in crowded company towns; furthermore, they found strict racial segregation difficult to impose in small towns of a few hundred residents, where African Americans and

Italians lived only a few hundred yards from whites in their own hollows, and where race mixing among adults and children could not be completely eliminated. Not only did men of all races mingle when the miners went underground, but they encountered one another frequently at the company stores, in saloons, and in brothels, as well as at union meetings in places like Paint Creek. See Corbin, *Life, Work, and Rebellion*, pp. 127–29.

24. Eller, *Miners, Millhands, and Mountaineers*, p. 183.

25. George G. Korson, *Coal Dust on the Fiddle: Songs and Stories of the Bituminous Industry* (Philadelphia: University of Pennsylvania Press, 1943), pp. 30–31. Quote in Richard J. Callahan Jr., *Work and Faith in the Kentucky Coal Fields: Subject to Dust* (Bloomington: Indiana University Press, 2009), p. 84.

26. Quote in Tams, *The Smokeless Coal Fields of West Virginia*, p. 58. Violence against women in mining towns has been neglected by historians until recently. For a study that does explore the problem in a smelting town near a copper minefield, see Laurie Mercier, *Anaconda: Labor, Community, and Culture in Montana's Smelter City* (Urbana: University of Illinois Press, 2001), pp. 124–27, 204–206.

27. Mary Lee Settle, *Addie: A Memoir* (Columbia: University of South Carolina, 1998), pp. 14–18, 46–50.

28. Quote in Callahan, *Work and Faith in the Kentucky Coal Fields*, p. 82.

29. Quote in ibid., p. 82, and Corbin, *Life, Work, and Rebellion*, pp. 120–21.

30. Corbin, *Life, Work, and Rebellion*, p. 67.

31. Eller, *Miners, Millhands, and Mountaineers*, p. 202; Tams, *The Smokeless Coal Fields of West Virginia*, pp. 81–83; Ken Sullivan, "Justus Collins," in Sullivan, ed., *The West Virginia Encyclopedia*, p. 155.

32. Letter from Justus Collins to Jairus Collins, Goodwill, WV, September 18, 1896, cited in Keith Dix, *Work Relations in the Coal Industry: The Hand-Loading Era, 1880–1930*, West Virginia University Bulletin, series 78, no. 7-2 (Morgantown, WV: Institute for Labor Studies, West Virginia University, 1977), p. 43.

33. In 1901, the rate of productivity for 16,000 pick miners was 5.14 tons of coal per day "man day," and the rate for 3,967 machine miners was 4.50 tons of coal per day "man day." By 1912, the number of machine miners would increase to 21,697, virtually the same as the total number of pick miners. By then, machine miners would be rated as slightly more productive. Ibid., tables on pp. 20, 28.

34. E. P. Thompson, "Time, Work-Discipline, and Industrial Capitalism," *Past & Present* 38 (December 1967): 91–95. On the emergence of measured time as the basis of wage payment, see David Brody, "Time and Work during Early American Industrialism," *In Labor's Cause: Main Themes on the History of the American Worker* (New York: Oxford University Press, 1993), pp. 3–42.

35. Kenneth R. Bailey, "A Judicious Mixture: Negroes and Immigrants in the West Virginia Mines, 1880–1917," *West Virginia History* 34 (1973): 144.

36. Ronald L. Lewis, *Black Coal Miners in America: Race, Class, and Community Conflict, 1780–1980* (Lexington: University Press of Kentucky, 1987), p. 135.

37. Corbin, *Life, Work, and Rebellion*, pp. 35–36. Also see Herbert G. Gutman, *Work Culture and Society in Industrializing America* (New York: Knopf, 1976), pp. 1–32.

38. Kenneth R. Bailey, "Hawk's Nest Coal Company Strike, January, 1880," *West Virginia History* 30, no. 4 (July 1969): pp. 625–34. On the Molly Maguires, see Kevin Kenny, *Making Sense of the Molly Maguires* (New York: Oxford University Press, 1998); and on British miners, see Corbin, *Work, Life, and Rebellion*, p. 27.

39. Lewis, *Black Coal Miners in America*, p. 136; and Peter Rachleff, *Black Labor in Richmond, 1865-1890* (Urbana: University of Illinois Press, 1989), pp. 34-69.

40. Henry Demarest Lloyd, *A Strike of Millionaires Against Miners; or, The Story of Spring Valley* (Chicago: Belford-Clarke, 1890), pp. 30–31, 35, 38–39.

Chapter 2: The Miners' Angel, Winter 1890–Winter 1903

1. Quote in Tom Juravich, William F. Hartford, and James R. Green, *Commonwealth of Toil: Chapters in the History of Massachusetts Workers and Their Unions* (Amherst: University of Massachusetts Press, 1996), p. 27.

2. McAlister Coleman, *Men and Coal* (New York and Toronto: Farrar & Rinehart, 1943), p. 45.

3. Quote in ibid., p. 53.

4. Jon Amsden and Stephen Brier, "Coal Miners on Strike: The Transformation of Strike Demands and the Formation of a National Union," *Journal of Interdisciplinary History* 7, no. 4 (Spring 1977): 594, 604–14;

and Maier B. Fox, *United We Stand: The United Mine Workers of America, 1890–1990* (Washington, DC: United Mine Workers of America, 1990), pp. 13–27.

5. Corbin, *Life, Work, and Rebellion*, p. 53, and Lewis, *Black Coal Miners in America*, pp. 136–37.

6. Herbert Gutman, "The Negro and the United Mine Workers of America: The Career and Letters of Richard L. Davis and Something of Their Meaning, 1890–1900," *Work, Culture, and Society in Industrializing America*, p. 143. The attorney Herbert Hill criticized Gutman's interpretation of Davis's letters, claiming that Gutman had invented a myth of racial egalitarianism in the UMWA. Herbert Hill, "Myth-Making as Labor History: Herbert Gutman and the United Mine Workers of America," *International Journal of Politics, Culture, and Society* 2, no. 2 (Winter 1988): 132–200. For an effective rebuttal, see Stephen Brier, "In Defense of Gutman: The Union's Case," *International Journal of Politics, Culture, and Society* 2, no. 3 (Spring 1989): 382–95.

7. Gutman, "The Negro and the United Mine Workers," pp. 143–44, quotes on pp. 141, 143; and Rice and Brown, *West Virginia*, pp. 111–61.

8. Kenneth R. Bailey, "'Tell the Boys to Fall in Line': United Mine Workers of America Strikes in West Virginia, January–June, 1894," *West Virginia History* 32, no. 4 (1971): 224–37.

9. Brody, "Market Unionism: The Case of Coal," *In Labor's Cause*, pp. 86–87; Lewis, *Black Coal Miners in America*, pp. 136–37, 139–42.

10. Coleman, *Men and Coal*, pp. 59–60.

11. Quote in Corbin, *Life, Work, and Rebellion*, p. 25.

12. Brody, "Market Unionism: The Case of Coal," pp. 139–42.

13. Bruno Ramirez, *When Workers Fight: The Politics of Industrial Relations in the Progressive Era, 1898–1916* (Westport, CT: Greenwood Press, 1978).

14. Selig Perlman and Philip Taft, *History of Labor in the United States, 1896–1932* (New York: Macmillan, 1935), p. 326.

15. Corbin, *Life, Work, and Rebellion*, pp. 5, 177.

16. Elliott J. Gorn, *Mother Jones: The Most Dangerous Woman in America* (New York: Hill & Wang, 2001), pp. 11, 27.

17. Niall Whelehan, *The Dynamiters: Irish Nationalism and Political Violence in the Wider World, 1867–1900* (Cambridge and New York: Cambridge University Press, 2012).

18. The sketch of Mother Jones's life is based on Gorn's fine biography, *Mother Jones*, pp. 7–90. For more on Chicago during Mother Jones's time there, see James Green, *Death in the Haymarket: A Story of Chicago, the First Labor Movement, and the Bombing That Divided Gilded Age America* (New York: Pantheon Books, 2006).

19. Rosemary Feurer, "Mother Jones: A Global History of Struggle and Remembrance, from Cork, Ireland to Illinois," *Illinois Heritage* 16 (May–June 2013): 28–29; Gorn, *Mother Jones*, pp. 63–64.

20. Mother Jones, *Autobiography of Mother Jones*, edited by Mary Field Parton (Chicago: Charles H. Kerr, 1925), p. 36.

21. Gorn, *Mother Jones*, p. 65; Jones, *Autobiography of Mother Jones*, pp. 115–19; and Ray Ginger, *Eugene V. Debs: A Biography* (New York: Collier Books, 1962 [1949]), p. 212.

22. Jones, *Autobiography of Mother Jones*, p. 45.

23. Quoted in ibid., pp. 77–78.

24. William Roosevelt Hudnall, *Kelly's Creek Chronicles, Kanawha County, West Virginia: The Illustrated Diary of James Alexander Jones, Coal Miner, Kept during the Period 1870 to 1939* (New Canton, VA: Kelly's Creek Publishers, 2005), p. 27; also see wardwestvirginia.wordpress.com/

25. Settle, *Addie*, pp. 51–52.

26. The description of Jones's arrival on Kellys Creek is from Jones, *Autobiography of Mother Jones*, pp. 46–48, and from Mary Lee Settle's evocative family history, which focuses on the experiences and memories of her grandmother: Settle, *Addie*, pp. 14–15, 30–31, 43–47, 75–83.

27. Jones, *Autobiography*, pp. 46–47; Corbin, *Life, Work, and Rebellion*, p. 10.

28. Bert Castle interview with Bill Taft, Alum Creek, WV, June 19, 1973, CD recording of audiotape, West Virginia and Regional History Center, West Virginia University Library, Morgantown; and Luigi D. Trappano interview with John G. Morgan, reprinted in Perry and Payne, *The History of Eskdale*, p. 62. Quote in Gorn, *Mother Jones*, p. 123.

29. Quote in John Brophy, *A Miner's Life* (Madison: University of Wisconsin Press, 1964), p. 75.

30. Jones, *Autobiography of Mother Jones*, pp. 46–48.

31. This description of the places and people in the valley also relies on the valuable record of life and work in this area compiled and edited by Hudnall, *Kelly's Creek Chronicles*, p. 27.

32. Quotes in Settle, *Addie*, p. 78.

33. Quotes in Gorn, *Mother Jones*, p. 92.

34. Ibid.

35. Philip S. Foner, *The Policies and Practices of the American Federation of Labor 1900–1909*, vol. 3 of *History of the Labor Movement in the United States* (New York: International Publishers, 1964), pp. 26–27.

36. Corbin, *Life, Work, and Rebellion*, p. 48; Donald L. Miller and Richard E. Sharpless, *The Kingdom of Coal: Work, Enterprise, and Ethnic Communities in the Mine Fields* (Philadelphia: University of Pennsylvania Press, 1985), pp. 256–57, includes quote from Mitchell's letter to Jones.

37. Charles P. Anson, "A History of the Labor Movement in West Virginia" (PhD diss., University of North Carolina, 1940), p. 216.

38. Philip S. Foner, ed., *Mother Jones Speaks: Collected Writings and Speeches* (New York: Monad Press, 1983), pp. 86–88.

39. On the militancy and solidarity of black miners in West Virginia, see Stephen B. Brier, "'The Most Persistent Unionists': Class Formation and Class Conflict in the Coal Fields and the Emergence of Interracial and Interethnic Unionism" (PhD diss., University of California at Los Angeles, 1992).

40. Joe William Trotter Jr., *Coal, Class, and Color: Blacks in Southern West Virginia, 1915–32* (Urbana: University of Illinois Press, 1990), Table 1.4. Quote in Gorn, *Mother Jones*, pp. 98–99.

41. *Fayette Journal*, June 12, 1902, quoted in George Bragg and Melody Bragg, *Coal Mining Mayhem and Murder: The Incredible New River Coal Field, 1900–1912* (Beaver, WV: GEM Publications, 2010), p. 24.

42. *Fayette Journal*, September 4 and November 11, 1902, cited in ibid., pp. 14–15.

43. John A. Velke III, *The True Story of the Baldwin-Felts Detective Agency* (privately published, rev. ed. 2004), pp. 7, 18, 31–34, 42–43.

44. Jones, *Autobiography of Mother Jones*, p. 65.

45. Velke, *Baldwin-Felts Detective Agency*, p. 57; *Charleston Gazette*, August 31, 1902; quote in Stephen H. Norwood, *Strikebreaking and Intimidation: Mercenaries and Masculinity in Twentieth-Century America* (Chapel Hill: University of North Carolina Press, 2002), p. 132.

46. *Fayette Journal*, July 13, August 28, and September 4, 1902, quoted in Bragg and Bragg, *Coal Mining Mayhem and Murder*, pp. 14, 17–19.

47. Quote in Gorn, *Mother Jones*, p 125.

48. Settle, *Addie*, p. 77.

49. Velke, *Baldwin-Felts Detective Agency*, pp. 53–59; *United Mine Workers Journal* quoted in Norwood, *Strikebreaking and Intimidation*, p. 132; Gorn, *Mother Jones*, p. 98.

50. Piney Creek Gorge is described at www.wvexp.com/ondexphp/Piney_Creek; quote in Jones, *Autobiography of Mother Jones*, pp. 69–70.

51. Lois C. McLean, "Stanaford, Battle of," in Sullivan, ed., *The West Virginia Encyclopedia*, p. 674.

52. Jones, *Autobiography of Mother Jones*, pp. 234–35.

Chapter 3: Frank Keeney's Valley, Winter 1903–Winter 1907

1. Edward M. Steel, ed., *The Speeches and Writings of Mother Jones* (Pittsburgh, PA: University of Pittsburgh Press, 1988), p. 206.

2. Quote from a 1931 article, "Frank Keeney's Coal Diggers," reprinted in Edmund Wilson, *The American Earthquake: A Chronicle of the Roaring Twenties, the Great Depression, and the Dawn of the New Deal* (New York: Da Capo Press, 1996 [1958]), p. 327.

3. Payne and Perry, *The History of Eskdale*, p. 1; Conley, *History of the West Virginia Coal Industry*, p. 128; Payne, *Pictorial History of Cabin Creek*, p. 6.

4. Perry and Payne, *The History of Eskdale*, p. 97; Payne, *Pictorial History of Cabin Creek*, p. 7.

5. Brophy, *A Miner's Life*, pp. 38–50, quote on p. 39.

6. Description and quote from Thomas G. Andrews, *Killing for Coal: America's Deadliest Labor War* (Cambridge, MA: Harvard University Press, 2008), pp. 144–45. In 1906, 334 miners died from explosions caused when gas or dust ignited or as a result of mistakes made in the use of black powder used in pit-face blasting. William Graebner, *Coal-Mining Safety in the Progressive Period: The Political Economy of Reform* (Lexington: University Press of Kentucky, 1976), Table 1, p. 8.

7. Booker T. Washington, *Up from Slavery: An Autobiography* (Garden City, NY: Doubleday, 1900), pp. 20–28, 38; Louis R. Harlan, *Booker T. Washington: The Making of a Black Leader, 1856–1901* (New York: Oxford University Press, 1972), pp. 30–50.

8. Callahan, *Work and Faith in the Kentucky Coal Fields*, p. 106.

9. Korson, *Coal Dust on the Fiddle*, pp. 291, 414.

10. Dix, *Work Relations in the Coal Industry*, pp. 2–5.

11. Brophy, *A Miner's Life*, p. 45.

12. Ibid., p. 44; Dix, *Work Relations in the Coal Industry*, Table 2, p. 20; Paul H. Rakes, "Technology in Transition: The Dilemmas of Early Twentieth-Century Coal Mining," *Journal of Appalachian Studies* 5, no. 1 (Spring 1999): 42.

13. Price V. Fishback, *Soft Coal, Hard Choices: The Economic Welfare of Bituminous Coal Miners, 1890–1930* (New York: Oxford University Press, 1992), p. 4.

14. Brophy, *A Miner's Life*, p. 46.

15. Tams, *The Smokeless Coal Fields of West Virginia*, pp. 34–38.

16. Carter Goodrich, *The Miner's Freedom* (Boston: Marshall Jones Company, 1925), pp. 31, 42.

17. Ibid., pp. 56–58. Quotes in David Montgomery, *Workers' Control in America: Studies in the History of Work, Technology, and Labor Struggles* (Cambridge and New York: Cambridge University Press, 1979), pp. 11, 13.

18. Quote in Dix, *Work Relations in the Coal Industry*, p. 5; Brophy, *A Miner's Life*, p. 42.

19. Quote in Andrews, *Killing for Coal*, pp. 163–64. This practice had been introduced to the Kanawha Valley mines by the British and Irish miners who came from Pennsylvania and had organized the first trade unions in the region during the 1880s, after employers violated the square turn tradition by giving extra, or "free," mine cars to certain favorites—cars that rightfully belonged to others. Brier, "'The Most Persistent Unionists,'" pp. 115–17.

20. Korson, *Coal Dust on the Fiddle*, pp. 291, 414–15.

21. Brophy, *A Miner's Life*, pp. 38, 40–41.

22. Ibid.

23. Paul H. Rakes, "West Virginia Coal Mine Fatalities: The Subculture of Danger and a Statistical Overview of the Pre-enforcement Era," *West Virginia History* 2, no. 1 (Spring 2008): 15. In 1906, the first year the federal government compiled mine fatality statistics, 826 bituminous miners died from cave-ins, and another 578 died of other causes. Graebner, *Coal-Mining Safety*, Table 1, p. 8.

24. *New York Times*, March 6, 1900; Governor Atkinson quoted in Graebner, *Coal-Mining Safety*, p. 73.

25. Quote in Andrews, *Killing for Coal*, p. 172; Paul H. Rakes, "A Combat Scenario: Early Coal Mining and the Culture of Danger," in Egolf, Fones-Wolf, and Martin, eds., *Culture, Class, and Politics in Modern Appalachia*, pp. 61, 68–69.

26. Quote in E. P. Thompson, *The Making of the English Working Class* (New York: Pantheon, 1963), p. 418; Ramirez, *When Workers Fight*, pp. 71–75; Fox, *United We Stand*, p. 65.

27. Payne, *Pictorial History of Cabin Creek*, pp. 7, 159–63.

28. Velke, *Baldwin-Felts Detective Agency*, p. 138.

29. Foner, *History of the Labor Movement in the United States*, pp. 57–58, and Slason Thompson, "Violence in Labor Conflicts," *Outlook*, December 17, 1904, cited in George E. Mowry, *The Era of Theodore Roosevelt and the Birth of Modern America, 1900–1912* (New York: Harper & Row, 1958), p. 11.

30. Keeney interview quoted in Winthrop D. Lane, *Civil War in West Virginia: A Story of the Industrial Conflict in the Coal Mines* (New York: B. W. Huebsch, 1921), pp. 86–87.

31. Bryan's second loss to William McKinley "drove many of Bryan's followers to despair" and to lose hope that democracy could be saved from plutocracy without a revolution. Michael Kazin, *A Godly Hero: The Life of William Jennings Bryan* (New York: Knopf, 2006), p. 109.

32. Ginger, *Eugene V. Debs*, p. 252; Frederick A. Barkey, *Working-Class Radicals: The Socialist Party in West Virginia, 1898–1920* (Morgantown: West Virginia University Press, 2012), pp. 29–30. Quote in Ronald L. Lewis, *Transforming the Appalachian Countryside: Railroads, Deforestation, and Social Change in West Virginia, 1880–1920* (Chapel Hill: University of North Carolina Press, 1998), pp. 7, 9.

33. At the time Keeney embraced socialism, Wayland's paper reached more than 250,000 readers each week, a circulation comparable to that of the popular *Saturday Evening Post*. The *Appeal*'s folksy "One Hoss Editor" published lurid exposés, penned satirical poems, and satirized plutocrats, robber barons, party bosses, and phony reformers like President Theodore Roosevelt. True to his populist roots Wayland took the side of the producers against the "parasites" who enriched themselves at the expense of working people. Wayland featured Upton Sinclair's muckraking exposé *The Jungle* as a serial and published Eugene Debs's flaming editorial "Arouse Ye Slaves," in which Debs threatened to lead an armed uprising if three mine union leaders on trial in Idaho were convicted of murder on the testimony of a paid informer. Debs's call to arms angered President Roosevelt so much that he asked his attorney general if the government could "proceed criminally" against Debs and shut down Wayland's

paper. The postmaster general concluded, however, that there were no legal grounds for banning the *Appeal*. Wayland kept publishing, and subscriptions to his weekly soared as thousands of "salesmen soldiers" in the *"Appeal* Army" peddled the paper, selling socialism door-to-door. James R. Green, *Grass-Roots Socialism: Radical Movements in the Southwest, 1895–1943* (Baton Rouge: Louisiana State University Press, 1978), pp. 38–41; Elliott Shore, *Talkin' Socialism: J. A. Wayland and the Role of the Press in American Radicalism, 1890–1912* (Lawrence: University Press of Kansas, 1988), pp. 165–85, 214–15.

34. Goodrich, *The Miner's Freedom*, pp. 57–58. Quote in Steel, ed., *Speeches and Writings of Mother Jones*, pp. 38–39.

35. Perry and Payne, *The History of Eskdale*, p. 97.

36. Quote in ibid., p. 10; Eller, *Miners, Millhands, and Mountaineers*, p. 138.

37. John Alexander Williams, *West Virginia and the Captains of Industry* (Morgantown: West Virginia University Library, 1976), p. 181, and quote in Bert Castle interview with Bill Taft.

38. Lou Athey, *James Kay: His Life and Work, 1849–1934* (Charleston, WV: Kay Company, 2005), p. 155; Perry and Payne, *The History of Eskdale*, p. 107.

39. Barkey, *Working-Class Radicals*, p. 47; quote in Howard B. Lee, *Bloodletting in Appalachia: The Story of West Virginia's Four Major Mine Wars and Other Thrilling Incidents of Its Coal Fields* (Morgantown: West Virginia University, 1969), p. 188.

40. Velke, *Baldwin-Felts Detective Agency*, p. 138; Bert Castle interview with Bill Taft; quote in Corbin, *Life, Work, and Rebellion*, p. 51. On Cabell, see "Charles Arnold Cabell," *History of West Virginia, Old and New, and West Virginia Biography*, vol. 2 (Chicago: American Historical Society, 1923), pp. 589–90. Charles Cabell testimony, *Conditions in the Paint Creek District, West Virginia, Part 2*, Committee on Education and Labor, U.S. Senate, 63rd Congress, 1st Session (Washington, DC: Government Printing Office, 1913), p. 1444.

41. Wade Perry testimony, *Conditions in the Paint Creek District*, pp. 2236–37.

42. Perry and Payne, *The History of Eskdale*, pp. 87, 92.

43. Ibid., p. 96.

44. Herbert G. Gutman, "The Workers' Search for Power: Labor in the Gilded Age," in H. Wayne Morgan, ed., *The Gilded Age: A Reappraisal* (Syracuse, NY: Syracuse University Press, 1963), pp. 43, 47.

45. Graebner, *Coal-Mining Safety*, pp. 61, 87, 89.

46. Frederick L. Hoffman, "Coal Mine Mortality Statistics," *Coal Age*, January 6, 1912, pp. 398–400; www.wvminesafety.org/historicprod.htm and www.wvminesafety.org/disaster.htm.

47. Graebner, *Coal-Mining Safety*, pp. 42, 142.

48. Nathan Miller, *The U.S. Navy: An Illustrated History* (Annapolis, MD: Naval Institute Press, 1977), pp. 166–68.

49. Lawrence R. Lynch, "The West Virginia Coal Strike," *Political Science Quarterly* 29, no. 4 (December 1914): 629.

50. Eller, *Miners, Millhands, and Mountaineers*, pp. 137–38.

51. By 1908, the number of machine miners had grown to 14,377, as compared with 21,728 pick miners. Dix, *Work Relations in the Coal Industry*, Table 3, p. 28; Rakes, "Technology in Transition," pp. 40-45. Between 1897 and 1902, 596 men died in roof falls and 121 in explosions; see West Virginia Department of Mines, *Annual Report of the Department of Mines, 1908* (Charleston, WV: Tribune Printing Company, 1909), pp. 4, 7, 208.

52. Rakes, "Early Coal Mining and the Culture of Danger," pp. 56–57, 74.

53. Ibid.

54. To support their theory about the carelessness of immigrant miners, industry experts pointed out that during the deadly years of the early 1900s, foreign-born workers accounted for 49 percent of these deaths, yet constituted only 22 percent of the workforce in 1907. There were, of course, inexperienced, reckless miners who cut corners and took chances to load more coal. But according to historian William Graebner, "For every miner who initiated an explosion by shooting coal off the solid, there was a mine foreman who failed to measure the air currents or instruct the miners in proper technique, or an operator who allowed the dust in his mines to dry and accumulate." Graebner, *Coal-Mining Safety*, pp. 73, 122, quote on p. 113.

55. Ibid., Table 4, pp. 15–16, 73–74, 87.

56. J. Davitt McAteer, *Monongah: The Tragic Story of the Worst Industrial Accident in U.S. History* (Morgantown: West Virginia University Press, 2007), pp. 79–80, 125–26, 302; William B. Klaus, "Uneven Americanization: Italian Immigration to Marion County, 1900–1925," in Ken Fones-Wolf and Ronald L. Lewis, eds., *Transnational West Virginia: Ethnic Communities and Economic Change, 1840–1940* (Morgantown: West Virginia University Press, 2002), p. 199; Frank Haas, *The Explosion at Monongah Mines* (Fairmont, WV: Fairmont Coal Company, 1908), p. 3.

57. Quote in Rakes, "A Combat Scenario," pp. 56–58, 74–76.

58. Ibid., p. 56.

59. Quote in Michael McGerr, *A Fierce Discontent: The Rise and Fall of the Progressive Movement in America, 1870–1920* (New York: Oxford University Press, 2003), pp. 176–77.

Chapter 4: A Spirit of Bitter War, Winter 1908–Summer 1912

1. David Brody, *Steelworkers in America: The Nonunion Era* (Cambridge: Harvard University Press, 1960), pp. 96-137 and quote in ibid., p. 99.

2. Quote in Mowry, *The Era of Theodore Roosevelt*, p. 221; Stanley Lebergott, "Annual Estimates of Unemployment in the United States, 1900–1954," in *The Measurement and Behavior of Unemployment* (Princeton, NJ: National Bureau of Economic Research, 1957), Table 1, p. 215, available at www.nber.org/chapters/c2644.pdf.

3. *Charleston Gazette*, January 19, 25, 1908. Quoted in Barkey, *Working-Class Radicals*, p. 45.

4. Ibid., pp. 63–64; *Labor Argus* quotes in ibid., p. 46.

5. Fred Barkey, "Red Men and Rednecks: The Fraternal Lodge in the Coal Fields," *West Virginia History* 17, no. 1 (January 2003), available at www.wvculture.org/history/wvhs1701.html.

6. Quote from Barkey, *Working-Class Radicals*, p. 58.

7. Gary Jackson Tucker, *Governor William E. Glasscock and Progressive Politics in West Virginia* (Morgantown: West Virginia University Press, 2008), p. 27.

8. The following account is based on Frederick A. Barkey, "Here Come the Boomer 'Talys': Italian Immigrants and Industrial Conflict in the Upper Kanawha Valley, 1903–1917," in Fones-Wolf and Lewis, eds., *Transnational West Virginia*, pp. 161–90.

9. C. Belmont Keeney, "A Union Man: The Life of C. Frank Keeney" (MA thesis, Marshall University, 2000), p. 16.

10. David A. Shannon, *The Socialist Party of America: A History* (New York: Macmillan, 1955), p. 5; Green, *Grass-Roots Socialism*, p. 201; Mowry, *The Era of Theodore Roosevelt*, p. 292; Robert F. Hoxie, "The Rising Tide of Socialism," *Journal of Political Economy* 19 (October 1911): 609–31.

11. Quote in Corbin, *Life, Work, and Rebellion*, p. 26.

12. Fox, *United We Stand*, pp. 147–48; Eller, *Miners, Millhands, and Mountaineers*, p. 178.

13. Lynch, "The West Virginia Coal Strike," pp. 630–33.

14. Kenneth R. Bailey, "'Grim Visaged Men' and the West Virginia National Guard in the 1912–1913 Paint and Cabin Creek Strike," *West Virginia History* 41 (Winter 1980): 112; *Charleston Gazette*, April 19, 1912.

15. Lane, *Civil War in West Virginia*, pp. 86–87.

16. Brant Scott testimony, *Conditions in the Paint Creek District*, p. 499; Morton's testimony at the same hearing quoted in Payne, *Pictorial History of Paint Creek*, p. 108.

17. Lee, *Bloodletting in Appalachia*, p. 21; Fred Mooney, *Struggle in the Coal Fields: The Autobiography of Fred Mooney*, edited by J. W. Hess (Morgantown: West Virginia University Library, 1967), p. 32.

18. Scott testimony, *Conditions in the Paint Creek District*, p. 297.

19. Newt Gump testimony, *Conditions in the Paint Creek District*, pp. 432–33.

20. Ibid.

21. Mooney, *Struggle in the Coal Fields*, p. 16.

22. Quote from W. W. Phaup testimony, *Conditions in the Paint Creek District*, pp. 1372–74.

23. W. Bruce Reid, "More Battle Descriptions from the Paint Creek Region: Last Article by Gazette Man on Bloody Phase . . ." *Charleston Gazette*, June 16, 1912.

24. Velke, *Baldwin-Felts Detective Agency*, pp. 143–44.

25. Letter from J. C. Moiony, royal consul of Italy, to William E. Glasscock, Philadelphia, July 22, 1912; Glasscock's response to Moiony, July 26, 1912; Roy Smith to Glasscock, Clarksburg, WV, July 10, 1912, William Ellsworth Glasscock Papers, West Virginia and Regional History Collection, West Virginia University Library, Morgantown.

26. James Chace, *1912: Wilson, Roosevelt, Taft, and Debs—The Election That Changed the Country* (New York: Simon & Schuster, 2004), p. 57; Letter from Theodore Roosevelt to William E. Glasscock, New York, March 2, 1912, Glasscock Papers.

27. Jones, *Autobiography of Mother Jones*, p. 147; Gorn, *Mother Jones*, p. 165.

28. Jones, *Autobiography of Mother Jones*, pp. 148–49.

29. Letter from Roy Smith to William E. Glasscock, Clarksburg, WV, July 10, 1912, Glasscock Papers.

30. McGerr, *Fierce Discontent*, pp. 119–20. Quote in Adams, *Age of Industrial Violence*, pp. 32–33. Statistics from Rhodri Jeffreys-Jones, *Violence and*

Reform in American History (New York: New Viewpoints, 1978), appendix, pp. 199–201.

31. William E. Glasscock to Professor Virgil Lewis, Charleston, WV, July 22, 1912, and Glasscock to Moiony, July 22, 1912, Glasscock Papers.

32. *Charleston Daily Mail,* July 16, 26, 1912.

33. Mooney, *Struggle in the Coal Fields,* pp. 31–32.

34. W. W. Phaup testimony, *Conditions in the Paint Creek District,* pp. 1378–79. The strikers who had guarded the tracks that night told a very different tale of what happened. They insisted that Phaup's partner pulled the pistols from his holsters and opened fire as soon as he saw the men ahead on the tracks. No one was ever charged with murder in the case, so a jury never weighed the conflicting testimony as to who fired the first shots that night on the tracks. Mooney, *Struggle in the Coal Fields,* p. 33.

35. Phaup testimony, *Conditions in the Paint Creek District,* pp. 1378–80, 1391. The day after the incident, Elizabeth Fish, the nineteen-year-old daughter of a striker, let her curiosity cloud her judgment and decided that she and her friend would walk over and take a look at the body of the dead detective. "We were coming down the road, not saying anything, when these mine guards commenced to firing," Fish later testified. "They called us Rednecks and told us to wade the creek. The creek was pretty wide and was up to our waist. We didn't take off our shoes or stockings nor did we lift up our clothes. They wouldn't give us time. Once they told us to hurry, that we were too damned slow." Fish recalled being too scared to remember what else they hollered at her, but she knew they used profanity. "There were about nine of them, and they all had these long guns . . . drawn on us until we crossed the creek." This incident is one of several suggesting that the Paint Creek strike may have been the first time coal-mining people were branded as "rednecks." Fish quoted in Dale Payne, *The Mine War, 1912–1913: Cabin Creek & Paint Creek* (Fayetteville, WV: privately printed, 2011), p. 50.

Many of the Baldwin-Felts agents had worked as policemen and deputy sheriffs in southern towns where, during the 1890s, local residents began referring to poor white farmers as rednecks because of their sunburned necks. Like the word "hillbilly," which sprouted up about the same time, and the much older term "white trash," "redneck" was a designation wealthier or more powerful people—like mine guards and deputy sheriffs—used as a way of expressing contempt for lower- and working-class white people.

The word soon gained wider usage as a way of referring specifically to union miners who wore red bandannas around their necks as a way of identifying themselves to one another during strike actions. The fact that many of these workers were socialists probably added meaning to the epithet. Before long, though, union miners began using the term "redneck" to describe poor white strikebreakers from the rural South. Patrick Huber, "Red Necks and Red Bandanas: Appalachian Coal Miners and the Coloring of Union Identity, 1912–1936," *Western Folklore* 65, no. 1/2 (Winter–Spring 2006): 195–209; and Annalee Newitz and Matthew Wray, "What Is 'White Trash'? Stereotypes and Economic Conditions of Poor Whites in the United States," in Mike Hill, ed., *Whiteness: A Critical Reader* (New York and London: New York University Press, 1997), p. 170.

36. *Charleston Gazette*, July 27, 1912; Mooney, *Struggle in the Coal Fields*, pp. 31–34; Quote in Joseph Platania, "Three Sides to the Story: Governor Hatfield and the Mine Wars," *Goldenseal* 11 (Summer 1985): 55–56; *Huntington Herald*, July 28, 1912; *Charleston Daily Mail*, July 26, 1912. Last quote from Tucker, *William E. Glasscock*, p. 162.

37. Hudnall, *Kelly's Creek Chronicles*, p. 39.

38. *Huntington Herald-Dispatch*, July 28, 1912.

39. Ibid.

40. Ibid.

41. On Charles D. Elliott, see *Men of West Virginia*, vol. 1 (Chicago: Biographical Publishing Company, 1903), pp. 90–92; Chace, *1912*, pp. 162, 167.

42. General Elliott's report to the governor quoted in "Our Strike in West Virginia," *United Mine Workers Journal*, September 26, 1912.

Chapter 5: The Lord Has Been on Our Side, July 27–September 5, 1912

1. J. C. Tipton, *Charleston and Its Resources* (Charleston, WV: John T. Johnson, 1898), pp. 10–20; Otis K. Rice, *Charleston and the Kanawha Valley* (Woodland Hills, CA: Windsor Publications, 1981); and Deborah R. Weiner, *Coalfield Jews: An Appalachian History* (Urbana: University of Illinois Press, 2006), pp. 29–31. On O. J. Morrison stores, see *History of West Virginia, Old and New*, vol. 3, p. 473.

2. Elizabeth J, Goodall, "The Charleston Industrial Area: Development, 1797–1937," *West Virginia History* 30, no. 1 (October 1968): 380–81.

3. Keeney, "Union Man," pp. 18–19.

4. Mooney, *Struggle in the Coal Fields*, p. 27.

5. Jones, *Autobiography of Mother Jones*, pp. 152–53; Steel, ed., *Speeches and Writings of Mother Jones*, p. 6; leaflet reprinted in Cabell testimony, *Conditions in the Paint Creek District*, pp. 1450–51.

6. Steel, ed., *Speeches and Writings of Mother Jones*, pp. 74, 79.

7. Jones, *Autobiography of Mother Jones*, pp. 154–56.

8. J. E. Staton testimony, *Conditions in the Paint Creek District*, p. 1566; quote in Lynch, "The West Virginia Coal Strike," p. 635.

9. Staton testimony, *Conditions in the Paint Creek District*, p. 1570; Athey, *James Kay*, p. 183; Corbin, *Life, Work, and Rebellion*, p. 90.

10. A. C. Felts testimony in George S. Wallace, *In the Circuit Court of Marshall County, West Virginia: J. R. Shanklin Petitioner vs. Habeas Corpus* (Charleston, WV: Union Publishing Company, 1912), pp. 31–32, 46–53.

11. Jones, *Autobiography of Mother Jones*, pp. 156–57.

12. Felts's account is quoted in Wallace, *In the Circuit Court*, p. 32. Also see Gorn, *Mother Jones*, pp. 156–59, and Staton testimony, *Conditions in the Paint Creek District*, pp. 1566–68. On the legend of the Red Warrior incident, see Michael Kline, "Growing Up on Cabin Creek: An Interview with Arnold Miller," *Goldenseal* 7, no. 2 (April–June 1981): 35–43.

13. Cabell testimony, *Conditions in the Paint Creek District*, p. 1446.

14. Letter from Dr. M. L. Campbell to William E. Glasscock, Eskdale, WV, September 9, 1912, Glasscock Papers. On Dr. Campbell, see Perry and Payne, *The History of Eskdale*, pp. 17–18.

15. Payne, *The Mine War*, p. 140.

16. Barkey, "Here Come the Boomer 'Talys,'" in Fones-Wolf and Lewis, eds., *Transnational West Virginia*, p. 177.

17. G. H. Edmunds, "The Strike in West Virginia," *United Mine Workers Journal*, August 29, 1912, p. 3; Lewis, *Black Coal Miners in America*, pp. 140–42; quote in Corbin, *West Virginia Mine Wars*, pp. 104–105.

18. Lewis, *Black Coal Miners in America*, pp. 141–42.

19. Quote in Mooney, *Struggle in the Coal Fields*, pp. 29–31.

20. Ralph Chaplin, "Violence in West Virginia," *International Socialist Review* 13, no. 10 (April 1913): 729.

21. Quotes in Corbin, *Life, Work, and Rebellion*, pp. 162, 164.

22. Lee, *Bloodletting in Appalachia*, p. 27, and Tucker, *Governor William E. Glassock*, p. 159.

23. Dr. C. A. Ray testimony, *Conditions in the Paint Creek District*, p. 911.

24. *Charleston Daily Mail*, August 31, 1912.

25. Quotes from Wallace, *In the Circuit Court*, pp. 46–49; Stuart Seely Sprague, "Unionization Struggles on Paint and Cabin Creeks, 1912–1913," *West Virginia History* 38, no. 3 (April 1977): 194-95; Bailey, "'Grim Visaged Men,'" p. 116; and Tucker, *Governor William E. Glasscock*, p. 162.

26. Lynch, "The West Virginia Coal Strike," pp. 636–37.

27. Robert S. Rankin, *When Civil Law Fails: Martial Law and Its Legal Basis in the United States* (Durham, NC: Duke University Press, 1939), pp. 111–13; J. Anthony Lukas, *Big Trouble: A Murder in a Small Western Town Sets Off a Struggle for the Soul of America* (New York: Simon & Schuster, 1997), pp. 111–15, 138–52.

28. *Lee, Bloodletting in Appalachia, p. 32*

29. Quote from Cabell testimony, *Conditions in the Paint Creek District*, pp. 1454–55.

30. *Huntington Herald-Dispatch*, September 3, 1912; *Parkersburg Dispatch News*, September 5, 1912; *Fairmont West Virginian*, September 4, 1912.

31. *Charleston Gazette*, September 15, 1912; Bailey, "'Grim Visaged Men,'" p. 197.

32. Letter from William E. Glasscock to General George Baker, Charleston, WV, September 25, 1912, Glasscock Papers.

33. Bailey, "'Grim Visaged Men,'" p. 198.

34. Corbin, *Life, Work, and Rebellion*, pp. 107–108; John H. M. Laslett, *Labor and the Left: A Study of Socialist and Radical Influences in the American Labor Movement, 1881–1924* (New York: Basic Books, 1970), pp. 213–31.

35. Quotes in Foner, ed., *Mother Jones Speaks*, pp. 206–207, 210, 214.

36. Letter from J. Lewis Baumgartner to William E. Glasscock, Beckley, WV, September 6, 1912, Glasscock Papers.

37. *Dispatch News*, September 8, 1912.

38. Wallace, *In the Circuit Court*, pp. 19–25, 38. Also see Tor Ekeland, "Suspending Habeas Corpus: Article I, Section 9, Clause 2, or the United States Constitution and the War on Terror," *Fordham Law Review* 74, no. 3 (2005): 1482–88; and Richard D. Lunt, *Law and Order vs. the Miners: West Virginia, 1907–1923* (Hamden, CT: Archon Books, 1979), pp. 24–25.

39. Corbin, *Life, Work, and Rebellion*, p. 95.

40. Lee, *Bloodletting in Appalachia*, p. 33.

41. David Montgomery, *Citizen Worker: The Experience of Workers in the United States with Democracy and the Free Market during the Nineteenth Century* (Cambridge and New York: Cambridge University Press, 1993),

pp. 93, 103–104, and David P. Thelen, *Paths of Resistance: Tradition and Dignity in Industrializing Missouri* (New York: Oxford University Press, 1986), p. 106.

42. Mooney, *Struggle in the Coal Fields*, pp. 45–46.

43. Chace, *1912*, pp. 199–202.

44. Ibid., pp. 197, 225.

45. Eric Foner, *The Story of American Freedom* (New York: W. W. Norton, 1998), pp. 140–42, quote on p. 142.

46. Quotes in ibid., pp. 114, 116, and in Chace, *1912*, pp. 194–95.

Chapter 6: The Iron Hand, September 6, 1912–February 9, 1913

1. Tucker, *Governor William E. Glasscock*, p. 128.

2. Carolyn M. Karr, "Henry D. Hatfield," in Sullivan, ed., *The West Virginia Encyclopedia*, pp. 321–22; Rice and Brown, *West Virginia*, pp. 214–16.

3. Altina L. Waller, *Feud: Hatfields, McCoys, and Social Change in Appalachia, 1860–1900* (Chapel Hill: University of North Carolina Press, 1988), pp. 182–237.

4. Ibid., p. 237; Velke, *Baldwin-Felts Agency*, p. 107; Coleman C. Hatfield and Robert Y. Spence, *The Tale of the Devil: The Biography of Devil Anse Hatfield* (Chapmanville, WV: Woodland Press, 2003), pp. 263–65.

5. Letter from William E. Glasscock to J. M. Dixon, governor's office, Charleston, WV, September 28, 1912, Glasscock Papers.

6. Edward H. Kintzer, "Miners Play a Waiting Game," *International Socialist Review* 13, no. 5 (November 1912): 391–93.

7. Chace, *1912*, p. 223.

8. Houston speech quoted in *Conditions in the Paint Creek District*, pp. 2259–60.

9. Ralph Chaplin, *Wobbly: The Rough-and-Tumble Story of an American Radical* (Chicago: University of Chicago Press, 1948), pp. 116–17, 188–89.

10. Cabell testimony, *Conditions in the Paint Creek District*, pp. 1444–45.

11. Barkey, *Working-Class Radicals*, pp. 85–86.

12. Chace, *1912*, pp. 238–40.

13. Rice and Brown, *West Virginia*, p. 215.

14. Bailey, "'Grim Visaged Men,'" p. 121; *Huntington Advertiser*, November 4, 1912; Major John B. Payne quoted in Payne, *The Mine War*, p. 131.

15. Guy Levy testimony, *Conditions in the Paint Creek District*, p. 1617.

16. *Charleston Gazette*, November 15, 1912.

17. *Fairmont West Virginian*, November 13, 1912. Quote in Lee, *Bloodletting in Appalachia*, p. 34.

18. *Charleston Gazette*, November 21, 1912.

19. Payne, *The Mine War*, pp. 140–41.

20. Lee, *Bloodletting in Appalachia*, p. 35.

21. *Labor Argus*, December 12, 1912.

22. Bailey, "'Grim Visaged Men,'" p. 121; Phaup and Levy testimonies, *Conditions in the Paint Creek District*, pp. 1380, 1617; *Huntington Advertiser*, November 4, 1912.

23. Ibid.

24. Payne, *The Mine War*, p. 36; quote from Bert Castle interview with Bill Taft.

25. Jones, *Autobiography of Mother Jones*, pp. 35–36.

26. Steel, ed., *Speeches and Writings of Mother Jones*, p. 11.

27. Elliot quoted in *New York Times*, November 10, 1904. Jack London, "The Scab," *Atlantic Monthly*, January 1, 1904, available at www.theatlantic.com/magazine/archive/1904/01/the-scab/306194/. On London's popularity, see Caleb Crain, "Four Legs Good: The Life of Jack London," *New Yorker*, October 28, 2013, available at www.newyorker.com/arts/critics/books/2013/10/28/131028crbo_books_crain.

28. Walter Lippmann, "A Key to the Labor Movement," *Drift and Mastery: An Attempt to Diagnose the Current Unrest* (New York: M. Kennerly, 1914), pp. 60–61.

29. Jones mounted this one-woman campaign at a time when "no genuinely effective, legally enforceable right to freedom of speech" existed in the United States; a time when the Bill of Rights "had little bearing on the lives of most Americans," according to historian Eric Foner. Foner, *The Story of American Freedom*, p. 142.

30. Jones, *Autobiography of Mother Jones*, p. 161.

31. Chaplin, *Wobbly*, pp. 121–22.

32. Chaplin's song "Solidarity Forever" reprinted in Edith Fowke and Joe Glazer, *Songs of Work and Protest* (New York: Dover Publications, 1973), pp. 12–13.

33. Rice and Brown, *West Virginia*, p. 215.

34. Staton testimony, *Conditions in the Paint Creek District*, p. 1568.

35. Levy testimony in ibid., p. 1617; *Labor Argus*, January 23, 1913.

36. Corbin, *Life, Work, and Rebellion*, p. 96.

37. Barkey, *Working-Class Radicals*, p. 94, and Scott testimony, *Conditions in the Paint Creek District*, p. 491.

38. Levy testimony, *Conditions in the Paint Creek District*, pp. 1608–10.

39. Mooney, *Struggle in the Coal Fields*, p. 35.

40. Lee Calvin testimony, *Conditions in the Paint Creek District*, pp. 640–43.

41. Ibid.

42. Lois McLean, "Blood Flows on the Creeks," in Ken Sullivan, ed., *The Goldenseal Book of the West Virginia Mine Wars* (Charleston, WV: Pictorial Histories Publishing Company, 1991), pp. 25–26.

43. Ibid., pp. 26–27.

44. Chaplin, *Wobbly*, p. 124.

45. E. L. Bock testimony, *Conditions in the Paint Creek District*, pp. 1637–38.

46. Mooney, *Struggle in the Coal Fields*, p. 25.

47. Lippmann, "A Key to the Labor Movement," pp. 59, 66.

48. Ibid., p. 61.

49. *Charleston Daily Mail*, February 11, 1913.

50. *Charleston Gazette*, February 12, 1912. Quotes in Payne, *Pictorial History of Paint Creek*, p. 67, and Mooney, *Struggle in the Coal Fields*, p. 26.

51. Jones quoted in Lunt, *Law and Order vs. the Miners*, p. 29, and Gorn, *Mother Jones*, p. 189.

52. Barkey, *Working-Class Radicals*, pp. 96–97, and Scott testimony, *Conditions in the Paint Creek District*, p. 493.

53. Chaplin, *Wobbly*, pp. 126–27.

54. Mooney, *Struggle in the Coal Fields*, p. 21, and Jones, *Autobiography of Mother Jones*, p. 162.

55. On Henry Hatfield's early life, see Karr, "Henry D. Hatfield," pp. 321–22; Rice and Brown, *West Virginia*, pp. 214–16; Hatfield and Spence, *The Tale of the Devil*, pp. 265–72.

56. The following account of the court-martial proceeding is based on the introduction and documents in Edward M. Steel, ed., *The Court-Martial of Mother Jones* (Lexington: University Press of Kentucky, 1995), pp. 31–34, 99–100.

57. Ibid., pp. 31–32.

58. Quote in Williams, *Appalachia*, p. 268. Of course, newly emancipated black citizens had suffered from a far more serious and longer-term campaign of suppression after the Civil War and then during the overthrow of Reconstruction and the imposition of a Jim Crow regime in the Southern States.

Democratic public officials encouraged and abetted this repression, but the denial of civil rights to blacks was largely the work of white vigilantes and terrorists rather than the product of military justice imposed by governors and National Guard troops. See Eric Foner, *Reconstruction: America's Unfinished Revolution, 1863-1877* (New York: HarperCollins, 1988), pp. 412-589.

Chapter 7: Let the Scales of Justice Fall, March 7–July 29, 1913

1. *New York Times*, March 11, 1912.

2. Harold West, "The Mine Guards," *Survey*, April 5, 1913, reprinted in Corbin, ed., *Mine Wars*, pp. 19–21; Steel, ed., *The Court-Martial of Mother Jones*, p. 19.

3. Steel, ed., *The Court-Martial of Mother Jones*, p. 19.

4. Ibid., pp. 19, 65, 82.

5. Wallace quoted in ibid., p. 300.

6. Ibid., pp. 53–54, 297.

7. Cora Older, "The Last Day of the Paint Creek Court Martial," *Independent*, May 15, 1913, pp. 1085–88; *New York Times*, March 22, 1913; Gorn, *Mother Jones*, p. 354.

8. Steel, ed., *The Court-Martial of Mother Jones*, pp. 57–58.

9. Ibid., p. 59; *Coal Age*, April 26, 1913.

10. John Alexander Williams, *West Virginia: A Bicentennial History* (New York: Norton, 1976), pp. 134–35.

11. *Huntington Herald-Dispatch*, May 9, 10, 1913; *Charleston Gazette*, May 10, 1913; and David A. Corbin, *"The Socialist and Labor Star*: The Harassment of Heresy," *Gun Thugs, Rednecks, and Radicals: A Documentary History of the West Virginia Mine Wars* (Oakland, CA: PM Press, 2011), pp. 217–48. Also see John Nerone, *Violence Against the Press: Policing the Public Sphere in U.S. History* (New York: Oxford University Press, 1994).

12. M. Michelson, "'Sweet Land of Liberty!': Feudalism and Civil War in the United States of America, **NOW**," *Everybody's Magazine*, May 1913.

13. Steel, ed., *The Court-Martial of Mother Jones*, p. 60; letters from Jones to Senators Wilson and Borah in Foner, ed., *Mother Jones Speaks*, pp. 586–89.

14. *Globe* quoted in *Literary Digest*, May 10, 1913.

15. Foner, ed., *Mother Jones Speaks*, pp. 222–25.

16. David A. Corbin, "Betrayal in the West Virginia Coal Fields: Eugene V. Debs and the Socialist Party of America, 1912–1914," *Journal of American History* 64, no. 4 (March 1978): 993–94.

17. Ibid., pp. 998–1009. For a different treatment of the Debs committee's report, see Nick Salvatore, *Eugene V. Debs: Citizen and Socialist* (Urbana: University of Illinois Press, 1982), pp. 256–57.

18. *New York Globe* quoted in *Literary Digest*, May 10, 1913, reprinted in
Corbin, ed., *Mine Wars*, p. 49.

19. *Investigation of Paint Creek Coal Fields of West Virginia: Speeches of
Hon. John W. Kern of Indiana in the Senate of the United States, May 9 and 14,
1913* (Washington, DC: Government Printing Office, 1913), pp. 5, 25.

20. *Paint Creek Coal Fields, West Virginia: Speech of Hon. Nathan Goff of
West Virginia in the Senate of the United States, May 9, 14, 15, and 19, 1913*
(Washington, DC: Government Printing Office, 1913), pp. 4–5, 14–15. On
Goff's background, see Rice and Brown, *West Virginia*, pp. 206–10, 226.

21. *Paint Creek Coal Fields, West Virginia: Speech of Hon. Nathan Goff*, p. 53.

22. Barkey, *Working-Class Radicals*, pp. 108–109.

23. "Senators Hear Plea of Mine Operators," *New York Times*, June 10,
1913.

24. "Quinn Morton's Testimony" in Corbin, ed., *Mine Wars*, pp. 39–43;
Corbin, *Life, Work, and Rebellion*, pp. 40–41, 43; "Senator in a Row with
Mining Man," *New York Times*, June 17, 1913.

25. Cabell testimony, *Conditions in the Paint Creek District*, p. 1446; William E. Glasscock testimony, *Conditions in the Paint Creek District*, p. 373.

26. G. C. Cowherd testimony, *Conditions in the Paint Creek District*,
pp. 900–902, 905–909.

27. Ibid., pp. 901–902.

28. Quotes in Williams, *West Virginia*, p. 138.

29. Mooney, *Struggle in the Coal Fields*, p. 27.

30. Perry and Payne, *The History of Eskdale*, pp. 12–13, 130, and McLean,
"Blood Flows on the Creeks," pp. 30–31.

31. Lynch, "The West Virginia Coal Strike," pp. 640–41.

32. More strikers may have died in the fighting, according to one historian who maintains that the "miners usually quickly removed and buried
the dead in order to deny the companies that information." Tucker, *Governor William E. Glasscock*, p. 154.

33. Chaplin quoted in Corbin, *Life, Work, and Rebellion*, pp. 88, 127, and
Chaplin, *Wobbly*, pp. 120–21 126–27.

34. Quotes in Mooney, *Struggle in the Coal Fields*, p. 39, and Cabell testimony, *Conditions in the Paint Creek District*, pp. 1447–49.

35. Quote in *Conditions in the Paint Creek District*, p. 20.

36. Rankin, *When Civil Law Fails*, p. 136; "Has West Virginia a Republican Form of Government?" *Bar* (June–July 1913): 18–21.

37. Steel, ed., *The Court-Martial of Mother Jones*, p. 75.

38. Samuel Gompers, "Russianized West Virginia," *American Federationist*, October 1913, reprinted in Corbin, ed., *Mine Wars*, pp. 14–15, 17.

39. Mooney, *Struggle in the Coal Fields*, p. 39.

40. Collins quoted in Corbin, *Life, Work, and Rebellion*, p. 114.

41. Barkey, *Working-Class Radicals*, p. 119.

42. *Wheeling Intelligencer*, September 19, 1913.

Chapter 8: A New Era of Freedom, Winter 1914–Fall 1918

1. James R. Green, *The World of the Worker: Labor in Twentieth-Century America* (New York: Hill & Wang, 1980), pp. 35-42.

2. Barkey, *Working-Class Radicals*, pp. 108–11.

3. The following account is drawn from Mooney, *Struggle in the Coal Fields*, pp. 1–15.

4. Ibid., pp. 44–52.

5. The following account of the factional struggle in District 17 is based on Barkey, *Working-Class Radicals*, pp. 129–33.

6. Ibid., p. 133.

7. Mooney, *Struggle in the Coal Fields*, p. 39.

8. William E. Glasscock, *The State of West Virginia* (Charleston, WV: News-Mail, 1909), p. 6. A few years after the Big Sandy and other rivers in the Monongahela basin overflowed, causing $100 million worth of damage in 1907, the forester and conservationist A. B. Brooks stated what most mountaineers knew: Forests not only produce wood and wild game, but they also hold rainwater and melting snow and let the runoff drain gradually into streams. The destruction of West Virginia's verdant forests and the stripping of the hills in the coal-mining valleys spelled trouble, Brooks warned, and if conservation practices did not begin immediately, then "Floods surpassing everything known in this region heretofore would be sure to follow." Brooks quoted in Dave Saville, "Floods and Deforestation," *Mountain State Sierran*, May 2004.

9. This account based on *Charleston Gazette*, August 10, 1916, and Payne, *Pictorial History of Cabin Creek*, pp. 14–32.

10. The death toll on Cabin Creek was revised to nearly fifty: *Charleston Gazette*, August 16, 1916. An earlier 1901 deluge in Pennsylvania took one hundred lives. See David McCullough, *The Johnstown Flood* (New York: Simon & Schuster, 1968).

11. Quote in Payne, *Pictorial History of Cabin Creek*, p. 14.

12. Quotes in ibid., p. 52, and Barkey, *Working-Class Radicals*, pp. 183–85.

13. Quotes in Corbin, *Life, Work, and Rebellion*, pp. 121, 125, 126, 129, 130.

14. Bruttaniti quoted in ibid., pp. 135–36.

15. Arthur S. Link, *Woodrow Wilson and the Progressive Era, 1910–1917* (New York: Harper, 1954), pp. 241–50, and John Milton Cooper Jr., *Woodrow Wilson: A Biography* (New York: Alfred A. Knopf, 2009), pp. 341–59.

16. Cornwell ran against a progressive Republican opponent who had enjoyed strong support among union coal miners. Ira Robinson had won the workers' favor when, as a justice of the state supreme court, he dissented from the majority view that it had been legal for the governor to impose martial law on Cabin Creek by treating it as an enemy country. "Cabin Creek District has not seceded," Robinson declared in 1912, adding, "The militia is not an imperial army." Robinson quoted in Steel, ed., *The Court-Martial of Mother Jones*, p. 23; Rice and Brown, *West Virginia*, p. 217; John Hennen, "John Jacob Cornwell," in Sullivan, ed., *The West Virginia Encyclopedia*, p. 169; Mooney, *Struggle in the Coal Fields*, pp. 59–60.

17. Corbin, *Life, Work, and Rebellion*, pp. 183–184.

18. Proceedings of the UMWA 1916 Annual Convention, quoted in David Montgomery, *The Fall of the House of Labor: The Workplace, the State, and American Labor Activism, 1865–1925* (Cambridge and New York: Cambridge University Press, 1987), p. 363; Cooper, *Woodrow Wilson*, pp. 18–20, 50–64; Barkey, *Working-Class Radicals*, p. 141.

19. Wilson quoted in Link, *Woodrow Wilson and the Progressive Era*, pp. 276–77.

20. Wilson quoted in ibid., pp. 281–82.

21. *New York Times*, May 26, 1917.

22. Ronald L. Lewis, "Coal Industry," in Sullivan, ed., *The West Virginia Encyclopedia*, pp. 148–49.

23. Lebergott, "Annual Estimates of Unemployment in the United States," Table 1, p. 215, and Gorn, *Mother Jones*, pp. 244–45.

24. Steel, ed., *Speeches and Writings of Mother Jones*, Jones quoted on pp. 187, 190; Sandburg quoted on p. xv.

25. Quote in ibid., p. 190; Fox, *United We Stand*, pp. 178–80; Corbin, *Life, Work, and Rebellion*, p. 183.

26. Mooney, *Struggle in the Coal Fields*, pp. 60–61.

27. Ibid., and Corbin, *Life, Work, and Rebellion*, p. 184.

28. Chaplin, *Wobbly*, pp. 228, 244–66, and Ginger, *Eugene V. Debs*, pp. 403–40.

29. Gorn, *Mother Jones*, pp. 246–47; Barkey, *Working-Class Radicals*, pp. 205–206; quote in Corbin, *Life, Work, and Rebellion*, pp. 182, 189.

30. Corbin, *Life, Work, and Rebellion*, p. 181.

31. On U.S. military activity in France, see Arthur S. Link, *American Epoch: A History of the United States since the 1890s*, 2nd ed. (New York: Knopf, 1963), pp. 196–98. Russell L. Stultz, *History of the Eightieth Blue Ridge Division in World War I*, edited and revised by Bill J. Krehbiel (Kansas City, MO: Opinicus Publishing Company, 2012), CD-ROM.

32. American Battle Monuments Commission, *80th Division: Summary of Operations in the World War* (Washington, DC: Government Printing Office, 1944), and Boyd B. Stutler, *West Virginia Casualties in the War with Germany* (Charleston, WV: Jarrett Printing Company, 1924), p. 477.

33. Quote in Corbin, *Life, Work, and Rebellion*, p. 179.

34. Quote in Corbin, ed., *Mine Wars*, pp. 67–68.

35. Corbin, *Life, Work, and Rebellion*, p. 181.

36. Quote in ibid., p. 181. See also Albert H. Fay, *Coal-Mine Fatalities in the United States 1919* (Washington, DC: Government Printing Office, 1920), Table 25, p. 32.

37. Corbin, *Life, Work, and Rebellion*, pp. 184–86.

38. John C. Hennen, *The Americanization of West Virginia: Creating a Modern Industrial State, 1916–1925* (Lexington: University Press of Kentucky, 1996), p. 53.

39. Ibid., p. 47; Corbin, *Life, Work, and Rebellion*, p. 186.

40. Quote in Corbin, *Life, Work, and Rebellion*, p. 183; Fox, *United We Stand*, p. 180.

41. Quotes in Fox, *United We Stand*, p. 181; in Corbin, *Life, Work, and Rebellion*, pp. 187–90; and in Foner, *The Story of American Freedom*, p. 176.

42. Josiah Keeley, "After the War," *Coal Age*, November 7, 1918, p. 868.

43. American Battle Monuments Commission, *80th Division*, pp. 13–61, and quote in letter from Private Lawrence Wills to Mrs. Woodson Wills, Argonne Forest, France, September 18, 1918, reprinted in *Charleston Daily Mail*, October 26, 1918.

44. Robert H. Ferrell, *America's Deadliest Battle: Meuse-Argonne, 1918* (Lawrence: University of Kansas Press, 2007), p. 148.

45. Ibid., pp. 111, 138–39, 147.

46. For a description of the Meuse-Argonne military cemetery and monument, see www.abmc.gov/cemeteries/cemeteries/ma.php.

47. The phrase quoted was coined by the influential British writer H. G. Wells in books he published in 1914 and 1915. President Woodrow Wilson used similar words in one speech. William Safire, *Safire's Political Dictionary*, rev. ed. (New York: Oxford University Press, 2008), pp. 792–93.

Chapter 9: A New Recklessness, Winter 1919–Winter 1920

1. Montgomery, *Workers' Control*, Table 2, pp. 87, 388–89.

2. Hennen, *The Americanization of West Virginia*, pp. 78–79, 85–86; Evelyn L. K. Harris and Frank J. Krebs, *From Humble Beginnings: West Virginia State Federation of Labor, 1903–1957* (Charleston: West Virginia Labor History Publishing Fund, 1960), pp. 131–32.

3. Quote in Mooney, *Struggle in the Coal Fields*, p. 67.

4. On county governments in the Mountain State as "little kingdoms," see Williams, *Appalachia*, p. 137. On Chafin, see Lee, *Bloodletting in Appalachia*, pp. 87–121; the fawning portrait by George T. Swain, *The Incomparable Don Chafin* (Charleston, WV: Ace Enterprises, 1962); and Walter R. Thurmond, *The Logan Coal Field of West Virginia: A Brief History* (Morgantown: West Virginia University Library, 1964), p. 77.

5. Arthur Gleason, "Private Ownership of Public Officials," *Nation*, May 29, 1920, p. 724; Steel, ed., *Speeches and Writings of Mother Jones*, pp. 211, 215, 222–23; Lee, *Bloodletting in Appalachia*, p. 91; George T. Swain quoted in "On Dark and Bloody Ground: An Oral History of the UMWA in Central Appalachia, 1920–1935," unpublished manuscript (National Endowment for the Humanities Youth Grant Report, January 1973), p. 74, available at the West Virginia and Regional History Collection, West Virginia University Library.

6 Arthur Gleason, "Company-Owned Americans," *Nation*, June 12, 1920, p. 725.

7. Lewis, *Black Coal Miners in America*, p. 160.

8. Gleason, "Company-Owned Americans," p. 725.

9. Mooney, *Struggle in the Coal Fields*, p. 83.

10. Ibid., p. 63; Fox, *United We Stand*, p. 248.

11. Lunt, *Law and Order vs. the Miners*, pp. 76–77; Mooney, *Struggle in the Coal Fields*, p. 64.

12. The fight between the Hatfield and McCoy clans was transformed into legend by those who interpreted it as an expression of the region's "uncivilized" nature, a product of an ancient code that led mountaineers to take the law into their own hands and kill each other for trivial or incomprehensible reasons. But as Altina Waller's research shows, the violence associated with the Hatfield-McCoy feud had more to do with the economic and political modernization of the region than it did with family animosities and old codes of justice. In any case, the conflict ended before the coal industry transformed the Tug River Valley, and it had no direct bearing on the second mine war that would be fought out on the same rugged ground. See Waller, *Feud*. Also see Hatfield and Spence, *The Tale of the Devil*, pp. 187, 230, 267, 274, 276, 281–83.

13. C. Belmont Keeney, "Rank and File Rednecks: Radicalism and Union Leadership in the West Virginia Mine Wars," in Melinda M. Hicks and C. Belmont Keeney, eds., *Defending the Homeland: Historical Perspectives on Radicalism, Terrorism, and State Responses* (Morgantown: West Virginia University Press, 2007), p. 33.

14. John Spivak, *A Man in His Time* (New York: Horizon Press, 1967), pp. 51–58, 62.

15. Ibid., pp. 62–64, 67, 70.

16. Roger Fagge, *Power, Culture, and Conflict in the Coalfields: West Virginia and South Wales, 1900–1922* (Manchester and New York: Manchester University Press, 1996), p. 129; Mooney, *Struggle in the Coal Fields*, p. 65; Keeney quoted in William C. Blizzard, *When Miners March* (Gay, WV: Appalachian Community Services, 2004), p. 103.

17. Spivak, *A Man in His Time*, pp. 73–74; Keeney quoted in Lunt, *Law and Order vs. the Miners*, p. 78.

18. Spivak, *A Man in His Time*, pp. 78–79.

19. "The Revolt of the Rank and File," *Nation*, October 25, 1919, p. 540. On the 1919 strikes, see Jeremy Brecher, *Strike!* (San Francisco, CA: Straight Arrow Books, 1972), pp. 105–30.

20. Quote in Robert K. Murray, *Red Scare: A Study in National Hysteria, 1919–1920* (New York: McGraw Hill, 1964 [1955]), p. 129.

21. *United Mine Workers Journal*, May 1, 1919; Fox, *United We Stand*, p. 187.

22. Steel, ed., *The Speeches and Writings of Mother Jones*, pp. 206–207; quote in Fagge, *Power, Culture, and Conflict in the Coalfields*, p. 130.

23. The following account of Chafin's shooting is from Swain, *The Incomparable Don Chafin*, pp. 21–25; Gleason, "Private Ownership of Public Officials"; and Lee, *Bloodletting in Appalachia*, pp. 92–93.

24. Quote in Mooney, *Struggle in the Coal Fields*, p. 67.

25. Quote in Lunt, *Law and Order vs. the Miners*, pp. 79–80.

26. Swain, *The Incomparable Don Chafin*, pp. 21–25; Lee, *Bloodletting in Appalachia*, p. 93.

27. Ibid.

28. Harding quoted in Melvyn Dubofsky and Warren Van Tine, *John L. Lewis: A Biography* (New York: Quadrangle/New York Times Book Company, 1977), p. 36.

29. Quotes in Hennen, *The Americanization of West Virginia*, p. 94, and Lunt, *Law and Order vs. the Miners*, p. 82.

30. Quote in Murray, *Red Scare*, p. 156.

31. Quote in ibid., p. 162, and Dubofsky and Van Tine, *John L. Lewis*, pp. 44–45.

32. Quote in Lon Savage, *Thunder in the Mountains: The West Virginia Mine War, 1920–21* (Pittsburgh, PA: University of Pittsburgh Press, 1990), pp. 9–10.

33. Murray, *Red Scare*, pp. 211–13, 217.

34. On Lewis's ambition, see Saul D. Alinsky, *John L. Lewis: An Unauthorized Biography* (New York: Vintage Books, 1970), p. 38.

35. Keeney quoted in Lunt, *Law and Order vs. the Miners*, p. 78.

Chapter 10: To Serve the Masses without Fear, Winter–Spring 1920

1. Dix, *Work Relations in the Coal Industry*, pp. 14–66.

2. Ibid., p. 80. For a study of mechanization as a form of workplace control, see Richard Edwards, *Contested Terrain: The Transformation of the Workplace in the Twentieth Century* (New York: Basic Books, 1979), p. 20. This account of events in Mingo County relies heavily upon the meticulous scholarship of Rebecca J. Bailey, *Matewan before the Massacre: Politics, Coal, and the Roots of Conflict in a West Virginia Mining Community* (Morgantown: West Virginia University Press, 2008), quote on p. 94.

3. Vinson quoted in Corbin, *Life, Work, and Rebellion*, pp. 106, 113.

4. Bailey, *Matewan before the Massacre*, pp. 189–90.

5. Quote in ibid., pp. 194–95.

6. Ibid., pp. 91–93, quote on p. 106.

7. Ibid., pp. 101–13.

8. Quotes in ibid., p. 115.

9. "Hatfield Feud Renewed," *New York Times*, March 30, 1902.

10. Savage, *Thunder in the Mountains*, p. 9.

11. Ibid., pp. 11–13; Hatfield and Spence, *The Tale of the Devil*, pp. 231–33.

12. Bailey, *Matewan before the Massacre*, p. 168.

13. Ibid., p. 194.

14. Ibid., pp. 209–13.

15. Ibid., pp. 214–15; Mooney, *Struggle in the Coal Fields*, p. 71.

16. Lunt, *Law and Order vs. the Miners*, pp. 93–94.

17. Quotes in *Williamson Daily News*, April 27, 1920, and Bailey, *Matewan before the Massacre*, pp. 215–16.

18. Quotes in Bailey, *Matewan before the Massacre*, p. 217; Lunt, *Law and Order vs. the Miners*, pp. 92–93; and Richard Burgett interview, "On Dark and Bloody Ground," p. 105.

19. Elias Lieberman, *Unions before the Bar: Historic Trials Showing the Evolution of Labor Rights in the United States* (New York: Harper, 1950), p. 91.

20. Ibid., pp. 93–94; William E. Forbath, *Law and the Shaping of the American Labor Movement* (Cambridge, MA: Harvard University Press, 1991), p. 166; Melvyn I. Urofsky, *Louis D. Brandeis: A Life* (New York: Pantheon, 2009), pp. 487–88.

21. Quote in *Survey*, December 22, 1917, pp. 348–49.

22. Quote in Bailey, *Matewan before the Massacre*, p. 217.

23. Ibid., pp. 215–17; Mooney, *Struggle in the Coal Fields*, p. 72.

24. Mooney, *Struggle in the Coal Fields*, p. 72; *New York Times*, May 20, 1920; Murray, *Red Scare*, p. 251.

25. Quotes in Blizzard, *When Miners March*, pp. 131–32.

26. Lunt, *Law and Order vs. the Miners*, pp. 94–95.

27. Bailey, *Matewan before the Massacre*, p. 168.

28. Martelle, *Blood Passion*, pp. 52, 57, 62.

29. Mooney, *Struggle in the Coal Fields*, p. 32; C. E. Lively testimony, *West Virginia Coal Field Hearings Pursuant to S. 80, to Investigate the Recent Violence*

in the Coal Fields of West Virginia and Adjacent Territory and the Causes Which Led to the Conditions Which Now Exist in Said Territory, Committee on Education and Labor, U.S. Senate, 67th Congress, 1st Session (Washington, DC: Government Printing Office, 1921).

30. Quote in Bailey, *Matewan before the Massacre*, pp. 1–2.

31. Bill Hall interview, Matewan Oral History Project, Matewan Development Center, West Virginia Archives and History, Charleston, available at www.wvculture.org/history/labor/matewan03.html.

32. The following description of the events in Matewan on the afternoon of May 19, 1920, is drawn from Rebecca Bailey's account based on her reading of the transcript of Sid Hatfield's trial and oral histories she recorded with witnesses in ibid.; from Savage, *Thunder in the Mountains*, pp. 13–16, in which the author's interview sources are not referenced; and from Topper Sherwood, "The Dust Settles: Felts Papers Offer More on Matewan," in Sullivan, ed., *Goldenseal Book of the West Virginia Mine Wars*, pp. 51–52.

33. "Matewan Trial Transcript Offers Eyewitness Accounts of Mine Wars 'O.K. Corral,'" *West Virginia and Regional History Collection Newsletter* 23, no. 1 (Fall 2007): 3–4.

34. *New York Times*, May 20, 1920; *United Mine Workers Journal*, June 20, 1920.

35. Quote in Savage, *Thunder in the Mountains*, p. 17.

36. Lunt, *Law and Order vs. the Miners*, p. 106.

37. Blankenship quote in ibid., pp. 102–103.

38. Letter from Frank Keeney to William Green, June 16, 1920, cited in Corbin, *Life, Work, and Rebellion*, p. 202; *United Mine Workers Journal*, July 1, 1920.

39. Letter from James Doyle and Andrew Wilson to President John L. Lewis, June 12, 1920, *United Mine Workers Journal*, July 15, 1920, p. 11; Keeney to Green, June 16, 1920, cited in Corbin, *Life, Work, and Rebellion*, p. 202.

40. Daniel P. Jordan, "The Mingo War: Labor Violence in the Southern West Virginia Coal Fields, 1919–1921," in Gary M. Fink and Merl E. Reed, eds., *Essays in Southern Labor History* (Westport, CT: Greenwood Press, 1977), p. 108.

Chapter 11: Situation Absolutely Beyond Control, July 4, 1920–May 29, 1921

1. Vinson testimony, *West Virginia Coal Field Hearings*, pp. 10–11.

2. Harry Olmstead testimony in ibid., p. 226.

3. Lunt, *Law and Order vs. the Miners*, p. 100.

4. Quote in ibid., pp. 100–103.

5. Ibid., p. 104.

6. Ibid., pp. 104–105, and Savage, *Thunder in the Mountains*, p. 21.

7. Roger Fagge, "'Citizens of This Great Republic': Politics and the West Virginia Miners, 1900–1922," *International Review of Social History* 40 (April 1995): 140; and Anthony Patrick O'Brien, "The Depression of 1920–21," in David Glasner, Thomas Cooley, et al., eds., *Business Cycles and Depressions: An Encyclopedia* (New York: Garland Publishing, 1997), pp. 151–53.

8. John C. Hennen, "Ephraim Franklin Morgan," in Sullivan, ed., *The West Virginia Encyclopedia*, p. 499; Corbin, *Life, Work, and Rebellion*, p. 212; Bailey, *Matewan before the Massacre*, pp. 218–22.

9. Lunt, *Law and Order vs. the Miners*, p. 117.

10. Corbin, *Life, Work, and Rebellion*, p. 203; Savage, *Thunder in the Mountains*, p. 28; Neil Burkinshaw, "Labor's Valley Forge," *Nation*, December 8, 1920, p. 639; Merle T. Cole, "Martial Law in West Virginia and Major Davis as 'Emperor of Tug River,'" *West Virginia History* 43 (Winter 1982): 118–44.

11. Savage, *Thunder in the Mountains*, p. 28, Houston quoted on p. 27; Lunt, *Law and Order vs. the Miners*, p. 116.

12. Lunt, *Law and Order vs. the Miners*, p. 95.

13. *United Mine Workers Journal*, January 15, 1921; Savage, *Thunder in the Mountains*, pp. 29–30.

14. *New York Times*, December 6, 7, 1920; Burkinshaw, "Labor's Valley Forge," p. 629.

15. Dix, *Work Relations in the Coal Industry*, Table 3, p. 28; *Fourteenth Census of the United States, 1920: Volume XI—Mines and Quarries*, Bureau of the Census (Washington, DC: Government Printing Office, 1922), pp. 250, 271; and *Fourteenth Census of the United States, 1920: State Compendium—West Virginia, Statistics of Population, Occupations, Agriculture, Manufactures, and Mines and Quarries for the State, Counties, and Cities*, Bureau of the Census (Washington, DC: Government Printing Office, 1925), p. 107.

16. Dubofsky and Van Tine, *John L. Lewis*, pp. 68–69; Montgomery, *The Fall of the House of Labor*, p. 391.

17. Dubofsky and Van Tine, *John L. Lewis*, pp. 50–51; *New York Times*, January 21, 1921.

18. Quote in the *New York Times*, January 21, 1921.

19. Lon Savage, "The Gunfight at Matewan," in Sullivan, ed., *Goldenseal Book of the West Virginia Mine Wars*, pp. 45–46; and Savage, *Thunder in the Mountains*, p. 31.20. Sherwood, "The Dust Settles," pp. 51–52; Harry Berman interview with John Hennen, June 7, 1989, Matewan Oral History Project; and Statement of Henry Haywood, June 28, 1921, Williamson, WV, Logan Coal Operators Association Collection, West Virginia Archives and History, available at www.wvculture.org/hiStory/labor/matewan01.html.

21. *Huntington Herald-Dispatch*, June 2, 3, 1920.

22. Sherwood, "The Dust Settles," pp. 51–52.

23. *Logan Banner*, January 14, 1921; quote in Hatfield and Spence, *The Tale of the Devil*, p. 278; Savage, *Thunder in the Mountains*, pp. 31–35.

24. Savage, *Thunder in the Mountains*, p. 36.

25. Martelle, *Blood Passion*, p. 56; Spivak, *A Man and His Time*, pp. 91–92.

26. Savage, *Thunder in the Mountains*, p. 33.

27. Lunt, *Law and Order vs. the Miners*, p. 146.

28. This account of the trial has become part of Mingo County lore, but it seems more likely that the grand jury overreached by indicting so many men on the charge of murdering Albert Felts. According to one jury member, the panel found the evidence against Sid Hatfield convincing, but the jurors shrank from the prospect of convicting all the other Matewan men. Dr. Rebecca Bailey telephone interview with the author, January 8, 2008; Lee, *Bloodletting in Appalachia*, p. 62.

29. Savage, *Thunder in the Mountains*, p. 36; *Fairmont Times* quoted in Fagge, "'Citizens of this Great Republic,'" p. 143.

30. Lunt, *Law and Order vs. the Miners*, pp. 147–49.

31. Corbin, *Life, Work, and Rebellion*, p. 216.

32. Keeney, "Rank and File Rednecks," pp. 37–38.

33. Savage, *Thunder in the Mountains*, p. 36; *Fairmont Times* quoted in Fagge, "'Citizens of this Great Republic,'" p. 143.

34. Jordan, "The Mingo War," pp. 101–43.

35. James R. Brockus testimony, *West Virginia Coal Field Hearings*, pp. 344–49.

36. Corbin, *Life, Work, and Rebellion*, p. 205.

37. Quote in ibid., p. 207.

38. Savage, *Thunder in the Mountains*, p. 36; *Fairmont Times* quoted in Fagge, "'Citizens of this Great Republic,'" p. 143.

39. See Merle T. Cole, "'Mere Military Color': The State Police and Martial Law," *West Virginia Historical Society Quarterly* 17, no. 3 (July 2003): 130–32; Savage, *Thunder in the Mountains*, p. 55; Brockus testimony, *West Virginia Coal Field Hearings*, pp. 344–49.

40. Cole, "'Mere Military Color,'" pp. 118–23.

41. Olmstead and Brockus testimonies, *West Virginia Coal Field Hearings*, pp. 229, 339.

42. Cole, "'Mere Military Color,'" p. 134.

43. Arthur Warner, "Fighting Unionism with Martial Law," *Nation*, October, 12, 1921, p. 396.

Chapter 12: There Can Be No Peace in West Virginia, May 30–August 7, 1921

1. Frank Ingham testimony, *West Virginia Coal Field Hearings*, pp. 26–30.

2. Warner, "Fighting Unionism with Martial Law," p. 396.

3. *New York Times*, May 26, 27, 1920. Quote in Robert Shogan, *The Battle of Blair Mountain: The Story of America's Largest Labor Uprising* (Boulder, CO: Westview Press, 2004), p. 129.

4. Shogan, *The Battle of Blair Mountain*, p. 130.

5. Cain, "The Battle Ground of Coal," p. 152.

6. John E. Bodnar, *Remaking America: Public Memory, Commemoration, and Patriotism in the Twentieth Century* (Princeton, NJ: Princeton University Press, 1992), pp. 80–83.

7. Corbin, *Life, Work, and Rebellion*, pp. 208–209.

8. William Ball affidavit, *West Virginia Coal Field Hearings*, p. 167.

9. Quote in Fagge, "'Citizens of this Great Republic,'" p. 145; Corbin, *Life, Work, and Rebellion*, p. 209.

10. The first casualty numbers were calculated by investigators for the mine operators' association of Mingo County and based on state police and county coroners' reports. The association's spokesmen vowed that every death had been verified. Among the dead were one McCoy, a nonunion miner, and one Hatfield, a union man. Olmstead testimony, *West Virginia Coal Field Hearings*, pp. 268–69. Keeney, who estimated a death toll of one hundred, based his judgment on reports from the field. The Morgantown newspaper's mortality figure for the summer of 1920 is cited in Jordan, "The Mingo War," p. 109.

11. Cole, "'Mere Military Color,'" pp. 134, 138.

12. *West Virginia Coal Field Hearings*, p. 304.

13. Lunt, *Law and Order vs. the Miners*, p. 209.

14. Corbin, *Life, Work, and Rebellion*, p. 209.

15. Letter from Roger Baldwin to Frank Keeney, March 31, 1920, quoted in Lunt, *Law and Order vs. the Miners*, p. 146.

16. Lane, *Civil War in West Virginia*, p. 39. The quotes and paraphrases in the following three paragraphs are on pp. 13–15, 20, 83, 85, 88–89, 103–14.

17. Quotes in ibid., pp. 103–14, 124–25.

18. John R. Commons, introduction to ibid., pp. 9–10; Daniel Ernst, "The Yellow-Dog Contract and Liberal Reform, 1917–1932," *Labor History* 30, no. 2 (1989): 253, 258–59.

19. Quotes in *West Virginia Coal Field Hearings*, pp. 8–9, 11–14, Lively testimony on pp. 148–150.

20. Quote in ibid., p. 20.

21. Keeney testimony in ibid., p. 176.

22. *Charleston Gazette*, August 2, 1921, cited in Corbin, *Life, Work, and Rebellion*, p. 209.

23. Richard Slotkin, *Gunfighter Nation: The Myth of the Frontier in Twentieth-Century America* (Norman: University of Oklahoma Press, 1998), pp. 127–28, 144–45, 151, 245 and Cain, "West Virginia: A Mine-Field Melodrama," p. 144.

24. Savage, *Thunder in the Mountains*, p. 50.

25. The arrival of the Matewan party in Welch is described in the *Wheeling Intelligencer*, July 30, 1921, cited in Shogan, *The Battle of Blair Mountain*, p. 154.

26. *Wheeling Intelligencer*, July 30, 31, 1921.

27. This account of the events in Welch on August 1 is based on the *New York Times*, August 2, 1921; Lee, *Bloodletting in Appalachia*, pp. 65–68, which relies on reports in the *Bluefield Daily Telegraph*; Savage, *Thunder in the Mountains*, pp. 51–52; and Jessie Hatfield and Sallie Chambers testimonies, *West Virginia Coal Field Hearings*, pp. 737–39.

28. Chambers testimony, *West Virginia Coal Fields Hearings*, pp. 737–39.

29. *New York Times*, August 2, 1921.

30. This account of the funeral on August 3 is based on *Wheeling Intelligencer*, August 4, 1921, and *Charleston Gazette*, August 4, 6, 1921.

31. Quotes in *Wheeling Intelligencer*, August 4, 1921; *Charleston Gazette*, August, 2, 3, 1920; and Mooney, *Struggle in the Coal Fields*, p. 89.

32. "The Primitive Mountaineer," *New York Times*, August 3, 1921.

33. Waller, *Feud*, pp. 185, 233, 246–47.

34. William Lynwood Montell, *Killings: Folk Justice in the Upper South* (Lexington: University Press of Kentucky, 1986). Montell argues that Civil War–era guerrilla warfare left a "self-perpetuating imprint on local culture." This heritage and a variety of other historical causes of gun violence are brilliantly described and analyzed in Williams, *Appalachia*, pp. 157–97, 242–73, quotes on pp. 186–87.

35. Williams, *Appalachia*, pp. 157–97, 242–73, quotes on pp. 186–87.

36. Quote in Savage, *Thunder in the Mountains*, p. 56.

37. Ibid., pp. 75–80, quote on p. 56; Gorn, *Mother Jones*, p. 271; Mooney, *Struggle in the Coal Fields*, p. 62.

38. Shogan, *The Battle of Blair Mountain*, p. 164.

Chapter 13: Gather Across the River, August 8–August 25, 1921

1. Letter from Harold Houston to Everett Early, Charleston, WV, August 9, 1921, William C. Blizzard Collection, West Virginia Division of Culture and History, West Virginia State Archives, Charleston. *Blair Mountain Cultural Resource Survey and Recording Project*, no. 2 (Morgantown, WV: Institute for the History of Technology and Industrial Archaeology, 1992), pp. 18–20.

2. *Blair Mountain Cultural Resource Survey*, p. 21.

3. William Wiley testimony before the Senate Committee on Education and Labor, quoted in ibid., p. 20.

4. Lunt, *Law and Order vs. the Miners*, p. 124.

5. J. S. McKeaver testimony, *The State of West Virginia v. Walter Allen*, Jefferson County, West Virginia. Microfilm of transcript available at the West Virginia and Regional History Center, West Virginia University Library.

6. Charles Tucker testimony in ibid.

7. *New York Times*, August 21, 25, 1921; *Charleston Gazette*, August, 22, 24, 1921; *The United Mine Workers in West Virginia*, Bituminous Operators' Special Committee, U.S. Coal Commission (New York: Evening Post Job Printing Office, 1923), p. 91.

8. *New York Times*, August 20, 1921.

9. Heber Blankenhorn, "Marching Through West Virginia," *Nation*, September 14, 1921, reprinted in Corbin, ed., *Mine Wars*, pp. 107–108.

10. Ibid., p. 109.

11. Quote in Gorn, *Mother Jones*, p. 274.

12. Blizzard, *When Miners March*, pp. 281–83.

13. Mooney, *Struggle in the Coal Fields*, pp. 79–80.

14. Jones, *Autobiography of Mother Jones*, pp. 234–35; *New York Times*, August 25, 1921; *Charleston Gazette*, August 25, 1921; Lunt, *Law and Order vs. the Miners*, p. 124; Mooney, *Struggle in the Coal Fields*, pp. 90–91; quote from J. W. Meadows testimony, *The State of West Virginia v. Walter Allen*; *Blair Mountain Cultural Resource Survey*.

15. Gorn, *Mother Jones*, p. 274.

16. Quote in ibid., pp. 275–76.

17. Ibid.

18. Blankenhorn, "Marching Through West Virginia," p. 108.

19. Savage, *Thunder in the Mountains*, p. 59.

20. Corbin, *Life, Work, and Rebellion* p. 221.

21. In 1912, the Baldwin-Felts agents had referred to Cabin Creek strikers, and even to their children, as rednecks. It was their way of scorning what one guard called "the meanest class of people" he had ever encountered. By 1921, fears of communism and the effects of the Red Scare had given the term "redneck" added political significance.

22. *New York Times*, August 25, 1921; *Charleston Gazette*, September 3, 1921.

23. *Blair Mountain Cultural Resource Survey*, pp. 30-31; quote from Bert Castle interview with Bill Taft.

24. Keeney, "Rank and File Rednecks," pp. 36–37.

25. William C. Blizzard and Wess Harris, "A Biographic Sketch of Bill Blizzard," in Blizzard, *When Miners March*, p. 396; Mooney, *Struggle in the Coal Fields*, pp. 47, 53, 67.

26. *West Virginia: A Guide*, pp. 461–62.

27. *New York Times*, August 25, 1921; *Charleston Gazette*, August 26, 1921; *Huntington Herald-Dispatch*, August 27, 1921.

28. *Charleston Gazette*, August, 25, 1921.

29. Quote in Corbin, *Life, Work, and Rebellion*, p. 221.

30. *Blair Mountain Cultural Resource Survey*, p. 23.

Chapter 14: Time to Lay Down the Bible and Pick Up the Rifle, August 8–August 25, 1921

1. Clayton D. Laurie, "The United States Army and the Return to Normalcy in Labor Dispute Interventions: The Case of the West Virginia Coal Mine Wars, 1920–1921," *West Virginia History* 50 (1991): 1–24.

2. Shogan, *The Battle of Blair Mountain*, pp. 175, 198–99.

3. *Charleston Gazette*, August 26, 1921; Blankenhorn, "Marching Through West Virginia," pp. 109–10.

4. Bandholtz quoted in Mooney, *Struggle in the Coal Fields*, p. 92.

5. By 1921, unemployment had reached a frightening level of 11.7 percent. On international events, see Geoffrey Barraclough, ed., *The Times Atlas of World History* (London: Times Books, 1978), pp. 260–65, and on the new Communist Party USA, see Anthony Bimba, *The History of the American Working Class* (New York: International Publishers, 1927), p. 290.

6. Mooney, *Struggle in the Coal Fields*, pp. 91–95.

7. *Logan Banner*, August 26, 1921; *New York Times*, August 27, 1921.

8. Quote in "On Dark and Bloody Ground," p. 63.

9. Mooney, *Struggle in the Coal Fields*, pp. 95–99; Shogan, *The Battle of Blair Mountain*, p. 183.

10. Shogan, *The Battle of Blair Mountain*, pp. 184–85.

11. Reynolds testimony, *The State of West Virginia v. Walter Allen*; *Blair Mountain Cultural Resource Survey*, pp. 24–25.

12. Savage, *Thunder in the Mountains*, pp. 86–87.

13. Shogan, *The Battle of Blair Mountain*, p. 186.

14. *Blair Mountain Cultural Resource Survey*, pp. 28–29, 31.

15. Shogan, *The Battle of Blair Mountain*, p. 186.

16. Ibid., p. 184; Lunt, *Law and Order vs. the Miners*, pp. 129–30; *Charleston Gazette*, August 29, 1921; quotes in Michael M. Meador, "The Redneck War of 1921: The Miners' March and the Battle of Blair Mountain," in Sullivan, ed., *Goldenseal Book of the West Virginia Mine Wars*, p. 61.

17. *The United Mine Workers in West Virginia*, p. 45; *Blair Mountain Cultural Resource Survey*, p. 35.

18. *Huntington Advertiser*, August 29, 1921.

19. Editorials reprinted in ibid.

20. Shogan, *The Battle of Blair Mountain*, p. 191; *Huntington Advertiser*, September 3, 1921.

21. Early Ball interview with Michael M. Meador, "The Siege of Crooked Creek Gap," in Sullivan, ed., *Goldenseal Book of the West Virginia Mine Wars*, pp. 69–70.

22. Wilburn quoted in Savage, *Thunder in the Mountains*, pp. 97, 110.

23. Jack Brinkman testimony, *The State of West Virginia v. Walter Allen*.

24. *Huntington Advertiser*, August 31, 1912.

25. *Huntington Advertiser*, August 31, 1921; U.S. Department of Agriculture Weather Bureau, "Daily Temperatures for August, 1921," *Climatological Data: West Virginia Section* 29 (1922): 32.

26. Lunt, *Law and Order vs. the Miners*, p. 136; Dr. Milliken testimony, *The State of West Virginia v. Walter Allen*, p. 89.

27. *Blair Mountain Cultural Resource Survey*, p. 31; Bert Castle interview with Bill Taft, 1973.

28. Quote in Savage, *Thunder in the Mountains*, p. 111; *Huntington Herald-Dispatch*, August 31, 1921; *Charleston Gazette*, September 1, 1921.

29. Savage, *Thunder in the Mountains*, p. 41; *Charleston Gazette*, September 2, 1921; *Blair Mountain Cultural Resource Survey*, p. 40.

30. Quotes in Shogan, *The Battle of Blair Mountain*, p. 198.

31. John L. Lewis statement printed in *Huntington Advertiser*, September 1, 1921.

32. Quote in Mooney, *Struggle in the Coal Fields*, p. 99.

33. Ibid., and Lunt, *Law and Order vs. the Miners*, p. 132.

34. C. F. Keeney and Household, Ward 3, Charleston, Kanawha County, West Virginia (Bureau of the Census, 1920), Enumeration District 90, Image 239, Roll T625_1958, p. 13b, available at www.ancestry.com; Keeney, "Rank and File Rednecks," pp. 33, 35, 37.

35. *Blair Mountain Cultural Resource Survey*, p. 31; *Huntington Herald-Dispatch*, September 4, 1921.

36. Quote in *Even the Heavens Weep: The West Virginia Mine Wars*, directed by Danny L. McGuire (Charleston: WPBY-TV and the West Virginia Educational Broadcasting Authority, 1985). Also see Ball interview with Meador, "The Siege of Crooked Creek Gap," in Sullivan, ed., *Goldenseal Book of the West Virginia Mine Wars*, pp. 66–69.

37. *Charleston Gazette*, September 1, 1921; *Huntington Advertiser*, September 1, 2, 1921; Meador, "The Redneck War," p. 61. Harvard Ayres, an archaeologist who has researched the battlefield for years, visited two bomb craters still visible on Crooked Creek. Harvard Ayres correspondence with author, February 6, 2012.

38. Shogan, *The Battle of Blair Mountain*, pp. 199–200; *Charleston Gazette*, September 2, 1921.

39. *New York Times*, September 2, 1921.

40. Jeffrey Ostler, *The Plains Sioux and U.S. Colonialism from Lewis and Clark to Wounded Knee* (Cambridge and New York: Cambridge University

Press, 2004), p. 288, and Jerry Green, ed., *After Wounded Knee: Correspondence of Major and Surgeon John Vance Lauderdale while Serving with the Army Occupying the Pine Ridge Indian Reservation, 1890–1891* (East Lansing: Michigan State University Press, 1996), pp. 26, 301. Thanks to Josh L. Reid for this citation.

41. *Huntington Advertiser* and *Charleston Gazette*, September 2, 1921.

42. *Blair Mountain Cultural Resource Survey*, pp. 41–42.

43. *Huntington Advertiser*, September 2, 1921.

44. Quotes in *Bluefield Daily Telegram*, September 3, 1921, and *Huntington Advertiser*, September 4, 1912; *Blair Mountain Cultural Resource Survey*, pp. 43–44.

45. Boyden Sparkes quoted in Blizzard, *When Miners March*, pp. 317–23.

46. Boyden Sparkes quoted in Cabell Phillips, "The West Virginia Mine War," *American Heritage* 25 (August 1974): 93.

47. Blizzard and Harris, "A Biographic Sketch of Bill Blizzard," in Blizzard, *When Miners March*, p. 397; Wess Harris, ed., *Dead Ringers: Why Miners March* (Gay, WV: Appalachian Community Services, 2012), pp. 80–81; and C. Belmont Keeney, "Bill Blizzard," in Sullivan, ed., *The West Virginia Encyclopedia*, p. 66. Lon Savage, another journalist who studied the march, also believed that Keeney and Mooney directed operations from their hideout in Ohio. Savage, *Thunder in the Mountains*, p. 120.

48. *Huntington Advertiser*, September 4, 1921.

49. Laurie, "The United States Army and the Return to Normalcy," p. 10. The number of lives lost in the fighting has remained a mystery, according to W. C. Blizzard, a well-informed journalist who concluded that the number of wounded and dead "will never be known." Blizzard, *When Miners March*, p. 305. After the warfare ended on September 4, army patrols searched the hills for bodies, and it became apparent that fewer men had died than initial reports indicated. The death toll seemed surprisingly "light" to one reporter, given the length and intensity of the fighting (at least a million rounds were fired). Soldiers in both armies had used the terrain and dense woods to shield themselves from "hail storms of lead" they unleashed at each other, he remarked. The miners were "strong, rugged mountaineer-types" who were "well versed in the strategy of woods fighting and bushwhacking." Furthermore, a big percentage of the fighters were World War I veterans who had learned to "keep their heads down." *Huntington Advertiser*, September 6, 1921; Shogan, *The Battle of Blair Mountain*, p. 208.

If the battle had been fought on open ground, a terrible slaughter would probably have ensued, and the miners' army, more than twice the size of the defense force, might have prevailed and marched on to Mingo County. In any case, local authorities told reporters "the miners had carried their dead and wounded away with them," and that it was, therefore, difficult to determine exactly how many men had perished. Sheriff Chafin claimed that his forces killed fifty miners. One of Chafin's friends, a journalist who covered the battle for the *Logan Banner*, reinforced this claim. George T. Swain, *The Blair Mountain War: Battle of the Rednecks* (Chapmanville, WV: Woodland Press, 2009 [1927]), p. 57. More objective newspaper reporters who covered the battle intensively estimated a much lower death toll, because they relied only on officially recorded death notices. After a detailed study of the march and the battle, journalist Lon Savage concluded that sixteen men had died in the fighting—all but four of them miners. *Huntington Herald-Dispatch*, September 4, 1921; Savage, *Thunder in the Mountains*, p. 47.

50. *Huntington Herald-Dispatch*, September 4, 1921.

51. Burkinshaw, "Labor's Valley Forge," p. 639; Warner, "Fighting Unionism with Martial Law."

52. Blankenhorn, "Marching Through West Virginia," pp. 107–11; *Washington Star*, September 2, 1921.

53. *Huntington Herald-Dispatch*, September 5, 1921.

54. Ibid.

55. Laurie, "The United States Army and the Return to Normalcy," p. 10.

56. Lunt, *Law and Order vs. the Miners*, pp. 149–51.

57. Shogan, *The Battle of Blair Mountain*, p. 213.

Chapter 15: Americanizing West Virginia, Fall 1921–Fall 1930

1. Quotes in Cain, "West Virginia: A Mine-Field Melodrama," p. 149, and Lee, *Bloodletting in Appalachia*, p. 105.

2. Quote in Shogan, *The Battle of Blair Mountain*, p. 215.

3. Frank Walsh testimony, *West Virginia Coal Field Hearings*, pp. 603–604.

4. Ibid., pp. 731–41.

5. Shogan, *The Battle of Blair Mountain*, p. 215.

6. The following description is based on Hennen, *The Americanization of West Virginia*.

7. Ibid., pp. 2–3, quote on p. 4.

8. C. Belmont Keeney, "A Republican for Labor: T. C. Townsend and the West Virginia Labor Movement, 1921–1932," *West Virginia History* 60 (2004–2006), pp. 3–4.

9. Quote in Lunt, *Law and Order vs. the Miners*, p. 159.

10. Keeney, "A Republican for Labor," pp. 3–4.

Lunt, *Law and Order vs. the Miners*, p. 154.

11. Ibid., p. 158.

12. Billy Sunday speech, April 7, 1922, quoted in Corbin, *Life, Work, and Rebellion*, p. 151.

13. Quote in Brian McGinty, *John Brown's Trial* (Cambridge, MA: Harvard University Press, 2009), p. 110.

14. Keeney, "A Republican for Labor," p. 5.

15. Ibid., pp. 3–5, and quote from *Charleston Gazette* cited in *Literary Digest*, May 13, 1922, reprinted in Corbin, ed., *Mine Wars*, p. 136.

16. Lee, *Bloodletting in Appalachia*, p. 107.

17. Judge David Sanders, *The Jefferson County Court House from 1800 to the Present*, pamphlet (Jefferson County Clerk, n.d.).

18. James G. Randall, "The Miners and the Law of Treason," *North American Review* 216, no. 3 (September 1922): 322.

19. James M. Cain, "Treason—To Coal Operators," *Nation*, October 4, 1922, p. 333.

20. Blizzard, *When Miners March*, p. 297.

21. Keeney, "A Republican for Labor," pp. 61–62; Lee, *Bloodletting in Appalachia*, pp. 109–10; *New York Times*, May 22, 1922.

22. Summary of news reports in *Literary Digest*, June 17, 1922.

23. Lee, *Bloodletting in Appalachia*, pp. 110–11; Swain, *The Blair Mountain War*, pp. 52–53.

24. Cain, "Treason—To Coal Operators," p. 333.

25. Ibid.

26. Lunt, *Law and Order vs. the Miners*, p. 162.

27. Cain, "Treason—To Coal Operators," p. 333. When his assignment covering the miners' treason trials ended, Cain returned to Baltimore and his job as a beat reporter. A few months later, an editor, impressed by Cain's reports on these trials, offered him a commission to write a feature story on the mine wars for the prestigious *Atlantic Monthly*.

Cain threw himself into this new assignment by leaving his newspaper job in Baltimore and heading back into coal country. He found a job as a miner with the Kellys Creek Colliery Company in Ward and joined the UMWA. On his first day underground, a young collier prevented the writer's precious right hand from being smashed between two coal cars. His fingers saved, Cain returned to the mine the next day, and at lunchtime he sat with pencil in hand, taking notes as he listened to miners talk and joke on the gob pile, and then tried to find the words he needed to depict the violent lives these men led underground and on the picket lines aboveground. Drawn ever deeper into the world of these mountaineer miners, Cain decided to write a great American novel about their epic struggle with the mine operators.

When the superintendent of the mine realized he had a reporter on his payroll, he invited Cain to dinner in his big house. A gentleman himself, Cain was also a good journalist who wanted to get the boss's perspective on the mining business. The next morning, as the reporter sat down to breakfast at his boardinghouse, the miners who had befriended him "looked through him" and talked with each other as though he wasn't there. Cain soon realized that he had crossed a line by having dinner with the boss. Suspected now of being a boss's stooge, Cain "dared not go back in the mine," fearing that another day underground might cost him his life. He left Ward the next day without collecting his pay.

In pursuit of his story, Cain crossed the Kanawha River and went on to Marmet; from there he began to trace the steps the armed miners had taken when they marched out of Lens Creek Hollow the previous summer. He followed their trail across Boone County until he reached Sharples, where the state police raid had gotten the local miners up in arms. There in the shadow of Blair Mountain, Cain stayed with a friendly coal operator—one "who didn't believe miners were low, lazy rats"—and started to scribble notes for his novel.

Cain labored over two drafts of his manuscript before he realized that the epic novel he imagined was a pipe dream. "I didn't seem to have the least idea where I was going with it," he confessed to a friend. The "homely characters" the writer had created on paper "stumbled" and spoke back to him in "a gnarled and grotesque jargon" that would, he feared, befuddle and alienate his readers. Besides, he realized that his theme of labor struggle was really "a dead seed" for a novelist writing in the Jazz Age.

Cain's reporting on West Virginia appeared in two articles, "The Battle Ground of Coal" and "West Virginia: A Mine-Field Melodrama," both reprinted in Corbin, ed., *Mine Wars*. All quotes here are from these two articles. On Cain's background and his adventures in West Virginia, see Roy Hoopes, *Cain: The Biography of James M. Cain* (New York: Holt, Rinehart & Winston, 1982), pp. 89–90, 92–93, 99, 101–103; quotes on pp. 554–56. Additional quotes are from James M. Cain, *The Butterfly* (New York: Alfred A. Knopf, 1947), p. v; William Marling, *The American Roman Noir: Hammett, Cain, and Chandler* (Athens: University of Georgia Press, 1995), p. 179; and Edmund Wilson, "The Boys in the Backroom," *New Republic*, November 11, 1940, pp. 665–66.

28. Quote in Lee, *Bloodletting in Appalachia*, p. 111.

29. Quote in Montgomery, *The Fall of the House of Labor*, p. 407.

30. Fox, *United We Stand*, p. 234.

31. Harris and Krebs, *From Humble Beginnings*, p. 160.

32. Cain, "The Battle Ground of Coal." After he left West Virginia, Cain fell under the spell of the *Baltimore Sun*'s legendary columnist and the nation's leading cynic, H. L. Mencken, a writer who exerted an unrivaled influence among the educated classes. The acerbic master of the American idiom, Mencken skewered the nation's intolerant bourgeoisie, condemned Prohibition, and defended complete freedom of speech, but he remained a political pessimist and a virulent anti-Semite who regarded the common man as a fool. Cain devoured the pages of Mencken's sophisticated magazine *The Smart Set* and became infected with the old iconoclast's spirit.

Despite his initial sympathy for the miners and his outrage over their treatment by coal operators, mine guards, and county judges, James M. Cain lost whatever respect he had for his subjects. Condescension oozed from the sardonic article he wrote about the miners in the *Atlantic Monthly*. West Virginia's mountaineer miners were "lovable fellows," he wrote, "hospitable and respectful," but they were vigilantes by temperament. Grudges obsessed them and bred strange feuds with "incomprehensible causes." As time went on, he claimed, they interbred and they became what he called "an atrophied race, a weaker strain of American stock." In his final assessment of the miners and their enemies, Cain reduced them all to stock characters in a silent movie filmed on location: "A melodrama where men carry guns, often in leather holsters, and wear big black felt hats . . . Where they give each other three-fingered handshakes, and slips of paper pass from palm to palm. Where hoarsely whispered plots are met by counterplots, and detective agencies flourish. Where personal differences are settled by guns . . ."

Cain would go on to publish a wildly popular novel, but it would not be the story he had wanted to write about an angry West Virginia coal miner on the march. His potboiler, *The Postman Always Rings Twice*, became a bestseller in hardback and paperback, and eventually the basis of a play and a popular movie that would become a template for Hollywood film noir. His salacious murder mystery was set in Southern California's coastal towns, places far removed from the southern West Virginia coal towns he had visited as a reporter and aspiring novelist. Yet the novel exudes that same darkness that cloaked Cain's writing about the doomed characters he portrayed in the Tug River minefields. Scenes and characters from coal country would appear in Cain's later novels about Americans consumed by greed—the devil that he had found stalking the hills of West Virginia. "Money turns out to be death personified in much of my writing," he later remarked, "because that's the way I see it." Cain, "West Virginia: A Mine-Field Melodrama," and quote in Hoopes, *Cain*, pp. 554–56. Additional quotes are from Marling, *The American Roman Noir*, p. 179, and Wilson, "The Boys in the Backroom," pp. 665–66.

33. George Echols testimony, reprinted in Corbin, ed., *Mine Wars*, pp. 102–105.

34. Lunt, *Law and Order vs. the Miners*, p. 165.

35. Ibid., p. 153, and Lee, *Bloodletting in Appalachia*, pp. 117–18.

36. Mooney, *Struggle in the Coal Fields*, p. 127.

37. Lee, *Bloodletting in Appalachia*, p. 14.

38. Hudnall, *Kelly's Creek Chronicles*, p. 56.

39. Mooney, *Struggle in the Coal Fields*, p. 39. For a fuller account, see Fox, *United We Stand*, pp. 263–65.

40. "C. Frank Keeney," *Biographical Dictionary of American Labor Leaders*, edited by Gary M. Fink (Westport, CT: Greenwood Press, 1974), p. 86; Dubofsky and Van Tine, *John L. Lewis*, pp. 96–97.

41. Ibid.

42. McAlister Coleman, "A Week in West Virginia," *Survey*, February 1, 1925, pp. 532–33.

43. Ibid.

44. Hudnall, *Kelly's Creek Chronicles*, pp. 56–58.

45. Ibid., p. 61.

46. Gorn, *Mother Jones*, pp. 275–85.

47. Jones, *Autobiography of Mother Jones*, pp. 234–35.

48. Mooney, *Struggle in the Coal Fields*, p. 127.

49. Ibid., p. 67; Keeney, "Bill Blizzard"; and Shae Davidson, "Mother Blizzard," in Sullivan, ed., *The West Virginia Encyclopedia*, p. 66. On coalfield baseball, Paul J. Nyden, "Coalfield Baseball," in Sullivan, ed., *The West Virginia Encyclopedia*, pp. 152–53. Baseball became "the miners' sport" and the Sunday games became a grand diversion from the cares of the workaday world. Excitement reached its highest pitch in October of 1924 when the Cincinnati Reds conducted a barnstorming tour through the coal towns competing against local teams like the McDowell All-Stars. Perhaps no one noticed that the Cincinnati Reds arrived just a few months after the demise of Frank Keeney and Fred Mooney—the men who had unleashed what one Logan County mine owner had called an invading "army of Reds" three years earlier. Quote from Shiffert, *Life, Work, and Culture in Company Towns of Southern Appalachia*, p. 163; also see William E. Akin, "West Virginia Coal Field Baseball," in John B. Wiseman and Benjamin G. Rader, eds., *Joy in Mudville: Essays on Baseball and American Life* (Jefferson, NC: McFarland, 2010), pp. 97–98.

50. Slichter quoted in David Brody, *Workers in Industrial America: Essays on the Twentieth Century Struggle* (New York: Oxford University Press, 1980), p. 57. Also see Ronald Garay, *U.S. Steel and Gary, West Virginia: Corporate Paternalism in Appalachia* (Knoxville: University of Tennessee Press, 2011), and Charles A. Cabell, "Employees First: A Statement of Certain Living and Working Conditions Employed by a Modern Mining Corporation," *West Virginia Review* 3, no. 9 (June 1926): 308–309, 352. U.S. Coal Commission quoted in Williams, *West Virginia and the Captains of Industry*, p. 190.

51. Trotter, *Coal, Class, and Color*, pp. 115–16.

52. Hudnall, *Kelly's Creek Chronicles*, pp. 99, 127–29, 244–45.

53. Quote in ibid., p. 99. The KKK reached its peak of power in 1924, when it established a strong base not only in the small towns of rural America, but also in the cities and larger commercial towns like Logan and Bluefield. Kenneth T. Jackson, *The Ku Klux Klan in the City, 1915–1930* (New York: Oxford University Press, 1967), pp. 18–21, 65, 241, 251.

54. Trotter, *Coal, Class, and Color*, pp. 127–29, 244–45; Fox, *United We Stand*, p. 260; Sterling D. Spero and Abram L. Harris, *The Black Worker: The Negro and the Labor Movement* (New York: Atheneum, 1968 [1931]), p. 371.

55. Homer L. Morris, *The Plight of the Bituminous Coal Miner* (Philadelphia: University of Pennsylvania Press, 1934), p. 126.

56. Percy Tetlow and Thomas Townsend testimonies, *Conditions in the Coal Fields of Pennsylvania, West Virginia, and Ohio*, Committee on Interstate Commerce, U.S. Senate, 70th Congress, 1st Session (Washington, DC: Government Printing Office, 1928); Townsend quoted in Coleman, *Men and Coal*, p. 133.

57. Coleman, *Men and Coal*, p. 360.

58. Archie Green, *Only a Miner: Studies in Recorded Coal-Mining Songs* (Urbana: University of Illinois Press, 1972), pp. 135–40.

59. Bittner quoted in Bernstein, *Lean Years*, p. 362.

60. Malcolm Ross, *Machine Age in the Hills* (New York: Macmillan, 1933), p. 161.

61. Mooney, *Struggle in the Coal Fields*, pp. 142–47.

62. Hudnall, *Kelly's Creek Chronicles*, p. 63.

63. Quote in ibid., p. 64.

64. Gene Autry may have heard about the miners' angel while he worked as a union telegrapher on the Frisco line in eastern Oklahoma's coalfield. Green, *Only a Miner*, pp. 241–78.

65. Korson, *Coal Dust on the Fiddle*, pp. 65–66, 447.

Chapter 16: A People Made of Steel, Winter 1931–Spring 1933

1. Quote in Jerry Bruce Thomas, *An Appalachian New Deal: West Virginia in the Great Depression* (Lexington: University Press of Kentucky, 1998), pp. 42–43; Arthur M. Schlesinger Jr., *The Crisis of the Old Order, 1919–1932* (Boston: Houghton Mifflin, 1956), p. 171.

2. Edmund Wilson, "Frank Keeney's Coal Diggers," *New Republic*, July 8, 1931, reprinted in Wilson, *The American Jitters* (New York and London: C. Scribner's Sons, 1932), p. 315.

3. Mooney, *Struggle in the Coal Fields*, pp. 142–49; Bernstein, *Lean Years*, p. 381; Tom Tippett, "The Miners Try for a Clean Union: West Virginia Begins Again . . ." *Labor Age*, April 1931, pp. 5–6.

4. Tippett, "The Miners Try for a Clean Union," pp. 5–6.

5. Bernstein, *Lean Years*, p. 382; Wilson, "Frank Keeney's Coal Diggers," pp. 310–11.

6. Wilson, "Frank Keeney's Coal Diggers," pp. 317, 327.

7. Ibid., pp. 312–13, 321; Ross, *Machine Age in the Hills*, pp. 158–62; and Tippett, "The Miners Try for a Clean Union," pp. 5–6.

8. Wilson, "Frank Keeney's Coal Diggers," pp. 310–11, 318, 326–27.

9. Hudnall, *Kelly's Creek Chronicles*, p. 65.

10. David A. Corbin, "'Frank Keeney Is Our Leader, and We Shall Not Be Moved': Rank-and-File Leadership in the West Virginia Coal Fields," in Fink and Reed, eds., *Essays in Southern Labor History*, pp. 150–51; Green, *Only a Miner*, p. 255; Kim Ruehl, "'I Shall Not Be Moved'—Traditional: History of an American Folk Song," available at folkmusic.about.com/od/folksongs/qt/ShallNotBeMoved.htm.

11. Thomas, *An Appalachian New Deal*, p. 46; John C. Hennen, "William Gustavus Conley," in Sullivan, ed., *The West Virginia Encyclopedia*, pp. 160–61.

12. Corbin, "'Frank Keeney Is Our Leader,'" p. 150; Bernstein, *Lean Years*, p. 383.

13. Union constitution quoted in Corbin, *Life, Work, and Rebellion*, p. 162. During the first cruel years of the Depression, a Pentecostal revival swept across America. At a time when established Protestant denominations declined, thousands joined the Assemblies of God, the Churches of God, and other Holiness churches. Pentecostals often spoke in tongues, as Christ's apostles had done two millennia before on the day of the Pentecost, the Jewish day for celebrating the harvest. Like the ritual of serpent handling practiced in some Appalachian communities, speaking in tongues revealed that a believer was "Spirit-filled" and bound for salvation. Deep personal experiences of ecstasy and a shared feeling of holy community attracted followers to Pentecostal churches and to Holiness preachers, who told their followers that because the material world would soon pass away, they must prepare for life in the eternal world of the spirit. A. P. Carter, a musician who had been raised in the Poor Valley of Virginia near the Pocahontas coalfield, wrote the song "There's No Depression in Heaven," of which the Carter Family made a popular recording.

The Pentecostal leaders of West Virginia's Churches of God—whose members lived almost entirely in coal-mining towns—condemned labor unions and their worldly ends. This edict was one of many through which Pentecostal religion discouraged political activism and merely provided an escape from a depressing world corrupted by sinners. But in the coal camps of Appalachia, faith in the Holy Spirit took on a nuanced meaning, according to historian Richard J. Callahan. For mining people, Holiness religion became another form of work, the kind of work necessary to protect and ultimately save these people from the perils of an ever-changing world. The coal miners' faith protected them from disease and disaster, it provided them with healing hands to soothe their aching backs and bruised bodies, and it offered everyone a powerful means of grieving those who died in underground rock falls and explosions. Furthermore, Holiness religion constituted an intensely emotional form of communal worship for the working-class people who listened faithfully to their own blue-collar ministers, even when they contradicted church elders. In this special context, miner-preachers evoked the redemptive possibilities of unionism as a means of restoring moral order to the chaos of the coalfields.

Some scholars maintain that Holiness faith reflected a sense of fatalism and "ecstatic escape" from the realities of life in depressed mining camps; a chiliasm of despair that promoted social passivity. See, for example, Robert Maples Anderson, *Vision of the Disinherited: The Making of American Pentecostalism* (Peabody, MA: Hendrickson, 1979), pp. 229, 235, 240. But why would some of the same Appalachian coal miners who worshipped in Pentecostal chapels also join militant labor unions like those in Kanawha County—a union led by socialists who wanted to change the material world? The answer, according to Callahan, lies in the peculiar evolution of religious ritual and belief in the Appalachian coal camps. "What is remarkable is not the 'escapism' of Holiness believers," he maintains, "but rather their engagement with material and social conditions . . ." Callahan, *Work and Faith in the Kentucky Coal Fields*, pp. 111, 130, 156, quote on pp. 178–80. On Pentecostalism, see David C. Fisher, "Not by Might, Nor by Power: The Growth of the Assemblies of God, 1929–1939" (MA thesis, University of Massachusetts at Boston, 2009), p. 97; Darrin J. Rodgers, "Seize the Moment," *Assemblies of God Heritage*, 2009, available on the Flower Pentecostal Heritage Center website, ifphc.wordpress.com/2011/07/11/seize-the-moment/. On the Carter Family, see Bill C. Malone, *Don't Get Above Your Raisin': Country Music and the Southern Working Class* (Urbana: University of Illinois Press, 2002), pp. 65, 97, 280; Fisher, "Not by Might, Nor by Power,"

p. 102; Deborah Vansau McCauley, "Religion," in Straw and Blethen, eds., *High Mountains Rising*, p. 181.

14. Quote in Corbin, *Life, Work, and Rebellion*, pp. 165–66. This book provides an insightful discussion of how important coal miner–preachers were in the struggle for unionism in southern West Virginia.

15. Quote in ibid., pp. 165–66.

16. Ross, *Machine Age in the Hills*, p. 158.

17. Ibid.

18. Keeney quoted in ibid., pp. 158–59.

19. Quotes in Hudnall, *Kelly's Creek Chronicles*, p. 67.

20. Schlesinger, *The Crisis of the Old Order*, pp. 232, 248.

21. Bernstein, *Lean Years*, pp. 385, 423, 425; Howard Zinn, *A People's History of the United States, 1492–Present* (New York: Harper, 2005 [1980]), pp. 395–405.

22. Bernstein, *Lean Years*, pp. 437–48.

23. Quote in Robert S. McElvaine, *The Great Depression: America, 1929–1941* (New York: Times Books, 1984), p. 91.

24. Forbath, *Law and the Shaping of the American Labor Movement*, p. 159; Lunt, *Law and Order vs. the Miners*, p. 169.

25. George W. Norris, *Fighting Liberal: The Autobiography of George W. Norris* (New York: Macmillan, 1945), pp. 1–38, 59–68, 234–44.

26. Bernstein, *Lean Years*, pp. 397–99.

27. Ibid., p. 407; Schlesinger, *The Crisis of the Old Order*, p. 224.

28. Quote in Forbath, *Law and the Shaping of the American Labor Movement*, p. 161; text of the law in Bernstein, *Lean Years*, pp. 398–99.

29. Quote in Bernstein, *Lean Years*, p. 506.

30. Ibid., p. 407; Schlesinger, *The Crisis of the Old Order*, p. 224; Fox, *United We Stand*, p. 304; Alinsky, *John L. Lewis*, p. 55; Dubofsky and Van Tine, *John L. Lewis*, pp. 85, 110–11.

31. Alinsky, *John L. Lewis*, pp. 63–65.

32. Lewis quoted in James P. Johnson, *The Politics of Soft Coal: The Bituminous Industry from World War I through the New Deal* (Urbana: University of Illinois Press, 1979), p. 131.

33. Brody, "Market Unionism: The Case of Coal," p. 154; Bernstein, *Lean Years*, p. 360; Williams, *Appalachia*, p. 253; Schlesinger, *The Crisis of the Old Order*, p. 248.

34. On the Red Jacket company's failure, see "Here's Another Lesson," *United Mine Workers Journal*, January 15, 1933.

35. Bernstein, *Lean Years*, p. 360.

36. Eller, *Miners, Millhands, and Moutaineers*, p. 239; Bureau of Labor Statistics, *100 Years of U.S. Consumer Spending: Data for the Nation, New York City, and Boston* (May 2006), p. 15, available at www.bls.gov/opub/uscs/1934-36.pdf; Bureau of Foreign and Domestic Commerce, "Wages, Hours of Labor, and Employent," *Statistical Abstract of the United States, 1937* (Washington, DC: Government Printing Office, 1938), p. 316, available at www2.census.gov/prod2/statcomp/documents/1937-13.pdf.

37. Schlesinger, *The Crisis of the Old Order*, pp. 3–4, 181.

38. Dubofsky and Van Tine, *John L. Lewis*, pp. 132–33; Irving Bernstein, *Turbulent Years: A History of the American Worker, 1933–1941* (Boston: Houghton Mifflin, 1970 [1969]), p. 34.

39. Alinsky, *John L. Lewis*, p. 71; Bernstein, *Turbulent Years*, pp. 29–30; *United Mine Workers Journal*, June 15, 1933, p. 3.

40. Bernstein, *Turbulent Years*, p. 35.

41. Burgett interview, "On Dark and Bloody Ground," pp. 105–107, 135–37, quote on p. 108.

42. "William Blizzard," *United Mine Workers Journal*, June 1, 1933, p. 5; Blizzard and Harris, "A Biographic Sketch of Bill Blizzard," pp. 396–97.

43. Milton Hendrix interview with Bill Taft and Lois McLean, Raleigh County, WV, 1973, West Virginia and Regional History Center, West Virginia University Library, Morgantown.

44. "Tidal Wave of Enthusiasm," *United Mine Workers Journal*, July 1, 1933, p. 3.

45. Quote in Thomas, *An Appalachian New Deal*, p. 93.

46. Louis Stark, "The American Federation of Labor," *Atlantic Monthly*, April 1935, p. 489; Lunt, *Law and Order vs. the Miners*, p. 181.

47. On Blizzard's uncredited role in the 1933 organizing, see Wess Harris, "Victory on Blair Mountain," in Harris, ed., *Dead Ringers*, p. 82; and Corbin, "Frank Keeney Is Our Leader," p. 151.

48. Quote in Wilson, "Frank Keeney's Coal Diggers," p. 327. For a discussion of a similar situation in recent mining strikes, see Richard A. Couto, "The Memory of Miners and the Conscience of Capital: Coal Miners' Strikes as Free Spaces," in Stephen L. Fisher, ed., *Fighting Back in*

Appalachia: Traditions of Resistance and Change (Philadelphia: Temple University Press, 1993), pp. 165–94.

49. For a similar expression of nationalism in a different context, see Gary Gerstle, *Working-Class Americanism: The Politics of Labor in a Textile City, 1914–1960* (Cambridge and New York: Cambridge University Press, 1989), pp. 153–80.

50. Quote in "Tidal Wave of Enthusiasm," pp. 3–4.

51. Keen quoted in "On Dark and Bloody Ground," pp. 125–26.

52. Frank Dean interview in ibid., p. 155.

53. Quote from *New York Times* report reprinted in *United Mine Workers Journal*, July 1, 1933, p. 26.

Chapter 17: More Freedom than I Ever Had, Summer 1933–Fall 1934

1. Eugene Palmer, recording secretary, Local Union No. 5967, Logan, WV, letter to the editor, *United Mine Workers Journal*, August 15, 1933, p. 10.

2. Bernstein, *Turbulent Years*, p. 45; Conley, *History of the West Virginia Coal Industry*, pp. 235–36.

3. Conley, *History of the West Virginia Coal Industry*, p. 232.

4. Jenks's song is reproduced in Korson, *Coal Dust on the Fiddle*, pp. 304–305.

5. Conley, *History of the West Virginia Coal Industry*, pp. 234, 236–37 and Trotter, *Coal, Class, and Color*, Table 3.3. The black elite in the area had maintained its close relations with the coal companies. Some preachers were indebted to employers for building their churches and some teachers were grateful to them for building their schools. The region's successful black newspaper, *McDowell Times*, defended the interests of black coal miners, but its business manager, a black lawyer named T. Edward Hill, also directed a special Bureau of Negro Welfare to aid the operators in recruiting, maintaining, and stabilizing the small army of seven thousand African American miners working in the Pocahontas field. African American solidarity in southern West Virginia mining communities had its limits, because the local elite had to balance its own interests and those of the mine companies along with the needs of the black coal miners. As these workers "faced the limitations of their alliance with the black elite, they developed distinct strategies of their own," according to the historian Joe William Trotter Jr., and in 1933, these African American miners charted an entirely new course for themselves. Trotter, *Coal, Class, and Color*, p. 51.

6. On the first generation, see Lewis, *Black Coal Miners in America*, pp. 131-32. And see Herbert R. Northrup, *Organized Labor and the Negro*, 2nd ed. (New York: Harper & Bros, 1971 [1944]), pp. 159–60, 165, 167.

7. Mary Ann (Williams) Young, memoir (unpublished manuscript, n.d.), made available to the author by Young's granddaughter, Karilyn Crockett.

8. Lyrics to "I Can Tell the World" by the United Four quoted in Korson, *Coal Dust on the Fiddle*, pp. 305–306.

9. Ibid.

10. Green, *Only a Miner*, pp. 6, 387.

11. The lyrics to West's song are reprinted in Korson, *Coal Dust on the Fiddle*, pp. 321–22.

12. "Loyal Women Are Enthusiastic Over What the Good Old Union Has Done for Them," *United Mine Workers Journal*, May 15, 1935, p. 5.

13. Callahan, *Work and Faith in the Kentucky Coal Fields*, pp. 156–57; quote in "On Dark and Bloody Ground," pp. 135–37.

14. Bernstein, *Turbulent Years*, p. 44; Alinsky, *John L. Lewis*, p. 72.

15. Hickok quoted in Thomas, *An Appalachian New Deal*, p. 95.

16. Lorena A. Hickok, *Eleanor Roosevelt: Reluctant First Lady* (New York: Dodd, Mead, 1980), pp. 132–44; Eleanor Roosevelt, *This I Remember* (New York: Harper & Row, 1949), pp. 127–31; "Hears Story of Woe: Eleanor Roosevelt Pays Secret Visit to Scotts Run Coal Camp," *United Mine Workers Journal*, September 15, 1933; Dan Barry, "From New Deal to New Hard Times: Eleanor Endures," *New York Times*, December 24, 2009.

17. The captive mine owners signed the Appalachian Agreement in April 1934. *United Mine Workers Journal*, April 15, 1933, p. 3. Bernstein, *Turbulent Years*, pp. 46–52, 56–60, quote on p. 45; Rice and Brown, *West Virginia*, p. 234. Two provisions in the Appalachian Agreement would have far more serious consequences later on. First, the UMWA's negotiating team failed in its attempt to gain the "union shop." Under such an arrangement, every worker on unionized mine property would have been required to pay membership dues. In practice, however, union committeemen usually made sure that every man paid his dues, like it or not. A man working deep in a mountain with a crew of UMWA loyalists was in no position to sail along as a freeloader. Second, the UMWA decided to grant all management rights exclusively to employers, including, at least implicitly, the right to replace men with machines. Once higher wages

became uniform across the industry, owners could make big investments in mechanizing the mines and reducing the labor force, knowing they would face no competition from nonunion, low-wage coal produced by smaller mining companies. Eventually, these technological changes would bring an end to the personal freedom and job control colliers had enjoyed during the hand-loading era. But at the dawn of the New Deal, it was difficult for union members to foresee the future. Desperate to regain their union rights and to earn a living wage, rank-and-file miners did not insist on protecting the traditional forms of job control they had inherited in the old days. "It was only later," explained the scholar Keith Dix, that many veterans "realized what they had given up." Keith Dix, *What's a Coal Miner to Do? The Mechanization of Coal Mining* (Pittsburgh, PA: University of Pittsburgh Press, 1988), p. 192.

18. Lewis quoted in Bernstein, *Turbulent Years*, pp. 45–46.

19. "Labor Day Celebrated for the First Time in Many Localities, Due to the Right to Organize," *United Mine Workers Journal*, October 1, 1934, pp. 6–8.

20. Ernest Blankenship interview, "On Dark and Bloody Ground," pp. 140–41.

21. Statistics on mine fatalities from West Virginia Department of Mines, *Annual Report, 1942*, cited in William M. Boal, "Unionism and Productivity in West Virginia Coal Mining" (PhD diss., Stanford University, 1985), p. 65.

22. Tams, *The Smokeless Coal Fields of West Virginia*, pp. 96–97, quote on p. 71, and Thurmond, *The Logan Coal Field of West Virginia*, pp. 13–14.

23. Velke, *Baldwin-Felts Agency*, p. 308; Thomas, *An Appalachian New Deal*, p. 101.

24. Conley, *History of the West Virginia Coal Industry*, pp. 234–40; Corbin, *Life, Work, and Rebellion*, p. 5; C. Stuart McGehee, "Gary," in Sullivan, ed., *The West Virginia Encyclopedia*, p. 270; Garay, *U.S. Steel and Gary, West Virginia*, pp. 33–48.

25. Coleman, *Men and Coal*, p. 149; Johnson, *The Politics of Soft Coal*, p. 154; and Mark Myers, "Depression, Recovery, and Instability: The NRA and the McDowell County, West Virginia Coal Industry, 1920–1938," in Egolf, Fones-Wolf, and Martin, eds., *Culture, Class, and Politics in Modern Appalachia*, pp. 283–304.

26. "On Dark and Bloody Ground," p. 127. On the Youngstown Sheet and Tube mills in Ohio, see www.youngstownsteel.com/images/yst/youngstown.html.

27. The option of voting for a company union, which had been allowed under the National Industrial Recovery Act of 1933, was outlawed by the National Labor Relations Act. Bernstein, *Turbulent Years*, pp. 46–52, 56–60, 333; Rice and Brown, *West Virginia*, p. 234.

28. Ernest Galloway, "The C.I.O. and Negro Labor," *Opportunity* 14 (November 1936): 326–30. In union locals with significant numbers of black members, and there were many, the UMWA required a white miner to serve as president and a black miner as vice president on the grounds that white bosses would not negotiate with black officers. While this leadership "formula" allowed black miners a voice in local policy making, it did not give them full access to the power that top leadership would have given them. This unusual, though still inequitable, experiment in biracial government provoked attacks from white supremacists, who claimed that the UMWA indulged in the same race-mixing policies the Communists preached.

In many West Virginia UMWA local unions, however, members ignored the "formula" and elected African American miners as presidents, even in a few locals with white majorities. Italians and other immigrants often supported African Americans over whites because they were more sympathetic to foreigners, and in many cases, they were more literate than white Americans. Blacks also won a good share of district offices, and in most locals they served on three-man pit committees customarily comprising one white American, one black American, and one immigrant. According to a sociologist who studied race relations in the West Virginia minefields, white members no longer hesitated to call black members their brothers or to accept them as equals, at least in discussions of union affairs. West Virginia mine operators had depended upon the "judicious mixture" of men as "an insurmountable bar to unionism," but in the depths of the Great Depression, a time of desperate job competition, the UMWA effectively formed "a united front" of races and nationalities. Herbert R. Northrup, *Organized Labor and the Negro*, 2nd ed. (New York: Harper & Bros, 1971 [1944]), pp. 159–60, 165, 167; James T. Laing, "The Negro Miner in West Virginia," *Social Forces* 14, no. 3 (March 1936): 418; Philip S. Foner,

Organized Labor and the Black Worker, 1619–1973 (New York: International Publishers, 1974), p. 218; Trotter, *Coal, Class and Color*, p. 111.

29. "Labor Day Celebrated for the First Time," p. 6.

30. A. W. McClung, Danin, WV, letter to *United Mine Workers Journal*, January 15, 1938, p. 9.

31. Bernstein, *Turbulent Years*, pp. 769–70, 777.

32. Thomas, *An Appalachian New Deal*, pp. 103–106. Hatfield had appealed to these black voters in McDowell County, perhaps the largest concentration of registered African American voters south of the Mason-Dixon Line. He won the county by six thousand votes in 1928, but in 1934 he lost the county in his reelection bid by a margin of five thousand votes. Voting returns by county in *West Virginia Legislative Handbook and Manual and Official Register—1930*, compiled and edited by M. S. Hodges (Charleston, WV: Matthews Printing Company, 1930); *West Virginia Legislative Handbook and Manual and Official Register—1931*, compiled and edited by M. S. Hodges (Charleston, WV: Matthews Printing Company, 1931); *West Virginia Legislative Handbook and Manual and Official Register—1935*, compiled and edited by Charles Lively (Charleston, WV: Matthews Printing Company, 1935); *West Virginia Legislative Handbook and Manual and Official Register—1937*, compiled and edited by Charles Lively (Charleston, WV: Matthews Printing Company, 1937).

Epilogue

1. Paul J. Nyden, "Hundreds March to Blair Mountain," *Charleston Gazette*, June 6, 2011; Zack Harold, "Protesters Begin Weeklong March," *Charleston Daily News*, June 7, 2011; "Appalachia Rising," *RT News*, June 13, 2011, available at rt.com/usa/mountain-coal-companies-schultz/; Jon Gensler, "Blair Mountain II: The New Battle over Coal Mining in West Virginia," *Christian Science Monitor*, June 10, 2011. The UMWA did not endorse the march presumably because it had not been involved in the planning and because its leaders were committed to keeping jobs in West Virginia and to organizing the men who worked those jobs. But the union's international president, Cecil E. Roberts, knew more than anyone what Blair Mountain meant to union coal miners; his great-uncle was Bill Blizzard, the commander of the 1921 march. In recognition of that legacy, Roberts published an editoral in the *Charleston Gazette* calling for the preservation of Blair Mountain.

2. Paul J. Nyden, "Blair Mountain March Nears End," *Charleston Gazette*, June 11, 2011. For background on mountaintop removal and the struggle against it, see Shirley Stewart Burns, *Bringing Down the Mountains: The Impact of Mountaintop Removal on Southern West Virginia Communities* (Morgantown: West Virginia University Press, 2007); Michael Shnayerson, *Coal River* (New York: Farrar, Straus & Giroux, 2008); Jason Howard and Silas House, eds., *Something's Rising: Appalachians Fighting Mountaintop Removal* (Lexington: University Press of Kentucky, 2009); and Chad Montrie, *To Save the Land and People: A History of Opposition to Surface Coal Mining in Appalachia* (Chapel Hill: University of North Carolina Press, 2003).

3. "Blair Mountain Removed from National Register of Historic Places; Sierra Club Takes Action," available at archive.is/dhMbM; Harvard Ayres, Barbara Rasmussen, and Brandon Nida, "Battle of Blair Mountain Continues," *Charleston Gazette*, April 30, 2011, available at www.wvgazette. com/News/201104291601; Jeff Biggers, "Where's the National Outrage on Blair Mountain? Gov. Joe Manchin and Bilbo Legacy," *Huffington Post*, April 8, 2009, available at www.huffingtonpost.com/jeff-biggers/wheres-the-national-outra_b_184177.html.

4. Nicolaus Mills, "War in Tug River Valley: A Long and Bitter Miners' Strike," *Dissent* 37 (January 1986): 45–52. For a sharp portrait of Blankenship, who was born in the Tug Fork Valley just a few miles from Matewan, and a description of the anti-union tactics adopted by Massey Energy, see Shnayerson, *Coal River*, pp. 22–35 151–60.

5. "Blair Mountain Removed from National Register of Historic Places"; Ayres, Rasmussen, and Nida, "Battle of Blair Mountain Continues"; Biggers, "Where's the National Outrage on Blair Mountain?"

6. Shnayerson, *Coal River*, pp. 22–35, 151–60. Blankenship won most of his battles with the UMWA, including one victory in 1998 at Massey's Upper Big Branch mine in Montcoal, West Virginia, where the lethal explosion occurred on April 5, 2010. On December 6, 2011, the Mine Safety and Health Administration cited Massey Energy for 389 violations and assessed the company $10.8 million in fines. Liability suits followed. At the end of that month, Blankenship resigned as CEO of Massey Energy—with an $86 million severance package—and Massey's owners sold out to Alpha Natural Resources. Early in 2013, Blankenship was named as a coconspirator in a plot "to routinely violate safety standards and then cover up the

resulting workplace hazards." Clifford Krauss, "Under Fire since Explosion, Mining C.E.O. Quits," *New York Times*, December 3, 2010; Ken Ward Jr., "Former Massey Official Pleads Guilty in Safety Probe, Says He Conspired with CEO," *Charleston Gazette*, February 28, 2013.

7. C. Belmont Keeney interview with author, February 10 and June 9, 2011, and June 7, 2013; C. Belmont Keeney interview with Melinda Tuhus, "Recent March to Protect Blair Mountain in West Virginia Brought Coal Miners and Environmentalists Together," *Between the Lines*, August 10, 2011, available at www.btlonline.org/2011/seg/110819bf-btl-keeney.html; and C. Belmont Keeney, "What's Next for Blair Mountain," *Front Porch*, July 29, 2011, available at appvoices.org/2011/07/29/guest-blogger-chuck-keeney-what's-next-for-blair-mountain/.

8. On the general neglect of labor history in textbooks, see Jean Anyon, "Ideology and United States History Textbooks," *Harvard Educational Review* 49, no. 3 (Fall 1979): 373. Even two of the first and foremost left-wing historians of the labor movement ignored the mine wars. Anthony Bimba, a Marxist intellectual and a member of the Communist Party, emphasized the case of Sacco and Vanzetti when he reached the 1920s—a story that typically overshadowed all other events in left-wing narratives of the era. Bimba, *The History of the American Working Class*. Louis Adamic, the highly acclaimed writer and popular historian, also left the story out of his book, which is devoted exclusively to these kinds of episodes in labor history. Louis Adamic, *Dynamite: The Story of Class Violence in America* (New York: Viking Press, 1931).

The mine wars were discussed briefly in a pioneering scholarly study of American labor history in Perlman and Taft, *Labor Movements*. The authors' awareness of the events in West Virginia undoubtedly reflected the fact that they knew some of the key actors in the drama. Subsequently, however, the story disappeared from the national narrative of labor history, even in the accounts of radical historians like Richard O. Boyer and Herbert M. Morais, authors of the vivid *Labor's Untold Story* (New York: Cameron Associates, 1955). It was missing as well from the two standard surveys of the field—Foster Rhea Dulles, *Labor in America: A History*, 2nd ed. (New York: Crowell, 1955), and Thomas R. Brooks, *Toil and Trouble: A History of American Labor*, 2nd ed. (New York: Dell, 1971)—and from the government-sponsored collection Richard B. Morris, ed., *Bicentennial History of the American Worker* (Washington, DC: Government Printing

Office, 1976). I also neglected to include the story in my survey, James R. Green, *The World of the Worker: Labor in Twentieth-Century America* (New York: Hill & Wang, 1980). Like most historians of the post–World War I era, I focused mainly on the Lawrence Bread and Roses strike and the Ludlow massacre in discussing the Progressive Era, and missed the significance of the first mine war in West Virginia. In the postwar era, I emphasized the mass strike of 1919, the Red Scare of 1920, and the anti-union open shop movement that followed. The saga of the second mine war was obscured, in my mind, by those national trends.

Even more surprising is the fact that after the publication of David Alan Corbin's comprehensive book *Life, Work, and Rebellion in the Coal Fields* in 1981, authors of textbooks and labor histories continued to omit the West Virginia mine wars. See, for example, Ronald L. Filippelli, *Labor in the USA: A History* (New York: A. A. Knopf, 1984); Joshua Freeman et. al., *Who Built America? Working People and the Nation's Economy, Politics, Culture, and Society, Volume 2: From the Gilded Age to the Present* (New York: Pantheon Books, 1992); Steve Babson, *The Unfinished Struggle: Turning Points in American Labor History, 1877–Present* (Lanham, MD: Rowman & Littlefield, 1999); A. B. Chitty and Priscilla Murolo, *From the Folks Who Brought You the Weekend: A Short, Illustrated History of Labor in the United States* (New York: New Press, 2001); and, most recently, Philip Dray, *There Is Power in a Union: The Epic Story of Labor in America* (New York: Doubleday, 2010).

For a discussion of why American historians tend to dismiss the significance of ideologically motivated violence in our past, see Beverly Gage, "Why Violence Matters: Radicalism, Politics, and Class War in the Gilded Age and Progressive Era," *Journal for the Study of Radicalism* 1, no. 1 (2007): 99–100. For an exception to the tendency, see Jeffreys-Jones, *Violence and Reform in American History*. Another reason the mine wars have been neglected may be that historians who sympathize with the union cause are reluctant to shine too much light on what happened when strikers picked up rifles to fight against the usually superior armed forces mobilized by their employers. These writers tend to focus their attention on incidents when strikers were victims of violence, which was the case time after time from 1877 to 1937. Therefore, certain stories of such bloody defeats— the railway workers' uprising of 1877, the Haymarket bombing in 1886, the battle of Homestead in 1892, and the Ludlow massacre of 1914—are always included in labor history surveys and often mentioned in general American history textbooks.

9. For an excellent interpretation of how the mine wars have been used as a setting by poets, filmmakers, and novelists, see Duke, *Writers and Miners*, pp. 71–100.

Don West, Appalachia's legendary activist poet, wrote of "Cabin Creek, alive in heroic tales, unrecorded" and "Blair Mountain, 1921 / Ten thousand miners in struggle / bombs dropping from the air." West, who was born in Georgia, published his first short story in 1936, about a fictional Kentucky miner, and then recruited a group of real Appalachian mountaineers to join the Abraham Lincoln Brigade and fight for the Republicans in Spain. After a rich career as a radical activist and writer, West chose to live the last year of his life in an old coal miners' house on Cabin Creek. Moving to "one of the hubs of the infamous coal wars" was, two of his admirers wrote, "a symbolic act of moving back into the heart of his life's struggles." Don West, "Something of America," *No Lonesome Road: Selected Prose and Poems*, edited by Jeff Biggers and George Brosi (Urbana: University of Illinois Press, 2004), p. 192, quote on pp. xxix–xliii.

Mary Lee Settle, the acclaimed Charleston-born novelist, used the 1912 strike on Paint Creek as the basis of the fourth volume in her series the Beulah Quintet—a family saga set in the Kanawha Valley. The action, including the Bull Moose train's attack on the tent camp at Holly Grove, took place on land owned by one of her ancestors. "Out of the social world of my parents as adolescents," Settle recalled, came her impressive fresco of life in her native land, *The Scapegoat* (New York: Random House, 1980), and her intimate portrait of life in the mining communities along Kellys Creek, *Addie*, as told to her by her grandmother Addie Tompkins.

Denise Giardina was raised in the very coalfields where the mine wars occurred, but she never learned about these events in school. She discovered the story in some obscure self-published accounts that made her realize "West Virginians had fought back against their oppressors." A committed activist, Giardina believed the story was covered up. The reason, she said, was clear to anyone who grew up in the minefields where "the coal industry still controlled all." She decided to bring the story to light in a novel. Her book spans the time from Paint Creek to Blair Mountain as it narrates the story of the vivid coal town characters she created. When she sent the novel out for review in the early 1980s, no one in the publishing industry was interested in a novel about labor struggles in West Virginia. It took Giardina several years to find a house that would publish her novel. Quotes from www.denisegiardina.com/heaven.htm#syn.

When W. W. Norton published *Storming Heaven* in 1987, the book won rave reviews from critics like Pulitzer Prize–winning writer Annie Dillard, who called it "a gripping story of a real conflict," a stirring story told with "fierceness and passion." More Americans probably learned about the mine wars from Giardina's fictional account than from all previous works of scholarship taken together.

In the same year Giardina's novel appeared, John Sayles released his movie *Matewan*, the gripping story of a particularly bloody episode in the mine wars. Like the West Virginia writers who discovered the mine wars on their own, Sayles heard about the Matewan gun battle when he hitch-hiked through West Virginia several times during the 1960s. Some of the people who picked him up were coal miners who told him frightening stories of modern mine disasters and wild fluctuations in coal prices. Sayles later wrote, "But every miner I talked to would shake his head and say, 'Buddy, this aint nothin compared to what *used* to go on. I could tell you some *stories.*'" These were tales of old times the miners learned from their elders, stories that "had a lot of the Old West in them" and "a whole hunk of our history I'd never heard of, that a lot of people had never heard of."

Sayles returned to West Virginia to do research for his novel *Union Dues*. He was reading a book about the Hatfield-McCoy feud when he came across a mention of Sid Hatfield and the bloody shoot-out in Matewan. As he learned more about events surrounding the gun battle, Sayles realized, as he later put it, that "All the elements and principles involved seemed basic to the idea of what America has become and what it should be. Individualism versus collectivism, the personal and political legacy of racism, the immigrant dream and the reality that greeted it, monopoly capitalism at its most extreme versus American populism at its most violent, plus a lawman with two guns strapped on walking to the center of town to face a bunch of armed enforcers—what more could you ask for in a story?" There was more—the incomparable setting: the green hills of West Virginia, where the people and the music had "a mood and rhythm to them that need to be seen and heard to be felt completely." On this stage the "coal wars of the twenties" were fought in such a personal way that ideology became accessible in the story, made "immediate and emotional." It was this kind of immediacy that made Sayles think about making a movie about the events in Matewan.

The film Sayles made on a very small budget would, he hoped, lead viewers to question the violence in American labor history that is "condoned or condemned depending on which side of the picket line you stand on." He did this by introducing a fictional protagonist named Joe Keenahan, who appears as a pacifist, a character who would allow the film to break out of the classic western shoot-out genre its overall plot structure resembled.

Matewan attracted many viewers—liberals, sixties radicals, union activists, fans of Sayles's first film and novel, and others as well—but as an independently produced movie with limited distribution, it could make only so much noise to disturb the silence about the mine wars in the nation's recorded history. As Sayles later explained, his film, made for only $3 million, was not a mass-market movie that would be seen widely or affect the consciousness of many people. Labor historians were generally thrilled by the film but unhappy that it ended so abruptly after the shoot-out in Matewan, with no treatment of the civil war that followed. Sayles was, of course, aware of this shortcoming. The "big-budget version" of his film would have carried the story through Sid Hatfield's funeral, the march on Logan County, and the Battle of Blair Mountain; the film would have been "very raw" and would have addressed not only the question of why labor unions are needed but why they were needed in the first place. John Sayles, *Thinking in Pictures: The Making of the Movie* Matewan (Boston: Houghton Mifflin, 1987), pp. 9–10, 16. For a critical review of the film, see Stephen Brier, "A History Film without Much History," *Radical History Review* 41 (1988): 129–44. John Sayles telephone interview with Beverly Gage, March 6, 2008; photocopy of transcript courtesy of Beverly Gage.

10. Sullivan, ed., *Goldenseal Book of the West Virginia Mine Wars*; Rice and Brown, *West Virginia*, pp. 183–233; Williams, *Appalachia*, pp. 266–72; and Keeney, "Redneck Radicals."

11. Frank Blizzard quoted in "On Dark and Bloody Ground," p. 36.

12. Keeney, "Redneck Radicals," p. 42.

13. Phillips, "The West Virginia Mine War," p. 59.

14. On the UMWA decline after World War II, see Paul F. Clark, *The Miners' Fight for Democracy: Arnold Miller and the Reform of the United Mine Workers* (Ithaca: New York State School of Industrial and Labor Relations, Cornell University, 1981), pp. 16–25, and Curtis Seltzer, *Fire in the Hole:*

Miners and Managers in the American Coal Industry (Lexington: University Press of Kentucky, 1985), pp. 55–86.

15. Quote in Clark, *The Miners' Fight for Democracy*, p. 19.

16. Joseph E. Finley, *The Corrupt Kingdom: The Rise and Fall of the United Mine Workers* (New York: Simon & Schuster, 1972). On the grassroots opposition to the UMWA national officers, see Paul J. Nyden, "Rank-and-File Organizations in the United Mine Workers of America," *Critical Sociology* 8, nos. 2–3 (October 1978): 25–39.

17. Miller did combat at the pit face for five years until he was old enough to volunteer for the U.S. Army, just in time for the Normandy invasion in June 1944. Miller was severely wounded in France and spent nearly two years in hospitals, undergoing twenty surgeries. When he returned to Cabin Creek, he went back in the mines and won election as president of the same UMWA local his grandfather had led. Miller later said he grew up hearing stories of the mine wars and the exploits of Frank Keeney and Mother Jones who "walked up this holler," as he explained to a journalist who visited him on Cabin Creek in 1981. She called the Baldwin-Felts gunmen "all kinds of foul names and told them they didn't have the guts to pull the trigger, that she was going to conduct a rally whether they liked it or not. And she did. She was a fearless woman." Her bravery encouraged Cabin Creek miners like Miller's grandfather to stand up against the "Baldwin thugs" on Cabin Creek back in 1912. Kline, "Growing Up on Cabin Creek," pp. 35–43.

18. Barbara Ellen Smith, *Digging Our Own Graves: Coal Miners and the Struggle over Black Lung Disease* (Philadelphia: Temple University Press, 1987), pp. 114–18.

19. In one of his first acts as president, Arnold Miller restored the members' right to elect their own district officials. Forty-eight years after John L. Lewis placed District 17 in receivership, Miller restored its autonomy. The members then elected as their new district president a Miners for Democracy activist from Logan County who had founded the Black Lung Association with Miller. Clark, *The Miners' Fight for Democracy*, p. 35.

20. Ibid., pp. 26–30; *New York Times* quoted on p. 31. Also see Seltzer, *Fire in the Hole*, pp. 98–122.

21. The *Miner's Voice* was published in Charleston for the rank-and-file miners who supported the Miners for Democracy slate headed by Arnold Miller. The journalists in the *Miner's Voice* editorial group included Robert

Hauptman, David Morris, Robert Seltzer, Earl Dotter, and Matthew Witt, along with Anne Lawrence, who directed the project. They recruited apprentices under a youth grant from the National Endowment for the Humanities. Their unpublished report to the NEH appeared as a typescript in 1973 under the title "On Dark and Bloody Ground: An Oral History of the UMWA in Central Appalachia, 1920–1935." A rare copy is located in the West Virginia and Regional History Collection, West Virginia University Library. The quotes that follow are all from this publication.

Index

Page numbers in italics refer to illustrations.

WITHDRAWN

Ohio

Weirton

Wheeling

Ohio River

Parkersburg

Clarksbu

Little Kanawha

West Virgini

Huntington

Great Kanawha River

Kanawha
Coal field

Charleston

Guyan
Coal field

C & O Railroad

New River
Coal field

Big Sandy River

Guyandotte River

Logan

Winding Gulf
Coal field

New River

A L

Williamson
Coal field

Tug Fork

Kentucky

Pocahontas
Coal field

Bluefield